T0305233

Joint Research and Development under US
Antitrust and EU Competition Law

NEW HORIZONS IN COMPETITION LAW AND ECONOMICS

Series Editors: Steven D. Anderman, *Department of Law, University of Essex, UK*, and Rudolph J.R. Peritz, *New York Law School, USA*
This series has been created to provide research-based analysis and discussion of the appropriate role for economic thinking in the formulation of competition law and policy. The books in the series will move beyond studies of the traditional role of economics – that of helping to define markets and assess market power – to explore the extent to which economic thinking can play a role in the formulation of legal norms, such as abuse of a dominant position, restriction of competition and substantial impediments to or lessening of competition. This in many ways is the *new horizon* of competition law policy.
    US antitrust policy, influenced in its formative years by the Chicago School, has already experienced an expansion of the role of economic thinking in its competition rules. Now the EU is committed to a greater role for economic thinking in its Block Exemption Regulations and Modernisation package as well as possibly in its reform of Article 102. Yet these developments still raise the issue of the *extent* to which economics should be adopted in defining the public interest in competition policy and what role economists should play in legal argument. The series will provide a forum for research perspectives that are critical of an unduly expanded role for economics as well as those that support its greater use.
    Titles in the series include:

Intellectual Property and Antitrust
A Comparative Economic Analysis of US and EU Law
Mariateresa Maggiolino

A Legal Theory of Economic Power
Implications for Social and Economic Development
Calixto Salomão Filho

Collective Dominance and Collusion
Parallelism in EU and US Competition Law
Marilena Filippelli

Cartels, Competition and Public Procurement
Law and Economic Approaches to Bid Rigging
Stefan Weishaar

The Chinese Anti-Monopoly Law
New Developments and Empirical Evidence
Edited by Michael Faure and Xinzhu Zhang

Standardization under EU Competition Rules and US Antitrust Laws
The Rise and Limits of Self-Regulation
Björn Lundqvist

Joint Research and Development under US Antitrust and EU Competition Law
Björn Lundqvist

Joint Research and Development under US Antitrust and EU Competition Law

Björn Lundqvist

Associate Professor of Competition Law, Copenhagen Business School, Denmark

NEW HORIZONS IN COMPETITION LAW AND ECONOMICS

Edward Elgar
PUBLISHING

Cheltenham, UK • Northampton, MA, USA

© Björn Lundqvist 2015

All rights reserved. No part of this publication may be reproduced, stored in a retrieval system or transmitted in any form or by any means, electronic, mechanical or photocopying, recording, or otherwise without the prior permission of the publisher.

Published by
Edward Elgar Publishing Limited
The Lypiatts
15 Lansdown Road
Cheltenham
Glos GL50 2JA
UK

Edward Elgar Publishing, Inc.
William Pratt House
9 Dewey Court
Northampton
Massachusetts 01060
USA

A catalogue record for this book
is available from the British Library

Library of Congress Control Number: 2014957097

This book is available electronically in the **Elgar**online
Law subject collection
DOI 10.4337/9781784713010

ISBN   978 1 78471 300 3 (cased)
ISBN   978 1 78471 301 0 (eBook)

Typeset by Columns Design XML Ltd, Reading
Printed and bound in Great Britain by T.J. International Ltd, Padstow

Till mamma

Contents

Acknowledgements

During the last years, I have written and published a book about standardization ('Standardization under EU Competition Rules and US Antitrust Laws – The Rise and the Limits of Self-Regulation' (Edward Elgar, 2014)), while I still, diligently, have been updating the manuscript for this book, about R&D collaborations. I have removed and added chapters, for example, a text regarding the US 'unlicensed experiment defense' has been added and a long discussion about 'innovation market' is also presented in this book. Ultimately, I developed two fully-fledged stand-alone books. This one founded on my doctoral dissertation; while the other was inspired by the research I conducted for my dissertation.

They can be read separately or together, with a minimum of overlap, to obtain both detailed knowledge and a great overview of the antitrust treatment of pre-market collaborations and conduct. In fact, the two books contain a detailed and unique knowledge of innovation competition from all angles of antitrust law. So, I hope you will enjoy the work you are now holding in your hands.

I am very grateful to a number of individuals for the encouragement and advice leading up to this book. I wish to begin my debts of gratitude with my supervisors, Professor Hanns Ullrich and Professor Steve Anderman. I thank Professor Ullrich for his invaluable comments and his patience with a confused PhD student. I am very grateful to Steve for his invaluable advice and, in fact, for undertaking the burden of chaperoning my first steps into academic life as a lecturer at Stockholm University. I also wish to express many thanks to other European University Institute professors for their support, including Heike Schweitzer, Ernst-Ulrich Petersmann and Fabrizio Cafaggi. Furthermore, I am very grateful to professors outside the EUI, including foremost Daniel Halberstam at the University of Michigan Law School, Ann Arbor, for his inspiring work and encouragement. I am also in debt to Mathias Reinmann, JJ Prescott, Rebecca Eisenberg and Donald Regan (all at the University of Michigan Law School, Ann Arbor). I would also like to thank Edward Elgar Publishing for giving me the opportunity to publish this and my other books.

ix

The most heartfelt thanks goes to my mother, to whom I dedicate this work. Without her support and encouragement this book would not have been completed.

Table of cases

EU CASES AND CASES FROM MEMBER STATES

EU Cases

Cases from the Member States

Decisions by the EU Commission

US COURT CASES

FTC Cases

1. Introduction

The object of this book is to dissect the antitrust treatment in the US and under EU law of joint research and development (joint R&D), with some analysis of thereto connected agreements for the implementation of the result of such R&D collaborations, such as standardisation agreements. Special focus will be on the telecoms sector and the pharmaceutical and biotech industries. It is in these industries where collaboration into the creation and adoption of innovations seem to be 'booming' and is more common than in other industries; and where possible anticompetitive effects may also appear because of these collaborations. The book focuses on the evaluation and regulation of R&D collaborations under antitrust law, while the regulation of R&D ventures under merger regulations is left unchecked.

The book is divided into two main parts: firstly, US antitrust regulation and case law for R&D collaborations and, secondly, EU competition rules and case law applying to the same collaborations. The historical regulations and case law are analysed so that the contemporary rules and principles in both jurisdictions are presented in light of the relevant background. Under US antitrust law, I will therefore start by analysing the Justice Department's 1980 guide for R&D joint ventures, while the National Cooperative Research (and Production) Act thereafter is presented. Under EU competition law, the three R&D block exemptions will be presented, starting with the block exemption from 1985. The case law originating from the EU Commission, under the old exemption procedure for paragraph 3 of the prohibition for anticompetitive agreement (mainly Article 85(3) Rome Treaty, now 101(3) TFEU), and the scant case law of EU courts will be analysed. The regulation of R&D collaborations in the two jurisdictions is thereafter compared.

The general conclusion of the book is that R&D collaborations have been, historically and contemporarily, treated leniently under both US and EU antitrust rules. R&D collaborations to create monopoly positions on future markets have been allowed to form on both sides of the Atlantic. Analysing R&D collaborations has been thwarted with the difficulties of identifying anticompetitive effects on any existing and future markets. Since the innovation process is problematic to predict, and the difficulties vary immensely between different industries, making predictions about the potential anticompetitive effects of R&D collaborations is notoriously difficult. The analysis often focuses on the potential effects collaborations may have in the future, on product markets, while efforts have been invested in coming up with a test to analyse how R&D collaboration may have exclusionary or 'collusionary' effects on R&D as such. Scholars and competition authorities have come up with concepts such as 'innovation market' in attempts to have some kind of test or benchmark for identifying dominance and market power in the innovation process. While the notion of 'innovation market' has not been used by competition authorities since, and generally these efforts diminished by, the beginning of 2000, there are scholars that still discuss and promote the concept of innovation market. In fact, the 'innovation market' seems today to have some kind of revival in the scholarly debate. Moreover, the fact that the 2010 EU R&D block exemption presented some more strict rules indicates that the EU Commission shows a nascent interest in the anticompetitive and anti-innovation effects of collusive R&D collaborations.

The author suggests at the end of the book that R&D collaborations would benefit from a more intense antitrust scrutiny. The antitrust analysis should be based on conclusions from economic research in the creation and sustainment of innovation – innovation competition. The antitrust scrutiny would need to distinguish between, on the one hand, incremental innovation efforts by often large and specialised firms already present in the market where the product or technology to be invented will be inserted. Then possibly dominance, competitors and market power may be identified since it may be predicted with some certainty that the innovation will materialise and how the market will react to the innovation. On the other hand, efforts to create radical or disruptive innovations possibly conducted by R&D-intensive firms in collaboration with other firms or universities are often difficult to predict and are generally pro-competitive. In reference to joint R&D to create radical or disruptive innovations, identifying exclusionary effects on future markets or on R&D in the area as such seems very difficult.

Nonetheless, as discussed at the end of the book, R&D-specific firms, when collaborating with larger firms, need some kind of protection so that the larger incumbent firms do not 'shelve' or stop the development of the R&D-specific firms' disruptive inventions, for example an inventive compound, through long-term exclusive development or licensing agreements. Perhaps, if, for example, an R&D-intensive firm and a large pharma company enter into an exclusive development agreement, conduct identified as development for the aim to create the goal of the collaboration, for example a drug, needs to be taken within a three-year period of signing; otherwise, the R&D-specific firm may under competition law exit the exclusive agreement. It would be considered anticompetitive under the prohibition to shelve the drug and the R&D-specific firm's effort for a longer period. In fact, shelving innovations with or without the R&D-intensive firm's understanding of the intent of the pharma firm to stop or at least slow the development of the compound seems to turn around a similar strategy as the 'pay-for-delay' cases. The pharma firm possibly has a drug in the market and they try to prevent a competing drug from being developed by entering an exclusive agreement with the R&D-specific firm that developed the compound.

Apart from these hopefully rare situations, competition law should possibly only regulate the joint innovation efforts where the future market will, in all likelihood, materialise. However, to focus antitrust efforts on joint innovations where there is a clear indication of aim in the form of a distinct market and clear probability of success may encompass more efforts than perhaps perceived initially. Firstly, it would encompass the joint design efforts that today are common practice for many firms in order to develop the next model or generation of a current marketed product. Joint collaboration between current product market competitors to develop or design next year's model may be scrutinised, since such collaborations may shelter collusive effects, either by aligning prices and costs or by aligning the products and design efforts as such to prevent competitors from initiating more disruptive innovation efforts.

Secondly, there seem to be procedures in certain industries that make it possible to predict a distinct market and clear probability of success for the joint effort. Standard-setting in some sectors of the telecom and IT industries seems today to be pre-dated by joint R&D in the pre-standardisation phase, where large firms with voting power in the relevant standard-setting organisation come together to conduct joint R&D and agree on what technology or innovation should be selected for the standard with the standard-setting organisation. This may be enough to also prove that the joint R&D effort by these firms possibly is anticompetitive. It will exclude competing innovations and decrease the incentive to conduct independent R&D for firms not included in the pre-standardisation consortia. Moreover, for the pharmaceutical sector, the FDA procedure for approving drugs together with the patent rules creates transparent R&D processes, where firms know early on what R&D competitors are conducting and what markets these competitors are aiming for. This creates the possibility for firms and competition authorities to identify what firms are active in the sector of R&D and thus whether collaborations between them would likely decrease R&D efforts and competitive pressure or not.

2. Innovation economics

Greatest prosperity is created by the daily development of new and improved products and services, and not by daily competition to pursue efficiencies for the production and sale of the cheapest products. Even though it is somewhat obvious, innovation as a process is based on the method of 'trial and error', with often several errors before a short period of success.[1] There seems to be a general consensus between the economists of today's new economy and the philosophers of yesterday's 'old economy' that unfettered innovation far exceeds the potential gain of making markets more competitive by driving prices closer to marginal costs.[2]

Notwithstanding the consensus on this point, the US and EU policies in the field of research and development may provocatively be purported to be an experiment in Schumpeterian theory that monopolies create more innovations than systems governed by competition or rivalry.[3] It seems that the legislators in the USA and the EU (supported by both

---

[1] It was von Hayek who first clearly emphasised this dimension of competition with his concept of 'competition as a discovery procedure'. Starting with the assumption that the best solutions are often not known yet, competition is viewed as an evolutionary trial and error process, in which the firms try out different problem solutions and can learn from the feedback of the market which of their specific products and technological solutions are the superior ones. Two conclusions can be drawn: (1) Competition is a process, in which previously unknown knowledge is generated, and (2) the multiplicity and diversity of the (parallel trials of the) firms might be crucial for the effectiveness of competition as a discovery procedure. This leads to the policy question whether competition law should take these effects of competition into account. Friedrich A. von Hayek, 'The Meaning of Competition', in Friedrich A. v. Hayek (ed.), *Individualism and Economic Order* (University of Chicago Press, 1948), 92.

[2] Phillip Areeda & Herbert Hovenkamp, *Antitrust Law – An Analysis of Antitrust Principles and Their Application* (Aspen Publishers, 2005), 113 with many references. See also Monopolkommission, *Huaptgutachten: Wettbewerbspolitik vor neuen Herausforderungen* (Nomos Baden-Baden, 1990), 342 et seq.

[3] Schumpeter did not express himself in such simple terms, cf. Joseph Schumpeter, *Capitalism, Socialism and Democracy* (George Allen & Unwin, 1976 (first published in 1943)), 82 et seq.

lawyers and economists) purport that firms with market power and the non-intervention of antitrust courts and agencies spur the rate of innovation. Hence, there is a very lax attitude towards regulating competition or rivalry when dealing with joint R&D collaborations.

It is 'the later' Schumpeter, displayed in *Capitalism, Socialism, and Democracy*, that has had a profound impact on the current state of mind. Schumpeter conceived technological progress as emanating from the large industrial research laboratories. In the laboratories of the large firms, creativity, invention and innovation, in a linear fashion, were conducted. Large firms created wealth and innovation because they enjoyed positions of static market power. He argued that such firms would use their economic profits to finance risky, large-scale R&D activity that would simultaneously leave society better off, in a dynamic sense, and allow the firms to maintain positions of static product-market dominance:[4] R&D for Schumpeter seems to have been based on trial and error:

> As soon as we go into details and inquire into the individual items in which progress was most conspicuous, the trail leads not to the doors of those firms that work under conditions of comparatively free competition but precisely to the doors of the large concerns ... and a shocking suspicion dawns upon us that big business may have had more to do with creating that standard of life than with keeping it down.[5]

Today, the opposing view to Schumpeter is normally attributed to Kenneth Arrow. Arrow famously argued that a monopolist's incentive to

---

[4]   Stephen Martin & John T. Scott, 'The nature of innovation market failure and the design of public support for private innovation', (1999) 29 *Research Policy*, 437, 437 et seq.

[5]   Joseph Schumpeter, *Capitalism, Socialism and Democracy* (George Allen & Unwin, 1976 (first published in 1943)), 82. It is clear that Schumpeter in this section of his book discussed the downfall of capitalism as such, as an intermediate stop to a wholly foreclosed society for entrepreneurs and where freedom is lost; nonetheless, he purports that large firms are able to innovate more efficiently than smaller firms. Such firms would be more capable of financing investment in innovation, could take advantage of such economies of scale as might exist in the R&D process, and, because they typically produce a diversified range of products, would be more likely to find commercially viable applications for new technological developments. He also viewed risk as an inherent aspect of research, development and commercialisation, and saw market power as a way of providing 'insurance' against such risk. Cf. Stephen Martin & John T. Scott, 'The nature of innovation market failure and the design of public support for private innovation', (1999) 29 *Research Policy*, 437, 437 et seq.

innovate is less than that of a competing firm, due to the monopolist's disincentive to cannibalise on his pre-existing monopoly. An *e contrario* interpretation of Arrow's viewpoint would be that firms not holding market power would have higher incentive to innovate so to acquire market power, thus, competition spurs innovation since the firms that innovate hope to obtain appropriability by gaining market power.[6]

While these two viewpoints are not necessarily in disharmony,[7] a large strain of the academic economic debate seems to have focused on proving who of these two 'heavyweights' were right. In fact, as Peritz points out,[8] later researchers use Arrow's and Schumpeter's findings and views without showing that they did not wholeheartedly commit to either competition or monopoly. Instead, they made both of these researchers into caricatures and patron saints of two different strands in the academic debate. As discussed below, several economists have theorised about whether innovation is promoted or restricted by collaborative research, and when collaborators are dominant enough to find that the diminishing competitive pressure would reduce their incentive to innovate.[9] Some state that as long as the technical development is fast, joint R&D

---

[6] Kenneth Arrow, 'Economic Welfare and the Allocation of Resources for Invention', in R. Nelson (ed.), *The Rate and Direction of Inventive Activity: Economic and Social Factors* (National Bureau of Economic Research, 1962), 620 et seq.

[7] Carl Shapiro, 'Competition and Innovation: Did Arrow Hit the Bull's Eye?', in Josh Lerner and Scott Stern (eds), *The Rate & Direction of Economic Activity Revisited* (University of Chicago Press, 2012), 363 et seq.

[8] Rudolph J.R. Peritz, 'Thinking about economic progress: Arrow and Schumpeter in time and space', in Josef Drexl (ed.), *Technologie et Concurrence – Liber Amicorum Hanns Ullrich* (Bruxelles: Larcier Pub., 2009), 627.

[9] Cf., e.g., Josh Lerner & Robert Merges, 'The Control of Technology Alliances: An Empirical Analysis of the Biotechnology Industry', (1998) 46 *Journal of Industrial Economics*, 125; Michael Katz, 'An Analysis of Cooperative Research and Development', (1986) 17 *Rand Journal of Economics*, 527; Thomas Jorde & David Teece, 'Innovation and Cooperation: Implications for Competition and Antitrust', (1990) 4 *Journal of Economic Perspectives*, 75; Thomas Jorde & David Teece, 'Rule of Reason Analysis of Horizontal Arrangements: Agreements Designed to Advance Innovation and Commercialize Technology', (1993) Winter *Antitrust Law Journal*, 579; Thomas Jorde & David Teece, 'Acceptable Cooperation among Competitors in the Face of Growing International Competition', (1989) *Antitrust Law Journal*, 529; and generally Gene Grossman & Carl Shapiro, 'Research joint Ventures: An Antitrust Analysis', (1986) 2 *J. L. Econ. & Org.*, 315.

promotes social welfare irrespective of market power.[10] Other economists are more careful.[11] Part of their research indicates that collaborations among product market competitors, at least in the old economy, under certain strict circumstances are beneficial. They are beneficial when (i) the degree of product market competition is low, when (ii) there is a large R&D spillover in the absence of the cooperation, when (iii) a high degree of sharing is technologically feasible, and when (iv) the agreement concerns basic research rather than development activities.[12] As discussed below, the exemptions for R&D collaborations under US and EU antitrust law do not seem to be narrow enough to carve out these industries only, and the collaborative research that has, according to empirical research, been conducted since R&D exemptions were enacted is in industries that already showed a high degree of R&D spending before the exemptions were enacted.[13]

Apart from theoretical work, there has been much empirical research. It seems almost, generally stated, as if theories of industrial organisation typically predict that innovation should decline with competition; empirical work finds that it increases.[14] Actually, the early stages of the modern economic innovation literature on R&D were largely devoted to sorting out the implications of these two divergent positions purported by,

---

[10]   See, e.g., Thomas Jorde & David Teece, 'Innovation and Cooperation: Implications for Competition and Antitrust', (1990) 4 *Journal of Economic Perspectives*, 75, 85 et seq.; Thomas Jorde & David Teece, 'Rule of Reason Analysis of Horizontal Arrangements: Agreements Designed to Advance Innovation and Commercialize Technology', (1993) Winter *Antitrust Law Journal*, 579, 600 et seq.; Thomas Jorde & David Teece, 'Acceptable Cooperation among Competitors in the Face of Growing International Competition', (1989) *Antitrust Law Journal*, 529, 543 et seq.

[11]   See, e.g., Josh Lerner & Robert Merges, 'The Control of Technology Alliances: An Empirical Analysis of the Biotechnology Industry', (1998) 46 *Journal of Industrial Economics*, 125, 132 et seq.; Michael Katz, 'An Analysis of Cooperative Research and Development', (1986) 17 *Rand Journal of Economics*, 527, 537 et seq.

[12]   Michael Katz, 'An Analysis of Cooperative Research and Development', (1986) 17 *Rand Journal of Economics*, 527, 527, 542 et seq.

[13]   See discussion infra sections 3.2 and 3.3.

[14]   Philippe Aghion, et al., 'Competition and Innovation: An Inverted-U relationship', (2005) May *The Quarterly Journal of Economics* 701, 701, with many references.

on the one side, theorists and, on the other, empirical researchers, respectively. The debate remains a lively one.[15]

Some prominent researchers (using both arguments based on theory and empirical findings) argue the existence of an inverted U between competition and innovation.[16] Thus, the innovation rate is low when there is 'too much' competition or 'too much' monopoly power, while the golden middle way generates most innovation and wealth.

It seems that Frederic M. Scherer was the first, in the 1950s, to launch the idea that the interplay between competition and innovation could be compared with an inverted U.[17] Scherer introduced the idea that competitive pressure forces firms to invest more in R&D until the point where the competition is so intense that the anticipated post-innovation profit is so unlikely that it causes the firms to stop innovating altogether.

In fact, by using the inverted U, both Schumpeter's and Arrow's underlying ideas seem to be able to fit in the same model. Schumpeter argues that if there is (almost or close to perfect) competition in a market the firms will not possess the opportunity to innovate because they will not make any form of (supra competitive) profit to be able to break the permanent condition of perfect allocation of resources. Only if that condition is breached will the firms at least have an incentive to innovate. In case the situation of perfect competition is breached and there is incentive to innovate, the rate of innovation will increase with opportunity and appropriability, the rate of market power held by the firm on the market, until the point that the market tilts to a monopoly. Even though the monopolist will have the opportunity to innovate because of obtaining competitive profits, the incentive will not exist because any new innovation would cannibalise on the monopolist's current sales. Of course, if there were potential entrants, that is, a contestable market, perhaps the monopolist would continue to innovate, otherwise the literature seems to

---

[15] Stephen Martin & John T. Scott, 'The nature of innovation market failure and the design of public support for private innovation', (1999) 29 *Research Policy*, 437, 437 et seq. with references.

[16] Philippe Aghion, et al., 'Competition and Innovation: An Inverted-U relationship', (2005) May *The Quarterly Journal of Economics* 701, 701, with many references.

[17] Frederic M. Scherer, 'Firm Size, Market Structure, Opportunity, and the Output of Patented Inventions', (1965) 55 *AM. ECON. REV.* 1097; Frederic M. Scherer, 'Market Structure and the Employment of Scientists and Engineers', (1967) 57 *AM. ECON. REV.* 524; Frederic M. Scherer, 'Research and Development Resource Allocation under Rivalry', (1967) 81 *The Quarterly Journal of Economics*, 359.

suggest that the innovation rate would tumble when there is a monopolist in the market.

In addition, perhaps there could also be a difference in what sort of innovations the firms breaking out of a situation of perfect competition, on the one hand, and, on the other hand, a monopolist, would market. In fact, the literature seems to suggest that monopolistic and even oligopolistic conduct supports incremental innovations. Large firms have a high degree of employees that are specialised in parts of the innovation process, while that may not be inductive for radical innovation, but rather incremental innovations. Furthermore, incremental innovations will not cannibalise on current sales to the same degree as radical innovations, and the monopolist may also use its current market presence to defend market positions and gain shares. A new entrant or the firms that would like to break out of the situation of perfect competition would prefer a radical or disruptive innovation based perhaps on a new invention to create a new market.

So should the idea of the inverted U be accepted as a basis for developing a regulation of R&D collaborations under antitrust law? Carl Shapiro has recently dissected in detail the innovation literature in an article regarding competition policy in *merger* regulation.[18] Thus, Shapiro is not writing about looser forms of collaboration. Nonetheless, Shapiro raises some noteworthy aspects. Interestingly, Shapiro points to the fact that many industrial economists define competition or competitive pressure as *inter alia* 'less product differentiation'. According to Shapiro, these models therefore were never designed to study rivalry or competition to develop new and improved products and processes. They may help us to understand why we have many brands of toothpaste, but not innovation in the definition preferred by Shapiro.[19] Shapiro rejects not only a definition of competition as 'more imitation', but also more specifically the work based on the existence of an inverted U relationship between 'competition' and innovation.

Shapiro states that increased imitation implies reduced appropriability for the inventor. Likewise, 'less product differentiation' implies less appropriability. He concludes that if imitation is allowed under a judicial system, it reduces incentive to innovate. That is no surprise. But that is not equivalent to or comparable with the statement that increased competition would reduce innovation. Increased competition is not the

---

[18]   Carl Shapiro, 'Competition and Innovation: Did Arrow Hit the Bull's Eye?', in Josh Lerner and Scott Stern (eds), *The Rate & Direction of Economic Activity Revisited* (University of Chicago Press, 2012).
[19]   Ibid., 371.

same as or equivalent to an increase in imitation of products or services or 'less product differentiation'.

The result of the research of several of these industrial economists (including Aghion), which Shapiro criticises, in fact argues for the implementation of regulation protecting intellectual property, while it does not 'hit the bull's eye' according to Shapiro when it comes to creating a competition policy that increases innovation.[20]

Shapiro seems to give the compelling argument that antitrust law should primarily protect competition by *substitute* products or innovations, while competition through *imitation* should be prevented under intellectual property law.

It should be acknowledged that Shapiro discusses merger regulation (and not collaborative R&D), and should be read as criticism of a rather recent US merger case, *Genzyme/Novazyme*.[21] In this case, it seems that the Justice Department ended the experiment with the use of 'innovation market' in merger cases. This case may moreover be viewed as an acknowledgement of a Schumpeterian view of how innovation is best promoted, that is, by creating firms with market power, while neither synergy effects nor even efficiencies seem to have compelled the Justice Department to reach its decisions in this case.[22] Clearly, Shapiro is critical of the Justice Department's conclusions and of the general trend of not acknowledging that competition spurs innovation.[23]

Some of Shapiro's (explicit and implicit) conclusions may be transferred into the area of regulating R&D joint ventures. Firstly, if the legal system (for example patent law) prevents competition by imitation, the incentive to innovate and to invest in R&D should increase when competition increases. Therefore, under the assumption that the patent law system works (which, everyone knows by now, it does not), there should not be an inverted U relationship between competition and innovation. Increasing competition by and between substitute products or

---

[20] Ibid., 373 et seq.
[21] Referring to FTC review of the merger between Genzyme and Novazyme. Ibid. 368. The case is discussed infra section 3.2.3.
[22] Also see the US Horizontal Merger Guidelines that stipulate that the antitrust authorities may accept a merger even though it is clear that prices will increase in the short term if innovation is promoted long term. Justice Department and FTC, Horizontal Merger Guidelines (DOJ, FTC, 2010), sections 6; 6.4; and 10.
[23] Criticising Massimo Motta for doubting that competition spurs innovation. See Carl Shapiro, 'Competition and Innovation: Did Arrow Hit the Bull's Eye?', in Josh Lerner and Scott Stern (eds), *The Rate & Direction of Economic Activity Revisited* (University of Chicago Press, 2012), 366.

innovations should not discourage investment in R&D, while patent law should, generally, prevent competition by imitation (that may decrease the incentive to innovate). In these situations competition and appropriability both can co-exist. Secondly, 'competition' in the view of Shapiro is rivalry. That is quite revealing. That would imply that competition law also should be applicable before any existing relevant markets exist. Thirdly, even though promoting rivalry, Shapiro is not orthodox; he still promotes that a collaboration that restricts rivalry in R&D may still be benign from a competition law perspective because of synergy effects (for example that the parties may create new innovations that they may not achieve independently) and/or increase appropriability (for example economy of scale on R&D).[24]

In light of the above, it seems that the economists are not in agreement about what market structures foster the greatest innovations. Even though Shapiro is quite critical of the idea of an inverted U regarding the interaction between innovation and competition, neither supporters of the inverted U relationship nor, obviously, Shapiro argue that competition or rivalry should not be protected under antitrust law. Few economists, not even Schumpeter, seem to imply that the total elimination of competitive pressure from substitute innovations would increase the incentive to innovate. Some economists seem only to propose that firms need to have funding to conduct R&D in the first place. However, that seems to be an intellectual property law problem, rather then a competition law problem.

Notwithstanding the above, Arrow and Schumpeter were also in agreement on the underlying assumption. As Peritz points out,[25] their views seem to align insofar that they both agree on the goal, the premise of 'the more innovations and inventions, the better'. This also points to the finding that they both agree that progress equals economic growth, that is, progress can be measured as a quantitative goal. Of course, this could be viewed as a given for economists.

In the arenas of network and pharmaceutical industries, the underlying goal of economic progress is sometimes taken to its logical extreme: that commercial success does not always imply the qualitative best result for consumers or users. Because of network effects, tipping, historical accidents, but also standard agreements, a technology of less quality can

---

[24] Carl Shapiro, 'Competition and Innovation: Did Arrow Hit the Bull's Eye?', in Josh Lerner and Scott Stern (eds), *The Rate & Direction of Economic Activity Revisited* (University of Chicago Press, 2012), 368.

[25] Rudolph J.R. Peritz, 'Thinking about economic progress: Arrow and Schumpeter in time and space', in Josef Drexl (ed.), *Technologie et Concurrence – Liber Amicorum Hanns Ullrich* (Bruxelles: Larcier Pub., 2009).

still become more successful than a qualitatively better technology. From a profit maximisation perspective, the market value of a lifestyle drug may outweigh the 'larger' user value of a life-saving drug since the demand for the former stems from more affluent consumer groups than the latter.

If the goal of economic policy takes both quantitative and qualitative improvements into account, more inventions and market success cannot be taken as natural evidence of societal or economic progress. Qualitative improvements as a goal call for normative judgement and political engagement and not only industry self-regulation and profit maximisation. The question then arises whether the qualitative issue can be taken into account and how. It seems clear – even Arrow pointed this out – that real-world success stories often involve a mix between enterprises and government institutions. However, does that imply that competition law should pursue the goal of the, for society, 'best' technology should be invented and gain access to markets? This is an issue that will be discussed in this book.

2.1 NETWORK INDUSTRIES

According to Manuel Castell's three-band pioneering work 'Information Age' from the 1990s, the network society and the 'new economy' bring together several developments: new technological paradigms, globalisation, social movements and the demise of the sovereign nation-state.[26] His ideas were quite revolutionary at the time. Today we are all now aware of and affected by the paradigm shift the 'new economy' brought with it. Global markets and globalisation as a process are today facts of life for many, if not all, firms and individuals. The technology revolution of the shift from analogue to digital communication was absolutely necessary to enable globalisation as a large-scale process and transfer, and enabled outsourcing and the relocation of services and production between specialised firms in different nation-states and continents. The demise of sovereign nation-states was caused by the loss of public power and control over previously national firms and transactions due to globalisation. Power to regulate these organisations and transactions was relocated from nation-states to regional or global organisations (for example the EU or the WTO), or from the nation-states to the firms

---

[26] Manuel Castell, *The Rise of the Network Society, The Information Age: Economy, Society and Culture* Vol. I. (Cambridge, MA; Oxford, UK: Blackwell, 1996, 2nd ed., 2000).

themselves by deregulation or the acknowledgement of the benefits of self-regulation.[27]

Carl Shapiro and Hal Varian in their book *Information Rules* from 1999 discuss information economics and network effects and their implication on *inter alia* antitrust regulation.[28] And while they acknowledge the necessity of collaboration and cooperation in the new economy, where firms are specialised and dispersed on global markets, they also recognise the need for antitrust regulation of said collaborations. The telecommunications and the internet industries, in particular, require interconnection, standardisation, coordination and other sorts of cooperation between competitors to establish, create and develop innovations into markets. The pharma and biotech firms need to collaborate to, firstly, conduct research, and, secondly, to develop and transfer new compounds and substances from the R&D-specific firms to the larger pharma firms for evaluation, clinical trials, approval and drug production.

Thus, the 'new economy' seems to imply (now, in hindsight, also has implied) that specialised firms are active on global markets where interoperability, collaboration and communication is of essence both regarding creating innovations and also – and this is more important from an antitrust perspective – for the implementation of said innovations into society at large. Hence, implementation of innovations implies the global acceptance, adoption and consumption of these technologies or drugs by competitors, customers, governments and, ultimately, consumers, demands collaborations.

The new economy implies that firms need to collaborate more and that antitrust must accommodate for such collaborations. In fact, in Shapiro's and Varian's, and other economists', early works from the 1980s and 1990s, there is a clear concern that the US antitrust regulation would stand in the way of necessary collaborations in developing the new economy in the USA. Their remarks and concerns were acknowledged and several of their proposals seem to have been implemented by Congress or by the Justice Department. An exemption for R&D collaborations under US antitrust law under the National Collaborative Research

---

[27]   Castell states that the network society also inherently picked up on the libertarian and revolutionary strands or possibilities of the new technology paradigm and all this combined created the 'information age'. There is something anti-authoritarian with networks, while networks and collaborations imply constant agreement to continue the cooperation. Ibid.

[28]   Carl Shapiro & Hal R. Varian, *Information Rules* (Harvard Business School Press, 1999).

Production Act (NCRPA) was enacted and amended during the 1980s and 1990s and later extended to also include standard-setting activities. The EU was soon to follow with the implementation and extension of the block exemption for R&D collaborations and guidelines for cooperation between competitors. It reflected a general change in approach towards R&D collaborations and the implementation of the result of such collaborations. The difference between research and development seems to have been blurred in network industries. Collaboration in incremental development should be judged similarly to basic research under antitrust law, while R&D should be judged not as a linear development but rather as a collaborative dynamic development between several firms.[29]

The realisation of the importance of collaborative innovation and the concern that hampering the innovative and competitive process could have a detrimental effect on competition, limit access to markets and generally diminish the creation of wealth led to attempts to regulate and measure restriction of competition in the creation and adoption of innovations. The idea of the innovation market was born.[30] Interestingly, when (re-)introduced by economists active at the Justice Department, it was quickly heavily criticised.[31] It was mainly criticised based on the fact that there are no real innovation 'markets'. Before there is trade and products or services are exposed to customers and consumers, we will not know what products or services will create sales and compete or at what price. Thus, we do not know if there is a market at all and, furthermore, whether any firm or firms hold market power in such a market. Mainly because of this deficiency, the concept of the innovation market never got a strong foothold and has not been used extensively.[32] It

---

[29] Thomas Jorde's and David Teece's research in this regard will be analysed. See, e.g., Thomas Jorde & David Teece, 'Innovation, Cooperation and Antitrust', (1989) 4 *High Tech Law Journal* 1. See also Gene Grossman & Carl Shapiro, 'Research Joint Ventures: An Antitrust Analysis', (1986) 2 *J. L. Econ. & Org*, 315. For a more up-to-date analysis about the difference between the linear way of conducting research *vis-à-vis* the more chaotic and complex models, see, for example, G.M. Peter Swann's work, e.g. Birke, D.; Swann, G.M.P, 'Network Effects, Network Structure and Consumer Interaction in Mobile Telecommunications in Europe and Asia', (2010) 76 *Journal of Economic Behavior and Organization*, 153 et seq.

[30] See discussion infra section 3.2.2.

[31] See discussion infra section 3.2.2.

[32] There were other points of critique to see: see discussion infra section 3.2.3. See also Michael A. Carrier, *Innovation for the 21st Century: Harnessing the Power of Intellectual Property and Antitrust Law* (Oxford Scholarship Online, May 2009), 297 et seq.

was primarily used in merger cases and some scholars claim that the last
US merger case to refer to it is from 2000, that is, the last time the US
Justice Department launched an innovation market case.[33] Nonetheless,
the weary feeling that conduct and collaborations – pre-competition –
still affect competition and need to be regulated seems to have lingered
on in the scholarly community. This feeling also materialises from the
fact that in the 'new economy' competition is happening during the R&D
phase and not through economies of scale when the markets have already
been established. Furthermore, in other sectors of the economy such as
the standard-setting industry and technology transfer markets, the under-
regulation of R&D collaborations seems to cause parties to engage in
long-lasting litigation regarding accessing technologies. In fact, the
litigations under the 'patent war' in the telecoms and IT sector have
reached the stage that parties use(d) courts as price authorities to stipulate
the royalty rates for the patents that are essential to access the innovations that the large firms (system leaders) were allowed to develop in
collaboration under the R&D phase. Could the lax regulation of R&D
collaborations lead to only single technologies being developed, implemented and adopted on markets in the new economy and therefore firms
have to litigate to access these technologies on fair terms?

Baron and Pohlmann's recent in-depth research also shows that firms
with substitutable R&D programmes and patent portfolios are more
likely to be members of the same pre-standardisation consortium.[34] In
fact, Baron and Pohlmann's research, based on a database including all
ICT standards issued between 1992 and 2009, shows that consortia have
been formed for all standards with an unusually high number of patent
holders.[35] Indeed, through upfront R&D coordination under the consortium, firms that have the same business model can coordinate R&D and
better anticipate technology selection decisions in standards development
organisations (SDOs).[36] However, their research shows that R&D-
specific or technology specialists firms, possibly the SMEs, are not
members of the pre-standardisation consortia.[37] Baron and Pohlmann also

---

[33]   Michael A. Carrier, *Innovation for the 21st Century: Harnessing the Power
of Intellectual Property and Antitrust Law* (Oxford Scholarship Online, May
2009), 93.
[34]   Justus Baron and Tim Pohlmann, 'Who Cooperates in Standard Consortia
– Rivals or Complementors' (2013) 9 *Journal of Competition Law & Economics*,
905, 921, 928.
[35]   Ibid., 905, 912, 921 et seq., 928.
[36]   Ibid.
[37]   Ibid.

warn that if the major economic function of consortia is to reduce technological rivalry, competition authorities should monitor the interface between SDO membership and R&D or pre-standard consortia carefully.[38]

Some dispersed regulations of R&D collaborations have existed either through *per se* rules (indicating *per se* illegal or *per se* legal conduct) under antitrust law, or by trying to identify potential anticompetitive effects by pointing to the parties' strong market presence in existing technology or product markets. The discussion of the concept of innovation market has moreover not disappeared and it has been discussed over the years – and more so quite recently – both by lawyers and economists.[39] In fact, Michael A. Carrier even draws up a new test or framework for how to establish anticompetitive mergers in the pharmaceutical sector using the notion of 'innovation market' in his contribution from 2009.[40] Nonetheless, it does not seem that the antitrust authorities have reacted and adequately addressed the antitrust effects caused by collaborations in the pre-competition phase.

2.2 THE PHARMACEUTICAL INDUSTRY

The latest trend in the pharmaceutical sector is that R&D-intensive firms, often clustered around universities, conduct much research that they later exclusively license and co-develop with larger pharmaceutical firms.[41] Normally, the R&D-intensive firms seek partners or purchasers when they have conducted successful pre-clinical or even clinical tests of the relevant substance. The larger pharma companies are mainly needed to

---

[38]   Ibid., 928.

[39]   See, for example, Josef Drexl, 'Anticompetitive stumbling stones on the way to a cleaner world: protecting competition in innovation without a market', (2012) 8 *Journal of Competition Law & Economics*, 507 with several references. See also Michael A. Carrier, *Innovation for the 21st Century: Harnessing the Power of Intellectual Property and Antitrust Law* (Oxford Scholarship Online, May 2009), 297 et seq. Granieri, Massimiliano, and Andrea Renda, *Innovation Law and Policy in the European Union: Towards Horizon 2020* (Milan: Springer, 2012), 4 et seq.

[40]   Michael A. Carrier, *Innovation for the 21st Century: Harnessing the Power of Intellectual Property and Antitrust Law* (Oxford Scholarship Online, May 2009), 303 et seq.

[41]   Constance E. Bagley & Christina D. Tvarnø, 'Pharmaceutical public-private Partnership: Moving From Bench To the Bedside' (2014) 14 *Harvard Business Law Review*, 373-401.

administrate and conduct the lengthy and costly regulator processes (Phases I, II and III). Indeed, there is a great increase in the amount of collaborations entered into in the pharma and biotech sectors.[42] Even the largest firms cannot today conduct research, develop and market all drugs and treatments in-house. Instead, collaborations, in the form of license agreements, R&D ventures, co-marketing agreements and even mergers, to develop and market new and generic drugs are on the increase. Pharma and biotech firms are collaborating more and more. This exchange of information and ideas coupled with, firstly, complex agreements with terms, obligations and covenants that may exclude and restrict the parties and, secondly, with the market transparency due to patent and market approval procedures creates a rather distinctive setting for competition law.

Carrier acknowledged that the economist community is not in agreement regarding which market structure fosters innovations, but believes that that should not prevent competition authorities from acting.[43] Interestingly, Carrier presents a rebuttal to the idea that the innovation market should not be used. Carrier wants to use a narrow version of the innovation market concept for the pharmaceutical industry. He states that unknown innovators do not carry out innovation in the pharma sector. The barriers to entry are high because of several patents and the lengthy regulator process for approving drugs. In fact, the patent thicket and the very high costs associated with the regulator process minimise the number of actors that can be active on a pharmaceutical innovation market. Moreover, at least historically, the higher amount of R&D inserted on an innovation market in the pharmaceutical sector, the higher the number of R&D results was gained. Possibly today in the biotech sector, this almost linear notion between investment in R&D and R&D results is not true anymore. However, possibly it still holds true for the general pharma sector where firms may utilise a trial-and-error R&D that would render results based on the number of tries conducted. In other words, generally, one may possibly predict some form of outcome from R&D, even though very few projects will in the end result in marketed

---

[42]   Robinson, D. T. & Stuart E. T., 'Financial Contracting in Biotech Strategic Alliances', (2007) 50 *Journal of Law and Economics*, 559-596. See also Gjalt de Jong and Rosalinde JA Klein Woolthuis, 'The Content and role of formal contracts in high-tech alliances', (2009) 11 *Innovation: Management, Policy & Practice*, 44-59.

[43]   Michael A. Carrier, *Innovation for the 21st Century: Harnessing the Power of Intellectual Property and Antitrust Law* (Oxford Scholarship Online, May 2009), 298 et seq.

drugs. Furthermore, pharmaceutical R&D typically does not suffer from the duplication that afflicts other industries, while it is almost impossible to duplicate even when striving to cure the same illness.[44]

The majority of the R&D conducted in the pharmaceutical sector covers products and not processes, implying that the innovations and patents are often broad and public in comparison with process innovations. Technical opportunity and appropriability are also quite high in the pharmaceutical industry; while foremost the innovations are drastic or disruptive, implying that they create new markets when marketed.[45]

Even though the products (drugs) marketed are disruptive, the very lengthy regulator procedure, interplaying with the pharmaceutical firms' need to patent their compound at an early stage of the development to do clinical testing, implies that innovation efforts in the pharmaceutical market are transparent. Firms in the industry know about their competitors' R&D efforts years before any drugs are marketed and this creates the possibility of anticompetitive collaboration for the creation of drugs even though it represents disruptive innovations.

Carrier even uses his modified framework to show that there are at least mergers between pharmaceutical firms where they both had drugs under evaluation in the regulatory procedure and that, by prohibiting these mergers, the US antitrust authorities have also upheld competition between the later approved drugs. There was a clear risk that the firms, if allowed to merge, would eliminate one of the efforts and therefore create a monopoly position.

2.3 COMPETITION AS AN EVOLUTIONARY PROCESS

From statistics it seems clear that joint R&D ventures are popular. Historically, there seems to be more joint R&D today, while the level of investment in R&D has stayed the same since the Second World War.[46]

Notwithstanding the above, research – starting with von Hayek's legendary statement that 'competition is a discovery procedure' – seems to emphasise diversity or an evolutionary process of parallel search for

---

[44]   Ibid., 303 et seq.
[45]   Ibid.
[46]   More developed in Björn Lundqvist, *Standardization under EU Competition Rules and US Antitrust Laws – The Rise and the Limits of Self-Regulation* (Edward Elgar, 2014), 45 et seq.

new solutions.[47] Wolfgang Kerber recently analysed much theoretical and empirical data regarding mergers and joint R&D ventures starting out with the broad question: what are the benefits of competition?[48] According to Kerber, the basic presumption of a market economy is that competition between firms is usually the best way to ensure that the consumers get their problems solved as sufficiently and cheaply as possible. The main problem, though, according to Kerber, is that in a changing world most often there is no objective knowledge of what the best products for the current preferences of consumers are and how to produce and distribute them with the least possible cost. However, the industrial economics literature on innovation usually assumes that the firms know the best products and technologies or what the current preferences are.[49] Therefore, the experimental dimension of competition, or the need for diversity and a multitude of R&D poles, as emphasised by Hayek and Farrell[50] – that is, that several firms try out different research approaches, make mistakes and learn from each other's experiences – is not dealt with in modern game-theoretic industrial economics.

Kerber's review of the economic research paints a picture that from empirical studies there is an overwhelmingly negative effect of mergers on innovation in comparison with generally more positive innovation effects of R&D joint ventures. The positive effects of joint R&D ventures may possibly differ on whether the parties are still allowed to conduct parallel or even competing R&D while conducting the R&D venture and thereafter. Kerber concludes, therefore, that while more empirical research needs to be conducted, it seems clear that both mergers and R&D joint ventures can reduce the effectiveness of competition as a process of parallel experimentation and therefore might raise concerns from a competition law perspective.[51]

---

[47]   Friedrich A. von Hayek, 'The Meaning of Competition', in Friedrich A. v. Hayek (ed.), *Individualism and Economic Order* (University of Chicago Press, 1948), 92.

[48]   Wolfgang Kerber, 'Competition, Innovation and Maintaining Diversity Through Competition Law', in J. Drexl, W. Kerber and R. Podszun (eds), *Economic Approaches to Competition Law: Foundations and Limitations* (Edward Elgar, 2010), 173.

[49]   Ibid.

[50]   Joseph Farrell, 'Complexity, Diversity, and Antitrust', (2006), 51 *Antitrust Bulletin*, 165.

[51]   Wolfgang Kerber, 'Competition, Innovation and Maintaining Diversity Through Competition Law', in J. Drexl, W. Kerber and R. Podszun (eds), *Economic Approaches to Competition Law: Foundations and Limitations* (Edward Elgar, 2010), 173.

Pure R&D ventures where firms, even competitors, let their research intermingle in order to exchange ideas and jointly try to solve problems would be pro-innovation. However, joint R&D ventures are often conducted with restrictions. The researchers seldom meet at all because the innovation process is divided up and different specialised groups of researchers address different parts of the research. The firms are often committed not to conduct competing research. Moreover, very little research has been done on the interface between joint R&D ventures and standards or clinical testing. Joint R&D conducted in the pre-standardisation phase by the firms holding a voting block, or even a majority position, in the technical committee of the relevant standard-setting organisation (SSO) or SDO may prevent new innovation from entering markets and may thus lessen the incentive for innovators not having access to the joint R&D venture to commit to conducting research.[52] In the pharmaceutical industry research is often transparent because of patent applications and clinical testing, so the firms know about what research is conducted and how close the firms are to succeeding and getting drugs approved under the national or regional drug approval systems. This information may act as a disincentive to invest in research and also make firms understand how to reach out to collude in R&D so that competing research tracks are eliminated.

While it is certain that the economists are not in agreement regarding the interlink between competition and innovation, the question is whether agencies or plaintiffs using competition law should take a step back, or whether competition scholars and courts should acknowledge that innovation and innovation rate is so important that we cannot risk not intervening when it seems clear that a concentration through a joint R&D collaboration will combine perhaps the only of the likely and interested innovators on the market. The intuitive feeling that innovation flourishes better if there is rivalry means that monopoly is in certain cases perhaps enough to, at least, prompt an analysis of the R&D collaboration or merger; what test to establish what concentration should be prohibited is a grander question to answer. Moreover, joint R&D can be combined with standard agreements or clinical testing and approval systems which in combination may be used to foreclose innovations to access markets.

---

[52] See generally Justus Baron and Tim Pohlmann, 'Who Cooperates in Standard Consortia – Rivals or Complementors' (2013) 9 *Journal of Competition Law & Economics*, 905.

2.4 INDUSTRIAL ECONOMICS, INTELLECTUAL PROPERTY LAW AND COMPETITION LAW

Arrow and Schumpeter (and other economists) disagree on the method to attain it, but they seem to agree that economic growth and thereby progress should be measured and valued by the quantitative increase of innovations and inventions and their market success, that is, economic wealth.[53] While, theoretically, quantitative increase of inventions is the target, from an objective legal perspective, when analysing the regulation, agencies' conduct and cases, it seems that we are pursuing a proxy. Neither intellectual property law nor competition law seems to pursue a goal of increased inventions or innovations; rather, the goal seems to be the increase of the amount of intellectual property rights, especially patents. But, it is quite clear that intellectual property rights, not even patents, always reflect innovations or inventions. Several authors and commentators have discussed the proliferation of patents and the reasons; therefore it will not be discussed at length here.[54] The unfortunate result of lowering the standard for obtaining patents is that patent rights have come to be treated and now *de facto* are an end in itself, rather than a means to encourage and protect invention.[55]

The underlying reason for why governments allow for the proliferation of patents and also for patents to increase in strength can, generally, be attributed to the exaggerated profit logic that emerged in the 1980s.[56] The idea seems to be that increased protection of the right-holders would automatically lead to more inventions since the incentive to invent would increase with the increase of protection. While such reasoning does not diminish the idea that a well-developed public domain of knowledge

---

[53]   Rudolph J.R. Peritz, 'Thinking about economic progress: Arrow and Schumpeter in time and space', in Josef Drexl (ed.), *Technologie et Concurrence – Liber Amicorum Hanns Ullrich* (Bruxelles: Larcier Pub., 2009), 627; and Rudolph J.R. Peritz, 'Freedom to Experiment: Towards a Concept of Inventor Welfare', (2008) 90 *Journal of the Patent and Trademark Office Society*, 245, 246 et seq.

[54]   Björn Lundqvist, *Standardization under EU Competition Rules and US Antitrust Laws – The Rise and the Limits of Self-Regulation* (Edward Elgar, 2014), 16 et seq. with several references.

[55]   Rudolph J.R. Peritz, 'Freedom to Experiment: Towards a Concept of Inventor Welfare', (2008) 90 *Journal of the Patent and Trademark Office Society*, 245, 253 et seq.

[56]   Ibid., 250 et seq.

increases the rate and amount of innovations, pursuing profit maximisation in order to increase the incentive to invent in an exaggerated manner, tilts the fragile balance between these twin engines for progress.[57]

One way that the balance was tilted in the US in the 1980s (and onwards) was that the case law based on the unlicensed experimental use defence under US intellectual property laws was restricted and limited. The requirements for the defence have been more difficult to fulfil after some landmark cases, starting with the *Bolar* case in 1984.[58]

The case law based on the US unlicensed experimental use defence has its origins in two cases from 1813, *Whittemore v. Cutter*[59] and *Saw v. Guild*,[60] and Justice Story's identification of a 'philosophical experimental' use exemption including experiments in the arts and sciences up to a point of making 'of a machine fit for use and with the design to use it for profit'.[61] It is the latter part of that rule where the courts have shifted, from a lenient approach towards the follow-on inventor in the identification of 'for profit', to a more stringent attitude, where every person having a 'business interest' in the experiment is fulfilling the 'for profit rule'. The Federal Circuit, soon after its inauguration as the US prominent patent court, made clear in *Bolar* that the experimental use defence allows a narrow range of conduct and nothing beyond dilettante affair.[62] It later confirmed and extended this rule in the famous *Madey v. Duke University* case, were educating and enlightening students and faculty participating in research furthered the institution's legitimate business practice.[63]

---

[57] Ibid., 246 et seq.
[58] *Roche Prods. v. Bolar Pharma. Co.* 733 F.2d 858 (Fed. Cir. 1984). Rudolph J.R. Peritz, 'Freedom to Experiment: Towards a Concept of Inventor Welfare', (2008) 90 *Journal of the Patent and Trademark Office Society*, 245, 250 et seq.
[59] *Whittemore v. Cutter* 29 F. Cas. 1120 (C.C.D. Mass. 1813) (No. 17,600).
[60] *Saw v. Guild* 21 F. Cas. 554 (C.C.D. Mass. 1813) (No. 12,391).
[61] *Whittemore v. Cutter* 29 F. Cas. 1120, 1121 (C.C.D. Mass. 1813) (No. 17,600), *Saw v. Guild* 21 F. Cas. 554, 555 (C.C.D. Mass. 1813) (no. 12,391). Rudolph J.R. Peritz, 'Freedom to Experiment: Towards a Concept of Inventor Welfare', (2008) 90 *Journal of the Patent and Trademark Office Society*, 245, 250 et seq.
[62] *Roche Prods. v. Bolar Pharma. Co.* 733 F.2d 858 (Fed. Cir. 1984).
[63] *Madey v. Duke University*, 307 F.3d 1351, 1362-63 (Fed. Cir. 2002).

Peritz concludes that under the current doctrine, the experimental use defence to patent infringement has become no more than a mirage.[64] The right to exclude is now not exclusively connected to the invention or product, but also to the process of obtaining the invention. The need to have a licensee to experiment will presumably lead to higher costs for accessing the invention process, which will imply that innovations that could have been developed, had we implemented a more inclusive experimental use defence, will not be developed.[65]

There is also a statutory experimental use exception. Congress, as a response to the restrictions put in place by the Federal Circuit in *Bolar* and *Madey*, enacted 35 U.S.C. § 271 (e) which exempts from infringement uses reasonably related to the development and submission of information under the Federal Food, Drug and Cosmetic Act (FDA Act). The statute is for the benefits of generic producers to conduct (drug) tests in preparation for the FDA regulatory procedure and approval. In 2005, in *Merck*, the Supreme Court seems to have interpreted the statute beneficially for the generic producers including any research, also pre-clinical research, reasonably related to the development and the submission of any information to the FDA.[66] The Supreme Court thereby not only disregarded any desire to make the exception available only for non-business aims, it also implemented a broad definition of 'experiment'.

There has also been empirical research on whether US research has suffered because of the narrow common law defence for unlicensed experimental use. Interestingly, the empirical research shows that it has not, because of a number of reasons.[67] It seems, firstly, that research culture does not correlate to such a narrow defence as displayed in *Madey*. Patents did not seem to deter researchers from conducting

---

[64] Rudolph J.R. Peritz, 'Freedom to Experiment: Towards a Concept of Inventor Welfare', (2008) 90 *Journal of the Patent and Trademark Office Society*, 245, 250 et seq.

[65] An interesting discussion regarding whether it is possible to make an economic analysis similar to a theory/graph about 'perfect competition', but instead based on the notion and aim of 'perfect invention'. Thus, where resources are allocated in the right way so as to enable quantitatively and qualitatively the most and best inventions. See ibid., 252 et seq.

[66] *Merck KGaA v. Integra Lifesciences I*, Ltd., 545 U.S. 193 (2005).

[67] See John P. Walsh et al., 'Where Excludability Matters: Material versus Intellectual Property in Academic Biomedical Research', (2007) 36 *Res. Pol'y* 1184, 1188 et seq. See also National Research Council, *Reaping the Benefits of Geonomic and Proteomic Research: Intellectual Property Rights, Innovation and Public Health* (2006).

research in the fields covered by patents, and patentees did not react with such hostility that *Madey* gives them the right to do. Patentees did not seem to impose restrictive licensing terms. Moreover, as Carrier discusses, even the (in-)famous research tools did not generate litigations since, in the end, actually few drugs were ever deduced or created by these tools in the biotech sector, and the potential damages for patentees to obtain were correspondingly quite minimal.[68]

Notwithstanding that research shows that *Madey* and *Bolar* have not (yet) had any profound effect in the pharma and biotech industries, under these judgments, a 'greenfield' innovator, outside the area of the FDA Act, and without any prior activities in the technology, most likely needs a licence from the patentee to use and experiment with the patent-protected information. In light of the prevailing US patent jurisprudence under *Madey* and *Bolar*, there is only a limited experimental use defence under US patent law jurisprudence. Thus, from a US perspective, an inventor, even connected to a university, needs to take out a licence. Otherwise, the researcher is already in violation of the patent when conducting research into how he can invent around the patent.[69]

From a European perspective, the experimental use exemption is statutory and, for the first time, will be unified in almost all EU member states. The Unified Patent Court Agreement (UPCA), which has been signed by 25 of the EU's 28 member states, stipulates an experimental use exception. Article 27 (b) UPCA stipulates:

The rights conferred by a patent shall not extend to any of the following:

(a) […]
(b) acts done for experimental purposes relating to the subject-matter of the patented invention;
(c) […]

---

[68] Michael A. Carrier, *Innovation for the 21st Century: Harnessing the Power of Intellectual Property and Antitrust Law* (Oxford Scholarship Online, May 2009), 261, et seq.

[69] However, as with many pools, the MPEG LA licences are limited to certain fields of conduct. In the MPEG-2 case it seems that the licensees may manufacture, sell and in most cases use the technology. Possibly use implies R&D, otherwise it actually seems that any firm wanting to conduct research in the field of the MPEG-2 needs to obtain individual licences from each member of the pool. See generally MPEG-2 pool Business Review Letter from Joel Klein to Gerrard Beeney dated June 26, 1997. See http://www.usdoj.gov/atr/public/busreview/215742.htm, last visited 20090407.

There is no case law yet regarding Article 27 (b), but it seems unlikely that the Unified Patent Court would demand a non-commercial requirement (in fact, there is a privately, non-commercial stand-alone exemption stipulated in Article 27 (a)). National case law regarding the experimental use exemption, even though not binding on the UPC, is scarce but does not seem to support a non-commercial requirement.[70] However, for the exemption to be applicable, the research conducted needs to be experimental and to understand the subject-matter of the patented invention. Most probably, this is a narrower definition of 'experimental' than what the Supreme Court acknowledged in *Merck* or even in *Bolar*.[71]

Moreover, there is a *Merck* experimental use exemption for generic drug producers in the Directive 2004/27/EC of 31 March 2004, which establishes a Community code relating to medicinal products for human use. Section 10.6 of the Directive stipulates an exception to patent infringement related to unlicensed experimentation, to pre-clinical trials and to clinical trials made with the aim of obtaining regulatory approval for a generic drug. This rule has, when implemented, influenced the general experimental use exemption in EU member states. For example, the national rule in Germany is not only applicable to generic producers, but to drugs in general, as in the US, while that is not the case in the UK.[72]

However, where did this lead us? The US antitrust regulation of R&D collaborations and innovation will be discussed in this book together with the similar and corresponding regulation under EU competition law. This will be done by scrutinising the development to establish exemptions for R&D collaborations under EU and US antitrust laws, respectively. However, the playing field is somewhat different, not levelled, between the US and EU for when, generally, intellectual property law regulates rivalry to the point when competition law starts to apply. In the EU, the

---

[70]   See, for example, the UK *Monsanto/Stauffer* (RPC [1985] 515) case: an exempted act can have 'an ultimate commercial purpose', while the experimental purpose must have a 'real and direct' connection with the subject matter of the patent.

[71]   The German experimental use exception is more generous than the UK equivalent. See Candi J. Soames, '"Experimental use" and "Bolar" exemption in the EU – how far do these provisions extend?', 2009 http://www.lexology.com/library/detail.aspx?g=0057f1d5-24ad-4b07-a56c-ed9254da6854. Accessed 9 September 2014.

[72]   Ibid.

experimental use exemption is wider in one sense than the US experimental use defence and therefore firms are obliged in the US to enter, at
least, licence agreements with patentees so as to enable them to conduct
R&D in the field that is covered by the patents. These licence agreements
can be scrutinised under US antitrust laws and could in theory be
prohibited, null and void, while equivalent research may be conducted
under the statutory exemption under the UPCA in the EU. Thus,
competing research cannot be conducted in the US, while in the EU it
would be performed. Moreover, the limited US defence also forces
competitors to collaborate. They need to extract licences from each other,
which could then give these firms incentives to collude.

In practice, the question is whether the playing field is unlevelled and
whether the scenarios discussed above will ever materialise. The licence
to conduct research as such would very seldom be found to be anticompetitive by the US antitrust agencies; only the ancillary restraints
might be found to violate competition law. Blanket R&D licences
between competing firms, even with strong market presence, will probably not be found to violate US antitrust law. Universities and firms also
seem to allow for competitors to conduct infringing R&D in the US
without filing infringement suits. Furthermore, the narrow interpretation
of experimental on the 'subject-matter of the patent' limits the EU
exception in a way that does not correspond in the US defence.
Therefore, the field is more level than one may first perceive. Moreover,
under global technical standards or under global patent pools, US
essential patents will almost certainly always be present, implying that
the US experimental use defence, being the most narrow, will presumably
restrict European firms with global aspirations. They would also need to
take out US licences to conduct experiments.

In the end, I will return to the issue of the experimental use
restrictions. Below, the antitrust regulation of R&D collaborations will be
scrutinised. Relevant decisions regarding R&D joint ventures by US
courts, the Justice Department under the business letter review system,
while, in addition to scant EU case law, the EU Commission's decisions
under the old system of notifying R&D collaborations and the comfort
letters published by the EU Commission, will be analysed. Interestingly,
this analysis shows that several of the high-profile cases in the technical
industries actually deal more with the establishment of standards than
with R&D collaborations, while we have seen very few R&D collaboration antitrust cases originating from the pharmaceutical sector. Thus, the
development to establish exemptions for R&D collaborations and for the
joint implementation and adoption of the results of such collaborations
will be described and analysed in this book. In the end, I will return to

the interplay between economics and law discussed in this chapter and draw some conclusions on what rules and principles could be beneficial to implement.

3. Research and development agreements under US antitrust law and EU competition rules

3.1 INTRODUCTION

Simply stated, research ventures which minimise transaction costs, prevent overlapping research and create economies of scale even between competitors with market power are accepted and promoted under contemporary application of US antitrust law and EU competition law; these are seen as preventing inefficiencies or wasted investments. Joint research ventures might, of course, be beneficial for other reasons: joint research might create great synergies and the basis for researchers to exchange ideas.[73] The meeting of minds has always been a way to enhance innovation and having competing researchers interact might be beneficial. Joint efforts might furthermore encourage the participants to take larger economic risks than single firms could.[74]

The above holds true for the contemporary antitrust policy *vis-à-vis* R&D collaborations. However, joint R&D efforts have historically been judged against a more stringent antitrust benchmark.

Obviously, joint R&D make the parties co-owners of a common result, that is, creating a common profit centre, which they need to price together, whereas independent research would create different results,

---

[73] For benefits of joint research ventures, see, e.g., Alan S. Gutterman, *Innovation and Competition Policy – A Comparative Study of the Regulation of Patent Licensing and Collaborative Research & Development in the United States and the European Community* (Kluwer Law International, 1997) 106 et seq.; Joseph Brodley, 'Joint Ventures and Antitrust Policy', (1981–1982) 95 *Harvard Law Review*, 1521, 1527 et seq. Cf. Andreas Fuchs, *Kartellrechtliche Grenzen der Forschungskooperation* (Nomos Verlaggesellschaft, 1989), 72 et seq.
[74] This statement might be contested. See John T. Scott, 'Diversification versus Cooperation in R&D Investment', (1988) 9 *Managerial Decision Economics* 173, 183 et seq.

that is, different potential profit centres with different prices.[75] Cooperation into research implies that neither of the parties is capable of securing a technology advantage over the other and thereby improves its position in the market in comparison with its R&D colleague.[76] If the parties are small or medium-sized firms, this would, of course, not create any problems. Then there would always be other firms or new entrants to ensure rivalry and instigate the competitive pressure needed for firms to invent and for the best innovation to win the competitive race. Nonetheless, older US case law *may* be interpreted that collaboration between parties to create a joint profit centre in a market may be considered anticompetitive *per se* if the plaintiff can show that the members of the collaboration would have entered the market independently, but for the collaboration.[77]

There are, generally, three types of distinct anticompetitive conduct within the sphere of joint R&D:

(i)   collusion between (often dominant) joint R&D parties forming an agreement to limit or exclude research or research avenues, or to limit potential competition in R&D, that is, naked agreements, or agreements to that effect, not to do research or to suspend or limit the discovery of innovations and in the end to lower the quality of the successful innovation;[78]

(ii)   exclusion, or access discrimination, of third parties from R&D results, denying them use of *essential* resources, that is, denying other firms access to the result of the R&D venture; and

(iii)   spillover collusion manifested in price or royalty cartels, excluding third parties from product markets; or the use of too intrusive collateral (ancillary) restraints.[79]

---

[75]   Cf. Joseph Brodley, 'Joint Ventures and Antitrust Policy', (1981–1982) 95 *Harvard Law Review*, 1521, 1524.

[76]   Commission, Report on Competition Policy 1978, 78.

[77]   See discussion *infra* in connection with the presentation of *United States v. Penn-Olin Chemical Co.* 378 U.S. 158, 84 S.Ct.1710 (1964).

[78]   See *United States v. Automobile Mfrs. Ass'n* 307 F.Supp. 617 (C.D. Cal. 1969) appeal dismissed *sub nom. City of New York v. United States*, 397 U.S. 248 (1970), modified *sub nom. United States v. Motor Vehicle Mfrs. Ass'n*, 182-82 Trade Cas. (CCH) 65,088 (C.D. Cal. 1982).

[79]   Cf. Andreas Fuchs, *Kartellrechtliche Grenzen der Forschungskooperation* (Nomos Verlaggesellschaft, 1989), 75 et seq. See also Commission, Report on Competition Policy 1994, 105 et seq.

These forms of conduct – to be regarded as anticompetitive – require that the parties may somehow exclude firms from the relevant market created or developed as a result of the R&D. This may be done by the use of intellectual property rights or by being dominant either in the research area or in the relevant market to the extent that power to exclude exists, and that there is the potential effect of exclusion.

Given the positive perception of innovation, both US and EU legislators try and have tried to facilitate pioneering and market-leading innovations. In fact, when analysing the legislators' efforts, the similarity of the effects of new acts and guidelines and their almost joint timing is striking. On both sides of the Atlantic, the legislators have tried to create more lenient treatment for joint R&D and similar collaborations. A short comparative historical exposé of the legislative amendments would look like this:

- US NCRA 1984 – enacted as an exemption for pure R&D collaborations;
- EU R&D block exemption 1984 – not only exempted pure R&D collaborations but also joint production;
- amendment to include joint production in US NCRPA 1993;
- amendment to include joint sales in EU R&D Block Exemption 1993;
- early–mid-1990s patent pools (MPEG-2 and DVD pools) are publicly accepted and exempted under both US and EU antitrust law;
- four technology safe zones in US Licensing Guidelines 1995;
- four technology thresholds in the EU Licensing Guidelines 2000;
- R&D block exemption 2000 – 25 per cent ceiling for R&D collaborations, but a seven-year total exemption for breakthrough R&D;
- three technology safe zones in US Licensing Guidelines 2000;
- in 2004, the US Standard Development Organization Advancement Act includes standard-setting activities with IP arrangements under the NCRPA;
- new horizontal guidelines and block exemptions for R&D and specialisation agreements in 2010/11, developing the exemption for standardisation agreements;
- new rules regarding patent pools in the TT Guidelines from 2014.

The points above indicate legislative efforts to facilitate joint R&D or thereto connected collaborations. In this chapter the above developments in the US and EU approaches to R&D collaborations and standard-setting agreements will be discussed. The positive and negative aspects of joint

R&D from an antitrust perspective will be analysed. Firstly, the US antitrust case law and regulation of R&D, the NCRPA, will be analysed. It has developed from a limited exemption for joint R&D to include the whole process from innovation creation through to exploitation. Thereafter the equivalent EU regulation will be considered. Finally, the two different legal systems will be compared.

3.2 THE US NATIONAL COOPERATIVE RESEARCH AND PRODUCTION ACT OF 1993

3.2.1 Historical Background

(i) Case law

Ensuring that joint R&D ventures would be subject to the rule of reason and not the *per se* rule was a central thrust of the original National Cooperative Research Act (NCRA) in 1984.[80] Proponents of the legislation argued that joint R&D ventures, because they involved two or more venture partners, were necessarily subject to section 1 of the Sherman Act. Even if a joint R&D venture was pro-competitive, these proponents contended, it nonetheless could be found to be *per se* illegal because of either faulty antitrust rules or judicial mistake in the application of these rules. Moreover, according to John Scott, especially if the venture threatened to be successful in creating new products or technology that would leapfrog the existing technology – the very kind of venture that society should encourage – competitors outside the venture would have an incentive to file antitrust actions to stop or, at least, impede the venture. Proponents argued that this threat of litigation and of *per se* illegality was hindering US technological progress and contributing to poor performance in increasingly international competition. Without the threat of *per se* illegality, proponents concluded, more US firms would form joint R&D ventures, increase the nation's technological activity and improve US economic performance.[81]

Scott makes several observations about the purported existence of a *per se* rule prior to 1984. First, although some joint ventures had been found to be *per se* unlawful before 1984, none of them were joint R&D

---

[80] Cf. John Scott, 'The National Cooperative Research and Production Act', in ABA (ed.), *Issues in Competition Law and Policy* (ABA Section of Antitrust Law 2008), 1300.

[81] Ibid.

ventures.[82] The fear of *per se* illegality may have stopped some firms from forming pro-competitive joint R&D ventures, but the fear could not have been based on actual antitrust attacks on such ventures. Second, the rule of reason applies automatically to all joint ventures covered by the Act. No filing or application needs to be made by the venture to have the protection of this portion of the statute. Third, while the original NCRA contained a list of factors for applying the rule of reason to a covered joint venture, it provided no guidance as to how these factors were to be weighed in the analysis. Therefore, according to Scott, the rule of reason invented in 1918 by Justice Louis Brandeis in *Chicago Board* was available for all joint R&D ventures and is still available under the NCRPA.[83]

The case law described as inhibiting joint R&D ventures and the source for the special legislation for joint R&D ventures originates from the early 1950s. As stated by Scott, these cases do not appear to be describing or prohibiting joint R&D ventures. This notwithstanding, the agreements scrutinised were sometimes labelled joint ventures; they amounted to either hard-core price cartels, patent pools or intra-enterprise conspiracies between parent firms and foreign subsidiaries or affiliates (that is, transactions within the business groups).[84] Few of these ventures,

---

[82]   John Scott, 'The National Cooperative Research and Production Act', in ABA (ed.), *Issues in Competition Law and Policy* (ABA Section of Antitrust Law 2008), 1300 et seq.

[83]   Ibid. See also *Chicago Board of Trade v. United States*, 246 U.S. 231, 238 (1918). Whether this is an accurate interpretation depends on the analysis of the amendment made to the NCRA in 1993. Possibly, the NCRPA then was given a special rule of reason, or there is a different environment for its application. See discussion *infra* section 3.2.3(vi) and 3.2.3(vii).

[84]   The most obvious case is the *Timken Roller* case in which the Supreme Court stated that, '[a]greements between legally separate persons and companies to suppress competition among themselves *and others* cannot be justified by labelling the project a "joint venture"' [italic by the author]. From the ruling one cannot distinguish who would be 'the others'. However, the Supreme Court hints at the fact that the global agreement on dividing markets and price between the Timken companies was part of a bigger cartel. The US parent firm held only minority share positions in the other Timken firms (UK and French), so it is difficult to state whether these agreements would have been exempted today under the intra-enterprise exemption now prevailing since *Copperweld Corp. v. Independence Tube Corp.* 467 U.S. 752 (1984). For the *Timken Roller* case, see *Timken Roller Bearing Co. v. United States*, 341 U.S. 593, 598 (1951). The *Timken* decision provoked great controversy and Justice Robert Jackson dissented, doubting that it should be unreasonable restraint of trade to organise foreign subsidiaries. See Wyatt Wells, *Antitrust and the Formation of the Postwar*

if any, concerned research, and their focus, from the beginning, was in general on manufacturing, commercialisation or both. Over time they were transformed into explicit price and output cartels for foreign markets. These collaborations also displayed the natural expansion of large enterprises into foreign countries through subsidiaries, save the fact that the subsidiaries were sometimes jointly owned with a competitor.[85] Thus, even though the cases display price collusion between stand-alone firms, the courts also struck down agreements between parent firms and their foreign subsidiaries since clearly the doctrine of economic unity had not yet been adopted by the US courts.

A seminal case of this era, and referred to as inhibiting the creation of joint R&D ventures, was the *National Lead* case concerning the world-wide patent pool holding the rights to a process for developing paint.[86] The titanium paint process was invented almost simultaneously in three different places: in the US by Barton and Rossi, in Norway by Jebsen and in France by Blumenfeld. The innovations and the process patents held by each party were competing technologies. In each place the patents were assigned to different firms, although already by 1920 the US firm National Lead and the Norwegian firm holding Jebsen's original patent had entered into an exclusive cross-licensing agreement for all current and future patents. The parties to this agreement effectively

---

World (Columbia University Press, 2002), 135. Nonetheless, the *Timken* ruling seems to be based on the *per se* rule for horizontal market division. This is, however, uncertain since the parties also agreed on price. Cf. Lawrence Sullivan & Warren Grimes, *The Law of Antitrust: An Integrated Handbook* (Thomson/ West 2006), 251. See also *United States v. Minnesota Mining & Manufacturing Co. et al* 92 F. Supp. 947 (D. Mass. 1950), where what seems to have been an export cartel, or an agreement among competitors that jointly owned foreign manufacturing plants (firms), should not directly export to the relevant markets, thus restricting exports from the US, not only from the participants, but also by blocking other US firms, that is, non-parties of the agreement. These cases seem to have been partially revoked by the intra-enterprise exemption prevailing since the *Copperweld* case (see above). Cf. also Daniel M. Crane, 'Joint Research and Development Ventures and the Antitrust Laws', (1984) 21 *Harvard Journal of Legislation*, 405, 411 et seq., and Douglas Ginsburg, 'Antitrust, Uncertainty and Technological Innovation', (1979) 24 *Antitrust Bulletin* 635, 677 n. 93.

[85]   Cf. Lawrence Sullivan & Warren Grimes, *The Law of Antitrust: An Integrated Handbook* (Thomson/West, 2006), 698, discussing that managerial intimacy can facilitate output reduction and price enhancement between competitors and, over time, can transform itself into an explicit price cartel, referring to *inter alia* the *Timken Roller* case, see *Timken Roller Bearing Co. v. United States*, 341 U.S. 593 (1951).

[86]   *United States v. National Lead Co. et al.* 63 F. Supp. 513 (1945).

divided the world market for titanium (paint) into two parts: North America for National Lead and the rest of the world for the Norwegian firm. The agreement not only contained a cross-licensing obligation but also covenants regarding the exchange of patent applications and know-how, and a non-challenge clause regarding the validity of the patents of the other party. Meanwhile, DuPont had obtained the US rights to the French process patents.[87] In the US, National Lead and DuPont competed vigorously, although their joint control of patents prevented the emergence of any other challenger or any new entrant to the market.

The early international cross-licensing/joint exchange of information agreements between the US and the Norwegian and the French firms were the starting point for several similar agreements and collaborations including, for example, German and Japanese firms in the paint industry. The agreements ultimately formed a network which slowly divided the global market into exclusively assigned territories. The process of establishing exclusive territories was also accompanied with transfers of minority and eventually majority share interests in several of the foreign contracting firms. Many firms also established jointly owned firms (subsidiaries) in third countries. This development continued until the entire world was included. It formed what District Judge Rifkind would later call a 'cartel' that controlled all commerce in titanium: '[e]very pound of it is trammelled by privately imposed regulations.'[88]

It should be pointed out that many features of the National Lead network resemble the collaborations that can be seen today under global patent pools and networks and represents the natural development of multinational firms on global markets. Such collaborations should thus not be regarded as *per se* anticompetitive. However, District Judge Rifkind, when resolving the *National Lead* case eventually brought by the Justice Department, stated it was of little significance whether the form of the association is called a cartel, an international cartel, a patent

---

[87] Wyatt Wells, *Antitrust and the Formation of the Postwar World* (Columbia University Press, 2002), 126 et seq.

[88] He went on to state that the channels of this commerce have not been formed by the winds and currents of competition, but are instead artificial canals, privately constructed. 'The borders of the private domain in titanium are guarded by hundreds of patents, procured without opposition, and maintained without litigation.' He concluded by stating that: '[i]t was more difficult for the independent outsider to enter this business than for the camel to make its proverbial passage through the eye of a needle.' See *United States v. National Lead Co. et al.* 63 F. Supp. 513, 521 (1945).

pool or a 'technical or commercial cooperation'.[89] The agreements
embraced 'acknowledgment of patent validity in respect to patents not
issued, or applied for, and concerning innovation not yet even conceived'.[90] 'While it has been held that the owner of a patent may license
whom he will, or refuse to license, it is now well settled law that a
license may not be used to extend patent monopoly beyond its term.'[91]

In fact, when District Judge Rifkind decided the case, the original
rights had expired and the firms relied on various incremental improvements in the production to keep competition at bay.[92] '[T]he newcomer is
confronted by a veritable jungle of patent claims through which only the
very powerful and stouthearted would venture,' Rifkind continued, commenting on the initial investment required to acquire the rights from the
pool and enter the market.[93] Rifkind believed the law in this case was
violated to the same extent as when several firms combined and agreed
not to do business with a particular customer or class of customers. He
therefore ordered the firms to license their patent at a reasonable royalty
to all applicants.[94] The Supreme Court, after limiting the reach of the
precedent, later affirmed the judgment of the District Court.[95]

---

[89]   See *United States v. National Lead Co. et al.*, 63 F. Supp. 513, 523
(1945).

[90]   *United States v. National Lead Co. et al.*, 63 F. Supp. 513, 524 (1945).

[91]   Ibid.

[92]   Wyatt Wells, *Antitrust and the Formation of the Postwar World* (Columbia
University Press, 2002), 127.

[93]   See *United States v. National Lead Co. et al.*, 63 F. Supp. 513, 532
(1945).

[94]   *United States v. National Lead Co. et al.*, 63 F. Supp. 513, 532 et seq.
(1945).

[95]   However, both the Justice Department and the Supreme Court acknowledged that Judge Rifkind had gone too far in his condemnation of patent pools.
See *United States v. National Lead Co. et al.*, 332 U.S. 319, 67 S. Ct. 1634
(1947). Several courts during this time acknowledged that their decisions rested
on law rather than on economics. Even Judge Rifkind stated that under the patent
pool the technology had rapidly advanced, production had increased and prices
had decreased. Nonetheless, according to District Judge Rifkind, the major
premise of the Sherman Act is that suppression of competition in international
trade is in itself a public injury, or at any rate that injury of suppression of
competition is greater than any benefits the conduct in the case secured.
Accordingly, he declined to acknowledge any efficiency defence. Since the
Supreme Court did not seem at this time to have acknowledged an efficiency
defence, it is also difficult to state whether there actually were any efficiencies
derived from the pool. The Justice Department did not need to rebut the
proposition that efficiencies existed to win either this or other cases from this era.

Given the extended definition of R&D in current legislation, the exchange of know-how and the covenant of cross-licensing of future patents, which Judge Rifkind commented upon so fiercely and considered to be *per se* violation of the Sherman Act, may be considered joint R&D or at least part of joint R&D under the contemporary exceptions.[96]

In perhaps the most famous joint venture case from the 1960s, the *Penn-Olin* case, the joint venture was ultimately exonerated, by the Supreme Court, after six years of litigation.[97] Penn-Olin Chemical Company was formed in 1960 as a 50/50 joint venture formed by Pennsalt Chemicals Corporation, a producer of sodium chlorate but established outside the relevant geographic market of the south-eastern US, and Olin-Mathieson Chemical Corporation, a large conglomerate which did not produce sodium chlorate. The parents of the joint venture, Penn-Olin Chemical Company, signed an agreement to construct a plant in Kentucky for the production of sodium chlorate, a chemical used in bleaching wood pulp to be sold in the south-eastern United States.

Prior to the formation of the joint venture, the sodium chlorate industry in the south-eastern US comprised two companies, holding over 90 per cent of the market. Pennsalt, which had its manufacturing facilities in Portland, Oregon, had marketed some sodium chlorate in the south-eastern US through a sales agreement with Olin, but was absorbing high transport costs.[98] Pennsalt was estimated to have a market share of 9 per cent of the relevant geographic market.

In 1961, the Justice Department challenged the Penn-Olin joint venture under section 7 of the Clayton Act and section 1 of the Sherman Act. The Justice Department argued, primarily, that the Penn-Olin joint venture eliminated the possibility that the parent firms would both enter the relevant market independently. The District Court found that both Pennsalt and Olin would not have entered the market unilaterally, that is, would not have built plants in the south-east if the joint venture had not been created. The District Court continued and stated that there was no basis for concluding the Penn-Olin joint venture had the effect of substantially lessening competition. The Supreme Court reversed, and held the District Court applied the wrong standard (under section 7

---

[96] See, for example, the definition of joint venture in NCRPA or joint R&D in the R&D block exemption.
[97] *United States v. Penn-Olin Chemical Co.* 378 U.S. 158, 84 S.Ct.1710 (1964).
[98] Robert Pitofsky, 'Joint Ventures under the Antitrust Laws: Some Reflections on the Significance of "Penn-Olin"', (Mar., 1969) 82(5) *Harvard Law Review*, 1007, 1009 et seq.

Clayton Act). While accepting the finding of the District Court that both would not have entered the market, it argued the test or benchmark should instead be whether one of the parents independently would have entered the south-east market. The Supreme Court therefore sent the case back to the District Court. It stated that the District Court had failed to consider whether elimination of the threat of potential competition by the other parent constituted a lessening of competition sufficient to violate section 7. Thus, both scenarios (going in together versus one building a factory and the other staying outside the market as a potential entrant) included the construction of a factory in the relevant market, while the second alternative was more beneficial to competition since potential competition would also prevail. Upon remand, the District Court determined that the government failed to establish that *either* company would have built the facility without the joint venture, and dismissed the complaint.[99]

The *Penn-Olin* case did not deal with an R&D joint venture; however, it signifies where the centre of attention was for the competition law courts at the time: the question of whether the collaborating parties were competitors or potential competitors, or whether they would enter the relevant market unilaterally or at least act as a potential entrant, and, hence, represent a potential competitive pressure on the incumbent firms. The *Penn-Olin* case as well as writers at the time seemed to purport that if both firms were committed to enter the market or committed to unilaterally conduct what is needed to enter the market independently, entering the market jointly could amount to a *per se* violation of competition law, without the need to check for monopoly power or whether there were efficiencies that would match any anticompetitive effects.[100]

Even though the Supreme Court in *Penn-Olin* applied merger analysis to the joint venture, voices purporting to represent US industry claimed that the *National Lead*, *Penn-Olin* and other cases[101] made use of the *per*

---

[99]   *United States v. Penn-Olin Chemical Co.* 378 U.S. 158, 84 S.Ct.1710 (1964).

[100]   Robert Pitofsky, 'Joint Ventures under the Antitrust Laws: Some Reflections on the Significance of "Penn-Olin"', (Mar., 1969) 82(5) *Harvard Law Review* 1007, 1044 et seq.

[101]   Also *Topco* 405 U.S. 596 (1972), where the Supreme Court used the *per se* rule to strike down an agreement stipulating total territorial protection under a franchise/distribution system, was heavily criticised at this time. The Topco brand had been founded in the 1940s by small supermarket chains that wanted to obtain merchandise under private labels to compete against larger national and

se rule to the extent that firms also refrained from entering pro-competitive and benign collaborations.[102]

After the *Penn-Olin* case, the Supreme Court entering the 1980s was soon to depart from using the *per se* rule, and decided three joint venture cases where the Court seemed to be embracing the rule of reason standard for joint ventures, even when competitors or potential competitors were collaborating: *Broadcast Music, Inc. v. Columbia Broadcasting System, (CBS) Inc.*;[103] *NCAA v. Board of Regents of the University of Oklahoma*;[104] and *Northwest Wholesale Stationers, Inc. v. Pacific Stationery and Printing Co.*[105]

In *BMI*, decided in 1979, the television network CBS, as a plaintiff, contended that blanket copyright licences for music provided by the collecting society BMI constituted illegal *per se* price fixing, and the Second Circuit Court agreed. The Second Circuit held that, since BMI negotiated the price of the blanket licence and also distributed royalties to the copyright holders, it was a form of horizontal price-fixing between the copyright holders. The Supreme Court rejected this use of the *per se* rule. It directed the Court of Appeal to apply the rule of reason. The Supreme Court found that the rule of reason should be used in this joint venture because the individual copyright owners were not precluded from

---

regional chains. Each new member of the association was only permitted to sell Topco brand products in the territory in which it was licensed. A member's market share in its licensed territory was only about 6 per cent. Although *Topco* has never been overruled, it is widely criticised and not infrequently honoured in the breach. See Herbert Hovekamp, *Federal Antitrust Policy – The Law of Competition and its Practice* (Thomson Reuters 4 ed. 2011), 226. It should be noticed that the *per se* rule does not apply to licensing of intellectual property (at least not to patents).

[102] Then Assistant Attorney General Thomas E. Kauper stated in a letter to the Arch Both Chief Executive Officer, U.S. Chamber of Commerce, that, '[t]he allegation that businesses feel discouraged [to form joint ventures] goes to their state of mind and is obviously impossible to verify or refute. On the other hand, the known facts tend to refute any concrete assertion about the inhibitory effect of antitrust laws.' See Daniel M. Crane, 'Joint Research and Development Ventures and the Antitrust Laws', (1984) 21 *Harvard Journal of Legislation*, 405, 411 fn. 30. See also John Anthony Chavez, 'Joint Ventures in the European Union and the U.S.', (Winter 1999) *Antitrust Bulletin*, 959.

[103] *Broadcast Music, Inc. v. Columbia Broadcasting System, (CBS) Inc.*, 441 U.S. 1 (1979).

[104] *NCAA v. Board of Regents of the University of Oklahoma*, 468 U.S. 85 (1984).

[105] *Northwest Wholesale Stationers, Inc. v. Pacific Stationery and Printing Co.*, 472 U.S. 284 (1985).

entering individual licensing agreements, the pricing arrangement was essential for the establishment of the new product (the blanket licences) and the joint venture increased economic efficiency.[106]

In 1984 in *NCAA*, the Supreme Court judged the joint negotiation of TV rights for college football. It held that the restraints by the joint venture on member colleges to not negotiate and sell, *inter alia*, TV rights to their individual (home) games, were not illegal *per se*, even though it created a horizontal restraint upon price competition and also restricted output by having a ceiling on the number of games televised. The Supreme Court possibly, even though not utilising the *per se* rule, still found the restraints to be naked restraints on price and output. In the end NCAA lost the case since the restraints put in place were too far-reaching (limiting the number of times an NCAA football team could have its games televised).[107]

The third case from 1985, *Northwest Stationers*, involved a retail office supply store that had been expelled from a cooperative that wholesaled products to member retailers. The record did not show why the retailer had been expelled. The Supreme Court held that the Ninth Circuit had incorrectly applied the *per se* rule. The Supreme Court thus reversed and substantially increased the plaintiff's burden in the association's refusal to deal with cases by stating that 'the plaintiff challenges expulsion from a joint buying cooperative, some showing must be made that the cooperative possesses market power or unique access to a business element necessary for effective competition.'[108]

As with the *National Lead* case, none of the cases referred to above directly addressed the question of whether specifically a joint *research* effort should be judged under the *per se* rule or the rule of reason.[109]

---

[106]   *Broadcast Music, Inc. v. Columbia Broadcasting System, (CBS) Inc.*, 441 U.S. 1 (1979).

[107]   *NCAA v. Board of Regents of the University of Oklahoma*, 468 U.S. 85, 104–107 (1984).

[108]   *Northwest Wholesale Stationers, Inc. v. Pacific Stationery and Printing Co.*, 472 U.S. 284, 297–98 (1985).

[109]   In only one of the cases did the Court seem to elaborate on the issue of whether the conduct was to be judged according to the *per se* rule or the rule of reason. In the *Imperial Chemical Industries* case, which also dealt with a worldwide patent pool between ICI and DuPont, the defendants were accused of dividing and eliminating competition in the global market for chemical products related to explosives, sporting arms and ammunition. The alleged conspiracy was based on several agreements which succeeded each other. The Court concluded that neither joint manufacturing nor joint commercialisation ventures are *per se* unlawful, but become unlawful only if their purpose or their effect is restraining

Instead, they concerned patent pools, technology standardisation arrangements, joint production or distribution. In contemporary antitrust jurisprudence, licensing future patents, establishing patent pools, which does not license third parties and agreeing on technology standards are not *per se* violations of US antitrust law.[110] Indeed, such collaborations, even though possibly objectionable, should generally be judged under the rule of reason.[111]

However, there is a Second Circuit case from around the 1980s that actually deals with joint R&D ventures. In *Berkey Photo Inc. v. Eastman Kodak Co.*,[112] two joint research ventures between, on the one hand,

---

or monopolising trade. The Court went on to state that when competitors or potential competitors set up jointly owned companies for the commercialisation of the products under the scheme of a joint cross-licence agreement, the Court in fact seriously questioned the presumed *per se legality* of such joint ventures. However, the Court found that the very purpose for which the firms organised themselves in this manner and the circumstances around the creation of the joint ventures place them 'under the bar'. See *United States v. Imperial Chemical Industries Limited et al.*, 100 F. Supp. 504, 557 et seq. (1954). The Court was here referring to the exemption for establishing jointly owned export trading companies. See 15 U.S.C.A. para 40001-03. From this case, it seems evident that the Court was not using the *per se illegality* test for either joint manufacturing or joint commercialisation. On the contrary, it even presumed *per se legality* for jointly owned exporting companies. However, the Court did not allow for an efficiency defence. Cf. Wyatt Wells, *Antitrust and the Formation of the Postwar World* (Columbia University Press, 2002), 130.

[110] Generally patent pools should be judged under the rule of reason, implicitly requiring that the plaintiff can show either market power or direct anticompetitive effects. Thus, a patent pool should be judged according to the rule of reason, at least if it does not hold market power. See DOJ/FTC, *Antitrust Guidelines for the Licensing of Intellectual Property*, 6 April 1995 (hereinafter IP Guidelines, 2), 28, which indicate that pool agreements generally need not be open to all who would like to join.

[111] However, could the collaboration in the *National Lead* case be regarded as a joint R&D under the NCRPA? The definition of research under the NCRPA is wide and possibly an agreement to share future know-how and intellectual property rights could be regarded as joint R&D under the NCRPA. While the *National Lead* case still represents valid law, parts of the collaboration considered *per se* anticompetitive in *National Lead* would clearly have enjoyed the protection of the NCRA enacted in 1984. Moreover, even more parts of the *National Lead* collaboration would be encompassed by the contemporary NCRPA. See generally *United States v. National Lead Co. et al.*, 63 F. Supp. 513 (1945).

[112] *Berkey Photo Inc. v. Eastman Kodak Co.*, 603 F.2d 263 (2d Cir 1979) cert. denied.

Kodak and, on the other, Sylvania Electric and General Electric, respectively, to develop the flash attachment 'Magicube' and a crystal flash 'PE' to hand-held cameras, respectively, were found to have violated the rule of reason under section 1 of the Sherman Act.

The plaintiff, Berkey, purported that Kodak's agreements with the Magicube and PE manufacturers, Sylvania and GE, respectively, violated section 1 of the Sherman Act. In particular, it charged that although Kodak did not make any meaningful technological contribution to either system, the confidentiality agreements it extracted from GE and Sylvania prevented other camera makers from competing in the production of cameras that could connect with the new flash devices. Evaluating all the evidence presented on these issues, the jury and the District Court found Kodak's conduct to be unreasonable restraints of trade.

Kodak appealed and challenged these verdicts with a rather straight-forward defence: it argued that both projects 'involved millions of dollars of research and development expense by Kodak' and 'led directly to the introduction of innovative new products' that 'gained wide success'.

The Second Circuit started with stating that an agreement among a few firms to restrict to themselves the rewards of innovation is not immune to examination under section 1 of the Sherman Act. Kodak's claim that it is 'not a "restraint of trade"', reasonable or unreasonable, to jointly develop a new product was dismissed and the Court explained that where a participant's market share is large, 'we believe joint development projects have sufficient anticompetitive potential to invite inquiry'. Referring to a standard work at the time,[113] the Court continued by stating that if several substantial firms in an industry join in research at a scale the remaining firms could not attain, and if the others are not permitted to join the group, the favoured competitors might obtain a decisive and unjustified advantage over the rest.

The Court thereafter states that Kodak and GE were not direct competitors, and Kodak and Sylvania were 'at best' potential competitors when the Magicube was being developed. Nevertheless, because of Kodak's market power over cameras, 'the exclusionary potential of horizontal research pools was present'. Moreover, GE had under the joint development agreement kept a desirable innovation (the PE flash) off the market for two years solely to suit Kodak's convenience, not to cannibalise on the sale of the Magicube flash. There was, according to the Court, a hollow ring to a claim of justification by appeal to the need to promote

---

[113]   L. Sullivan, *Handbook of the Law of Antitrust* (St Paul, MN: West Publishing, 1977), 298 et seq.

innovation, where the result of the conduct was such a clear loss to consumers.

The Second Circuit thereafter claimed that it did not hold that joint development agreements between a monopolist and a firm in a complementary market were *per se* violations. Nevertheless, joint ventures involving a monopolist have sufficient anticompetitive potential that they must be scrutinised with care so they not are permitted to fortify the already substantial entry barriers inherent in a monopolised market. The relevant variables might, according to the Court, include: the size of the joint ventures; their share of their respective markets; the contributions of each party to the venture and the benefits derived; the likelihood that, in the absence of the joint effort, one or both parties would undertake a similar project, either alone or with a smaller firm in the other market; the nature of the ancillary restraints imposed and the reasonableness of their relationship to the purposes of the venture. The list was not intended to be exhaustive.

The *Berkey* case is (historically) interesting because of several findings by the Second Circuit: firstly, R&D collaborations are not *per se* legal, in the sense that if the parties hold market power, the joint R&D ventures may be considered anticompetitive if exclusionary effects are likely to materialise. Secondly, it seems that the parties to the joint R&D only need to be potential competitors, active on complementary markets, and still be exposed to the rule of reason Sherman Act section 1, as long as one party to the agreement holds a monopoly position in the market to which access or competition is dampened. Thirdly, the Court clearly indicates that confidentiality and other covenants that cause outsiders not to be able to access the result of such joint R&D or a joint decision to stall introduction of a new innovation may be violations under the rule of reason of section 1 of the Sherman Act.

The cases referred to above indicate that joint R&D ventures most likely would not be judged under the *per se* rule. Moreover, the overall development of the time was clearly to decrease the use of the *per se* rule. Why the older case law therefore caused Congress to enact the NCRA is somewhat unclear. Possibly the reason could be that the legislators also found that the treatment of joint ventures, in general, and of joint R&D in particular, by the Courts under the *rule of reason* was not lenient enough. Nonetheless, it would take some time between when these cases were decided until legislation was actually enacted. The Justice Department first tried to give some guidance through a non-legislative measure.

(ii)   The research guide

Even though antitrust law treatment of joint ventures under US law can be traced back to early case law,[114] the notion that cooperative research should be treated differently from other collaborations stems from 1979. That year President Jimmy Carter gave the Justice Department the assignment to explain and clarify the present state of antitrust law in relation to research conducted in cooperation. In response, the Justice Department in 1980 published a guide concerning joint R&D ventures (the Guide).[115]

From the outset the Guide was based on the principle that the more competitive the industry is, the greater the incentive to innovate is likely to be.[116] According to the Guide, competition was both a cause and an effect of new and improved products and services and more efficient production processes. Investment in research increases competition, for a successful innovator gains a competitive advantage over its rivals, who must then imitate the innovation or develop innovations of their own in order to keep up in the competitive race.

Indeed, the antitrust theory, as displayed in the Guide, was based on competition as the driving force for innovation. The antitrust laws strive to keep markets competitive in order to promote and encourage innovation, which in turn promotes more competition.[117] Even so, the Justice Department in the Guide admitted that no pure joint R&D venture without so-called anticompetitive ancillary restraints had ever, to that date, been challenged by the Antitrust Division.[118]

The Guide spelled out what anticompetitive conduct to look for under the rule of reason procedure envisioned by the Justice Department. The Guide stated three different ways a joint R&D cooperation can affect

---

[114]   See cases referred to *supra* under the previous heading. See also generally, e.g., *Standard Oil Co. v. United States*, 283 U.S. 163 (1931), *Chicago Board of Trade v. United States*, 246 U.S. 231 (1918), and *Broadcast Music v. Columbia Broadcasting System*, 441 U.S. 1 (1979).

[115]   US Department of Justice, *Antitrust Guide Concerning Research Joint Ventures* (1980) (earlier defined as the Guide).

[116]   The Guide, 3, with reference to Fredric Scherer, *Industrial Market Structure and Economic Performance* (Houghton Mifflin Company, 1980), 428–9. It seems as if Scherer has somewhat modified his view, see F.M. Scherer & David Ross, *Industrial Market Structure and Economic Performance* (Houghton Mifflin Company, 1990), 613 et seq.

[117]   The Guide, 3. Cf. F.M. Scherer & David Ross, *Industrial Market Structure and Economic Performance* (Houghton Mifflin Company, 1990), 613 et seq.

[118]   The Guide, 2.

competition: first (i) the essential elements of the joint R&D venture would lessen existing or potential competition between the participating firms. Second (ii), the venture agreement, or other related agreements between the participants, could contain specific restrictions that restrain competition. If these restrictions are not essential elements of the project, or unwarranted in scope or duration, they present antitrust concerns under the ancillary restraints doctrine. Finally (iii), limitations on access to participation in joint research or to the fruits of that research cause antitrust problems if the effect of those limitations is the creation or abuse of market power in the hands of the participants. Indeed, antitrust law in the field of joint R&D ventures should prevent the creation of market power, collusion and abuse of market power.

(a) Market power When discussing whether the essential element of the agreement lessens real or potential competition between the participants under the rule of reason, the Guide made reference to the then prevailing Merger Guidelines.[119] The Guide stated that research joint ventures might be regarded as benign, or even pro-competitive, even though creating a joint market share which would, presumably, be considered anticompetitive according to the Merger Guidelines.[120] This more lenient treatment was based on the notion that joint ventures are short-lived, one-time 'problem solving mechanisms' compared with mergers. The Guide also admitted that the rule of reason evaluation under section 1 of the Sherman Act bears many similarities to the application of section 7 of the Clayton Act. Hence, the level of concentration in the market or markets that are affected by the contemplated research was of great importance when establishing whether the main purpose of the joint R&D venture was anticompetitive or not. The Guide stated that the elimination of research competition between major firms raised antitrust concerns.[121]

Primarily this meant that the antitrust law would be triggered if the parties were actual or potential competitors. Would the loss of competitive pressure significantly decrease overall competition in the market? In other words, if the market for the contemplated result of the research was concentrated, the barriers to entry high and if the joint R&D venture

---

[119] See DOJ/FTC, The Horizontal Merger Guidelines issued in 1992 and revised in 1997, and the non-horizontal Merger Guidelines issued in 1984. See http://www.usdoj.gov/atr/public/premerger.htm. Accessed 9 May 2010.

[120] The Guide, 7 et seq.

[121] See *United States v. Penn-Olin Chemical Co.*, 378 U.S. 158, 84 S.Ct.1710, 1718 (1964) for the method for identifying competitors.

combined two competitors that jointly held market power and thus further concentrated the market, the Justice Department would have scrutinised the research.[122] Moreover, the potential competitor doctrine derived from the *Penn-Olin* case created a wide definition of what constituted potential competition.[123] Interestingly, even though the definition of competitor was wide, it does not appear that under the Guide the competitive relationship between the parents and the joint venture was analysed under the plaintiff's *prima facie* case. Instead, the issue whether, for example, the contemplated research was such that the parents were not able to perform it unilaterally was considered a justification for the defendants to put forward rather than part of the plaintiff's *prima facie* case.

The Guide did not specify which markets to identify. Indeed, by making reference to the Merger Guidelines, the Guide was firmly established in 'conventional' antitrust markets, that is, markets for products or services. The 'innovation market' had not yet been conceptualised by the Justice Department.

In the case where the Justice Department did find the parties to be competitors or potential competitors and that the relevant market(s) were concentrated, and enclosed by barriers to entry, the Department considered, as a second step to building a *prima facie* case, the nature of the research: whether the joint R&D venture was aimed towards basic, applied or developmental research, or directed to externality effects (spillover effects).[124]

The reason for such an analysis was essentially connected to the market power of the joint venture. The anticompetitive test in the Guide was based on the philosophy that the more basic the contemplated joint research, the less dangerous it was from an antitrust perspective, and thus higher concentration of market power would be tolerated.[125] The logic was based on the fact that the more basic the research, the more useful the knowledge created would be to firms from different industries. Put differently, the closer the aim of the joint R&D venture was to an actual marketed technology, product or service, for example, research into the development or design of a product, the more likely a joint effort would have anticompetitive effects, for example, cost communalities or even

[122] Andreas Fuchs, *Kartellrechtliche Grenzen der Forschungskooperation* (Nomos Verlaggesellschaft, 1989), 112 et seq.
[123] See *United States v. Penn-Olin Chemical Co.*, 378 U.S. 158, 84 S.Ct. 1710, 1718 (1964).
[124] The Guide, 7 et seq.
[125] See the Guide, 3.

price collusion. The closer the joint research was to the end product, that is, applied research, the less likely the partners in the joint R&D venture would have anything to gain from the joint effort except when close competitors. Thus, joint efforts in applied or developmental research should be allowed only if the parties had no or minor combined market power. Therefore, the Guide refused to stipulate any firm market share thresholds for when a joint research was anticompetitive or not. Instead, the tolerated combined market power was dependent on where in the value chain the collaboration took place.[126]

In the current NCRPA this difference appears to have been eliminated.[127] The contemporary act acknowledges that commercial research today is rather performed closer to the end products. The contemporary logic is that new products are not developed in a linear fashion, where innovations grow out of an R&D department. Instead, today's products are modifications and development of old products or the result of interactions – networks – between several departments and firms closer to the end market. The era of scientists in white coats in R&D departments envisioning the breakthrough products of the future is a

---

[126] Barry Hawk stated: 'There is an antitrust benefits/risk spectrum with basic research joint venture at one end and a marketing joint venture at the other. The best way to understand treatment of joint ventures in the EEC (and in the US) is to view a simple arrangement and a complex arrangement as raising differences in degree along a continuous spectrum. Again, at one end is the basic research joint venture where there is a particular need for close cooperation and few antitrust concerns. As one moves across the spectrum toward the marketplace, the need for close cooperation generally diminishes and antitrust exposure generally rises.' See Barry Hawk, *United States, Common Market and International Antitrust: A Comparative Guide* (New York, 1985), 45 et seq.

[127] See discussion *infra* section 3.2.3. The elimination of this 'rule of thumb' was presumably because of the academic contribution by Jorde and Teece, cf., e.g., Thomas Jorde & David Teece, 'Innovation, Cooperation and Antitrust', (1989) 4 *High Tech Law Journal*, 1; Thomas Jorde & David Teece, 'Acceptable Cooperation among Competitors in the Face of Growing International Competition', (1989) *Antitrust Law Journal*, 529; Thomas Jorde & David Teece, 'Innovation and Cooperation: Implications for Competition and Antitrust', (1990) 4 *Journal of Economic Perspectives*, 75; and Thomas Jorde & David Teece, 'Innovation, Cooperation, and Antitrust', in Thomas Jorde & David Teece (eds), *Antitrust, Innovation, and Competitiveness* (Oxford University Press, 1992), 47 et seq. *Contra*, see generally Joseph Brodley, 'Antitrust Law and Innovation Cooperation', (1990) 4 *Journal of Economic Perspective*, 97.

thing of the past. With it also the old truism that joint research closer to the end product is automatically more suspicious than research into basic science.[128]

The Guide continues and states that if the plaintiff could show that the parties were competitors or potential competitors in existing markets and that their combined market share in the light of the nature of the research would risk anticompetitive effects, it had fulfilled the requirements for a *prima facie* antitrust case. According to the Guide, the next step was to evaluate the justifications for the collaboration. Closely connected to this issue was whether the parties involved would have performed the contemplated research on their own, absent the joint venture. Indeed, the Guide acknowledged that even though the participants exerted significant power on existing markets, the venture could be exempted if the parties showed that the contemplated research was of such a character that the parties would not independently have performed it. The parties were not only considered blocked from individually performing the research by, for example, patent barriers, or lack of know-how, but also by large economic risks which would prevent the participants from doing the necessary individual investment.[129] It implies, for example, that copyright-protected software could be such a barrier that a joint R&D venture was allowed in order to bridge it.

In comparison, today, the plaintiff bears the burden of proof for whether the parties are not able to perform the research as such independently.[130] Indeed, under the 'innovation market' and otherwise concept, two firms not able to conduct a contemplated collective research

---

[128]   See generally the article that started the argument that applied and basic research should be judged similarly under US antitrust law: Thomas Jorde & David Teece, 'Innovation, Cooperation and Antitrust', (1989) 4 *High Tech Law Journal*, 1. Under EC competition law the parties can justify an R&D venture by showing that the research is of a basic nature. Then the R&D is presumed to fall outside Article 101(1) TFEU. If the research is close to the end product, there is no presumption that the research is anticompetitive; however, it will be scrutinised more carefully. Guidelines on the application of Article 81 of the EC Treaty to horizontal cooperation agreements, OJ C 3, 06/01/2001, 2 (the 2001 Horizontal Guidelines), para 24. See, now, Guidelines on the application of Article 101 on the functioning of the European Union to horizontal cooperation agreements, OJ C 11, 14/01/2011, 1 (Horizontal Guidelines), paras 129 et seq.
[129]   The Guide, 8 et seq. After the innovation of the R&D market or innovation markets, this analysis should be included in the establishment of whether the parties were competitors or potential competitors. See *United States v. Penn-Olin Chemical Co.*, 378 U.S. 158, 84 S.Ct. 1710, 1718 (1964).
[130]   See *infra* section 3.2.3(v).

independently would not be competitors and the plaintiff needs to show that firms are competitors to build a *prima facie* case that the collaboration will decrease output and/or increase prices, or lessen innovation.

It is interesting to note that the Guide did not stop with the issue of whether the parties could perform the contemplated research on their own. It also raised the question of what research the participants would have performed absent the joint research.[131] Although it was clear that the parties would not be able unilaterally to perform the jointly envisaged research, they would have performed some kind of research which would be forsaken in favour of the joint effort. According to the Guide, these unilateral hypothetical efforts should be weighed against the collective effort when assessing whether research was anticompetitive or not. The primary reason is that such unilateral research could create two innovations and thereby more intense competition, especially under the assumption that the collaborators were already competitors on some downstream market. The unilateral efforts could also create more 'innovation' than the contemplated joint innovation, even though the contemplated joint innovation would amount to a longer innovative leap.

In contemporary antitrust jurisprudence, trying to determine and take into account alternative research avenues, hypothetically taken by the parties absent the joint R&D venture, is symptomatically absent from the antitrust test, under both US and EU antitrust law. The current predominant question to determine is instead whether the parties would be likely to perform the contemplated research independently. If at least one of the parties is not able independently to conduct the agreed research, it is presumed that the parties are not competitors (under EU competition law) or that the concentration on the innovation market will not increase (under US antitrust law).[132] They are then – presumably – not in violation of either section 1 of the Sherman Act or Article 101(1) of the Treaty on the Functioning of the European Union ('TFEU').

(b) Ancillary restraints   The 1980s Guide stated that under the rule of reason even though the essential elements of the joint R&D venture are not on balance anticompetitive in themselves, some collateral restraints might be unreasonable.[133]

---

[131]   The Guide, 9.

[132]   See the definition of 'competitors' under the DOJ/FTC, 'Antitrust Guidelines for Collaborations Among Competitors', issued in 2000 (hereinafter Collaboration Guidelines), 2. *Contra*, The Horizontal Guidelines, para 23.

[133]   The Guide, 16 et seq.

If the main purpose of the venture agreement, according to the test discussed above, is benign, because, for example, the parties do not hold market power, the effect of the agreement could still be anticompetitive. Some restraints could, according to the Guide, even be considered *per se* anticompetitive. Restricting the participant's freedom to stipulate down-stream prices (price-fixing), agreeing on the division of the market, tying arrangements and group boycotts should be considered *per se* violations, irrespective of whether the parties were competitors or of their combined market power. Accordingly, such conduct would render the whole venture unlawful. Other collateral restrictions, reasonably related to a legitimate business transaction, were judged according to the rule of reason under the ancillary restraints doctrine. An ancillary restraints test included a full factual inquiry to resolve whether the restrictions (i) were ancillary to a lawful main purpose and (ii) have a reasonable scope and duration and (iii) were not part of a pattern of restrictive agreements that has unwarranted anticompetitive effects.

Interestingly, the Guide stated that joint manufacturing can be considered necessarily ancillary, depending on the contemplated result of the research.[134] Joint marketing was also, under certain circumstances, permissible according to the Guide.[135] However, the Guide stated that restrictions to forgo independent research in competition with the joint venture constitute an unreasonable competitive restraint.[136]

The Guide clearly envisioned the courts weighing the possible benefits of the contemplated innovation with the anticompetitive effect of the restraints. Indeed, the doctrine of the less restrictive alternative would be applicable irrespective of market power held by the joint R&D venture.[137] It was a sliding scale dependent both on the importance of the contemplated innovation and on the necessity of the restrictive clause.

There is no sliding scale for establishing whether there are less restrictive alternatives under the contemporary US standard for establishing anticompetitive conduct. The joint R&D effort, if fulfilling the requirements of the NCRPA, will not fall outside the NCRPA by stipulating covenants which would make the joint R&D anticompetitive under the rule of reason. The limitations for private plaintiffs still prevail

---

[134]   The Guide, 16 et seq., 48 et seq.
[135]   The Guide, 48 et seq.
[136]   Ibid.
[137]   Cf. Gabe Feldman, 'The Misuse of the Less Restrictive Alternative Inquiry in Rule of Reason Analysis', (2009) 58 *American University Law Review*, 561.

irrespective of market power by the participants or the lack of benefits of the contemplated innovations.

(c) Access for third parties   The Guide also raised the question of access to innovation: should the joint R&D venture or the result of the joint R&D be accessible for the competitors and other firms? According to the Guide, joint ventures set up to engage in research on externality problems presented a special issue with respect to collateral restraints. Restraints on public knowledge concerning the subject matter of the joint R&D venture on externalities should seldom be permitted; such restraints can prevent the regulators or the public from learning of substantial progress by one or more ventures towards attaining a regulatory goal, and thus inhibit adequate determination of the public interest.[138] The Guide specifically stipulated that firms are not allowed to prevent the dispersion of positive externalities in society. For example, all-industry joint R&D ventures must openly present their findings. The Guide expressed the belief that competition law not only benefitted society by upholding a requirement for creating efficiency between the parties involved, but also promoted competition from third parties. Some knowledge had to be given to the public.[139]

The Guide acknowledged that there can be anticompetitive concerns with limitations on access to the venture or the result created by the venture.[140] The Guide did not mention the notion of 'essential facility'. Instead, it stated that principles, developed in antitrust cases and dealing

---

[138]   The Guide, 18. However, the Guide had little to say about the exploitation of the result of the venture. It stated that joint exploitation is likely to raise the greatest danger of antitrust risk, especially if the joint venture includes participants representing a significant share of the relevant market. Therefore, it is not certain whether a patent pool, where the former research parties exploit their combined result by bundling rights, was anticompetitive or not according to the Guide.

[139]   Ibid. Presumably, there is an underlying patent law theory behind the standpoint that all-inclusive research should not create remunerating patents. The patent law requirements of novelty and obviousness would not be fulfilled, if all firms 'skilled in the art' were involved in creating the innovation. Thus, there was a patent law reason why the Guide, in practice, required publication of certain R&D results.

[140]   Ibid., 19. *Associated Press v. United States*, 326 U.S. 1, 17 (1945). However, see *Verizon Communication Inc. v. The Law Offices of Curtis V. Trinko LLP* 124 S. Ct. 872 (2004). Pooling confidential information was particularly suspect in a joint project dealing with externalities. Thus, pooling confidential information prevents free-riding (copying). However, the Guide tried to protect

with joint facilities established by competing firms, suggest that if a joint R&D venture becomes the key to competing effectively in the markets served by the participants, and if the research effort is not practicably or effectively duplicable by excluded firms, access to the venture (or its result) on reasonable terms may be mandated by the Sherman Act.[141] Of course, this is in stark contrast to the Supreme Court's refusal in 2004 to acknowledge an essential facility doctrine under US antitrust law in *Trinko*.[142]

Finally, the Guide recognised that collective denial of access, or of licences, particularly by major competitors in regard to actual or potential competitors, raised serious potential problems under section 1 of the Sherman Act. Such actions could constitute a group boycott or concerted refusal to deal. If the collective decision cannot be justified on legitimate grounds unrelated to the competitive interests of the parties, it would have to be treated as *per se* illegal. A right for individual members of the venture to exclude third party applicants was particularly likely to be found illegal.[143] However, access has not always been a prerequisite for success of a technology. Access should therefore not be granted if the firms in the venture were not dominant prior to the new technology development.

(d) Conclusion   The guiding principle for the antitrust evaluation was, according to the Guide, that elimination of research competition should not exceed that reasonably necessary to meet the needs of effective research.[144] It is interesting to note that the guiding principle was based on effective rather than efficient research. Despite acknowledging that the reason for joint R&D ventures often is based on the notion of efficiency and costs savings, the Guide is remarkably silent regarding the existence of an efficiency defence as a justification for minimising competition in research or, for that matter, innovation. Arguably, this is because of

---

such free-riding. Accordingly, such information should be made public. Regarding patent and know-how restraints, the Guide found that pooling patents, not 'reasonably necessary' for the work of the joint venture, raised antitrust problems.

[141]   The Guide, 19, making reference to *United States v. Terminal R. Assn.*, 224 U.S. 383, 409–410 (1912).

[142]   *Verizon Communication Inc. v. The Law Offices of Curtis V. Trinko LLP* 124 S. Ct. 872 (2004).

[143]   See *Worthen Bank Trust Co. v. National Bank America, Inc.*, 485 F.2d 119 (8th Cir. 1973), cert. denied, 415 U.S. 918 (1974).

[144]   The Guide, 8.

incompatible fit between the model of perfect competition and innovation. It must therefore be concluded that the Guide was based on the belief that antitrust law should protect a high innovation rate by promoting rivalry, even at the expense of efficiency. Competition could only be restrained by a joint effort, provided that innovation was promoted.

An efficiency defence became available under the NCRA. Moreover, the NCRA introduced a safe harbour and, foremost, a different test for determining anticompetitive collaborations.

3.2.2 The National Cooperative Research and Production Act and Innovation Market

(i) Introduction

In 1984, Congress enacted the National Cooperative Research Act (the NCRA).[145] The NCRA was the first antitrust statute to address joint research cooperation. The act was amended in 1993 to also include joint production ventures and the word 'production' was added to the name, that is, National Cooperative Research and Production Act (the NCRPA). The Act clarified that courts had to measure joint R&D ventures against the rule of reason standard, regardless of whether the joint research was attacked under federal or state antitrust laws. It introduced that a plaintiff needed to prove anticompetitive restraints on an R&D market.[146] Moreover, the Act stipulated *inter alia* that if the Attorney General or the FTC

---

[145]   For analyses of the Act, see Alan H. Blankenheimer, 'Strategic Alliances: Antitrust Issues', (July 1997) 1002 *PLI/CORP* 547; John A. Maher, 'National Cooperative Production Amendments of 1993: Limited Cartelism Invited!', (1994) 12 *Dick. J. Int'l.* 195; Maher & LaMont, 'National Cooperative Research Act of 1984: Cartelism for High-Tech Ventures (and Others?)', (1988) 7 *Dick. J. Int'l.* 1; Foster, et al., 'The National Cooperative Research Act of 1984 as a Shield From the Antitrust Laws', (1985) 5 *J.L. & Commerce* 347; Veronica M. Dougherty, 'Antitrust advantages to joint ventures under the National Cooperative Research and Production Act', (1999) Winter, *The Antitrust Bulletin*, 1007 with references. See also Hanns Ullrich, *Kooperative Forschung and Kartellrecht* (Verlag Recht und Wirtschaft 1988), 91 et seq. See also Andreas Fuchs, *Kartellrechtliche Grenzen der Forschungskooperation* (Nomos Verlaggesellschaft 1989), 92 et seq.

[146]   The relevant legal text states, 'such conduct shall be judged on the basis of its reasonableness, taking account all relevant factors affecting competition, including, but not limited to, effects on competition in properly defined, relevant R&D markets.' See section 3 NCRA. The text seemed to imply that an R&D market always needs to be identified where at least some anticompetitive conduct is manifest. The text was later altered in the NCRPA, see discussion *infra* section 3.2.3(v).

was notified about the joint venture, the parties were not obliged to pay treble damages should the joint venture eventually be regarded as anticompetitive in a court of law. Instead, they would be liable for actual damages, caused by the anticompetitive harm, created by the collaboration.[147] Finally, the NCRA stipulated provisions obliging the losing plaintiff to pay the attorneys' fees of the prevailing defendant.

These changes had rather profound effects. It was not only a clear theoretical break with the previous application of antitrust law to R&D collaborations under the Guide. Private antitrust enforcement in the area of R&D collaboration was also severely limited. From the very beginning, it should have been clear to Congress that the Act eliminated the incentive for private plaintiffs and limited the incentives for the antitrust enforcement agencies to launch any suits based on antitrust law in the field of R&D. Congress created a 'safe harbour' for R&D collaboration.

In addition, it should be mentioned that the NCRA and later the NCRPA is applicable under all 'antitrust laws', both federal and state, and thus also under, for example, section 2 of the Sherman Act. R&D joint ventures were perhaps not of such great interest, but in the latest amendment, standards development organisations (SDOs) were included under the NCRPA and for such organisations the non-application of the NCRPA under section 2 of the Sherman Act and its equivalent is of interest.[148]

(ii) Definition of research venture

The NCRPA defines 'joint ventures' as a group of activities engaged in by two or more legal persons for the purpose of:[149]

(i)   theoretical analysis, experimentation, or systematic study of phenomena or observable facts;
(ii) the development or testing of basic engineering techniques;
(iii) the extension of investigative findings or theory of a scientific or technical nature into practical application for experimental and

---

[147]   An amendment provided that a plaintiff could still obtain treble damages in circumstances in which a joint venture violated not only the antitrust laws but also violated a court or FTC order concerning the conduct of the joint venture. See Thomas W. Queen, 'Recent Development in Federal Antitrust Legislation', (1984–1985) 53 *Antitrust Law Journal*, 443, 448.

[148]   It seems that the NCRPA is applicable under the Sherman Act and the Clayton Act, but not the FTC Act, see 15 U.S.C.A § 4301, making reference to 15 U.S.C.A § 12.

[149]   15 U.S.C.A § 4301(a)(6).

demonstration purposes, including the experimental production and testing of models, prototypes, equipment, materials, and processes;

(iv) the production of a product, process, or services;[150]

(v)   the testing in connection with the production of a product, process, or services by such venture;

(vi) the collection, exchange, and analysis of research or production information; or

(vii) any combination of the purposes specified in the paragraphs above, and may include the establishment and operation of facilities for the conducting of such a venture, the conducting of such a venture on a protected and proprietary basis, and the prosecution of applications for patents and the granting of licences for the results of such ventures.

During the legislative process the definition of joint venture was altered a few times.[151] The Senate gave special weight to the definition of 'joint research and development programme' when discussing the NCRA bill. According to their definition a 'joint research and development programme' included theoretical analysis, exploration or experimentation, or the extension of basic scientific knowledge into practical application, including prototype development.[152] The Senate thought that this definition gave the bill a sound basic balance that allowed joint R&D programmes to be structured in effective, efficient ways while still clearly laying out the intended scope of the exemption. The Senate intended 'the programme' to encompass single research programmes or projects. Hence, the NCRPA was to exempt vehicles for developing single innovation, technology or solving a problem. However, when the bill was returned to the House of Representatives, the text was changed to 'joint [research and development] ventures', thus losing some of its decisive feature as an exemption for single research efforts. Instead it became a vehicle for exempting long-term and even non-determined projects.[153]

---

[150] Production was added with the 1993 amendment; see the National Cooperative Production Amendments of 1993, Pub. L. No. 103-42, amended the National Cooperative Research Act of 1984, Pub L. No. 98-462, renamed it the National Cooperative Research and Production Act of 1993. For the leading production joint venture precedents, see *In re* General Motors 103 F.T.C. 374 (1984) and, see also *In re* General Motors 116 F.T.C. 1276 (1993).

[151] See H.R. REP. 98-1044, *reprinted* 1984 U.S.C.C.A.N. 3131, 3132; S. REP. 98-427, *reprinted* 1984 U.S.C.C.A.N. 3105, 3106, 3109 et seq.

[152] Ibid.

[153] Ibid.

There is no limitation for how long a venture may utilise the NCRPA. However, after ten years the ventures should, presumably, be notified as a merger.[154]

The First Circuit noted in *Addamax Corporation v. Open Software Foundation* the phrase joint venture is 'often used to describe a venture, other than one engaged in naked *per se* violations (like a price-fixing cartel), that represents a collaborative effort between companies – who may or may not be competitors – to achieve a particular end (e.g., joint research and development, production of an individual product, or efficient joint purchasing).'[155] Although the definition of joint venture is wide, most antitrust attorneys would agree that an agreement stipulating that the parties agree not to innovate should be regarded as a *per se* illegal sham agreement. Such a naked restriction of innovation demands the *per se* standard. This is especially true in light of the fact that restraining the pace or development of innovation can have far more negative effects on prosperity than price-fixing cartels.[156]

Early case law reflects this view. In the *Automobile Manufacturers Association* case, the US car manufacturers were alleged to have conspired in order to eliminate competition in research, manufacturing and installation of air pollution control equipment.[157] The government and the car manufacturers entered into a consent decree. Therefore, the case was never tried on its merits, but an agreement not to research existed between the manufacturers which were considered anticompetitive by the Justice Department.[158]

---

[154]   Collaboration Guidelines 5, fn. 10. As a comparison, the EU block exemption for R&D ventures limits the collaboration to seven years. See Article 4 (1) of the R&D block exemption.

[155]   *Addamax Corporation v. Open Software Foundation, Inc.*, 152 F.3d 40, 50 n.3 (1st Cir. 1998).

[156]   See, e.g., Phillip Areeda & Herbert Hovenkamp, *Antitrust Law – An Analysis of Antitrust Principles and Their Application* (Aspen Publishers 2005), 113, § 2115b2.

[157]   *U.S. v. Automobile Manufacturers Association, Inc.*, 307 F. Supp. 617, 13 Fed. R. Serv.2d 731, 1970 Trade Cases P73, 070. *United States v. Mfrs. Aircraft Ass'n, Inc.*, 1976-1 Trade cas. (CCH) 60,810 (S.D.M.Y. 1975). Also making reference to the R&D cartel, implying that it must have contained patent pool features. See *United States v. Automobile Mfrs. Ass'n* 307 F. Supp. 617 (C.D. Cal. 1969) appeal dismissed *sub nom. City of New York v. United States*, 397 U.S. 248 (1970), modified *sub nom. United States v. Motor Vehicle Mfrs. Ass'n*, 182-82 Trade Cas. (CCH) 65,088 (C.D. Cal. 1982).

[158]   Hanns Ullrich, *Kooperative Forschung and Kartellrecht* (Verlag Recht und Wirtschaft 1988), 53 et seq. with references.

Furthermore, according to the Supreme Court, the parties cannot just caption an anticompetitive agreement 'research and development cooperation' and expect the agreement to pass antitrust scrutiny.[159] The aim of the joint research should imply that the result can be protected under patent law or at least that relevant know-how is created. Nonetheless, it is evident that neither the Justice Department nor the FTC has ever considered a *pure* joint R&D venture as anticompetitive. Thus, as long as the parties have a specific idea to pursue, the joint research will not be condemned.

Apart from the clear-cut cases, where the parties agreed not to research, there is a variety of hypothetical anticompetitive conduct: the parties can agree to perform the research in question, but not with the eagerness and efficiency one might expect. They can invent with the view of not introducing the product until the current sold product is obsolete, or when faced with competition from a third party.[160] As long as the parties agree to conduct some kind of joint research, the implied elimination of other research avenues, denied access for third parties and also restrictive ancillary restraints between the R&D parties will be judged under the rule of reason standard. Hence, the parties risk being considered anticompetitive only if they hold market power.

It should also be pointed out that the definition of joint venture does not differentiate between different R&Ds. By *not* making a distinction between basic and applied research, Congress granted a wide scope for what constitutes a joint R&D programme. By abandoning the notion of different treatment under the Act of basic, applied and developmental research, Congress made the NCRA applicable to both basic science and applied design features. It thereby took a step away from the basic idea under the old rule of reason. In the Guide, the Justice Department did not want to stipulate a clear market share threshold for when a joint R&D venture should be regarded as monopolising the market. The reason for not stipulating a market share threshold was the conviction that basic research must be judged differently from applied research. Firms conducting basic research in collusion can be pro-competitive and pro-innovation, even though these firms might hold substantial market power

---

[159] See *Timken Roller Bearing Co. v. United States*, 341 U.S. 593, 598 (1951) and the Guideline, 10 et seq.

[160] Cf., generally, regarding obsolescence as anticompetitive conduct, Jeremy Bulow, 'An Economic Theory of Planned Obsolescence', (1986) 101 *The Quarterly Journal of Economics*, 729, and cf. Michael Waldman, 'A New Perspective on Planned Obsolescence', (1993) 108 *The Quarterly Journal of Economics*, 273.

on downstream product markets. Correspondingly, jointly conducted applied research, that is, research close to the end product, can have extensive effects on the end product market, for example, same or similar prices, and, hence, reduce competition on the relevant product market even though there exist several other poles of similar research in the market or globally. Therefore, the market share threshold should be less for applied research than basic research. Congress, however, made the NCRA, and the thresholds or safe harbours thereby enacted, available for all R&D efforts equally. In addition, Congress stipulated in the legal history that four joint venture efforts constituted the threshold for when a venture might raise anticompetitive concerns.[161] The four-venture threshold was later adopted by the antitrust agencies and inserted in, for example, the Justice Department's and FTC's 'Antitrust Guidelines for the Licensing of Intellectual Property' from 1995 (hereinafter the IP Guidelines).[162]

(iii)   Why the need for an act of Congress?

Legislative history shows three major reasons for enacting the NCRA.[163] A first reason was to inform the business community that engaging in joint R&D ventures would not endanger the parties by holding them in violation of any *per se* standard of antitrust law. Secondly, to inform business that in light of the fact that research was increasingly more expensive, US firms must be able to eliminate wasteful duplication of research efforts. Finally, for the US to maintain its competitiveness, US firms should be able to conduct cooperative research to the same extent as firms based in other jurisdictions.[164]

In the years before the enactment of the NCRA, several bills were pending before Congress regarding the exemption of R&D from the ambit of the antitrust laws.[165] These bills all stem from an uneasy feeling

---

[161]   See discussion *infra* section 3.2.2(vii).

[162]   DOJ/FTC, Antitrust Guidelines for the Licensing of Intellectual Property issued 1995 (earlier defined as IP Guidelines).

[163]   See H.R. REP. 98-1044, *reprinted* 1984 U.S.C.C.A.N. 3131 et seq.; S. REP. 98-427, *reprinted* 1984 U.S.C.C.A.N., 3105 et seq. Interestingly, any economic theory regarding research cooperation is conspicuously absent from the reasons stated for enacting the NCRA. Congress also acknowledged that the Justice Department has never challenged a pure R&D joint venture without ancillary restraints.

[164]   Ibid.

[165]   Cf. Andreas Fuchs, *Kartellrechtliche Grenzen der Forschungskoopera-tion* (Nomos Verlaggesellschaft, 1989), 92 et seq. Cf. also Daniel M. Crane, 'Joint Research and Development Ventures and the Antitrust Laws', (1984) 21

that US business was losing ground in the face of international competition, especially from Japanese firms. One perceived difference
between Japanese and American industry was the Japanese method of
organising legal stand-alone firms in business groups and the promotion
and guidance of such collaborations by different Japanese governmental
bodies. Thus, from an American perspective, the Japanese collectively
performed certain tasks, such as research, instead of conducting them
through competition. A reason why American firms did not collaborate
was the perceived restriction imposed by US antitrust law. However, as
discussed (*supra*) under the early case law, the claims that US antitrust
law prohibited collective research efforts were based on controversial
case law which, some commentators contended, did not discourage
legitimate research joint ventures.[166]

Scott stated the NCRPA was not needed to dictate that R&D ventures
should be judged under the rule of reason.[167] That said, it should be
pointed out that the Reagan administration bill, which eventually laid the
groundwork for the NCRA, suggested that *all* intellectual property
licensing agreements, including patent pools, should be exempted from
the ambit of the *per se* rule under the proposed act. The Reagan bill also
suggested circumscribing the patent misuse doctrine only to encompass
antitrust violations.[168] The NCRA in the end became narrower, dealing
with joint R&D and joint licensing derived therefrom. Nonetheless, it
should be stressed that the bill supported by the Reagan administration
did not only include research activities, but also all licensing activities in
technology markets. All restrictions in reference to licensing, for

---

Harvard Journal of Legislation, 405, 442 et seq.; see Thomas W. Queen, 'Recent
Development in Federal Antitrust Legislation', (1984–1985) 53 *Antitrust Law
Journal*, 443, 445 et seq. See also Jr. James H. Wallace, 'Recent Development in
Federal Antitrust Legislation', (1983) 52 *Antitrust Law Journal*, 479, 480 et seq.

[166] Then Assistant Attorney General Thomas E. Kauper stated in a letter to
the Arch Both Chief Executive Officer, U.S. Chamber of Commerce, that, '[t]he
allegation that businesses feel discouraged [to form joint ventures] goes to their
state of mind and is obviously impossible to verify or refute. On the other hand,
the known facts tend to refute any concrete assertion about the inhibitory effect
of antitrust laws.' See Daniel M. Crane, 'Joint Research and Development
Ventures and the Antitrust Laws', (1984) 21 *Harvard Journal of Legislation*, 405,
411 fn. 30.

[167] John Scott, 'The National Cooperative Research and Production Act', in
ABA (ed.), *Issues in Competition Law and Policy* (ABA Section of Antitrust Law
2008), 1300 et seq.

[168] Cf. Thomas W. Queen, 'Recent Development in Federal Antitrust Legislation', (1984–1985) 53 *Antitrust Law Journal*, 443, 445 et seq.

example, the restrictions in the patent pool cases above, should be judged according to the rule of reason. In the light of such a broad exemption from the *per se* rule, the early case law needed to be overturned.

It should also be recognised that the amendment in 1993 creating the NCRPA, enacted under President Bill Clinton, mirrored the original Reagan bill, thus including also joint production of R&D results under the more lenient treatment. The last amendment in 2004, enacted under President George W. Bush, in which standard-setting agreements were included under the Act, in fact widened the immunity even further than intended by the Reagan administration. With the latest amendment, IP arrangements under standard development organisations where patentees that have conducted unilateral R&D publicly state or agree on terms for licensing third parties are encompassed by the NCRPA.[169]

From the perspective of exempting patent pools and IP arrangements, the *National Lead* case and its equivalents did enforce a *per se* rule. However, in light of the fact that the NCRA and later NCRPA revolved around research ventures, these cases did not directly reflect any limitation for such ventures. They did not directly concern research ventures. Interestingly, the political movement that initiated the enactment of the NCRA was thus based on fears that stem from cases which actually did not primarily deal with R&D. Nonetheless, the NCRPA today encompasses much more than joint R&D. It must be viewed as rendering obsolete many parts of *National Lead* and the other classical patent pool or cartel cases originating from the end of the 1940s.[170]

(iv)   The exemption

Whether the NCRPA in fact is an exemption rather than stipulating a limited immunity is a question of degree and viewpoint.[171] There is indubitably no incentive for a private plaintiff to initiate proceedings under the Act. Indeed, the parties that engage in activities encompassed

---

[169]   Discussed *infra* section 3.2.4.

[170]   Discussed *infra* section 3.2.4.

[171]   Members of the House of Representatives actually used the notion of 'immunity' from federal and state antitrust laws, see Report from the House Committee on Science, Space, and Technology. H. Rpt. 98-571, pt 1. The notion that NCRPA creates limited immunity was acknowledged by representatives of the Justice Department, see speech by Gerald Masoudi, 'Efficiency in Analysis of Antitrust, Standard Setting, and Intellectual Property', paper given at High-Level Workshop on Standardization, IP Licensing, and Antitrust 2007, TILEC, University of Tilburg. See http://www.usdoj.gov/atr/public/speeches/220972.htm, accessed 21 April 2012.

by the Act are shielded from private antitrust suits. The limitation of frivolous private suits, or more precisely unfounded class actions, was an important reason for enacting the NCRPA. However, the exemption also came to preclude any well-founded suits. For example, the Act is applicable within the collaboration. Suits initiated by either joint venture party in the attempt to declare the joint R&D or specific covenants void are also encompassed by the NCRPA.

The exemption in the NCRPA for joint R&D against private third party litigation was created mainly by way of three limitations. The first cornerstone of the exemption is the limitation whereby a successful private plaintiff would only be rewarded actual damages, not treble damages under the Act, if the joint R&D has been notified under section 4303 of the Act.[172] This is in contrast with the prevailing US antitrust philosophy. Furthermore, in connection with the other general limitations under antitrust law, the plaintiff faces difficulties quantifying the damages for several reasons. Firstly, the question is, how can a plaintiff prove actual damages for anticompetitive R&D? Knowledge is seldom traded. How do such damages accrue? Presumed damages will arise in the future, in different markets, long after the alleged harmful conduct was committed, and long after it could have been challenged and undone. Secondly, actual damages imply direct antitrust injury.[173] A competitor may find it very difficult to be rewarded damages from a court for not being able to gain access to an anticompetitive joint research venture, and the ultimate consumer would probably be barred from any compensation. Thirdly, how does anyone really concerned, that is, active in a research market, get standing in the first place? Standing is only given to plaintiffs who can show that they incurred direct antitrust harm, but that is, in light of the above, almost impossible to prove.[174] Moreover, it should be noted that the limitation to actual damages also applies to joint production of products, processes and services if such joint production takes place

---

[172]   See 15 U.S.C.A § 4303. Interestingly, states are allowed to recover total damages, see 15 U.S.C.A. § 4303 (b). For an analysis of the notifying requirement see Veronica M. Dougherty, 'Antitrust advantages to joint ventures under the National Cooperative Research and Production Act', (1999) Winter, *The Antitrust Bulletin*, 1007, 1021 et seq.

[173]   See generally *Brunswick Corp. v. Pueblo Bowl.-O-Mat, Inc.*, 429 US 477, 489, S. Ct. 690, 50 L. Ed. 2d 701 (1977).

[174]   Cf. Lawrence Sullivan & Warren Grimes, *The Law of Antitrust: An Integrated Handbook* (Thomson/West, 2006), 959 et seq., discussing causation, antitrust injury and standing. See also *Illinois Brick Co. v. Illinois*, 431 U.S. 720, 97 S. Ct. 2061, 52 L. Ed. 2d 707 (1977).

within the US and the venture and the parties controlling the venture are either US persons or foreign persons from a country that treats US persons no less favourably than domestic persons under its antitrust laws.[175]

The second reason to prevent private litigation was that a defendant in some cases is able to win their costs.[176] This is a concept alien to US antitrust law traditions.[177] It gives the defendant an incentive to prolong litigation, and it adds to the rather extreme uncertainties facing a potential antitrust plaintiff. The difficulties should also be seen in light of the fact that the typical antitrust plaintiff has considerably fewer assets than the defendant. Moreover, smaller firms, for example R&D-only firms, may be discouraged from both entering R&D agreements and trying to exit anticompetitive agreements, given the risk of having to pay the other party's litigation costs.

The third restriction creating the exemption is the interaction between the rule of reason and the concept of 'innovation market'. The restriction of the *per se* rule implies that the plaintiff needs to show either direct anticompetitive harm or likely anticompetitive effects with evidence of, or due to, substantial market power.[178] Direct antitrust harm caused by collaborative research will be difficult to show, so a plaintiff needs to establish market power in a research, development or other relevant market to be successful. The third restriction not only limits private parties but also the Justice Department and the FTC in their pursuit of alleged anticompetitive collaborations.

(v) The R&D or Innovation Market under the NCRA[179]

The NCRPA does not stipulate a new rule to be applied to joint R&D ventures. Since the incumbent rule was the rule of reason, the enactment

---

[175] See 15 U.S.C.A § 4306. Interestingly, the requirement that the place of production should be in the US would probably disqualify the US from treating foreign firms any less favourably under its antitrust laws.

[176] See 15 U.S.C.A § 4304 (a) (2), 'if the claim, or the claimant's conduct during the litigation of the claim, was frivolous, unreasonable, without foundation, or in bad faith'.

[177] However, reimbursement for legal fees for the plaintiff is standard civil law procedure in civil law countries.

[178] For the rule of reason approach under the NCRPA, see Thomas Jorde & David Teece, 'Innovation, Cooperation and Antitrust', (1989) 4 *High Tech Law Journal*, 1, 62 et seq. with references.

[179] This part is based in part on Björn Lundqvist, *Standardization under EU Competition Rules and US Antitrust Laws – The Rise and the Limits of Self-Regulation* (Edward Elgar, 2014), 153 et seq.

of the NCRA implied no different treatment of research ventures.[180] However, the governing rule was not the innovative part of the NCRA and later the NCRPA. It is, according to current academic thought, similar to the rule of reason invented in the *Chicago Board of Trade* case.[181] Instead, the innovative part of the NCRA was the establishment of a new environment for its application. The full ambiguity of the rule of reason in this field of law only reveals itself after a closer analysis of the concepts of 'research and development market' or 'innovation market'.

The NCRA introduced the notion of 'research and development markets'.[182] Before that, technology, service and product markets, or any markets where arm's length sales take place, had been acknowledged under the antitrust laws as relevant markets. But by creating the concept of R&D markets, Congress opened up a new competitive dimension. Firms, which do not compete in the relevant product or technology markets, can compete in an R&D market.

Legal history argues that an R&D market should include all firms with the ability and incentive, either individually or in collaboration with other firms, to undertake research comparable to that of the joint programme in question.[183] Incentive should be judged objectively. Firms, thus, did not have to compete with each other at the production or marketing stage in order to be competitors in the R&D market. Market shares in current markets or in projected future markets were not to determine a firm's ability or incentive to compete in the relevant R&D market. Rather, the crucial aspects of whether the firms were competitors consisted of the facilities, technologies and other assets to which firms had access.[184]

---

[180] John Scott, 'The National Cooperative Research and Production Act', in ABA (ed.), *Issues in Competition Law and Policy* (ABA Section of Antitrust Law 2008), 1300 et seq. See generally *Chicago Board of Trade v. United States*, 246 U.S. 231, 238 (1918). Jorde and Teece might have been somewhat successful in getting the rule of reason under the NCRPA somewhat more structured. Cf. Thomas Jorde & David Teece, 'Innovation, Cooperation and Antitrust', (1989) 4 *High Tech Law Journal*, 1, 62 et seq. See discussion *infra* section 3.2.3(vi) and 3.2.3(vii).

[181] Ibid.

[182] S. REP. 98-427, *reprinted* 1984 U.S.C.C.A.N. 3105, 3107 et seq. For an analysis, see, e.g., Andreas Fuchs, *Kartellrechtliche Grenzen der Forschungs-kooperation* (Nomos Verlaggesellschaft, 1989), 119 et seq., or Lawrence B. Landman, 'Did Congress Actually Create Innovation Markets?', (1998) 13 *Berkeley Technology Law Journal*, 721.

[183] S. REP. 98-427, *reprinted* 1984 U.S.C.C.A.N. 3105, 3107 et seq.

[184] S. REP. 98-427, *reprinted* 1984 U.S.C.C.A.N. 3105, 3109 et seq.

When introduced in the NCRA, the concept of R&D market attracted some attention.[185] In 1993–95, after having been (re-)introduced in the NCRPA and the IP Guidelines, the concept of 'innovation markets' became the subject of heated discussions.[186]

The concept of 'innovation market' brought with it a new, or, at least, gave more focus to, specific anticompetitive conduct. Firms that are able to decrease spending on R&D because of the fact that the innovation market becomes too concentrated through their joint R&D collaboration are in fact entering into an anticompetitive agreement.

The definition of an 'innovation market' is a market consisting of R&D, directed at particular new and improved goods or processes, and at the close substitutes for that R&D. Close substitutes are R&D efforts, technologies and goods that significantly constrain the exercise of market power with respect to the scrutinised R&D. For example, research limiting the ability and incentive of a hypothetical monopolist to slow down the pace of R&D.[187] When introduced, the theory was that an innovation market was identified through an analysis of the set of R&D activities that a monopolist would profitably be able to reduce by a small yet significant reduction in R&D spending.[188] Thus, a monopolist was defined as a firm able profitably to decrease R&D spending on an innovation market. If there would be no other R&D efforts to compete with and, hence, to force the monopolist to invest in research – logically

---

[185]   Jorde and Teece made some contribution to the R&D market concept, which probably partly caused the adjustment of the R&D market concept in the 1993 amendment. See Thomas Jorde & David Teece, 'Innovation, Cooperation and Antitrust', (1989) 4 *High Tech Law Journal*, 1, 65 et seq., with references.

[186]   Two Deputy Assistant Attorneys initiated the discussion in an article, outlining the innovation market concept, see Richard Gilbert & Steven Sunshine, 'Incorporating Dynamic Efficiency Concerns in Merger Analysis: the Use of Innovation Markets', (1995) 63 *Antitrust Law Journal*, 569, 574 et seq. Several commentators have commented and criticised their views. See, e.g., Robert Hoerner, 'Innovation Markets: New Wine in Old Bottles?', (1995–1996) 64 *Antitrust Law Journal*, 49; George Hay, 'Innovations in Antitrust Enforcement', (1995–1996) 64 *Antitrust Law Journal*, 7; and Richard Rapp, 'The Misapplication of Innovation Market Approach to Merger Analysis', (1995–1996) 64 *Antitrust Law Journal*, 19. See also Gilbert and Sunshine's reply: Richard Gilbert & Steven Sunshine, 'The Use of Innovation Markets: A Reply to Hay, Rapp, and Hoerner', (1995–1996) 64 *Antitrust Law Journal*, 79.

[187]   IP Guidelines, 11.

[188]   Thus, appealing similarities to the SSNIP test, see Richard Gilbert & Steven Sunshine, 'Incorporating Dynamic Efficiency Concerns in Merger Analysis: the Use of Innovation Markets', (1995) 63 *Antitrust Law Journal*, 569, 594.

it could decrease its R&D spending. The test, as introduced by the economists at the Justice Department, Richard Sunshine and Steven Gilbert, focused on whether a firm was able to decrease R&D investments by a small but significant amount without losing market share. If the firm was able to decrease R&D investments by, for example, 5–10 per cent without losing any market share, it should be considered holding monopoly, or market, power.[189]

Sunshine and Gilbert's definition of innovation market, relying on the logic of the significant non-transitory increase in relative price (SSNIP) test,[190] thus acknowledged actual market power in real product markets. According to Sunshine and Gilbert, only if the parties could limit the output effect of a reduction in innovation in classic goods or service markets, the conduct would have to be considered anticompetitive.[191] Thus, the parties would be dominant in the research market if they were able to limit R&D investment and continue to defend their market share in the relevant end markets.

The above shows that the definitions of an innovation market and an R&D market in the beginning were somewhat different.[192] The R&D market concept in the NCRA was more focused on a non-market definition. Thus, it was not based on a reversed SSNIP test or on market power the parties held in the product or service market and how that affected innovation. Instead, the R&D market concept in the NCRA focused on which firms had the assets necessary to perform the research in question. One way of viewing this is that R&D market under the NCRA actually was a broader concept than innovation market, or that the Justice Department in fact identified narrower 'future goods markets' under the notion of innovation markets, rather than actual competition in innovation.[193] However, the concepts intertwine and possibly the introduction

---

[189]   Cf. Richard Gilbert & Steven Sunshine, 'Incorporating Dynamic Efficiency Concerns in Merger Analysis: the use of Innovation Markets', (1995) 63 *Antitrust Law Journal*, 569, 594 et seq.

[190]   See generally Commission Notice on the definition of the relevant market for the purposes of Community competition law, OJ C372, 9.12.1997, 5 et seq.

[191]   Richard Gilbert & Steven Sunshine, 'The Use of Innovation Markets: A Reply to Hay, Rapp, and Hoerner', (1995–1996) 64 *Antitrust Law Journal*, 79.

[192]   Cf. Thomas Jorde & David Teece, 'Innovation, Cooperation and Antitrust', (1989) 4 *High Tech Law Journal*, 1, 65 et seq., for the even broader notion of R&D market.

[193]   Lawrence B. Landman, 'Competitiveness, Innovation Policy and the Innovation Market Myth: A Reply to Tom and Newberg on Innovation Markets as the "Centerpiece" of "New Thinking" on Innovation', (1998) 13 *St. John's Journal of Legal Commentary*, 223.

of innovation market added a prerequisite of establishing market power. In comparison with the R&D market in order to establish market power in an innovation market, dominance needs to be established also in a connected downstream product market.

In comparison, according to the IP Guidelines the market shares in related product markets are of great interest when establishing market power in an innovation market.[194] The definition of innovation market, relying on a reversed SSNIP test for R&D investment, made use of the actual market power in real product markets and whether it would be lessened. According to Sunshine and Gilbert, only if the parties can prevent the transmission of the reduction in innovation into an output effect in 'classic' goods or service markets should the conduct be considered anticompetitive.[195]

Notwithstanding the above, today the concepts of 'research market' under the NCRPA and innovation market must be similar. Thus, the innovation market concept as presented in the IP Guidelines should also be used under the NCRPA. However, that does not automatically imply that the market is narrower. The plaintiff still needs to prove market power on a wide market.

In most cases, the innovation market encompasses more firms than the connected product or technology markets.[196] An innovation market is only in rare circumstances narrower, containing fewer participants, than the product or technology markets. Of course, this implies two things: firstly, one can find overlapping activities where, using product and technology market definitions, one would find that the parties are non-competitors, since they are active in different geographic or product markets.[197] If the parties have similar facilities and other R&D assets, they are competitors even though producing different products. However, secondly, by increasing the market, any market power held by the parties in, for example, separate but connected product markets is bound to be

---

[194]   IP Guidelines, 10 et seq.

[195]   Richard Gilbert & Steven Sunshine, 'The Use of Innovation Markets: A Reply to Hay, Rapp, and Hoerner', (1995–1996) 64 *Antitrust Law Journal*, 79.

[196]   Cf. Richard Gilbert & Steven Sunshine, 'The Use of Innovation Markets: A Reply to Hay, Rapp, and Hoerner', (1995–1996) 64 *Antitrust Law Journal*, 81. See also Thomas Jorde & David Teece, 'Innovation, Cooperation and Antitrust', (1989) 4 *High Tech Law Journal*, 1, 66: 'Markets for know-how are almost always going to be broader in scope than markets involving commercialization.'

[197]   See *United States v. General Motors Corp.* No 93-530 (D. Del filed Nov. 16, 1993) referred to in Richard Gilbert & Steven Sunshine, 'The Use of Innovation Markets: A Reply to Hay, Rapp, and Hoerner', (1995–1996) 64 *Antitrust Law Journal*, 77.

less in an innovation market since it is, by definition, almost always larger, encompassing more firms holding similar assets but active in several product markets. Thus, as a general rule, more firms representing in total larger turnover and larger overall R&D investments are represented in the innovation market than in the downstream technology and product markets.

Interestingly, the notion of innovation market when introduced was mostly criticised for the fact that such markets were not real markets where a purchaser and a seller transferred products or services at market value,[198] that the doctrine of 'potential competition' could also encompass innovation markets,[199] and that the Justice Department was to use the new innovation market as a way to attack conglomerate mergers.[200] However, the early critique appears to have been somewhat oblivious of the most striking feature of the concept. In almost all cases, firms' product market influence or dominance diminishes in the larger innovation markets. By increasing the size of the relevant market in all respects, that is, the number of technologies or products to be encompassed, the geographic scope and also the period of (future) time to be analysed, very few firms can be regarded as holding market power. Innovation markets are a way to diminish the effect of the conduct of large firms in the innovation race. Indeed, the concept opens up for large firms, system leaders, to collaborate in, for example, R&D or standard-setting while claiming to have no market power in the innovation market. In fact, it may be therefore that innovation market in practice soon developed into a 'future goods' market,[201] where the future product

---

[198] See, e.g., John Temple Lang, 'European Community Antitrust Law: Innovation Markets and High Technology Industries', in Fordham University School of Law (ed.), *International Antitrust Law & Policy* (1996), 557 et seq. Lang also claims that there is a right to compulsory licence under Article 81 EC Treaty (now 101 TFEU), see ibid., 570. See also Robert Hoerner, 'Innovation Markets: New Wine in Old Bottles?', (1995–1996) 64 *Antitrust Law Journal*, 49, 53.

[199] George Hay, 'Innovations in Antitrust Enforcement', (1995–1996) 64 *Antitrust Law Journal*, 7, 9 et seq. Richard Rapp, 'The Misapplication of Innovation Market Approach to Merger Analysis', (1995–1996) 64 *Antitrust Law Journal*, 19, 21.

[200] Robert Hoerner, 'Innovation Markets: New Wine in Old Bottles?', (1995–1996) 64 *Antitrust Law Journal*, 49, 55 et seq.

[201] Landman identified that the innovation market was used by the antitrust agencies rather as a future goods market than such innovation market proposed by the legal history. It named it the 'Innovation Market Myth'. See Lawrence B. Landman, 'Competitiveness, Innovation Policy and the Innovation Market Myth:

market was identified rather than the actual 'pure' innovation market as envisioned by the authors of the legal history to the NCRA and the NCRPA. In fact, the argument by Sunshine and Gilbert, that the reduction in R&D investment and the anticompetitive effects must be potentially visible in a classic goods or service market, also actually limits the room for the innovation market.

(vi) The Innovation Market under the NCRPA

The relevant section of the NCRPA states:

> In any action under the antitrust laws, or under any State law similar to the antitrust laws, the conduct of any person in making or performing a contract to carry out a joint venture shall not be deemed illegal *per se*; such conduct shall be judged on the basis of its reasonableness, taking into account all relevant factors affecting competition, including, but not limited to, effects on competition in properly defined, relevant *research, development, product, process, and service markets.* For the purpose of determining a properly defined, relevant market, *worldwide capacity* shall be considered to the extent that it may be appropriate in the circumstances [emphasis added].[202]

The NCRA stipulated that an R&D joint venture should be judged on the relevant R&D market.[203] The legal history (that is, the *travaux*

A Reply to Tom and Newberg on Innovation Markets as the "Centerpiece" of "New Thinking" on Innovation', (1998) 13 *St. John's Journal of Legal Commentary*, 234 et seq.

[202] See 15 U.S.C.A § 4302.

[203] IP Guidelines, 12 et seq. Example 4 is an illustrating example of the contemporary application of US antitrust law to R&D joint ventures (note, e.g., that there is no analysis of whether the participants in the joint R&D could have conducted the research independently): 'In this case, a relevant market is an innovation market – R&D for biodegradable (and other environmentally friendly) containers. The Agency would seek to identify any other entities that would be actual or likely potential competitors with the joint venture in that relevant market. This would include those firms that have the capability and incentive to undertake R&D closely substitutable for the R&D proposed to be undertaken by the joint venture, taking into account such firms' existing technologies and technologies under development, R&D facilities, and other relevant assets and business circumstances. Firms possessing such capabilities and incentives would be included in the R&D market even if they are not competitors in relevant markets for related goods, such as the plastics currently produced by the joint venturers, although competitors in existing goods markets may often also compete in related innovation markets. Having defined a relevant innovation market, the Agency would assess whether the joint venture is likely to have anticompetitive effects in that market. A starting point in this analysis is the

préparatoires) is silent as to the reason(s) for the literal alteration of the market definition between the NCRA and the NCRPA, but probably the academic writings of Jorde and Teece, and Shapiro and Grossman, respectively, affected the new version of the NCRPA.[204]

Shapiro and Grossman suggested already in 1986 implementing a guideline for how the rule of reason should be applied by courts under the NCRA.[205] According to them, such a guideline was necessary even though Congress, by enacting the NCRA, had diminished the antitrust risks considerably. Some uncertainties remained, not the least of which

---

degree of concentration in the relevant market and the market shares of the parties to the joint venture. If, in addition to the parties to the joint venture (taken collectively), there are at least four other independently controlled entities that possess comparable capabilities and incentives to undertake R&D of bio-degradable plastics, or other products that would be close substitutes for such new plastics, the joint venture ordinarily would be unlikely to adversely affect competition in the relevant innovation market, (plausible, the right amount is three other independently controlled entities possessing comparable capabilities, see the Collaboration Guidelines, 26). If there are fewer than four other independently controlled entities with similar capabilities and incentives, the Agency would consider whether the joint venture would give the parties to the joint venture an incentive and ability collectively to reduce investment in, or otherwise to retard the pace or scope of, R&D efforts. If the joint venture creates a significant risk of anticompetitive effects in the innovation market, the Agency would proceed to consider efficiency justifications for the venture, such as the potential for combining complementary R&D assets in such a way as to make successful innovation more likely, or to bring it about sooner, or to achieve cost reductions in R&D. The Agency would also assess the likelihood that the joint venture would adversely affect competition in other relevant markets, including markets for products produced by the parties to the joint venture. The risk of such adverse competitive effects would be increased to the extent that, e.g., the joint venture facilitates the exchange among the parties of competitively sensitive information relating to goods markets in which the parties currently compete or facilitates the coordination of competitive activities in such markets. The Agency would examine whether the joint venture imposes collateral restraints that might significantly restrict competition among the joint venturers in goods markets, and would examine whether such collateral restraints were reasonably necessary to achieve any efficiencies that are likely to be attained by the venture.'

[204] Cf., e.g., Thomas Jorde & David Teece, 'Innovation, Cooperation and Antitrust', (1989) 4 *High Tech Law Journal*, 1, and Gene Grossman & Carl Shapiro, 'Research Joint Ventures: An Antitrust Analysis', (1986) 2 *J. L. Econ. & Org.*, 315. *Compare* H.R. REP. 103-94, *reprinted* 1993 U.S.C.C.A.N. 176, 178 et seq.

[205] Cf. Gene Grossman & Carl Shapiro, 'Research Joint Ventures: An Antitrust Analysis', (1986) 2 *J. L. Econ. & Org.*, 315.

was the rule of reason approach. They proposed a two-part test where the initial market share should be identified not only in the relevant research market but also on the relevant product market. The size of the barriers to entry should be determined. It should only be possible to establish a violation under the NCRA if the participants held market power in both the relevant research market and the relevant product market.[206]

In hindsight, given the size of innovation markets, if a plaintiff is able to prove market power on an innovation market, the participants together with the joint venture would likely also hold market power on relevant downstream markets. However, a defendant showing that it does not hold market power on any downstream market should be able to rebut the *prima facie* case.

Shapiro and Grossman argued that, in the research market, activities such as basic research, applied research or product development are performed.[207] They stated that these stages of R&D take place in sequence for each new commodity, and that they are all input factors in the ultimate production process for a final product or service. The potential of spillover is greatest for basic research, decreases as it moves down the spectrum to more applied discoveries, and is smallest for the development of specific products or prototypes. Therefore, according to Shapiro and Grossman, the potential for efficiency gains are greatest when a research joint venture concentrates its activities on basic research projects.[208] In almost all cases, the firms participating in the research market are similar to those active in producing and marketing final goods. In measuring R&D competition, both in-house research and stand-alone R&D firms should be included. The asset-oriented R&D market concept of the NCRA became the innovation market concept described in the NCRPA and IP Guidelines.[209] Likewise, since knowledge can be dispersed easily and without cost, Shapiro and Grossman believe that the geographic market should be global, and potential

---

[206]   Ibid., 317.

[207]   Shapiro and Grossman state some of the benefits of joint research and acknowledge that in practice so-called wasteful duplication of research presumably avoided by joint research is very difficult to establish and measure, especially since two projects having the same objective and running parallel can achieve very different results, cf. Gene Grossman & Carl Shapiro, 'Research Joint Ventures: An Antitrust Analysis', (1986) 2 *J. L. Econ. & Org.*, 315, 319 with references.

[208]   Ibid.

[209]   Jorde and Teece had also seen that a market share safe harbour of 20–25 per cent was enacted. Cf. Thomas Jorde & David Teece, 'Innovation, Cooperation and Antitrust', (1989) 4 *High Tech Law Journal*, 1, 63.

entrants into the research market should be taken into consideration. Grossman and Shapiro make clear that the requirement of having market power not only on the innovation market but also in the downstream markets was a coveted change of the NCRA.[210]

Jorde and Teece went further and proposed that the NCRA should be amended so that, *inter alia*, first, the rule of reason became more structured and, second, that a market share safe harbour should be enacted.[211] However, when implementing the innovation market concept proposed by Jorde and Teece,[212] it is likely that even the market power prominent product market monopolist can diminish in light of the connected innovation market. Only a firm capable of monopolising a whole industry for the whole engineering cycle can monopolise an R&D market if the definition of Jorde and Teece should be utilised.[213]

Jorde and Teece argued that the rule of reason under the NCRA was too muddled.[214] Accordingly, monopoly power under the Act should only be found where a firm was able to sustain sales for a whole engineering cycle without competitors introducing a new product that significantly

---

[210]   Gene Grossman & Carl Shapiro, 'Research Joint Ventures: An Antitrust Analysis', (1986) 2 *J. L. Econ. & Org.*, 315, 330 et seq.

[211]   Thomas Jorde & David Teece, 'Innovation, Cooperation and Antitrust', (1989) 4 *High Tech Law Journal*, 1, 61 et seq., especially 63 et seq. Jorde and Teece also suggested (i) that the market definition should be tailored to the context of innovation and that the product market should only become relevant when commercialisation was included within the scope of the collaboration. They furthermore (ii) suggested that the limitation of liability and possibility of getting awarded attorneys' fees under the NCRPA should be made available for collaborators without need of registering the collaboration with the Justice Department.

[212]   Thomas Jorde & David Teece, 'Innovation, Cooperation and Antitrust', (1989) 4 *High Tech Law Journal*, 1, 66. The authors did not discuss potential competition, but included it in the market definition. Richard Gilbert & Steven Sunshine, 'Incorporating Dynamic Efficiency Concerns in Merger Analysis: the Use of Innovation Markets', (1995) 63 *Antitrust Law Journal*, 569, 595.

[213]   Thomas Jorde & David Teece, 'Innovation, Cooperation and Antitrust', (1989) 4 *High Tech Law Journal*, 1, 66.

[214]   Cf., e.g., Thomas Jorde & David Teece, 'Innovation and Cooperation: Implications for Competition and Antitrust', (1990) 4 *Journal of Economic Perspectives*, 75, 85 et seq.; Thomas Jorde & David Teece, 'Rule of Reason Analysis of Horizontal Arrangements: Agreements Designed to Advance Innovation and Commercialize Technology', (1993) Winter *Antitrust Law Journal*, 579, 600 et seq. Thomas Jorde & David Teece, 'Acceptable Cooperation among Competitors in the Face of Growing International Competition', (1989) *Antitrust Law Journal*, 529, 543 et seq.

affected price or output.[215] Geographically the market should be global, since knowledge is disbursed without incidental travelling costs.[216]

The definition of research is wide under the Act. It includes the spectrum from basic research to applied research of the end product. Before the NCRPA, the Justice Department viewed joint basic research more positively than joint research closer to the end product. This was caused by the fact that basic research could still create a diversity of end products. Joint research into applied research was more suspect. It implied that the parties were competitors in the product market, that is, product diversity could diminish and they could end up having similar cost structures which could lead to similar end prices.

The NCRPA is, however, equally available for all kinds of joint research and so are the safe harbours in the IP Guidelines and the Justice Department's and FTC's Antitrust Guidelines for Collaborations Among Competitors from 2000 (hereinafter Collaboration Guidelines).[217] Even though it is possible under the rule of reason to argue that applied

---

[215]   Thomas Jorde & David Teece, 'Innovation, Cooperation and Antitrust', (1989) 4 *High Tech Law Journal*, 1, 66.

[216]   Thomas Jorde & David Teece, 'Rule of Reason Analysis of Horizontal Arrangements: Agreements Designed to Advance Innovation and Commercialize Technology', (1993) Winter *Antitrust Law Journal*, 579, 609 et seq. From this platform Jorde and Teece introduced the notion of the 'hedonic method' for establishing relevant markets, cf. Thomas Jorde & David Teece, 'Rule of Reason Analysis of Horizontal Arrangements: Agreements Designed to Advance Innovation and Commercialize Technology', (1993) Winter *Antitrust Law Journal*, 579, 612 et seq. Jorde and Teece do not state whether research should be regarded as an attribute, but add that a market to establish a relevant market in antitrust matters in markets where price is not essential, the agencies should calculate using 'attributes' with a coefficient of 25 per cent. Hence, if supply decreases when research spending is decreased by a coefficient of 25 per cent, the product(s) accruing increase in demand and the scrutinised product are in the same market concerning *research*. Likewise, when 'decreasing' the design by 25 per cent the product acquiring the increase in demand and the scrutinised product are perhaps in competition in the development market (or design market). While Jorde and Teece do not actually propose that the hedonic method would imply that a product or service actually competes on several different markets, i.e., a market for innovation, one for design, price, etc., which could be one interpretation of how to make use of the rule of reason text in the NCRPA, their hedonic method taken to its logical end does seem to lean towards such a conclusion. Thus, a product may be dominant in the research attribute (market), but less dominant in the development attribute (market) or in the price attribute (product market).

[217]   DOJ/FTC, 'Antitrust Guidelines for Collaborations Among Competitors', issued 2000 (earlier defined as Collaboration Guidelines).

research is more likely to be anticompetitive than basic research, the overall exemption – and safe harbour – is equally available to all kinds of research.[218] The breadth of the definitions of research and innovation market makes it possible for competitors to engage in joint R&D in applied development close to the end product and still not be considered dominant. Their combined market power should be judged in an innovation market including both basic and applied research even tenuously connected to the scrutinised research. Jorde and Teece,[219] by arguing that research is not done in a linear sequence anymore but instead in dynamic fashion with interaction between research, application, manufacturing and even commercialisation, gave the principal reasons for why the NCRPA should not differentiate between basic science and applied research. According to Jorde and Teece, the NCRA was not sufficiently permissive.[220] The NCRA implicitly accepted the serial model and not the dynamic or simultaneous model of innovation, paying no attention to the special characteristics of the innovation process in a quickly changing industry. Accordingly, Jorde and Teece argued that the basic notion should instead be that collaboration in industries with rapid technology change is unlikely to injure competition at all.[221]

It should be noted that neither the IP Guidelines and the Justice Department's and FTC's report 'Antitrust Enforcement and Intellectual Property Rights: Promoting Innovation and Competition' (hereinafter IP

---

[218] Recent commentators argue that the rule of reason under the NCRPA is the same rule of reason as for the rest of US antitrust law. Given such statements it should be possible to argue that applied research is more dangerous than basic research. Cf. John Scott, 'The National Cooperative Research and Production Act', in ABA (ed.), *Issues in Competition Law and Policy* (ABA Section of Antitrust Law 2008), 1300 et seq.

[219] Cf., e.g., Thomas Jorde & David Teece, 'Innovation, Cooperation and Antitrust', (1989) 4 *High Tech Law Journal*, 1, 13 et seq.; Thomas Jorde & David Teece, 'Innovation and Cooperation: Implications for Competition and Antitrust', (1990) 4 *Journal of Economic Perspectives*, 75, 86. See also Thomas Jorde & David Teece, 'Innovation, Cooperation and Antitrust', (1989) 4 *High Tech Law Journal*, 1, 4 et seq. See Joseph Brodley, commenting on Jorde and Teece's article and proposition by stating he can find no economic or legal academic consensus supporting the conclusion that high technology markets are immune to anticompetitive risk, see Joseph Brodley, 'Antitrust Law and Innovation Cooperation', (1990) 4 *Journal of Economic Perspectives*, 97, 98.

[220] Ibid.

[221] Ibid.

2 Report),[222] nor the Collaboration Guidelines – as far as the author has discovered – discuss research as such and, hence, does not differentiate between basic research and applied development from an anticompetitive perspective. Whether, as Jorde and Teece argued, all research shall be judged similarly, and, for example, the same market share threshold on the innovation market should apply regardless of the development of the contemplated research, is too early to determine given the lack of case law. Nonetheless, the academic contributions of Jorde and Teece clearly have influenced the perception of what research is potentially anti-competitive.

Interestingly, in contemporary innovation-driven industries, the linear notion of R&D is making a comeback. At least, R&D-only or technology-only firms are proliferating and they are clearly in a vertical relationship with many of their customers and counterparts when entering joint R&D agreements where their customers often outsource specific research to these firms. In fact, several of the private–public partnerships for R&D implicitly are based on the idea that research is conducted before development and design.[223]

(vii)   The safe harbour

The enactment of the NCRA and later the NCRPA also brought about the creation of a safe harbour. Where, according to the legislative history, four comparable R&D efforts are under way or completed, anti-competitive effects are unlikely and the antitrust agencies should abstain from investigating the joint effort.[224] Similarly, the IP Guidelines still

---

[222]   DOJ/FTC, 'Antitrust Enforcement and Intellectual Property Rights: Promoting Innovation and Competition', in (U.S Dep't of Justice & Fed. Trade Comm'n, 2007). (Hereinafter IP 2 Report.)

[223]   Other commentators have criticised the concept of an innovation market based on the fact that 'market power' in an innovation market is only interesting in relation to the ability to use that power on product or service markets, or, at least, on an independent market where purchasers and sellers meet under market conditions. Hence, innovation markets and the market power expressed in them are only an intermediate stop for evaluating market power in product or service markets. See, e.g., Monopolkommission, *Huaptgutachten: Wettbewerbspolitik vor neuen Herausforderungen* (Nomos Baden-Baden, 1990), 343 et seq.

[224]   S. REP. 98-427, *reprinted* 1984 U.S.C.C.A.N. 3105, 3109 et seq. This also implies that compulsory access to a joint effort cannot be enforced by antitrust law when there are at least three or four other R&D poles. Interestingly, by stating that an R&D programme should not be obliged to accept all aspiring participants so that competition might be enhanced, and the absence of comment on right to access the result, Congress indicates a departure from the standpoint

state a safety zone of four or more independently controlled close substitute research efforts when challenging a restraint in an intellectual property licensing arrangement,[225] or in R&D joint agreements.[226]

The safe harbour has expanded. According to the Collaboration Guidelines, the antitrust enforcement agencies should not challenge an R&D collaboration on the basis of its effect on competition in an innovation market in case there are three or more independently controlled close substitute research efforts, in addition to the effort under scrutiny.[227] In determining close substitutes, the agencies will consider the nature, scope and magnitude of the research efforts: their access to financial support, to intellectual property or to other specialised assets.

Between the publication of the IP Guidelines (1995) and that of the Collaboration Guidelines (2000), the number of independent research poles needed for the scrutinised effort to be encompassed in the 'safe harbour' decreased from four to three. Interestingly, this decrease is not consistent with the Congressional intent when enacting the NCRA, which stated four different controlled research efforts apart from the joint venture under scrutiny.[228] Moreover, it creates an awkward difference between the legal history, which presumably influences private plaintiffs, and the guidelines of the antitrust enforcement agencies, which govern the antitrust enforcement agencies rather than the courts.

The difference between the IP Guidelines and the Collaboration Guidelines is confusing. Arguably it can be interpreted to mean that three research efforts on the innovation market will constitute the threshold for when R&D collaboration may concentrate the relevant innovation market. However, for joint licensing of the result of the joint R&D to be within the safe zone, there should be four other competing alternative technologies. If this was an intended difference, it should have been written more clearly.

---

stated in the Guide. The Guide acknowledged a right to access – probably derived from the *per se* rule regarding group boycotts – i.e., a right to a free ride and duplicate. Joint R&D ventures, especially research efforts creating externalities, were obliged, e.g., to publish their findings.

[225]   See the IP Guidelines, 22 et seq. See also IP Guidelines, 12 et seq., Example 4.

[226]   IP Guidelines para 3.2.3, 13.

[227]   Compare Collaboration Guidelines, 26 et seq. and IP Guidelines, 13, 23, which state four or more independent research efforts in addition to the scrutinised effort.

[228]   See IP Guidelines, 23, fn. 31, which specifically refer to the Congressional intent when enacting the NCRA. Compare S. REP. 98-427, *reprinted* 1984 U.S.C.C.A.N. 3105, 3109 et seq.

Moreover, economic theory between 1995 and 2000 does not appear to have developed in a way that would suggest that the threshold should be three R&D efforts instead of four.

In addition, the general safe zone of a 20 per cent market share stipulated in the Collaboration Guidelines should be kept in mind.[229] Presumably, joint R&D between firms that do not jointly or unilaterally hold a 20 per cent market share of any relevant downstream market are in the safe harbour even though the joint venture would hold a larger market share on the innovation market.

(viii)   Too large and spacious?

Is the safe harbour too large and spacious? It is of some interest to theorise about these numbers. Analysing the NCRPA in the light of the Guidelines implies that, for example, GM, Ford and Chrysler can engage in a joint R&D venture to innovate a new bio-fuelled hybrid engine as long as there are three other similar efforts in the world. For example, if there are Japanese, European and perhaps university-based efforts, the hypothetical big three joint R&D venture can fit within the safe harbour. Thus, in the light of the threshold stated in the Guidelines, it would be a joint R&D agreement that raises no anticompetitive risks and presumably is benign or even pro-competitive.

The antitrust enforcement agencies are restricted by the three technology safe harbours and the general safe zone of 20 per cent on the downstream markets. The Justice Department and the FTC have therefore voluntarily limited themselves. Such a self-imposed restriction creates certainty for the joint ventures and has clear benefits for the participants.

According to Scott, several economists have theorised about whether innovation is promoted or restricted by collaborative research, and when collaborators are dominant enough to find that the diminishing competitive pressure would reduce their incentive to innovate.[230] As stated above,

---

[229]   Collaboration Guidelines, 26.

[230]   Cf., e.g., Josh Lerner & Robert Merges, 'The Control of Technology Alliances: An Empirical Analysis of the Biotechnology Industry', (1998) 46 *Journal of Industrial Economics*, 125; Michael Katz, 'An Analysis of Cooperative Research and Development', (1986) 17 *Rand Journal of Economics*, 527; Thomas Jorde & David Teece, 'Innovation and Cooperation: Implications for Competition and Antitrust', (1990) 4 *Journal of Economic Perspectives*, 75; Thomas Jorde & David Teece, 'Rule of Reason Analysis of Horizontal Arrangements: Agreements Designed to Advance Innovation and Commercialize Technology', (1993) Winter *Antitrust Law Journal*, 579; Thomas Jorde & David Teece, 'Acceptable Cooperation among Competitors in the Face of Growing

some argue that as long as the technical development is fast, joint R&D promotes social welfare irrespective of market power,[231] but others are more careful.[232] Industrial organisation models often examine the interaction between product market competition and joint R&D. These models examine cost-reducing R&D and associated spillover and the result varies depending on the amount of spillover. The amount of spillover indicates the amount of knowledge transferred between the two collaborators or to the general public that does not necessarily concern the joint R&D venture but is beneficial for overall development. Part of this research indicates that collaborations among product market competitors are beneficial when the degree of product market competition is low, when there is R&D spillover in the absence of cooperation, when a high degree of sharing is technologically feasible, and when the agreement concerns basic research rather than development activities.[233]

Several scholars, however, have, as stated in the introduction, recently criticised these results and the modelling used by the theorists in this area. They claim that the industrial organisation literature reaches different conclusions depending on the specific modelling assumptions.[234] According to this criticism the specialisation within this area of economic research has become so great that it is difficult to see its usefulness. One economist analysing specifically the economic research into joint R&D

International Competition', (1989) *Antitrust Law Journal*, 529; and generally Gene Grossman & Carl Shapiro, 'Research Joint Ventures: An Antitrust Analysis', (1986) 2 *J. L. Econ. & Org.*, 315.

[231]   See, e.g., Thomas Jorde & David Teece, 'Innovation and Cooperation: Implications for Competition and Antitrust', (1990) 4 *Journal of Economic Perspectives*, 75, 85 et seq.; Thomas Jorde & David Teece, 'Rule of Reason Analysis of Horizontal Arrangements: Agreements Designed to Advance Innovation and Commercialize Technology', (1993) Winter *Antitrust Law Journal*, 579, 600 et seq. Thomas Jorde & David Teece, 'Acceptable Cooperation among Competitors in the Face of Growing International Competition', (1989) *Antitrust Law Journal*, 529, 543 et seq.

[232]   See, e.g., Josh Lerner & Robert Merges, 'The Control of Technology Alliances: An Empirical Analysis of the Biotechnology Industry', (1998) 46 *Journal of Industrial Economics*, 125, 132 et seq.; Michael Katz, 'An Analysis of Cooperative Research and Development', (1986) 17 *Rand Journal of Economics*, 527, 537 et seq.

[233]   Michael Katz, 'An Analysis of Cooperative Research and Development', (1986) 17 *Rand Journal of Economics*, 527, 527, 542 et seq.

[234]   Kathryn L. Combs & Albert N. Link, 'Innovation Policy in Search of an Economic Foundation: The Case of Research Partnership in the United States', (2003) 15 *Tech. Analysis & Strategic MGMT*, 177, 181.

concluded that, 'theoretical research... is largely self-contained activity, firmly insulated from vagaries of evidence about the subjects it analyses'.[235]

There is, however, according to Scott, substantial empirical research of joint R&D collaboration agreements that has been notified under the NCRPA.[236] These studies suggest that there has been a dramatic increase in the number of research partnerships during the last two decades. Donald Siegel presumes that the relaxation of antitrust enforcement caused this increase.[237] Also, in the empirical research there are many assumptions, for example, the joint venture agreements are not available. The research conducted identifies the industries in which the joint research is conducted, the possible market power of the participants and from these facts academic research tries to conclude whether the joint research is pro-innovation or not. Interestingly, many observers therefore conclude that from these empirical studies it is difficult to find a clear answer as to whether joint R&D is welfare-enhancing. The main issue is whether the welfare-enhancing spillover effects are substantial, something which is difficult to quantify and measure.[238]

For example, in a research project in the mid-1980s, Scott[239] examined all NCRA filings over an 18-month period (61 R&D projects) and found that R&D collaborations were not occurring in industries where research probability was likely to be low. Instead, collaborations were more common in industries where concentration was high, productivity growth

---

[235]   Stephen Martin, 'The Evaluation of Strategic Research Partnerships', (2003) 15 *Tech. Analysis & Strategic MGMT*, 159, 159.

[236]   For a review of the empirical research, see generally Donald Siegel, 'Data Requirements for Assessing the Private and Social Returns of Strategic Research Partnerships: Analysis and Recommendations', (2003) 15 *Tech. Analysis & Strategic MGMT*, 207.

[237]   Ibid.

[238]   Cf. Suzanne E. Majewski, *How Do Consortia Organize Collaborative R&D? Evidence from the National Cooperative Research Act* (SSRN 2004), 3 et seq., 8 et seq. and 12 et seq.; and generally Suzanne E. Majewski & Dean V. Williamson, *Endogenous Spillovers, Strategic Blocking, and the Design of Contracts in Collaborative R&D: Evidence from NCRA filings of R&D Joint Ventures* (SSRN 2002).

[239]   John T. Scott, 'Diversification versus Cooperation in R&D Investment', (1988) 9 *Managerial Decision Economics*, 173, 183 et seq. Cf. also John Scott, 'The National Cooperative Research and Production Act', in ABA (ed.), *Issues in Competition Law and Policy* (ABA Section of Antitrust Law 2008), 1300 et seq.

strong and firms were already engaged in diversified R&D in order to be able to exploit R&D spillover across the industry.[240]

In his study, Scott did not find that research, after the enactment of the NCRA, increased in those industries where it would have been beneficial.[241] R&D did not increase in industries where there was little or no innovation before the enactment, that is, where there was a market failure causing no or little innovation to happen.[242] In other words, neither the NCRA, nor presumably the NCRPA, has had a pro-innovative effect on these industries. On the contrary, it may, according to Scott, have caused substantial losses in competition stimulus and only minimal gains because the industries in which the research collaborations occurred were those industries in which collaborations were not needed and where collaboration, theoretically, did more harm than good.[243]

Scott also provided an economic theory on why joint R&D would likely lead to less innovation than would be stimulated by competition. According to Scott, diversification of R&D is primarily a tool to escape the normal return implicit in the final equilibrium of pure price competition. Therefore, it is a natural incentive for firms to innovate. The problem for firms is that they do not know how much their competitors spend on research. They therefore spend more than would be efficient from their firm's perspective compared with a situation where they knew about the spending of their competitors.[244] However, since all firms think in a similar way, they all 'over-invest' or 'overbid' from their own perspective in innovation.[245] Although firms generally earn less in return, over-investment creates more innovation for the society as a whole. More spillover of new knowledge will presumably be created and disbursed in society.

---

[240] In light of these revelations, Joseph Brodley concluded that the NCRA might already have caused substantial losses in competitive stimulus. Joseph Brodley, 'Antitrust Law and Innovation Cooperation', (1990) 4 *Journal of Economic Perspectives*, 97, 101.

[241] John T. Scott, 'Diversification versus Cooperation in R&D Investment', (1988) 9 *Managerial Decision Economics*, 173, 183 et seq.

[242] See John Hagedoorn, Albert N. Link & Nicholas S. Vonortas, 'Research Partnership', (2000) 29 *Res. Pol'Y* 567, 582 et seq.

[243] Ibid.

[244] Cf. Susanne Scotchmer, *Innovation and Incentives* (The MIT Press 2004), 113, verifying this in theory.

[245] Cf. also William Baldwin & John Scott, *Market Structure and Technological Change* (Psychology Press 1987), where they develop the notion of overbidding to the benefit of society, 11, 19 et seq.

This was the basic logic behind the early antitrust treatment of joint R&D: increased competition creates more innovation and even though the parties could not unilaterally achieve the goal of the proposed joint R&D, a court should take into consideration such hypothetical unilateral research into other areas since such R&D would create innovations too. In the end the Court needed to weigh what situation could create the most innovation.[246]

One common justification for promoting cooperation in R&D is that it may decrease wasteful duplication. Scott in 1988, however, suggested that cooperation may decrease R&D spending even more than the costs saved by eliminating duplication.[247] Since firms in collaboration know the amount of the investment of their competitors, they, according to Scott's earlier research, spend less on innovation for natural profit-seeking motives. Thus, no 'overbidding' on future products occurs. According to Scott's model, it is likely that the decrease in investment in R&D will be larger than the cost saved by preventing duplicate research. Moreover, duplication of research may only happen in some industries. More often two R&D groups given the same goal and resources will create different results.

In a competitive environment, firms overbid for innovation rewards (the contemplated result) as they try to pre-empt one another from reaching the profitable innovation, and as they look only to their own profitable opportunities without regard to the erosion of the total expected profits in the particular area of R&D. It is possible that the additional incentive to do R&D because of overbidding will offset the tendency towards poorer appropriability conditions, and result in a competitive R&D environment closer to socially optimal levels of innovative investment. Because cooperation eliminates more investment in overbidding than is saved by the increase of appropriability and the decrease of truly duplicative R&D, it is still possible for cooperative solutions to be socially inferior to the competitive solution.[248]

Scott's basic theoretical point in 1988 was that independent diversified firms may create equilibrium with higher social net present value than cooperation would create, because the increase in appropriability result-ing from cooperation is incomplete. Society would gain from the additional imperfectly correlated research efforts of competing firms,

---

[246] See discussion *supra* section 3.2.2(i).
[247] Ibid.
[248] Ibid.

even though, from the standpoint of the cooperating firms, the marginal value of such efforts falls short of their marginal cost.[249]

Scott concluded that the NCRA led to less R&D spending, and less diversification of products, which implied less competition and in the end less wealth. This in turn lowered the investment in R&D from a stage of social optimum to less than optimum. His research did not attract much interest at the time and lately he seems to have changed his mind a bit. In light of the above, Scott concludes that we do not know whether the NCRPA promotes welfare and innovation or not.[250]

In later research, Scott seems to have reached somewhat contradictory conclusions in comparison with the research discussed above. According to Scott's own research, regarding environmental issues/problems facing an industry or the society, industry-wide research could yield more dividends to society than R&D done in competition or rivalry.[251] Secondly, the effect of learning from other firms should also be regarded as highly beneficial. Research partnerships are sources of absorptive capacity. Together the research partners are better able to learn from each other and develop successful innovations. Moreover, as discussed below, collaborations between private and public researches may be highly beneficial since including universities may warrant spillover effects, that is, that the result of the collaborations will 'trickle down' and out in society through the publications of publicly employed scientists. Thus, Scott – even though still agreeing with his old critique from 1988 – and the more theoretical researchers seem to, at least, agree that joint industry-wide research may be beneficial when certain specific requirements are fulfilled. As stated in the introduction to this book, they are beneficial when (i) the degree of product market competition and R&D

---

[249] Ibid.

[250] John Scott, 'The National Cooperative Research and Production Act', in ABA (ed.), *Issues in Competition Law and Policy* (ABA Section of Antitrust Law 2008), 1317 et seq.

[251] It must be mentioned that research of a somewhat older date indicates that joint ventures in manufacturing, at least during the analysed period of 1960–71, were set up between firms with only slight horizontal and vertical relationships, were motivated by developing anticompetitive linkages. The authors conclude: 'while joint venture activity is also predicted by technological considerations, the substantial predictive power of market structure for horizontal joint ventures, and resource interdependence for joint ventures, generally, indicate that technological considerations do not, by themselves, satisfactorily account for observed joint venture activity. It appears that substantial additional antitrust enforcement activity is warranted.' See Pfeffer & Nowak, 'Patterns of Joint Venture Activity: Implications for Antitrust Policy', (1976) 21 *Antitrust Bull.*, 315, 339.

rivalry are low, when (ii) there is large R&D spillover in the absence of cooperation, when (iii) a high degree of sharing is technologically feasible, and when (iv) the agreement concerns basic research rather than development activities.[252] The debate between theorists and empirical researchers remains a lively one and will probably continue for several more years.[253]

Even though, from a legal perspective, at first glance, the idea that competition spurs innovation seems somewhat obvious, it can only be realised with an intelligent and well-balanced property law system. Without a property law system, R&D with large spillover effects would not be conducted. Notwithstanding this, Scherer (and Scott) purports that also with patent law protection, there exists an inverted U, and that if competitive erosion of post-innovation profits is severe enough firms will avoid R&D.[254] From a lawyer's perspective, this may happen if the breadth of the patent protection is not sufficient and that imitation may be marketed. Or, more theoretically, and perhaps seldom seen, where substitute technologies may co-develop on a single market and they still cause 'tipping effects'. So, when new innovation enters the market, it gains almost total market power but very quickly becomes obsolete because of a substitute innovation launched by a competitor that likewise tips the whole market to its advantage. I guess if the time between the new innovations is too short for the innovators to reap benefits from their innovations, there may be too much competition so as to erode the incentive to compete on that market, and firms may exit. However, before an inventor would exit, the natural reaction for these firms would be to try to contractually bind customers beyond the introduction of new competing innovations (for example, the game console market and the exclusive agreements between console builders and game developers).

---

[252]   Michael Katz, 'An Analysis of Cooperative Research and Development', (1986) 17 *Rand Journal of Economics*, 527, 527, 542 et seq.

[253]   Shapiro states (in a resigned manner) that this issue will not be resolved during his lifetime. Carl Shapiro, 'Competition and Innovation: Did Arrow Hit the Bull's Eye?', in Josh Lerner and Scott Stern (eds), *The Rate & Direction of Economic Activity Revisited* (University of Chicago Press 2012), 380.

[254]   Frederic M. Scherer, 'Firm Size, Market Structure, Opportunity, and the Output of Patented Inventions', (1965) 55 *AM. ECON. REV.* 1097; Frederic M. Scherer, 'Market Structure and the Employment of Scientists and Engineers', (1967) 57 *AM. ECON. REV.* 524; Frederic M. Scherer, 'Research and Development Resource Allocation under Rivalry', (1967) 81 *The Quarterly Journal of Economics,* 359. See John Scott, 'The National Cooperative Research and Production Act', in ABA (ed.), *Issues in Competition Law and Policy* (ABA Section of Antitrust Law 2008), 1306. Making reference to Scherer's articles.

In light of the above, the conclusion by Shapiro, as discussed in the introduction of this book, seems accurate. From a competition *policy* perspective the outset should be that competition in R&D spurs innovation and restricting competition/rivalry in innovation lessens the production of innovation (leaving intellectual property law to the side for a moment). Collaboration that restricts rivalry in R&D may still be benign from a competition law perspective if there is a 'market' failure on the innovation 'market': synergy effects are great (for example, that the parties may create new innovations that they may not achieve independently) and/or increase appropriability (for example, economy of scale on R&D) and outweigh the negative effects of decreasing competition in creating innovations.[255] The idea or the existence of an inverted U should not interfere with that conclusion. That firms stop conducting R&D due to competitive pressure and thus exit the market is part of the competitive process, or the failure of the intellectual property law system.

Notwithstanding the above, R&D collaboration to be anticompetitive under a case-by-case analysis needs to lessen the competitive pressure to innovate, generally, that is, the collaboration needs to create or enhance a monopoly or dominant position that would erode the incentive to innovate and the likelihood of innovation, or directly cause the erosion of innovation and innovative incentives.

(ix) How to use the rule of reason under the NCRPA

(a) Competitors or rivals   The interaction between the innovation market and the rule of reason to establish a *prima facie* antitrust case is the key to the exemption under the NCRPA. The restriction of the *per se* rule under the NCRPA implies, as stated above, that the plaintiff, in order to establish a *prima facie* case, needs to show either direct anticompetitive harm or (the risk of) anticompetitive effect with evidence of substantial market power.[256] Direct antitrust harm of a contemplated collaborative research will be difficult to show, so a plaintiff, to be successful in its antitrust *prima facie* case, needs to establish proof that the joint R&D will create market power in a research, development or other relevant

---

[255]   Carl Shapiro, 'Competition and Innovation: Did Arrow Hit the Bull's Eye?', in Josh Lerner and Scott Stern (eds), *The Rate & Direction of Economic Activity Revisited* (University of Chicago Press, 2012), 368.

[256]   For the rule of reason approach under the NCRPA, see Thomas Jorde & David Teece, 'Innovation, Cooperation and Antitrust', (1989) 4 *High Tech Law Journal*, 1, 62 et seq. with references.

market to a degree that anticompetitive effects are likely to occur.[257] The plaintiff needs to show, presumably, that the parties to the collaboration are competitors and that the collaboration creates or increases monopoly power.

Interestingly, the *Madey* and *Bolar* cases concerning the unlicensed experimental use exemption could be weighed in when identifying whether firms were competitors or not. If a patent held by one firm would cover the R&D object of the other firm, and that firm may not benefit from the now restricted unlicensed experimental use defence, then these firms would presumably not be competitors. The patent *de lege lata* blocks these firms from being competitors, or rivals, in this specific research/experiment under US antitrust law.[258]

Moreover, a plaintiff needs to prove that there are less than three (or four) other similar R&D poles or clusters able to conduct similar research in the world to get the defendant out of the safe harbour. However, possibly the plaintiff needs to show even more to establish market power under the rule of reason.[259]

(b)   Market power under the rule of reason   The idea of innovation markets is commendable. Certainly, such 'markets' exist in certain circumstances today perhaps more than in the 1980s. Specific firms focusing on providing R&D services are now a reality in many industries. These

---

[257]   What the rule of reason actually encompasses or includes is highly disputable and fluctuates depending on the economic theory currently in use by the antitrust courts and authorities. Nonetheless, put simply, under the rule of reason, a plaintiff needs to show, to have a *prima facie* case, that the alleged anticompetitive conduct either caused direct antitrust harm or that the collaboration had market power in combination with a (likely) anticompetitive antitrust effect, e.g., exclusion of competitors. See the foregoing fn. Cf. Mark Patterson, 'The Role of Power in the Rule of Reason', (2000) 68 *Antitrust Law Journal*, 1.

[258]   *In re* Summit Tech. Inc., 127 F.T.C. 208 (1998). In re VIXS Inc., 127 F.T.C. 136 (1999).

[259]   In addition, a successful plaintiff should show that it is likely that the collaborators can decrease R&D investments without losing sales or market share or at least point to other likely anticompetitive conducts or effects. If the plaintiff is able to meet this burden of proof, the defendant can rebut the *prima facie* case by showing, e.g., that there are more research poles that can and are likely to conduct competitive research, or that the contemplated innovation would create efficiencies to a level that the anticompetitive effects should be tolerated. In the end, the court should weigh the pro-competitive and anticompetitive effects of the joint R&D. Regarding rebuttals available for an R&D joint venture defending itself under the rule of reason, cf. Thomas Jorde & David Teece, 'Innovation, Cooperation and Antitrust', (1989) 4 *High Tech Law Journal*, 1, 66 et seq.

R&D-specific firms have often sprung up around universities and are specifically focused on conducting research on the behalf of clients that engage them for their services and/or to pursue their own research interest with the aim to obtain inventions and patents to market to firms. Multinationals or vertically integrated firms may outsource R&D to these firms or enter into joint R&D ventures with these firms. Likewise, public–private partnerships in joint R&D are also common. These agreements or conduct are taking place on 'innovation markets' or R&D service markets. Here trade is taking place. Firms purchase R&D services.

Moreover, even outside the area of firms purchasing research services, innovation market is easy to grasp, at least conceptually. If there is rivalry or competition between firms to develop new and improved products and processes (and the firms themselves certainly perceive that there is competition to develop new inventions and innovations), one would imagine that there is also a market where this competition is played out. Nonetheless, innovation markets clearly do not exist in the same manner as product markets since there is no trade regarding inventions or innovations. If such trade should take place, there would be a market.

However, proponents of the concept of innovation market address the problem from the wrong point of view. Arguably, a plaintiff or a court should first establish the relevant end markets, that is, the market where the result is eventually marketed. When two firms 'join' their R&D departments, either through a merger or a joint venture, the point of departure, in establishing whether they and the joint venture hold market power, should not be trying to establish what research will be performed and what research facilities potentially could perform the same research. Instead, the analysis should begin by identifying whether there are potential investors or purchasers of the service rendered by the analysed R&D collaboration. Are there any other firms willing to buy the contemplated innovations? Thus, will the merger or joint venture create a monopsony or 'oligopsony' in the market for purchasing the identified research service?[260] Are there other firms, for example competitors to the parents, who are interested in the research that will be performed in the joint effort as an input to their business or are the scrutinised firms

---

[260] Possibly SSOs should be judged under a similar test. Regarding monopsonies and oligopsonies, see generally Roger Blair & Jeffrey Harrison, *Monopsony Antitrust Law and Economics* (Princeton University Press, 1993), 36 et seq. and 158 et seq. See also Richard Gilbert & Steven Sunshine, 'The Use of Innovation Markets: A Reply to Hay, Rapp, and Hoerner', (1995–1996) 64 *Antitrust Law Journal*, 79.

the only plausible investors in that R&D? Under the notion of 'bidders' market', the issue would be whether the firms contemplating the joint research will be the only *de facto* 'bidders' in the market.[261] To establish market power, the court needs to consider whether there are any other potential purchasers of the contemplated innovation, other than the parents of the joint R&D effort. These purchasers can be located globally. If there are no other purchasers, the joint R&D should be considered as holding market power on the innovation market, since their incentive would be to 'bid' less in that market because of their combined position as the only interested purchaser of the said R&D service.

The second step, after establishing that there are other purchasers, or not, is to establish whether these other potential purchasers can perform the contemplated research independently, jointly or by outsourcing the R&D to a third party. For example, R&D-focused firms can possibly perform the relevant R&D but these firms might not have the proper means to produce or distribute the result. It is at this stage the test purported in the IP Guidelines should be utilised, that is, a control of whether there are entities that possess comparable capabilities and incentives to undertake the research in question. Indeed, now the three or four technology safe harbours should be applicable. Consequently, the first question should be whether there are any competitors to the purchasers of the result of the analysed joint R&D venture. The second question is whether there are other facilities able to perform the competing R&D and according to that analysis the specific existence and effect of background patents should be taken into consideration.

The above analysis follows the innovation market concept and is admittedly quite theoretic in approach. However, to make it simpler and perhaps more relevant, the analysis of market power on the innovation market needs to take any existing standardisation agreement into consideration.

Standardisation agreements, if decided by the relevant SDO, may define the boundaries for the relevant innovation market and indicate the relevant technologies and the essential background intellectual property rights. In fact, successful standards often attract much R&D investments so as to create standard essential patents. Shapiro and Grossman discussed how to establish market power in the research market and concluded that it was dependent mostly on the availability of patents

---

[261]   For definition and analysis of bidders' markets see generally Szilágyi Pál, 'Bidding Markets and Competition Law in the European Union and the United Kingdom Part I', (2008) 1 *E.C.L.R*, 1.

between the parties.[262] If they hold essential patents on the contemplated technology market created by a consortia that aims both to establish a standard and joint R&D, they should *prima facie* be regarded as having market power. Patentees holding an essential patent in reference to a standard may even be considered *ipso facto* dominant under EU competition law.[263]

Holders of essential patents to the identified standard could, logically, be regarded as having market power on the relevant technical market and innovation market. Joint R&D between such patentees should be considered a combination of market power on such markets. The result of such joint R&D would be standard essential patents (SEPs) that would imply power to either exclude or increase market barriers for other firms to the relevant markets identified by the standard. Only if the contemplated R&D would create a new market (new standard) should these firms be considered not holding market power.[264]

Thus, membership in the relevant standard-setting organisation (SSO) and background patents should be taken into consideration. The collaborating patentees may historically have had influence in an SSO. Perhaps they even represent a majority of the voting power of the relevant technical committee or even of the SDO. Such facts should be taken into consideration since it *de facto* reflects the power to exclude competing inventions and innovations, and, hence, power to exclude on the 'innovation' market through the governance influence of the relevant SSO (in fact, not market power, but public power).

Consequently, the monopoly or dominance analysis should be focused on the power of the participants as purchasers of contemplated inventions and innovations, on the relevant end market and on essential patents and technology standards, rather than which entities generally have the facilities to conduct similar research. The general criteria for establishing market power set out in the IP Guidelines should be followed only if there are no background patents, no relevant standardisation agreements and the joint R&D aims to create a new market.[265]

---

[262]   Cf. Gene Grossman & Carl Shapiro, 'Research Joint Ventures: An Antitrust Analysis', (1986) 2 *J. L. Econ. & Org.*, 315.

[263]   See Commission decision Case No COMP/M.6381 Google/Motorola Mobility, 13.02.2012.

[264]   See generally the *BMI* case, *Music v. Columbia Broadcasting System* 441 U.S. 1 (1979). And from an EU perspective the *Nungesser* case, Case 258/78, *L.C. Nungesser KG and Kurt Eisele v. Commission*, [1982] ECR, 2015.

[265]   Thus, if the contemplated innovation concerns a great leap forward, such joint research should not be considered dominant if the parties cannot perform

(c)   Anticompetitive conduct or effect   After establishing market power, the anticompetitive effects of the research as such should be analysed. The issue forwarded in the Guidelines is whether the joint venture would give the parties to the joint venture an incentive and ability collectively to reduce investment in, or otherwise to retard the pace or scope of, R&D efforts.[266] In addition, the likelihood that the joint venture would adversely affect competition in other relevant markets, including markets for products produced by the parties to the joint venture, should be assessed. The test is, in other words, ambiguous; however, the statement by Shapiro and also the research made by Scott, for example, fits. The idea that joint R&D may reduce incentive and create the ability, collectively, to reduce investment in, or otherwise to retard the pace or scope of, R&D efforts, should be considered anticompetitive.

Generally, the main goal would be to try to prevent exclusion of competition, or the exclusion of competitive pressure – that the joint R&D with thereto connected covenants and agreements would erode innovation, innovative incentives or investment in R&D. Of course, joint R&D can cause product or technical market collusion, for example price cartels. Such 'spillover' effects will be dealt with below under 'Ancillary restraints', while here the effort is to try to identify when the core of the R&D collaborations may cause anticompetitive effects.

For example, consortia where the parties are holders of essential patents under a *de facto* or *de jure* standard should perhaps not be allowed to conduct R&D under the relevant technology standard if the collaboration can be predicted to have exclusionary effects by causing an erosion of competitive pressure to conduct research. Holders of essential patents, individually, as Shapiro and Grossman developed,[267] hold market

---

the joint R&D independently, there are at least three other likely R&D poles that can conduct the contemplated research and it is likely that the joint venture may achieve the object of the R&D. The great leap requirement can be indicated with reference to whether the contemplated result would be within a standard or whether the firms claim to start competing with the governing technology. The question should be whether the joint research is 'for' the market, or creates a new market, rather than a step in the competition within the market. If no standard exists, the long leap requisite would be dependent on its relation to previous patents and in reference to the amount of prior art. Regarding the economic discussion about bidders' markets, auction markets and competition for and in markets, see, e.g., generally Paul Klemperer, 'Auction theory – A guide to the literature' (SSRN, 1999).

[266]   IP Guidelines, 13.

[267]   See discussion *supra*.

power on the relevant 'innovation' markets as defined correlation to the technology market stipulated in the standardisation agreement.

In fact, the agreement and implementation of successful standards will likely erode the incentive for firms to conduct competing R&D in the effort to come up with a substitute standard, while increasing the likelihood for some firms to conduct R&D under the successful standard in an effort to obtain standard essential patents (SEPs). There are two different incentives for obtaining SEPs. Firstly, to obtain a somewhat safe royalty stream. Successful standards, that is, standards with market power, are safe investments for holders of SEPs since many firms active on the connected product markets must enter into licence agreements with SEP holders. Secondly, product manufacturers under successful standards would also like to obtain SEPs since they may use these in their negotiations to obtain cross-licence arrangements with other SEP holders.

In fact, successful standards change the incentive for firms. They create the incentive of pursuing an effort to obtain patents covering, not a substitute technology, but the technology already developed and standardised, that is, parts of the standardised technology not yet covered by patents; or, to create imitative technology. Thus, an as efficient competitor to the firms collaborating would probably end efforts to pursue a new standard, while either exiting the market or pursuing the effort to obtain SEPs under the standard selected. To only pursue an effort to produce a product under the standard would most likely not be profitable. In an effort to uphold competition on the technology and product markets and to prevent non-holders of SEPs from exiting these markets, joint R&D between SEP holders to create new SEPs under the relevant standard should be considered anticompetitive. They may erode the incentive for other firms as efficient as they are to pursue competing in that technology. Only if they are able to prove great efficiencies should such joint R&D be allowed.

Apart from the specific standard-driven R&D discussed above, and irrespective of what the IP Guidelines state, the general guiding principle when analysing a dominant R&D collaboration must be whether there had been more and better innovations without it, that is, will a larger demand be created by the joint effort compared with the 'counter-factual'?

Only if the objective of the joint R&D is to create a break-through invention which would create a new demand and a separate relevant market should a more free or disconnected analysis be conducted. The question of what research should be regarded as anticompetitive or not should be addressed by weighing pro-competitive and anticompetitive risks and effects of the collaboration.

Several issues should be analysed: first, the issue of what research the parties could have performed independently should be addressed. Based on the previous patents applied for by the firms and the agreed-upon technology in the standard, it would, perhaps, be possible to evaluate what unilateral research the parties might have conducted and what will be disregarded because of the joint effort. If the issue of whether the parties could have performed the contemplated research independently has not been addressed under the market power analysis, it could be addressed here. In an ideal world, there would not only be a quantitative test, but a 'quality test' should also be conducted. If the joint effort of a consortia will with all likelihood create a successful standard, such effort may of course be exempted because of its efficiencies, but if the contemplated innovation compared with the innovations is disregarded because of the joint effort, the 'quality test' should be whether the contemplated joint result would create a larger market or demand than two individual research results.

Secondly, a court can also evaluate – in light of the prevailing standard – whether the parties will actually license under the standard or whether the research effort is only aimed at excluding other firms.

Thirdly, if the participants in a joint R&D effort have identified the standard technology for the future, joint research efforts outside this technology could have as an objective the foreclosure of other technologies and to promote the agreed standardised technology. Thus, perhaps, the aim is to create strategic patents, that is, patents only to foreclose competing technical avenues. Such competitive strategic conduct could, perhaps, under these settings, be considered an abuse of dominance, monopolisation of the joint R&D venture.

Ultimately the court needs to weigh the anticompetitive features against the pro-competitive features of the joint R&D venture. The guiding principle for the antitrust evaluation was, according to the Guide, that elimination of research competition should not exceed what is reasonably necessary to meet the needs of effective research.[268] The issue changed with the introduction of the NCRPA. Under the NCRPA and the innovation market concept, the guiding principle is instead whether investment in R&D will decrease or otherwise whether the joint R&D will retard the pace or scope of R&D.

The question is whether the above issues should fall within the *prima facie* case and hence be a burden for the plaintiff to prove or whether these issues could be used for the rebuttal by the defendant. Under the

---

[268]   The Guide, 8.

Guide they were the burden for the defendant. However, the introduction of the innovation market, and the obligation of the plaintiff to address not only the R&D capacity of the scrutinised joint venture but also other equivalent R&D centres in the world, implies that these issues might already have been necessary to address by the plaintiff in the *prima facie* case to establish dominance. Indeed, these issues would in any case have needed to be addressed by the plaintiff under the NCRPA and, thus, for the rebuttal, the defendant can focus on showing efficiencies gained by the joint R&D venture.

I am the first to acknowledge that analysing pure R&D ventures under competition law is very difficult and a court will never or very rarely find antitrust violation in reference to such collaborations. However, if there is a successful standard in the technology which the collaborators own, both dominance and abuses may be detected.

(x) Ancillary restraints

The above analysis of dominance and anticompetitive effect was only directed towards the main aim of the joint research, not at individual covenants in the R&D agreements. Presumably, if the joint R&D under the suggested step-by-step analysis would be considered anticompetitive, the ancillary restraints do not need to be scrutinised separately. However, if the joint effort is considered benign or even pro-competitive, the covenants in the R&D agreement should still be scrutinised. Especially if the analysis reveals that the joint R&D does not possess market power, the ancillary restraints doctrine should be utilised. There is a list of covenants in the NCRPA not to be utilised at the risk of the R&D venture having to exit the NCRPA, but presumably there are other covenants which might be considered anticompetitive under the ancillary restraints doctrine or for that matter under the less restrictive doctrine.[269] The list is also not R&D specific. It does not specifically aim at identifying those restraints that, for example, might inhibit R&D-only firms from growing:

(i)   the obligation to exchange commercial information, for example, costs, and prices, of any product sold by the parties if not reasonably necessary to conduct the research;

---

[269]   For definition and discussion, see Gabe Feldman, 'The Misuse of the Less Restrictive Alternative Inquiry in Rule of Reason Analysis', (2009) 58 *American University Law Review*, 561.

(ii)	restrictions regarding the marketing or distribution of products, other than distribution of goods from the venture to the parents or the commercialisation of intellectual property;

(iii)	restrictions limiting the output of other products, services or innovation not produced by the venture and also requiring the sale, licensing or sharing of other innovations not encompassed by the venture (restricting grant-backs);

(iv)	restrictions on the parties not to research unless appropriate to restrict the use of proprietary information contributed by one party to the venture, or to require that party to conduct certain research;

(v)	agreement on allocation of markets with a competitor;

(vi)	the obligation to exchange information regarding the production of products or services other than those produced by the venture;

(vii)	requirements to use existing facilities to produce the product, service or process in question unless it involves the production of a new product or technology; and

(viii)	apart from (ii), (iii) and (vii), restricting or requiring participation of a participant to the joint effort of unilateral or joint activity, if not reasonably required.

According to the Collaboration Guidelines, this list expresses the *per se* violations of US antitrust law.[270] The NCRPA therefore creates a rather peculiar situation where there is a 'black list' of covenants that should not be used; however, all other covenants, which the parties or their counsels can imagine, are encompassed by the Act and thus exposed to the more lenient treatment.

---

[270]	See Collaboration Guidelines, 13, fn. 37. The Collaboration Guidelines stipulate an *e contrario* presumption for activities that fall outside the definition of joint R&D in the NCRPA. If the participants decide jointly to market the goods or service produced, or to limit the independent sale of goods produced outside the exempted collaboration, this should at least presumably be judged according to a *per se* standard according to the Collaboration Guidelines. In light of the legislative history, this seems to be a hasty presumption. According to the legislative history of the NCRPA, situations may exist where such a joint sale may be regarded as benign. Thus, it does not seem that joint sales from joint ventures should be judged as *per se* violation of section 1 of the Sherman Act, rather it should be judged under a rule of reason. This was also the case under the Guide, *ex ante* the enactment of the NCRA, see the Guide, 48 et seq. Otherwise, the Collaboration Guidelines are remarkably silent in regard to the NCRPA. For the legislative history see H.R. REP. 98-1044, *reprinted* 1984 U.S.C.C.A.N. 3131, 3133.

What is missing, *de lege ferenda*, is a list of covenants or agreements which should be judged under the rule of reason, but which does not benefit from the NCRPA. Such a list would not be of much use for a third party litigator, but it could be of great use, for example, to university-based firms specialising in R&D. When such firms enter into R&D agreements such a list could be useful when drafting and negotiating the R&D agreements with larger vertically integrated firms.

The quite limited list stipulated in the NCRPA should therefore – read *e contrario* – be regarded as giving the parties extended possibilities of restricting each other in the use of the result of the research and with reference to the 'background patents'.

Interestingly, even R&D agreements to slow research should be judged under the rule of reason, if the parties are able to circumvent condition (iv) above. This should, however, be under the condition that the agreement on stalling R&D is a legitimate R&D agreement and not a sham agreement.[271] The definition of R&D, *de lege ferenda*, could be improved by qualitative requirements on the research, that is, that the contemplated result should create more or a new demand, or at least be protectable under patent law. This could prevent sham agreements.

The 'ancillary restraint' doctrine and the 'less restrictive' doctrine are applicable also under the NCRPA. Restraints not necessary or too restrictive for the aim of the joint R&D should be considered anticompetitive also under the NCRPA. To my knowledge the connection between these doctrines and the NCRPA has not been discussed in the literature, but presumably the participants in an R&D venture cannot restrict themselves beyond what is necessary and reasonable to achieve the goal of the contemplated research. The lack of guidance in these issues may cause limitations in efficiency exactly where inefficiencies for society should not appear. R&D-only firms and technology-only firms are often restricted under R&D agreements with larger vertically integrated firms with covenants that most likely would have been anticompetitive under a rule of reason analysis outside the NCRPA. In particular, these firms are often prevented from unilateral use of the result in further research and commercialisation.

---

[271]   See Antitrust Guidelines for Collaborations Among Competitors Issued by the Federal Trade Commission and the U.S. Department of Justice April 2000, 9. Whether an agreement is a sham agreement or not should be dependent on whether the contemplated result implies an inventive step, e.g., the result can gain protection under patent law.

(xi)   Access to joint venture

When introducing the NCRA, Congress clarified that joint R&D may not be overly inclusive.[272] It is necessary to ensure adequate R&D competition when applying the rule of reason. Interestingly, by stating that an R&D programme should not be obliged to accept all comers, and by not commenting on right to access either the research or the result, Congress indicated a departure from the general rule stated in the Guide. The Guide acknowledged a right to access, which arguably is derived from the *per se* rule regarding group boycotts, that is, a right to free ride and duplicate the result of the R&D in certain incidents.[273] Joint R&D ventures, especially research efforts creating externalities, were obliged to publish their findings.[274]

The IP Guidelines erase the notion of any right of access to the result of joint research as was envisioned in the Guide. According to the IP Guidelines, the agencies will not require the owner of intellectual property to create competition in its own technology.[275] The issue is whether this rule also applies to joint R&D ventures: are joint ventures required to create competition in their 'own' technology? One can argue that under US antitrust law concerted refusal to deal or boycotts are *per se* violations. Therefore, there can be a right to access of the result *joint* efforts under fair and non-discriminatory terms.[276] However, that is not certain given the current climate after *Trinko*.

(xii)   Joint licensing

It is worth noting that as the NCRPA is now structured, the independent firms that participate in a joint venture can jointly market the researched and produced R&D results. According to Scott, they can either form a new entity that purchases the intellectual property rights from the joint venture and thereafter produces the relevant product or service, or they can jointly license the R&D result on the technology market.[277]

---

[272]   S. REP. 98-427, 1984 U.S.C.C.A.N. 3105, 9 et seq.

[273]   Joseph Brodley, 'Joint Ventures and Antitrust Policy', (1981–1982) 95 *Harvard Law Review*, 1521, 1533 et seq.

[274]   The Guide, 18 et seq.

[275]   The IP Guidelines, 7.

[276]   See, e.g., *Associated Press v. United States*, 326 U.S. 1 (1945).

[277]   John Scott, 'The National Cooperative Research and Production Act', in ABA (ed.), *Issues in Competition Law and Policy* (ABA Section of Antitrust Law 2008), 1300.

Under the NCRPA the joint venture can patent and license the result of the joint R&D.[278] For example, the venture can license the intellectual property and set a royalty rate and other licensing terms that reflect the market power held by the joint venture on the technology market. The NCRPA can, according to Scott be considered a national cooperative research, production, marketing and sales act with regard to the ventures' activities covered by the NCRPA.[279] He states 'that although certainly the participants in the ventures gain, society may lose valuable competitive pressure – even when, if society could make the investment decisions for the monopolist, it would indeed choose a monopolist to do the research because of efficiencies of scale and scope.'[280] Even though joint production may contain anticompetitive risks, joint licensing, under, for example, R&D pools, may be very useful tools to control markets.

Given the possibility of jointly licensing the result of the R&D, the participants can obtain supra-competitive profits from the technology market. For example: the two firms, collaborating in their joint R&D efforts, can use the patents they acquired, and their background intellectual property rights, in order to stipulate a *de jure* or create a *de facto* technology standard. The intellectual property rights thereby made essential in the joint venture can be used to extract royalties from third parties that operate under the standard. In theory, they are even able to extract all supra-competitive profits from the product market into the joint R&D venture if not the notion of FRAND royalty will become applicable.[281] That is a reason why third firms would likely exit the market. The two participants obtain profits from the royalty streams that stem from that third firm. It is obvious that the third firm, the non-member of the joint venture, could lose the profit it used to gain on the product market to its rivals.

In the example above, the two firms participating in the joint effort might lose incentives to innovate further. A new solution invented by either of them individually would very likely be competing with the result of the joint R&D. A competing technology would decrease the

---

[278]   See 15 U.S.C.A § 4301.

[279]   John Scott, 'The National Cooperative Research and Production Act', in ABA (ed.), *Issues in Competition Law and Policy* (ABA Section of Antitrust Law 2008), 1316.

[280]   Ibid.

[281]   Cf. Susanne Scotchmer, *Innovation and Incentives* (The MIT Press 2004), 137 et seq. Cf. also Stephen Maurer & Suzanne Scotchmer, 'Profit Neutrality in Licensing: The Boundary Between Antitrust Law and Patent Law', (2006) 8 *American Law and Economics Review*, 476, 484 et seq.

overall price on the technology market. Or, if the innovation is a follow-on innovation, the one firm not holding patent rights to it could prevent its marketing if the new innovation infringes the essential patents from the joint effort. In the end it is, thus, possible – not taking into consideration external activities – that the participants are better off not to invent before the patents of the joint effort have expired.[282]

That patentees are able to extract supra-competitive profits is a natural consequence of the intellectual property law system and is thus the price society has to pay for the new invention created by the joint effort. However, in the example above, the profit gained is derived partly from the innovation and partly from the market power of the joint venture, that is, from the fact that the new technology becomes a technology standard.[283] Thus, if there is a standard that reflects a penetration consisting of a market, SEP holders to a joint R&D effort to obtain more essential patents under such a standard could, logically, be considered dominant and abusing their dominant position.

3.2.3   Cases and Business Review Letters

(i)   Introduction

Apart from the *Berkey Photo Inc. v. Eastman Kodak Co.* case discussed above, the *Automobile Manufacturings Association* case, and, perhaps, the *Open Software Foundation* case, there is little case law regarding pure R&D collaborations and the use of innovation markets.[284] The *Automobile Manufacturing's Association* case seems to deal with a clear-cut agreement between large car manufacturers not to conduct certain R&D. It is rather unique as a 'naked' agreement not to develop a technology. Other forms of agreement may implicitly or explicitly state not to develop certain (competing) technology as an ancillary restraint to an agreement where they regulate a joint R&D venture to develop a

---

[282]   In the 1960s Kenneth Arrow had already explained that monopolists were less likely to innovate because of the cost of cannibalism. Cf. Kenneth Arrow, 'Economic Welfare and the Allocation of Resources for Invention', in R. Nelson (ed.), *The Rate and Direction of Inventive Activity: Economic and Social Factors* (National Bureau of Economic Research, 1962), 609 et seq.

[283]   Cf. Mark Patterson, 'Inventions, Industry Standards, and Intellectual Property', (2002) 17 *Berkeley Technology Law Journal*, 1043, 1056 et seq. Patterson argues that SDOs should therefore be allowed to negotiate with the patentees so as to decrease the royalty rate to only reflect the inventive step in the essential intellectual property right.

[284]   See also *Open Software Foundation Inc et al. v. United States Fidelity and Guaranty*, 307 F.3d 11 (1st Cir. 2002).

technology. A covenant to the effect that the partners in an R&D collaboration or standardisation agreement should not conduct any competing R&D has been accepted as benign and pro-competitive by the antitrust authorities.[285] The commendable idea is that firms would not engage in joint R&D if they would be allowed to confidentially have a separate unilateral competing R&D programme. In the *Open Software Foundation Inc et al. v. United States Fidelity and Guaranty* case, Addamax, a producer of security software, unsuccessfully alleged that the joint R&D/standard-setting venture between Hewlett-Packard, IBM and Digital Equipment, called the Open Software Foundation, engaged in horizontal price fixing by conspiring to force input prices (the price of security software) below the competitive price.

Even though there are few pure R&D joint ventures that have been declared anticompetitive, there are certainly several high-profile price cartel cases where the parties have been involved in R&D collaborations.

In the semiconductor memory market, both the Justice Department and the EU Commission have, for example, investigated and also launched successful actions against firms being involved in cartels.[286] The Justice Department charged four companies (Samsung, Infineon, Hynix and Elpida) with fixing prices for dynamic random access memory (DRAM). The charge stated that the firms' executives had discussed the price of DRAM at joint meetings, agreed to fix prices and exchanged information with competitors. According to Goeree and Helland, Micron, who was a co-conspirator, sought amnesty from prosecution under the US leniency policy, and hence was not subject to charges in exchange for information on the other conspirators. Samsung, Hynix, Elpida and Infineon pleaded guilty and agreed to pay more than $732 million in collective fines, the second highest total obtained in an investigation aimed at one industry. These companies had been involved in various research joint ventures with overlapping membership, including Sematech, of which Micron was a member, which seem to have been the starting points also for the price cartels.[287] Thus, this is a case that gives some indications that joint R&D may spill over into price cartels. Disturbingly, Scott in an earlier article

---

[285]   See for example Article 5 in the EU R&D Block Exemption.

[286]   For the EU Commission investigation see press release regarding settlement from 19 May 2010, http://europa.eu/rapid/press-release_IP-10-586_en.htm accessed 3 February 2013.

[287]   See Michelle S. Goeree and Eric Helland, 'Do Research Joint Ventures Serve a Collusive Function?', *Working Paper Series* (Institute for Empirical Research in Economics University of Zurich Working Paper Series, July 2012).

actually hailed the Sematech R&D collaboration as an attempt to both collaborate and uphold rivalry.[288]

In addition, the high-profile LCD cartel case involved parties that had previously engaged in R&D collaborations, while older case law, regarding industrial pumps for example, shows similar patterns.[289]

The above cases show that there is clearly an interface between competitors engaging in joint R&D and cartels. In fact, Goerre and Helland also find an interesting correlation between the introduction of the new leniency programme in the USA in 1993 and a sharp drop in notification of joint R&D collaborations under the NCRPA. When the new leniency programme was developed, fewer firms seem to have been keen to enter into joint R&D ventures with their competitors.[290]

(ii) Merger cases where the Innovation Market was used
There are few cases where primarily the FTC has referred or used the concept of competition in research and development or the innovation market. According to Michael A. Carrier, neither the Justice Department nor the FTC has brought any innovation market cases recently.[291] There have been a number of challenges to mergers in innovation markets, and, according to Carrier, all except a few occurred in the pharmaceutical sector.[292]

---

[288] John Scott, 'The National Cooperative Research and Production Act', in ABA (ed.), *Issues in Competition Law and Policy* (ABA Section of Antitrust Law 2008), 1308, fn. 57.

[289] There have been various joint R&D ventures to develop the LCD technology. For the EU cartel case see http://ec.europa.eu/competition/antitrust/cases/dec_docs/39309/39309_3580_3.pdf accessed 3 February 2014. Regarding pump cases, see *infra*.

[290] Michelle S. Goeree and Eric Helland, 'Do Research Joint Ventures Serve a Collusive Function?', *Working Paper Series* (Institute for Empirical Research in Economics University of Zurich Working Paper Series, July 2012).

[291] Michael A. Carrier, *Innovation for the 21st Century: Harnessing the Power of Intellectual Property and Antitrust Law*, (Oxford Scholarship Online, May 2009), 93. See also Michael A. Carrier, 'Two Puzzles Resolved: Of the Schumpeter-Arrow Stalemate and Pharmaceutical Innovation Markets' (2008) 93(2) *Iowa Law Review*, 393 et seq. For a great analysis of merger and other cases where innovation market competition in innovation has been an issue, see generally Marcus Glader, *Innovation Markets and Competition Analysis*, (Cheltenham, Edward Elgar, 2006). As Glader analyses there are several EU pharmaceutical cases where innovation competition or R&D poles have been utilised.

[292] Ibid., 312 et seq. It should be noted that several of these mergers have also been scrutinised under the EU merger regulation. They will be scrutinised *infra*.

These cases were resolved by consent orders by the FTC under section 7 of the Clayton Act and section 5 of the FTC Act, and, obviously, do not concern R&D collaboration judged under the Sherman Act. Nonetheless, they can give some indications of how a joint R&D agreement would be judged on an innovation market if it were to be judged under the Sherman Act.

The FTC, when identifying the relevant innovation market in these cases, is rather blunt. It identifies the relevant market by a compound or future drug connected to the treatment of an illness. For example, in the Upjohn/Pharmacia merger from 1996, the FTC identified the relevant market as the 'research, development, manufacture and sale of topoisomerase I inhibitor for the treatment of colorectal cancer'.[293] In the Roche/Genetech merger from 1990 the FTC identified the relevant market as 'CD4-based therapeutics for treatment of AIDS and HIV infection'.[294] In the Glaxo/Wellcome merger it identified 'non-injectable 5HT-1D agonists' for the treatment of migraine attacks.[295]

Thereafter, the FTC describes the market structure often quite shortly, establishing that the acquisition would lessen competition, for example in the Glaxo/Wellcome merger, by, among other things:

a. Eliminating actual, direct and substantial competition between Glaxo and Wellcome in the relevant market;
b. Decreasing the number of research and development tracks for non-injectable 5HT ID agonists; and
c. Increasing Glaxo's ability to unilaterally reduce research and development of non-injectable 5HT ID agonists.[296]

In the Upjohn/Pharmacia merger the FTC simply states that Upjohn and Pharmacia are two of only a very small number of firms currently in the advanced stages of developing topoisomerase I inhibitors for the treatment of colorectal cancer. Upjohn product in development (CPT-11) is expected to be the first inhibitor for the treatment of colorectal cancer on the market in the United States. Pharmacia is soon to seek FDA approval for its inhibitor. The FTC continues and states that it is difficult and time-consuming to enter the relevant market. Entry is governed by the requirements of the FDA and the lengthy clinical trial periods, time-consuming data collection, and so on. The effect of the merger would therefore be:

---

[293] In the Matter Upjohn Co., et al. 121 FTC 44, 47–48 (1996).
[294] *In re* Roche Holding Ltd., 113 FTC 1086 (1990).
[295] In the Matter Glaxo PLC, 119 FTC 815 (1995).
[296] Ibid., 817.

a. Eliminating actual, direct and substantial competition in research and development between Upjohn and Pharmacia in the relevant market;

b. Potentially decreasing the number of research and development tracks for topoisomerase I inhibitors for the treatment of colorectal cancer; and

c. Eliminating the potential for actual, direct and substantial price competition between Upjohn and Pharmacia in the relevant market.[297]

The FTC clearly identifies the antitrust harm as suppression of competition and research efforts in these cases. But, is that a plausible harm to identify? Research is a difficult and risky business to conduct. Fortunately, Carrier has conducted a deepened analysis of the cases. By analysing the letters addressed to the FTC by the parties, annual reports from the time and other materials, he concludes, for example, in the Glaxo/Wellcome case that there were no non-injectable migraine treatments at the time of the merger. Glaxo did have an injectable migraine treatment, but more importantly Wellcome had a drug in Phase III clinical testing under the US FDA system. Glaxo was in either Phase II or III with its non-injectable drug.[298] Thus, a merger would have led to a decrease in rivalry.

According to the Carrier research, he proposes a new test under the innovation market concept especially catering to the pharmaceutical industry. He shows that the likelihood of success for drugs that have reached Phases II and III (especially III) is statistically high under the FDA system of approving drugs. From drugs in Phase III the likelihood of reaching the market was 57 per cent in Carrier's empirical research.[299] Suppression of research due to mergers is therefore a real possible danger.[300]

---

[297]   In the Matter Upjohn Co., et al. 121 FTC 44, 47–48 (1996). It should be noted that the Upjohn/Pharmacia merger was scrutinised also by the EU Commission under the EU merger regulation and cleared without commitments. The EU merger regulation did a different analysis of the relevant market and of innovative competition, in essence not finding rivalry or competition restrained in reference to research. See Case No IV/M.555 – Glaxo/Wellcome OJ C 65/3 (1995) also discussed by Marcus Glader, *Innovation Markets and Competition Analysis* (Cheltenham, Edward Elgar, 2006), 134 et seq.

[298]   Michael A. Carrier, 'Two Puzzles Resolved: Of the Schumpeter-Arrow Stalemate and Pharmaceutical Innovation Markets' (2008) 93(2) *Iowa Law Review*, 393, 433 et seq.

[299]   Ibid. Earlier research has shown slightly smaller numbers, see Marcus Glader, *Innovation Markets and Competition Analysis* (Cheltenham, Edward Elgar, 2006), 113, fn. 67, with several references.

[300]   Michael A. Carrier, *Innovation for the 21st Century: Harnessing the Power of Intellectual Property and Antitrust Law* (Oxford Scholarship Online, May 2009), 304 et seq.

Carrier continues, stating that the innovators in the pharmaceutical industry are easy to identify from the beginning. The interplay between the requirements to test drugs under the FDA procedure and the need of seeking patent protection also implies that the R&D is transparent. The antitrust agencies can therefore identify competing research efforts, as well as the merging parties' research efforts and how far the research and testing effort has endured. In fact, the same approach was used by the FTC in a number of other merger cases in the pharmaceutical industry, as, for example, in Amgen-Immunex (2002) and Pfizer-Pharmacia (2003).[301] Given the success rate for drugs that have reached at least Phase III to actually make it to the market, Carrier concluded that concentration on the innovation 'market' may be identified, even though not yet being a market where ascertained consumer demand can be identified.[302] Carrier's research is supported by decisions from the FTC and the EU Commission. In a case from 2000, *Glaxo Wellcome/ SmithKline Beecham*, also dealing with *inter alia* anti-migraine drugs, the EU Commission concluded that an acquisition of a research programme in Phase II could constitute a restriction of potential competition in light of Glaxo Wellcome's strong market power on the anti-migraine market.[303]

The focus on the innovation market prolonged during the 1990s. However, it was soon to change. In an interesting later case from 2003 and 2004, *Genzyme/Novazyme*,[304] the FTC analysed innovation competition in reference to two firms being the only source of research for a treatment for the rare Pompe disease. While both firms where in pre-clinical testing for a drug/treatment against the Pompe disease, the FTC commissioners were not in agreement and the FTC decision to close the case without remedies was heavily criticised by the dissenting commissioner and abstinent commissioner. The majority pointed to the fact that the FTC could not decline a merger simply based on the number of independent R&D programmes. Furthermore, there were substantial

---

[301]   Amgen and Immunex Docket no. C-4053 (2002) and Case No COMP/M. 2922 Pfizer/Pharmacia (2003) and FTC Pfizer and Pharmacia Docket No. C-4075 (2003).

[302]   Ibid.

[303]   Case No COMP/M.1846 – *Glaxo Wellcome/SmithKline Beecham* (2000).

[304]   See press release 13 January 2004, FTC Closes its Investigation of Genzyme Corporation's 2001 Acquisition of Novazyme Pharmaceuticals, Inc., http://www.ftc.gov/news-events/press-releases/2004/01/ftc-closes-its-investigation-genzyme-corporations-2001, last visited 12 January 2013. See also In the Matter of Genzyme Corp. Docket c 4126 File no 0410083 (2005).

efficiencies to be gained by the merger. The dissident concluded that a 'race to the market' would be eliminated, and at hand was, thus, a merger to monopoly. One of the commissioners also noted that the barriers to entry were high for this research and stated that, given the facts of the case, she was puzzled by the majority opinion.[305] It is also this case which made Shapiro write the article referred to at the beginning of this book.[306]

The then FTC Chairman Timothy Muris in this case explained the Commission's decision not to challenge the merger, and he explicitly relied on the proposition that the Commission did not use the innovation market analysis because 'economic theory and empirical investigations have not established a general causal relationship between innovation and competition'.[307] This statement, taken alone, is, as Shapiro noted, unobjectionable. Much of the theoretical and empirical literature on the relationship between market structure and innovation emphasises complexity while seeking to explain how different factors affect that relationship, recognising that both market structure and innovation are endogenous. Nonetheless, Shapiro argues with emphasis that we do know enough to warrant a presumption that a merger between the only two firms pursuing a specific line of research to serve a particular need is likely to diminish innovation rivalry, absent a showing that the merger will increase appropriability or generate R&D synergies that will enhance the incentive or ability of the merged firm to innovate.

In light of the *Genzyme/Novazyme* case, one may perhaps conclude that prohibiting mergers that concern not yet marketed pharmaceuticals *de jure* is difficult in the US. While the FTC disregarded the innovation market analysis, the use of the same and recognition of innovation competition in these cases should not make it impossible, and not solely in cases where two firms having Phase II or III drugs merge; but also mergers between firms having drugs in earlier stages of research and testing may in rare cases benefit from a prohibition.

---

[305] Ibid.

[306] See Section 2 above. Carl Shapiro, 'Competition and Innovation: Did Arrow Hit the Bull's Eye?', in Josh Lerner and Scott Stern (eds), *The Rate & Direction of Economic Activity Revisited* (University of Chicago Press, 2012), 371.

[307] See press release 13 January 2004, FTC Closes its Investigation of Genzyme Corporation's 2001 Acquisition of Novazyme Pharmaceuticals, Inc., http://www.ftc.gov/news-events/press-releases/2004/01/ftc-closes-its-investigation-genzyme-corporations-2001, last visited 12 January 2013. See also In the Matter of Genzyme Corp. Docket c 4126 File no 0410083 (2005).

Regarding the non-pharmaceutical cases, the FTC and the Justice Department have analysed the harm to innovation in existing markets in, for example, the proposed merger between the German firm ZF Friederichshafen purchasing General Motor's Allison Division.[308] The Justice Department opposed the merger and found GM and ZF to be the largest producers of medium and heavy automatic transmissions and, even though only competing in a few product markets in the US, the Justice Department still believed that the concentration threatened innovation (rate) in automatic transmissions. Innovation required constant feedback from production and GM and ZF were the only firms with the necessary production capacity. Historically, innovation had also occurred when the two firms continuously leapfrogged each other.[309] In the GM and ZF merger the Justice Department included the concerns for innovation in the market analysis. The case has been criticised because of the fact that by integrating the research and development factor, a merger that in the US at least did not seem to have many product market overlaps, became a concern. Thus, the identification of innovation market made two firms that were distant competitors into close competitors.[310]

A similar case also defined as a case regarding innovation in existing market was the market (and innovation for) ultra-high-pressure water jet intensifier pumps.[311] Marcus Glader has identified and classified different groups of mergers where the antitrust agencies are concerned with innovation and, as he indicates, it is difficult to distinguish between the cases where the agencies include innovation as a factor when analysing the product market competition, and where innovation competition has been treated as a stand-alone, or even as a market in itself.[312]

A similar case is the joint venture between Montedison and Shell, which also has the twist that it was analysed in both the US and the

---

[308] *US v. Gen. Motors Corp.*, Civ. No. 93-530 (D. Del Filed Nov 16, 1993).

[309] Marcus Glader, *Innovation Markets and Competition Analysis* (Cheltenham, Edward Elgar, 2006), 94 et seq.

[310] Lawrence B. Landman, 'Competitiveness, Innovation Policy and the Innovation Market Myth: A Reply to Tom and Newberg on Innovation Markets as the "Centerpiece" of "New Thinking" on Innovation', (1998) 13 *St. John's Journal of Legal Commentary*, 234, 244.

[311] *US v. Flow Int'l Corp.*, Civ. No. 93-530, 949 referred to and discussed by Lawrence B. Landman, 'Competitiveness, Innovation Policy and the Innovation Market Myth: A Reply to Tom and Newberg on Innovation Markets as the "Centerpiece" of "New Thinking" on Innovation', (1998) 13 *St. John's Journal of Legal Commentary*, 234, 243 et seq.

[312] Marcus Glader, *Innovation Markets and Competition Analysis* (Cheltenham, Edward Elgar, 2006), 98.

EU.[313] Montedison and Shell entered into an agreement to form and acquire equal interests in a joint venture that would merge the majority of Shell's and Montedison's worldwide polyolefins businesses. The proposed joint venture, designated by Montedison and Shell as 'Montell', combines assets valued at over $6 billion. Under the terms of the agreement between Montedison and Shell, Shell would retain outside the proposed joint venture polypropylene assets of Shell Oil (Shell subsidiary in the USA), including Shell Oil's polypropylene catalyst and polypropylene resin production facilities, Shell Oil's rights and obligations under a 1983 Cooperative Undertaking Agreement with Union Carbide Corporation pursuant to which Shell Oil and Union Carbide research, develop and license polypropylene technology and polypropylene catalyst worldwide, and Shell Oil's interest in the Seadrift Polypropylene Company, a partnership with Union Carbide which produces polypropylene resin. Nonetheless, Shell would control Shell Oil as well as Montell, and the proposed joint venture would create a common interest between Shell and Montedison. The FTC defined several relevant product and technology markets, but also referred to the research and development conducted by the parties on or for these markets. In fact, the parents to the joint venture did control the two competing technologies in the industry.[314] The FTC approved of the joint venture after the parties had made substantial commitments.

In the military airline sector, the Justice Department in 1998 denied a merger between Northrop and Lockheed, where the director of operations and merger enforcement, Robinson, explicitly emphasised the need 'to maintain a number of firms with the capability of innovating to meet future national security challenges' and concluded 'protecting variety in innovation is critically important'.[315]

---

[313]   *In re* Montedison 119 FTC 676 (1995) and EU: Case No IV/M.269 – Shell/Montecatini, OJ 332/48 (1994).

[314]   Which in fact was the conclusion made by the EU Commission in this case. Also the EU Commission demanded commitments by finding that the merger (full-functioning JV) would create a dominant position on the technology market. (Case No IV/M.269 – Shell/Montecatini, OJ 332/48 (1994)). Glader concludes that the Commission did not identify R&D as a stand-alone factor, but rather included the R&D factor as an aspect of competition on the technology market. See Marcus Glader, *Innovation Markets and Competition Analysis* (Cheltenham, Edward Elgar, 2006), 101.

[315]   Wolfgang Kerber, 'Competition, Innovation and Maintaining Diversity Through Competition Law', in J. Drexl, W. Kerber and R. Podszun (eds), *Economic Approaches to Competition Law: Foundations and Limitations* (Edward Elgar, 2010), 173.

While the non-pharmaceutical cases above concern taking innovation into consideration on the relevant market, or taking incremental innovations into consideration for products that were already marketed, the *Sensormatic Electric* case deals with a future goods market where the parties possibly tried not only to align their R&D, but supposedly also tried to create and implement a new market and a new industry standard which could become dominant in the sense that both manufacturers and retailers in the clothes industry could be locked into a system controlled by the two merging firms.[316]

Sensormatic and Knogo, the concerned undertakings for the merger, were active in the market for electronic article surveillance (EAS) systems for retail stores. They agreed to partially merger, while Sensormatic would acquire all Knogo's assets outside North America along with the patents related to the technology named SuperStrip. Knogo would still remain active inside the US and would be granted a non-exclusive licence for the SuperStrip. Under the licence agreement, the parties agreed to grant each other, royalty-free, licences for any improvements to patents and trade secrets related to the technology. The SuperStrip related to a system where the manufacturers would insert alarms in the products (clothes) directly without the retail stores having to perform such activity. The retail stores and the manufacturers would use the same technology standard or interface, so that the retailers and manufacturers did not have to adapt the alarm or retail store surveillance system (source labelling).

The FTC found that the barriers to entry were high and that the competitive harm consisted of reducing Knogo's incentives to conduct research and development on disposable labels for source labelling, by decreasing the number of research and development tracks and by increasing Sensormatic's ability to unilaterally reduce R&D of disposable labels for source labelling.

All the cases referred to above are merger cases; nonetheless, the underlying logic for finding innovation (or future goods) market, concentration (or more specific elimination of plausible and likely research paths) and competitive harm can also be used in reference to joint R&D outside the realms of mergers. Even though a merger admittedly creates longer lasting structural effects, joint R&D may very well include a discontinuing of research paths similar to, for example, the Glaxo case. A joint R&D project where these parties, instead of merging, would join

---

[316] Lawrence B. Landman, 'Competitiveness, Innovation Policy and the Innovation Market Myth: A Reply to Tom and Newberg on Innovation Markets as the "Centerpiece" of "New Thinking" on Innovation', (1998) 13 *St. John's Journal of Legal Commentary*, 234, 245.

patent and R&D portfolios so as to pursue only one of the two Phase II/III approved drugs would diminish competition in the future market in the same manner as the proposed merger did.

A last string of cases,[317] where the FTC and the Court did take innovation into consideration, involves the Intel saga. Intel was accused in three incidents of having used its market power in the semiconductor industry to force access to patents that the proprietors believed that Intel had infringed. Several of these cases were resolved by settlement agreements, while the *Intergraph* case[318] went to court. In these cases the FTC as well as the Court indicated that innovation and access to future innovation made by Intel were important and Intel's conduct of not granting access to information, and technical data and future innovation diminished the incentive of Intel's three customers in these cases to develop new innovations relating to the microprocessor technology.

Interestingly, the settlement agreement with one of these customers (Digital) implied that assets were transferred to Intel from Digital and that Intel got somewhat of an exclusivity of the technology held by Digital. The FTC consented to the joint venture only after Digital and Intel had agreed to other parties being able to license the technology. The FTC also, when analysing this settlement/joint R&D/licence agreement, defined an innovation market.[319]

(iii)   Business review letters

Interestingly, the business review letter procedure is applicable if the parties of a joint R&D or SDO are not sure whether they are in breach of antitrust law or may use the exemption in the NCRPA. Under the business review letter procedure, which is separate from the NCRPA, parties can informally ask the Justice Department how it would consider a proposed arrangement from an antitrust perspective. The Justice Department is not bound to make a decision and, if it does, it is not legally bound to follow it in the future. However, the procedure is an efficient and informal way to have *ex ante* control of a proposed joint venture before the parties commit to it through investments. They can still also make use of the NCRPA, even if they apply for a business review letter.

---

[317]   Starting with the FTC investigation in *In re* Intel Corp. 128 FTC 213 (1999).

[318]   *Intel Corp. v. Intergraph Corp.*, 195 F.3d 1346 (Fed. Cir. 1999).

[319]   See *In re* Digital Equipment Corp. 126 FTC 1 (1998). Marcus Glader, *Innovation Markets and Competition Analysis*, (Cheltenham, Edward Elgar, 2006), 103 et seq.

A positive business review letter does not formally eliminate the risk that the Justice Department will later charge the collaborators with violating the antitrust laws; however, in practice, the risk is minimal.[320] Therefore, the combination of the NCRPA and the business review system enables the joint ventures to become immune against both private and public suits. The elegance of this system is paramount, especially in reference to an antitrust jurisprudence, which often is not very clear-cut. However, the elegance is somewhat tarnished by two elements: first, the R&D market or innovation market concept is vague. It is difficult to distinguish whether a joint effort is conducting R&D within an innovation market that contains other competitors. For an adequate analysis the Justice Department would need more information than will be provided under the NCRPA or under the business review letter procedure. R&D is often conducted under strict confidence.

This ambiguity can also be detected in the Justice Department's decisions under the business review letters scheme after the enactment of the NCRA in 1984. After the enactment, firms seek acceptance for all industry-wide joint R&D effort since they are clearly outside the safe harbour.

Second, and more problematic from an antitrust perspective, is that collaborations, which fall under the NCRPA and inside the safe harbour, can restrict both the innovation rate and competition.[321] Thus, innovation and competition can be restricted not only by joint research notified under the business review letter scheme, but also by research falling under the NCRPA and the three technology threshold.

The Justice Department has in some instances delivered opinions regarding R&D joint ventures under its business review letter procedure. Of course, these opinions are of little legal value and are neither binding courts nor the antitrust enforcement agencies. They represent the administrative treatment of proposed R&D joint ventures disconnected from the court system and also the NCRPA. Nonetheless, given that the NCRPA prevents private litigants from accessing courts, the administrative procedure under the business review letter procedure becomes an important tool for analysing joint R&D. If the collaborators receive a positive

---

[320] To the author's knowledge, no collaboration approved under a business review letter has later been challenged by the Justice Department.

[321] This thesis points out several situations where collaborations exempted under the NCRPA can be anticompetitive. For more economic research focused on R&D collaborations cf. John Scott, 'The National Cooperative Research and Production Act', in ABA (ed.), *Issues in Competition Law and Policy* (ABA Section of Antitrust Law 2008), 1300 et seq. with references.

business review letter, they, in practice, have to fear neither private nor public litigants. In practice, a letter gives *carte blanche* to the collaboration.

The business review letters concerning joint R&D can be divided in two groups: first, joint research ventures which would be encompassed under the safe harbour and/or directly by the amendments of either 1993 or 2004 to the NCRPA, that is, production joint ventures and standardisation agreements. In other words, a body of 'case law' that today is somewhat obsolete under the antitrust jurisprudence under the NCRPA and the IP and Collaboration Guidelines since these collaborations are in practice exempted.

The second group contains the joint R&D ventures which are not directly encompassed by the safe harbour and, thus, where the parties have decided to submit the agreement under the business review letter scheme to the Justice Department in order to obtain reassurance that the collaboration was not in violation of the antitrust laws.

Below, the letters regarding R&D agreements which have been scrutinised by the Justice Department under the business review letter scheme and which presumably fall outside the safe harbour will be analysed. Generally, they concern industry-wide research efforts, since those do not fall within the safe harbour of at least three (or four) different research poles, as stated in the legal history of the NCRPA and in the Collaboration Guidelines and IP Guidelines, respectively.[322]

When analysing the business review letters from 1968 onwards, it is evident that the early scrutinised joint ventures were focused on specific problems. Generally, the problem was of a basic nature, the period of contemplated research was short, and it often involved the relevant trade association and, at least, the majority of the firms active in that industry.[323]

---

[322]   Compare Collaboration Guidelines, 26 et seq. and IP Guidelines, 13, 23, which state four or more independent research efforts in addition to the scrutinised effort. See discussion *supra* section 3.2.3(vii).

[323]   For example, in a business review letter sent by then Associate Assistant Attorney Thomas Kauper on April 21, 1976, a joint research was approved which amounted to an investment of approximately $4,000 and was predicted to last three months. The research was only to concern basic industry information, and the result was to be made available to all industry members regardless of their membership in the trade association. In a business review letter dated June 7, 1976, a research venture was similarly approved by the Justice Department through Thomas Kauper. The venture was to conduct joint research into toxic hazards of chemicals, set up by the leading member of the industry (but also open for anyone wanting to become a member). The information approximated

Some joint research was triggered by the revelation that one of the components, necessary for the manufacture of the product, was no longer readily available. For example, in 1976 the producers of capacitors teamed up to do research in order to find a substitute when their impregnate compound PCB was found to be toxic.[324]

A feature of almost all the early notified research efforts was that the result of the joint effort was immediately made available to all firms in the industry. Neither the result nor the research itself was considered confidential or a competitive tool. Instead, it was considered basic knowledge and all members gained from accessing it to no or minimum royalty fees.[325] Indeed, research with large spillover effects was often allowed to be conducted collectively. It is evident that the Justice Department gave weight to the fact that the research was basic. None of the participants were likely to conduct the R&D alone because it was not commercially feasible or attractive for an individual firm due to the large spillover effects.[326]

A recurring feature in these cases is also the participation of a public entity, for example, the technical department of a university, in the joint research.[327] Often the technical department of a university conducts the joint R&D on behalf of a group of competing firms. Thus, the competing

---

by the research would be accessible for everyone and published. [The business review letters are on file with the author.]

[324] PCB business review letter dated October 15, 1976. The PIMA research was a variation of joint research due to the revelation that one of the used compounds was toxic and the industry needed to rethink. The industry as a whole needed not to find a substitute chemical for CFC (Freon), but a joint centre to help the entities in the polyisocyanrate foam industry jointly to test whatever they individually come up with as a substitute, see business review letter, dated Feb. 28, 1989. [The business review letters are on file with the author.]

[325] See also business review letter dated May 9, 1978, where the research on the medical effects of treated coal on psoriasis was approved, since the result and the patent would be placed in the public domain and licensed royalty free. [The business review letter is on file with the author.]

[326] Ibid.

[327] See, e.g., the notified research made by the Center for Advanced Television Studies, where MIT was the performing research institution. MIT was to hold any and all intellectual property rights to the result of the research. Business review letter dated Sept. 21, 1983. [The business review letter is on file with the author.]

firms outsource the R&D to the university.[328] Today, we would call that public–private partnership.

It is apparent that the Justice Department did and still today does not suspect collaborations including public entities to violate the antitrust laws. Instead, these outsourced R&D collaborations are viewed as a warranty against any knowledge or information being kept confidential (that is, not being made public or not being published). In more recent letters, the mere existence of a public department of a participating university appears to be sufficient to warrant that the R&D result eventually becomes public. The Justice Department approved most all-industry inclusive joint ventures where the intellectual property rights may be protected, royalties demanded and membership in the research effort can be, if not prohibited, at least stalled for new entrants as long as a university participated.[329]

There is another detectible development when analysing the business review letters from 1968 onwards. In earlier letters, the research was basic, while, in the later letters, the research, contemplated by the parties in the joint efforts, became more applied instead of basic research, even though it often has a public entity (university) conducting the R&D.[330]

---

[328]   Ibid. It was stated that the research concerned basic research but that specific projects have not been selected yet. The venture concerned making TV sets better and less costly to produce. The conclusion that competing firms outsource R&D to third parties is also supported by research conducted on R&D ventures that were notified under the NCRPA but where the parties did not apply for a business review letter. See Suzanne E. Majewski, *How Do Consortia Organize Collaborative R&D? Evidence from the National Cooperative Research Act* (SSRN 2004), 12 et seq.

[329]   See, e.g., the GPRI business review letter from Joel Klein to Rufus Oliver, dated April 23, 1997, regarding joint R&D outsourced to a university in Texas by six members of the oil industry (referred to as 'major oil companies'). The university department conducted the research on behalf of the prominent oil companies. The parties stated that they would comply with the NCRPA and that the joint R&D was open for anyone wanting to join and the university was allowed to license third parties for remuneration. [See http://www.usdoj.gov/atr/public/busreview/1104.htm, last visited 2009-04-21.] A similar letter was given in 2007; see the AEC business review letter from Thomas O. Barnett to Rufus Oliver dated Aug. 23, 2007, where seven oil companies outsourced R&D to a university in Texas. In contrast with the 1997 joint venture, the 2007 joint venture is not open to any comer and the parties can prevent the result from being licensed to third parties. [See http://www.usdoj.gov/atr/public/busreview/225511.htm, last visited 2009-04-21.]

[330]   See, e.g., business review letter dated June 25, 1985 (press release June 26), regarding the CAM-I research among software and computer firms, which

Thus, basic research, which supposedly is best from a societal point of view for joint research because it creates spillover knowledge, the interaction of ideas, is not performed jointly. Instead, applied research regarding issues closer to the end product or service is conducted jointly, while the basic research has already (presumably) been conducted by the participating university department from the university at an earlier stage.

Furthermore, when comparing business review letters from the 1980s to the letters written at the beginning of the 1970s, it is evident that the notified research efforts during the 1980s were predicted to last for a longer time. Some were even recurrent, and, above all, they were larger projects that involved more assets and larger investments than the joint R&D efforts of the 1970s.

United Technologies business review letter from 1983 relating to a joint venture formed to develop and manufacture an advanced jet engine is one, according to commentators, of the important agency statements of that time. The joint venture was formed among major jet engine manufacturers. The Justice Department analysed the probable effect on competition in the market in which the venture proposes to operate (future goods market) and any effect upon competition in any other markets in which the venture partners compete or might compete. With respect to the first area of inquiry (the future goods market), the Justice Department considered the probability that any of the partners would enter the market independently and, if they would, the significance of any diminution of competition resulting from them entering jointly. Concluding that it was unlikely that more than one member of the consortium would incur the substantial cost and expense of developing and producing an advanced jet engine, the Justice Department concluded that the production of the planned engine would not diminish competition. Thus, the underlying (likely wrong) logic of the Supreme Court's *Olin-Penn* joint venture judgment seems to have been scrapped.[331]

After the NCRA was enacted in 1984, the Justice Department approved joint R&D ventures, which gave the joint venture not only the possibility of conducting joint research, but also jointly exploiting the result through licensing. For example, the jointly proposed formation of a

---

states that the venture concerns applied instead of basic research. [The business review letter is on file with the author.]

[331] See John Anthony Chavez, 'Joint Ventures in the European Union and the U.S.' (1999 Winter) *Antitrust Bulletin*, 959, referring to business review letter from William F. Baxter Ass't Attorney General, Antitrust Division to Irving B. Yoskowitz, Vice President and General Counsel, United Technologies Corp. (Oct. 27, 1983), Antitrust & Trade Reg. Rep. (BNA) No. 1138, at 726 (Nov. 3, 1983).

$220 million limited partnership in the machine tool industry stated that the limited partnership had an option to exclusively license the intellectual property that resulted from the research.[332]

Some review letters show arguments resembling the 'failing firm' defence. The competitors should be allowed to conduct joint R&D since the downturn in the industry prevents the participants from performing the R&D independently.[333] For example, the US pump industry ran into problems in the mid-1980s and made use of the failing firm defence. The proposed R&D venture involved all US pump manufacturers and it was approved because of *inter alia* the situation of the industry. The investment was not, as the Justice Department stated, extremely large and foreign research poles could act as a competitive incentive.[334] The contemplated research concerned applied science in the sense that it was based on already known technology.[335]

The requirement that the firms would only perform the intended research jointly was even more relaxed in the business review letter for joint research by Amoco, Arco, Exxon, Mobil, Shell and Texaco and Texas University Institute from 1997.[336] These founding members set up an institute for exploration and production research, open to any entity that received significant revenues from petroleum exploration or production activities. The institute would perform research which the parties

---

[332]   Business review letter dated Oct. 16, 1984. See also the business review letter from Sept. 21, 1983, concerning the Center for Advanced Television Studies, where MIT was the performing research institution. It admitted only firms whose original parent companies were from the US. [The business review letters are on file with the author.]

[333]   Business review letter dated July 5, 1985. [The business review letter is on file with the author.]

[334]   Ibid.

[335]   Scott states that the primary reason for joining together in a joint R&D is competition from foreign firms or from a dominant foreign or domestic firm. Cf. John T. Scott, 'Diversification versus Cooperation in R&D Investment', (1988) 9 *Managerial Decision Economics*, 173, 175 et seq.

[336]   See, e.g., the GPRI business review letter from Joel Klein to Rufus Oliver dated April 23, 1997, regarding joint R&D outsourced to a university in Texas by six members of the oil industry (referred to as 'major oil companies'). [See http://www.usdoj.gov/atr/public/busreview/1104.htm, last visited 2009-04-21.] A similar letter was given in 2007; see the AEC business review letter from Thomas O. Barnett to Rufus Oliver dated Aug. 23, 2007, where seven oil companies outsourced R&D to a university in Texas. In contrast with the 1997 letter, the joint venture is not open for any comer and the parties can prevent the result being licensed to third parties. [See http://www.usdoj.gov/atr/public/busreview/225511.htm, last visited 2009-04-21.]

found more expedient to perform jointly than individually. According to the joint venture agreement, they were still free to perform individual research. Nonetheless, the joint research performed by the institute can be of such character that it would be economically feasible to perform it individually.[337] According to the letter the joint R&D was encompassed under the NCRPA. If the research was successful, the intellectual property was to be held by the institute, which was obliged to license rights royalty-free to its members or to non-members for a fee. Whether the contemplated research was to be of basic or applied art was not stated.[338]

The institutional organisation of the scrutinised research efforts differs greatly. However, as mentioned above, there is one striking similarity in several of the all-industry joint R&D ventures scrutinised under the business review letter procedure: apart from the industrial members there is often a public entity, for example, a department of a university, which supervises the joint venture and is contracted to perform the research by the joint venture. When deciding what research to perform, the industry members often take an annual vote deciding on a small number of projects, or they are allowed to support different research efforts within an area of interest. However, after deciding what effort to pursue, the members are often disconnected and a research organisation, often connected to the participating university, is contracted to perform the specific research in question.[339] Thus, generally large competitors in an industry, 'system leaders', jointly outsource certain R&D through these collaborations to public entities that are at least partially publicly funded.[340]

---

[337] The parties stated that a majority of the members were not to contribute to the cooperative over any three-year period a sum which in the aggregate would exceed 10 per cent of each member's total research budget, see Petroleum E&P Research business review letter from Joel Klein to Rufus Oliver dated April 23, 1997. See http://www.usdoj.gov/atr/public/busreview/1104.htm, last visited 2009-05-06.

[338] See also the similar AEC business review letter from Thomas O. Barnett to Rufus Oliver dated Aug. 23, 2007, where seven oil companies outsourced R&D to a university in Texas. See http://www.usdoj.gov/atr/public/busreview/225511.htm, last visited 2009-04-21.

[339] See, e.g., PRT business review letter from Joel Klein to David William Livingston, dated March 20, 1998. See http://www.usdoj.gov/atr/public/busreview/1608.htm, accessed 5 May 2009.

[340] Cf. Suzanne E. Majewski, *How Do Consortia Organize Collaborative R&D? Evidence from the National Cooperative Research Act* (SSRN 2004), 12 et seq.

Probably, joint research in the US is not generally performed as in these cases. The majority of joint efforts are not filed to the Justice Department under the business review letter scheme. Instead, they are notified under the NCRPA and include less than all firms in an industry. The reviewed letter above shows the way to get an all-industry inclusive R&D effort approved by the Justice Department. Indeed, the reason for requesting a business review letter for these kinds of efforts, and to not only notify them under the NCRPA, is the over-inclusiveness or dominance of the industry participants. The four technology safe harbour is not applicable. The Justice Department allows these forms of joint research since, generally speaking, the research is of some basic nature, the members are still allowed to perform individual research, and the university participant 'warrants' dissemination of the result in society, at least within some years after discovery. Moreover, from a business point of view it is attractive to employ university institutions since they are at least to some extent publicly funded.

However, the method of organising the joint R&D, that is, competitors jointly outsourcing the research to a public entity, appears common not only when the members consist of the leading, or all, members of an industry. On the contrary, in one study the majority of the R&D joint ventures that were notified under the NCRPA consisted of competitors jointly outsourcing R&D to third R&D-specific firms or university institutes. Researchers at the Justice Department have on two occasions analysed R&D agreements which had been filed under the NCRPA so as to enable the participants to gain access to the safe harbour.[341] From data consisting of 142 joint R&D agreements, Suzanne Majewski concluded that most joint R&D agreements were entered into by product market competitors, that is, vertically integrated firms. These competing firms tended in their agreements to collectively outsource their R&D to third parties, often technical departments on university campuses. By outsourcing they benefit from shared costs and reduction in duplicative efforts. They also avoided spillover effects and opportunistic problems of having researchers from the firms interacting. However, by avoiding scientists interacting, supposedly welfare-enhancing exchange of ideas (spillover) was minimised. Synergy effects are lost if the parties do not conduct the research jointly. This was also supported by the fact that in

---

[341]   Suzanne E. Majewski, *How Do Consortia Organize Collaborative R&D? Evidence from the National Cooperative Research Act* (SSRN 2004), 12 et seq.; Suzanne E. Majewski & Dean V. Williamson, *Endogenous Spillovers, Strategic Blocking, and the Design of Contracts in Collaborative R&D: Evidence from NCRA filings of R&D Joint Ventures* (SSRN 2002), 20 et seq.

only 14 per cent of the analysed R&D joint ventures was a scientist allowed to rotate between the participating firms. Majewski's research also shows that there is a new sort of firm emerging: the R&D-only firms. These R&D-exclusive firms tend to cater to product market competitors but conduct their work exclusively in the innovation and technology markets and they often are closely connected to universities.

Interestingly, when analysing all letters from 1968 onwards, the Justice Department has never – ultimately – rejected any joint R&D ventures. Moreover, the general approach appears also to be more permissive today than previously. Arguably, this contrasts with the fact that privately funded basic research is becoming less and less common;[342] at least, private parties perform such research with less and less regularity.[343] It should therefore be natural to see a decline in the approval rate of the all-inclusive efforts. Apparently that is not the case. Instead, based on the joint R&D notified under the business review letter scheme, it seems that the research now performed industry-wide is more of applied art than basic science. In addition, the model where large vertically integrated firms jointly outsource R&D to universities or R&D-specific firms that at least to some extent are publicly funded would raise concerns, not only from an antitrust perspective but also from general capitalistic theory. Despite these concerns, the Justice Department has not changed the approach when analysing these cases.

What is also striking in these letters is the interaction between R&D collaborations and standardisation agreements. The argument that the purpose for setting up a joint R&D venture was the creation of a technology standard was increasingly invoked at the beginning of the 1990s.[344] Hence, the argument that the contemplated technology will dominate the industry was forwarded as an argument for conducting joint research.[345] Also, the Justice Department promoted standardisation in

---

[342]   See, e.g., the Economist March 3–9, 2007, The Rise and Fall of Corporate R&D, 69 et seq.

[343]   Ibid.

[344]   See, e.g., the business review letter from Charles James to Ky P. Ewing dated Nov. 12, 2002, addressing the 3G patent platforms for the third generation mobile communication systems. See also business review letter from Thomas O. Barnett to Robert A. Skitol, dated Oct. 30, 2006, regarding the standard-setting body of VITA.

[345]   See, e.g., the RIAA research into finding one system for limiting the ability to copy or 'burn' CDs. The copyright business as a whole wanted to implement a joint system and the Justice Department decided not to intervene. See RIAA business review letter of March 14, 1991. [The document is on file with the author.]

highly technical and investment-intensive industries, for example, the nuclear industry.[346] These cases show how far the development has gone. From the beginning of the 1980s when a Guide was published stipulating that competition should govern the innovative process, to a situation where the parties may as a reason for exempting the joint effort under antitrust law put forward the argument that the result of the effort will dominate the market as a standard.

3.2.4   The Latest Amendment to the NCRPA, Standard-setting[347]

(i)   Exempted SDOs
Congress decided in 2004 to amend the NCRPA with the Standards Development Organization Advancement Act, in order to extend the protection from the antitrust laws stipulated in the NCRPA to specified activities of standards development organisations (SDOs). If an SDO discloses the scope and nature of its activities to the Department of Justice, it may take advantage of the NCRPA.[348]

A standard development organisation (SDO) is a standard-setting organisation (SSO) that has been accredited with the International Organization for Standardization (ISO) or the International Electrotechnical Commission (IEC).

SSO is therefore a larger term including not only SDOs but also, for example, private consortia of firms joining together to advance a technical solution to become a standard. SSOs or consortia were using the NCRPA long before the 2004 amendment.[349] It was customary for standard consortia to be notified under the NCRPA given the wide definition of research stipulated in the NCRPA. SSO activities could thus

---

[346]   See, e.g., business review letter from Mark Gidley to Michael I. Miller dated Sept. 2, 1992, for setting up a standard-setting research effort in advanced reactor technology. See, http://www.usdoj.gov/atr/public/busreview/211283.htm, last visited 2009-05-23.

[347]   This part is based in part on Björn Lundqvist, *Standardization under EU Competition Rules and US Antitrust Laws – The Rise and the Limits of Self-Regulation* (Edward Elgar, 2014), 149 et seq.

[348]   For a background to the amendment and a scholarly argument in support of its implementations, see generally Mark Lemley, 'Intellectual Property Rights and Standard-Setting Organizations', (2002) 90 *California Law Review*, 1889 and specifically 1970.

[349]   See Carl Cargill, 'Intellectual Property Rights and Standard Setting Organizations: An Overview of Failed Evolution', (2002) 27 March *FTC/DOJ Hearings on Competition and Intellectual Property Law and Policy in the Knowledge-Based Economy*, 1, 1 fn. 1. [The document is on file with the author.]

fall under the definition of 'research'. SSOs could make use of the NCRPA and thereby limited their antitrust exposure.[350] This practice really put the emphasis on the fact that in practice the conduct of agreeing on future technology to employ, that is, what to conduct research about, may be done both in the setting of an SSO or under a joint R&D venture. Thus, the 2004 amendment instead foremost catered to the large and acknowledged SSOs, that is, the SDOs, while the consortia already used the NCRPA.

As I have discussed elsewhere,[351] according to the NCRPA, 'standard development activities' conducted by an SDO may include any action for the purpose of creating, developing or maintaining a consensus standard.[352] This is a wide definition. Any decision on what technology to use or not use and implicitly towards what aims the technology should develop falls under the definition.[353] Indeed, one purpose of the Standards Development Organization Advancement Act was that the exemption should cover the handling of the members' intellectual property rights by the SDOs.[354] Agreements on royalty rates or at least unilateral public announcements of royalty rates by patentees and SDO members are encompassed by the Act.[355] Interestingly, what can be included as

---

[350] Cf. Carl Cargill, 'Intellectual Property Rights and Standard Setting Organizations: An Overview of Failed Evolution', (2002) 27 March *FTC/DOJ Hearings on Competition and Intellectual Property Law and Policy in the Knowledge-Based Economy*, 1, 3 et seq. [The document is on file with the author.] Cf. also Jack Brown, 'Technology Joint Ventures to set Standards or Define Interfaces', (1992–1993) 61 *Antitrust Law Journal*, 921, 933.

[351] Björn Lundqvist, *Standardization under EU Competition Rules and US Antitrust Laws – The Rise and the Limits of Self-Regulation* (Edward Elgar, 2014), 149 et seq., 168 et seq.

[352] 15 U.S.C.A § 4301(c).

[353] The Supreme Court stated in *Allied Tube* that, 'agreement on a product standard is, after all, implicitly an agreement not to manufacture, distribute or purchase certain types of products. Accordingly, private standard-setting organizations have traditionally been objects of antitrust scrutiny.' *Allied Tube and Conduit Corp. v. Indian Head, Inc.*, 486 U.S. 492, 500 (1988).

[354] See H.R. REP. 108-125, *reprinted* 2004 U.S.C.C.A.N. 609, 610 et seq. It should be noted that Congress was (to a lesser extent) concerned with so-called 'patent ambush', i.e., firms which do not admit having filed for patents and try to steer the standard in order to create the highest impact for the patents.

[355] According to the amendment, the term 'standards development activity' does not only mean any action taken by a standards development organisation for the purpose of developing, promulgating, revising, amending, reissuing, interpreting or otherwise maintaining a voluntary consensus standard, or using such standard in conformity assessment activities, but also actions relating to the

'standard development activities' according to the NCRPA are *inter alia* standardisation agreements, and SSOs' IP policies or IP rules.[356] However, it seems as if the NCRPA now creates immunity for the SDOs in reference to the agreement among the licensors regarding the technology and the terms for licensing of intellectual property rights under the industrial or technology standard. An agreement can include the royalty at which and on what other terms third parties may license the essential patents.

Technology standards agreements are often preceded by joint R&D in the pre-standardisation phase. Joint R&D is conducted by technology or system leaders, but the parties do not need to conduct joint R&D for the NCRPA to be applicable to the SDO.[357] The NCRPA therefore grants limited immunity not only for R&D (and production joint ventures), but also to all industry agreements on technology and even to agreement on royalty rates for the standard essential patents.[358]

As a matter of fact, the standardisation process often starts with a pre-standardisation phase where often system leaders in small groups prepare standards *en petit comite* by entering joint R&D agreements, so as to present a joint solution for adoption as a standard.[359] These joint R&D ventures are encompassed by the NCRPA and are often rather exclusive groups.[360] The result of the joint R&D is either presented directly to an SDO or, firstly, an SSO is created and then the SSO tries to obtain approval for itself and the technology standard it governs by ISO, EIC or ANSA (or in certain industries a technology standard was not created, merely 'open specifications').[361] Given the market power of

---

intellectual property policies of the standards development organisation. See 15 U.S.C.A § 4301. (c). It should be noted that allocation of markets is not within the notion of standard-setting activities as it is not the agreement on price for any product or service. Though deciding price for the licensing of intellectual property rights seems *e contrario* to be included under the term 'standard development activity', see 15 U.S.C.A § 4301(c).

[356] It corresponds *inter alia* to the horizontal part of patent pool agreements, see discussion *infra* section 4.

[357] See discussion *infra* section 3.2.4(vi).

[358] Björn Lundqvist, *Standardization under EU Competition Rules and US Antitrust Laws – The Rise and the Limits of Self-Regulation* (Edward Elgar, 2014), 402 et seq.

[359] Maurits Dolmans, 'Standards for Standards', (2002) 26 *Fordham International Law Journal*, 163, 171 et seq.

[360] Ibid.

[361] See generally Cargill about the evolution of the standardisation process over the years, Carl Cargill, 'Intellectual Property Rights and Standard Setting

these system leaders, and their head start in the pre-standardisation phase, they can steer the relevant SDOs to adopt their technology or get their relevant SSO to become an SDO. This is, of course, most troublesome if the standard is a prescriptive or interoperability (or compatible) standard, where the standard can be matched towards certain patents.[362]

Interestingly, the antitrust enforcement agencies disregard the fact that the patentees who hope to get their patent under the standard may be influential members of the SDO. The issue that several members of the SDO might have set up pre-standardisation R&D ventures holding complementary patents making up a technology, which they want to get approved and implemented by the organisation simultaneously, was likewise overlooked by Congress when enacting the NCRPA.

In certain cases, one larger inventor can even set up its own standard, based on its technology, and attract smaller firms in order to create a standard. Moreover, it is not uncommon to use the 'consortia model' for the creation of a standard, that is, competitors come together to create both a standard and an SDO.[363]

(ii) What the NCRPA fails to address and what the Justice Department disregards

Theoretically the anticompetitive risks with consortia standards-setting are several: (i) open access to the standardisation process may be restricted or limited; (ii) over-standardisation, that is, the breadth and depth of the technology standard excludes new and competing technologies (in addition, the time aspect should be noted, implementing standards too early might suppress the development of alternative technologies); (iii) under-standardisation, that is, the technology is still regulated under the standard, however the breadth or depth of the standard is too narrow or shallow, creating exclusive fields of use for

---

Organizations: An Overview of Failed Evolution', (2002) 27 March *FTC/DOJ Hearings on Competition and Intellectual Property Law and Policy in the Knowledge-Based Economy*, 1, 2 et seq. [The document is on file with the author.]

[362]   Björn Lundqvist, *Standardization under EU Competition Rules and US Antitrust Laws – The Rise and the Limits of Self-Regulation* (Edward Elgar, 2014), 402 et seq.

[363]   For an interesting description of the patent and standard-setting process, see generally Scott Peterson, 'Patent and Standard Setting Process', in *FTC/DOJ Hearings on Competition and Intellectual Property Law and Policy in the Knowledge-Based Economy* (FTC, 2002). [The document is on file with the author.]

certain intellectual property holders; (iv) collusion in choice of tech-nology, that is, the technology selected under the technology standard is neither the 'best' nor the technology which should have been selected under a free innovation and competition process not influenced by the standardisation agreements; (v) the result of the standardisation process is not open for every firm to access; and (vi) spillover effects, information exchange between competitors, commercial collusion and market alloca-tion.[364]

In addition, also theoretically, pure vertical concerns regarding standardisation agreements may emerge: (i) IP policies of dominant SSOs can reduce incentives to innovate by firms focusing on R&D and (ii) compulsory licensing obligations, under the *eBay* line of case law, can be imposed on members of SSOs.

The NCRPA emphasises that the SDOs should employ a standard-isation process that is open, fair and transparent, and generally the above theoretical problems are solved by the good governance rules and by firms reaching some kind of an agreement.

The standardised technology may in the end not be the 'best' tech-nology alternative.[365] However, the SDOs imply a procedure to reach and create markets. The standardised technology does not need to reflect superior research and that the 'tipping' effects of a technology standard might elevate the technology to a market share and market power inadequate in reference to inventive steps inherent in the innovation, and to the most efficient dynamic competitive equilibrium. But, this is not an antitrust problem.

Furthermore, a single patentee can be exposed to a buyer cartel (monopsony) in the form of an SDO.[366] That a patentee needs *ex ante* to reveal his licensing terms or even agree to some licensing terms under the threat that the SDO otherwise will change the technology standard and

---

[364]   For a similar but different list, cf. the headings of Maurits Dolmans, 'Standards for Standards', (2002) 26 *Fordham International Law Journal*, 163. Cf. also Carl Cargill, 'Intellectual Property Rights and Standard Setting Organ-izations: An Overview of Failed Evolution', (2002) 27 March *FTC/DOJ Hear-ings on Competition and Intellectual Property Law and Policy in the Knowledge-Based Economy*, 1. [The document is on file with the author.]

[365]   This has been a complaint regarding formal SDOs for a long time. See Carl Shapiro, 'Setting Compatibility Standards: Cooperation or Collusion?', in Rochelle Dreyfuss, et al. (eds), *Expanding The Boundaries of Intellectual Property* (Oxford University Press, 2001), 84 and 89.

[366]   Mark Lemley, 'Intellectual Property Rights and Standard-Setting Organ-izations', (2002) 90 *California Law Review*, 1889, 1900, 1939 et seq.

make the patentee's innovation superfluous might, of course, be interpreted as a buyer cartel.[367] It creates foreclosure. It would also diminish innovation incentives for smaller firms.[368]

Finally, the spillover effects of R&D collaborations should not be underestimated. As Goerre and Helland have shown, there are ways in which R&D collaborations may lead to collusive product market behaviour.[369] They have found that several of the joint R&D ventures notified under the NCRPA are entered into between product market competitors. They also point to the fact that several of the high-profile cartel cases investigated by the Justice Department may have started as joint R&D collaborations. For example, in the oil and petroleum business, where many of the joint R&D ventures notified under NCRPA stem from, also have been investigated and found violating hard-core restriction of US antitrust law. They also find an interesting correlation between a (sharp) drop in the number of joint R&D collaborations notified under the NCRPA and the introduction of the new leniency programme in the USA in 1993.

3.2.5 Conclusion

Clearly, the NCRPA has served its purpose. There is almost no court case law where the Act has even been mentioned. In some cases the parties have stumbled over the Act without really making use of the exemption. In the few cases where the Act is mentioned, both the parties and the court appear bewildered about what to do with it.[370] Since the Act was

---

[367]   Several authors argue that SDOs should be allowed to negotiate with holders of essential patentees. See, e.g., Mark Patterson, 'Inventions, Industry Standards, and Intellectual Property', (2002) 17 *Berkeley Technology Law Journal*, 1043, 1078 et seq.

[368]   For a general discussion regarding oligopsony and SDOs, see Robert A. Skitol, 'Buyer Power and Antitrust: Concerted Buying Power: Its Potential For Addressing the Patent Holdup Problem in Standard Setting', (2005) 72 *Antitrust Law Journal*, 727. For an example of a monopsony case involving a European SDO, see Maurits Dolmans, 'Standards for Standards', (2002) 26 *Fordham International Law Journal*, 163, 176 et seq.

[369]   See Michelle S. Goeree and Eric Helland, 'Do Research Joint Ventures Serve a Collusive Function?', *Working Paper Series* (Institute for Empirical Research in Economics University of Zurich Working Paper Series, July 2012).

[370]   See the U.S. District Court case *Addamax Corp. v. Open Software Foundation Inc. et al.*, 888 F. Supp. 274 (D.Mass. 1995); and *Open Software Foundation Inc et al. v. United States Fidelity and Guaranty*, 307 F.3d 11 (1st Cir. 2002).

implemented, few courts have concluded that an anticompetitive R&D agreement has existed. However, this does not mean that the phenomenon is rare. Joint research ventures and joint production agreements are probably entered into every day, so not all of them are likely to be considered pro-competitive in case an analysis was conducted.

The innovation market definition introduced in 1984, and altered in 1993, is elusive and has never been utilised in reference to R&D joint ventures. The participants need to represent market power not only in the relevant research market, but also in at least one relevant downstream product market. Possibly, they also need to hold a dominant position on intermediate relevant development or process markets, before their restrictive joint venture would be considered anticompetitive. In addition, the participants can claim that efficiencies obtained in, for example, the manufacturing or development stage, should trump any anticompetitive build-up of market power in the R&D market. Combined market power above 20 per cent, or even more, in a technology or product market can be redeemed by showing competition in the innovation market.

However, the NCRPA includes more than joint R&D. From initially a safe harbour for joint R&D and joint licensing of the result, the Act has expanded over the years to include joint production and now finally joint standard activities, which include joint arrangements on how to give access to intellectual property rights.[371]

In order to implement an R&D scheme, the parties, after having performed the joint research, should approach the three or four other globally existing joint research ventures and agree on a joint standard. They can pool their patents under the relevant SDO. Then they are able to control both the innovation market, where the joint R&D is present, and the technology market, where the patents and the pool are active.

Interestingly, the parties can also do the opposite. They can first initiate an agreement on standards of technology in the pre-standardisation phase, and thereafter start performing joint research in smaller groups. They 'innovate' the result, apply for intellectual property rights and reveal the new technology system to the relevant SDO. The entire process evades antitrust scrutiny under the NCRPA.[372]

---

[371]   In addition, John T. Scott indicates that joint sales can be implemented by transferring the result of the joint R&D to a jointly owned firm. See John Scott, 'The National Cooperative Research and Production Act', in ABA (ed.), *Issues in Competition Law and Policy* (ABA Section of Antitrust Law 2008), 1316.

[372]   This is a common collaborative scenario in network markets. See Maurits Dolmans, 'Standards for Standards', (2002) 26 *Fordham International Law Journal*, 163, 171 et seq., especially 172.

When analysing the background of some of the high-profile patent pools scrutinised in business review letters from the end of the 1990s, for example the DVD pool collaboration between Koninklijke Philips Electronics N.V. (Philips), Sony Corporation of Japan (Sony) and Pioneer Electronic Cooperation of Japan (Pioneer), it becomes apparent that the participants jointly researched and developed the technology before setting up the SSO as well as the patent pool.[373] Philips and Sony have been jointly engaging in research under the supervision of the Japanese Government for a long period of time, coming up with technologies such as the VCR video, CD, minidisc and DVD.[374] These standards, including their accompanying patent pools, were first considered benign under both US and EU antitrust laws, but were later questioned in several jurisdictions. Apparently, at least regarding the CD-ROM technology, the parties later had to dissolve the relevant technology pool.[375] The main

---

[373] See the 3DVD pool business review letter from Joel Klein to Gerrard Beeney dated Dec. 16, 1998. See http://www.usdoj.gov/atr/public/busreview/ 2121.htm, last visited 2009-04-01.

[374] The background seems to be as follows: 'Sony and Philips worked together in the late 1970s to develop the audio CD. Philips' work on LaserDisc and Sony's digital error correction encoding resulted in a huge leap forward for consumer audio that delivered high quality sound on a durable medium with instant playback. In the early 1990s, the two companies began collaborating on an inexpensive new video version, called the MultiMedia Compact Disc. At the same time, a group led by Toshiba, and including Pioneer and JVC, introduced the SuperDensity Disc. For a year and a half, the companies tried without much luck to interest consumers in the two formats. In 1995, the groups united to form the DVD Consortium, later called the DVD Forum. That cooperation helped the single new DVD format to be adopted rapidly. DVDs use ISO standard MPEG-2 video compression and digital audio, typically delivered as Dolby Digital AC-3 or DTS surround sound. Using standard, interoperable formats based on patent pools from established technical leaders meant that DVDs could be delivered by any hardware manufacturer under reasonable and non-discriminatory licensing.' See http://www.roughlydrafted.com/2007/08/29/origins-of-the-blu-ray-vs-hd-dvd-war/. Accessed 8 February 2008.

[375] See EU Commission press release IP/03/1152; 07/08/2003, 'Commission clears Philips/Sony CD Licensing programme' and EC Commission press release IP/06/139, 09/02/2006, 'Commission closes investigation following changes to Philips CD-Recordable Disc Patent Licensing'. For the famous Chinese Taipei case see OECD roundtable discussions regarding Intellectual Property in 2004, 21 Jan. 2005, 117 *3*. http://www.oecd.org/dataoecd/61/48/3430 6055.pdf. The Chinese Taipei case resulted in very interesting litigation concerning patent rights and misuse of patent rights, see the ITC case Notice of Commission on Determination of No Violation of section 337, In the matter of Certain Recordable Compact Discs and Rewritable Compact Discs, Investigation

complaint by the licensees was that the patent pools contained patents that were not necessary or essential to produce products under the technology, and that the royalty fees amounted to more than 40 per cent of the end product price. This makes it impossible for licensees to produce products profitably. There was no competing technology and the available firms, which had the relevant know-how and assets to develop a competing technology, were already included in the pool as licensors.[376]

It is evident that global standards are derived from joint R&D ventures performed by very large firms. Undoubtedly, the VCR technology and CD technology have been beneficial to consumers. However, the question is whether such joint efforts are or should be encompassed by the NCRPA. Should large firms such as Sony and Philips be allowed to take advantage of the NCRPA? Would they not be able to defend themselves under the regular antitrust laws? Should competition only govern design or product diversification of the individual VCR recorders or CD recorders? From an antitrust law perspective it must be considered more beneficial if the parties perform research independently and both parties, under the pressure of competition, independently came to the conclusion that certain technologies are preferred. Thereafter they enter into agreements on standard. Is society not better off with Sony and Philips competing, not only in design and minor improvements of products, but also for the best technology for storing music or films?

Interestingly, in the pharmaceutical industry the opposite situation obtains. In the pharmaceutical industry, R&D firms are relatively small in comparison with the larger pharmaceutical firms, which are more focused on distribution and obtaining the approval of the different FDA authorities globally. There is anecdotal evidence that large pharmaceutical firms shelve new innovations by entering joint R&D agreements with exclusive

---

No. 337-TA-474. See also United States Court of Appeals for the Federal Circuit *U.S. Philips Corp. v. International Trade Commission*, 424 F.3d 1179 (Fed. Cir. 2005). For an even earlier case concerning Philips and Sony cooperation into VCR video technology, see Commission decision Videocassette recorders, OJ 1977 L 47/42. Cf. Maurits Dolmans, 'Standards for Standards', (2002) 26 *Fordham International Law Journal*, 163, 175. The US FTC also did an early analysis of the licensing agreements for CD-ROM pool in the 1980s. See Carl Shapiro, 'Navigating the Patent thicket: Cross Licenses, Patent Pools and Standard Setting', in Adam Jaffe, et al. (eds), *Innovation Policy and the Economy* (2001), 20.

[376]   The CD, DVD and Blu-ray patent pools are discussed in Björn Lundqvist, *Standardization under EU Competition Rules and US Antitrust Laws – The Rise and the Limits of Self-Regulation* (Edward Elgar, 2014), 251 et seq., 277 et seq.

joint exploitation covenants.[377] This eliminates the possibility for the exclusive R&D firms to market or address other firms in case their 'partner' in the R&D agreement refuses to make use of the R&D result, mostly derived from the smaller R&D firm. If such a pharmaceutical firm was considered dominant, such a covenant could have been declared anticompetitive under the antitrust laws. However, since the R&D agreement falls under the NCRPA, the R&D-focused firm is not likely to launch a private suit for the reasons discussed above.[378] The smaller firm in the example above cannot terminate the contract since an antitrust suit under the NCRPA is simply too burdensome.[379] It is too difficult to establish, for example, dominance by the larger firm. In the end, this can lead to the stiffening of the pharmaceutical sector as such, given that the larger firms do not conduct R&D with the same intensity as the smaller firms.[380]

The technology markets for electronic consumer goods and the mobile telephone markets can be profitably harvested, if the firms have the right essential patents under relevant standard. Hence, several firms have decided not to produce any products anymore, but only to conduct R&D, create technology standards and license patents (and trademarks) under technology standards. Philips and Qualcomm appear to be pursuing this strategy. Since they have in many circumstances exited the product market, they are, under the NCRPA, presumably not exposed to the same antitrust scrutiny as the producing firms. Therefore, they can negotiate and agree on conduct which the producing firms are not allowed to negotiate or agree upon. It remains to be seen whether this will provide an incentive for more innovation and for more firms to exit the product markets and focus on R&D.

---

[377]   See Saami Zain, 'Suppression of Innovation or Collaborative Efficiencies?: An Antitrust Analysis of a Research & Development Collaboration That Led to the Shelving of a Promising Drug', (2006) 5 *J. Marshall Rev. Intell. Prop. L*, 347, 350 et seq. with references. See also Davis Hamilton, 'Silent Treatment: How Genetech, Novartis Stifled a Promising Drug', (2005) *Wall. St. J.*, A1.

[378]   Good sources are hard to find. See, however, generally, Kurt M. Saunders & Linda Levine, 'Better, Faster, Cheaper-later: What Happens When Technologies are Suppressed', (2004) 11 *Mich. Telecomm. & Tech. L. Rev*, 23.

[379]   For discussion regarding such a case see Saami Zain, 'Suppression of Innovation or Collaborative Efficiencies?: An Antitrust Analysis of a Research & Development Collaboration That Led to the Shelving of a Promising Drug', (2006) 5 *J. Marshall Rev. Intell. Prop. L*, 347, 350 et seq.

[380]   See Davis Hamilton, 'Silent Treatment: How Genetech, Novartis Stifled a Promising Drug', (2005) *Wall. St. J.*, A1.

In the pharmaceutical industry the situation is different. The invention of new substances and drugs in collaboration may imply that the drug still gets suppressed by the firms which conduct the relevant approval and distribution service. Exclusive exploitation stipulations can be common covenants in the pharmaceutical industry. However, the anti-commons or the patent thicket do not exist in the pharmaceutical sector where the rule 'one product one patent' still applies.

Nonetheless, a similar development to the evolution in the pharmaceutical sector may also play out in the telecommunication and consumer electronic markets. R&D will be conducted by small specific R&D firms, often situated in connection to a university and at least partially funded by public means. The larger firms will instead employ and instruct these smaller R&D-exclusive firms in joint R&D ventures, while they provide the standards-setting and joint licensing service.[381] Manufacturing-only firms produce actual products under joint production ventures or on an assignment basis from the larger firms. They enter licensing agreements under IP arrangements or technology pools. The manufacturing-only firms also need to license trademarks from the larger firms focused on standards-setting.

All these collaborations in the electronic, telecommunication and pharmaceutical industries could presumably today be encompassed by the NCRPA. Interestingly, the NCRPA rather protects the stronger of the participants of the joint R&D venture or IP arrangement against the other party in that agreement from making use of the antitrust laws. Thus, if the above hypotheses are accurate, the NCRPA has developed into a protection for the system leaders within the R&D or production collaborations against antitrust suits from their counterparts rather than third parties or consumers in general.

---

[381] A difference between SDOs and SSOs is that SSOs often employ a 'pay to play' rule, and even though SDOs are inexpensive in comparison, SSOs are clearly in some industries winning in the competition against SDOs. Cf. Carl Cargill, 'Intellectual Property Rights and Standard Setting Organizations: An Overview of Failed Evolution', (2002) 27 March *FTC/DOJ Hearings on Competition and Intellectual Property Law and Policy in the Knowledge-Based Economy*, 1, 6.

3.3　THE EU ANTITRUST REGULATION OF RESEARCH AND DEVELOPMENT

3.3.1　Introduction

In the EU, the focus on R&D collaborations from an EU competition law perspective has fluctuated over the years. From a hesitant attitude during the very early years of the Community to a more intrusive application of EU competition law, with the introduction of the first block exemption in 1985 (Commission Regulation (EEC) No. 418/85 of 19 December 1984 on the application of Article 85(3) of the Treaty to categories of research and development agreements (hereinafter the 1984 or old block exemption)).[382] The EU Commission returned to a more lenient treatment of R&D collaborations in the contemporary jurisprudence, while we can still see that the Commission is less moderate in the latest block exemption and horizontal guidelines from 2010 compared with the block exemption and thereto connected guidelines from 2001.

The section is divided into the following parts. Initially the historical development will be analysed. Given that today neither the EU courts nor the Commission generate any great amount of case law or decisions, some older cases reflecting the Commission analysis of joint R&D collaborations under both the first and the third paragraph of Article 101 TFEU will be discussed. Secondly, the current legal regime consisting of the R&D block exemption and the applicable guidelines will be scrutinised so as to establish what conduct is prohibited by Article 101 TFEU and what is not. Thirdly, the interaction between technology or industrial standardisation and R&D collaborations is reviewed. Fourthly, I conclude.

3.3.2　The Origins of the R&D Exemption

(i)　Introduction

A research and development exemption under Article 101 of the TFEU can be traced back to a notice issued in 1968 where the Commission stated *inter alia* that pure R&D cooperations generally do not restrict competition, on the condition that the parties are free to pursue their own

---

[382]　Commission Regulation (EEC) No. 418/85 of 19 December 1984 on the application of Article 85(3) of the Treaty to categories of research and development agreements, OJ L 53 22.2.1985 p. 5 et seq. (hereinafter the 1984 or old block exemption).

research, and there is no restriction regarding the use of the R&D result (Notice concerning agreements, decisions and concerted practices in the field of cooperation between enterprises (hereinafter the 1968 notice)).[383] The parties should, normally, not be denied access to the results of joint research. The 1968 notice also stated that arrangements, solely between non-competitors, or arrangements between competitors that neither limit the parties' competitive behaviour nor affect the market position of third parties, should be deemed not to fall under the first paragraph.[384]

The notice was applicable for all firms, irrespective of their size and market share. It has been asserted that not limiting the notice to small and medium-sized undertakings was a mistake, and the exemption was later narrowed down, in practice, to apply only to these kinds of firms.[385] A useful argument for such an assertion was that collaborations between large firms, or any collaboration consisting of those holding market power, would almost automatically affect the market position for third parties. Larger collaborating enterprises therefore needed individual exemptions under the third paragraph to enter into R&D agreements.[386]

This development in approach can be detected in the first decisions of the Commission. In *Eurogypsum* the Commission cleared, as not infringing Article 85(1) (now Article 101(1) TFEU), an industry-wide joint research and study carried out by a trade association.[387] All the results

---

[383]   1968 notice, 3, (Notice concerning agreements, decisions and concerted practices in the field of cooperation between enterprises, OJ C 75/3 27.7.1968 3 (hereinafter the 1968 notice). See also Commission, Report on Competition Policy 1971, 46.

[384]   1968 notice, 3, paras 3 et seq.

[385]   According to the Commission, Report on Competition Policy 1971, 45, the notice should be utilised with discretion and certain reservations when dealing with large enterprises. See also Hanns Ullrich, 'Competitor Cooperation and the Evolution of Competition Law: Issues for Research in a Perspective of Globalisation', in Joseph Drexl (ed.), *The Future of Transnational Antitrust From Comparative to Common Competition Law* (2003), 188 et seq. See also Valentine Korah, *R&D and the EEC Competition Rules Regulation 418/85* (ESC Publishing Limited 1986), 13 fn. 2.

[386]   Hanns Ullrich, 'Competitor Cooperation and the Evolution of Competition Law: Issues for Research in a Perspective of Globalisation', in Joseph Drexl (ed.), *The Future of Transnational Antitrust From Comparative to Common Competition Law* (2003), 188 et seq. with references. The possibility of individual exemption under Article 101(3) has now been abolished. See Council Regulation (EC) No 1/2003 of 16 December 2002 on the implementation of the rules on competition laid down in Articles 81 and 82 of the Treaty, OJ L 1, 04.01.2003, 1 et seq. (hereinafter Regulation 1/2003).

[387]   Commission, Report on Competition Policy 1971, 46 et seq.

were made available to members, who were not restrained from carrying out their own research in the same or other fields of research. The trade association was also open to anyone who wished to become a member. Moreover, the result was not only accessible to the members but it was also widely published.[388] The research conducted by the parties was also of a 'basic' nature and did not concern product development or applied research.[389]

The Commission stated in *Henkel-Colgate* from 1971 that a joint research venture by two large enterprises active on a worldwide oligopolistic market for a homogeneous product (textile detergents), with high barriers to entry, can violate the prohibition stipulated in Article 85(1) (now Article 101(1) TFEU).[390] It stated that, in the market for textile detergent, competition is largely not performed with the price parameter, but with innovation and technical progress. A competitor can only acquire an advantage over his competitors by improving quality and use by means of research, and by showing that the product is technically superior through advertisement. Thus, an agreement where two competitors merge their R&D in such a market can limit competition. The agreement was considered a violation of Article 85(1).[391] The Commission, however, exempted the research under Article 85(3) (now Article 101(3) TFEU), indicating that the collaboration only concerned research, and not manufacturing and distribution. The parties would have access to the patents and know-how that stem from the joint research and sell the end product under separate trademarks. The Commission conditioned the collaboration on the parties giving information to the Commission regarding any changes in ownership or alteration of the rules for the cooperation.[392]

It is interesting to see that the Commission, even though stating in the 1968 notice that 'pure' R&D collaboration normally did not fall within

---

[388] Commission decision, Eurogypsym, OJ 1968 L 57/9.

[389] Commission, Report on Competition Policy 1971, 46 et seq.

[390] Commission decision 1971 Henkel-Colgate, OJ 1972 L 14/14. See Commission, Report on Competition Policy 1971, 47. See also Valentine Korah, *R&D and the EEC Competition Rules Regulation 418/85* (ESC Publishing Limited 1986), 13.

[391] The Commission, Report on Competition Policy 1971, 46 et seq.

[392] Ibid. Another early case was the *ACEC-Berliet* case, see Commission decision 1968 ACEC-Berliet, OJ 1968 L 201/7.

then Article 85(1), declared already in 1971 in *Henkel-Colgate* that such an agreement was in need of an exemption.[393]

(ii) Period of more intense scrutiny

At the end of the 1970s and the beginning of the 1980s, the Commission focused more on R&D agreements.[394] It began to examine cooperative research efforts, initiated by large enterprises that acted on markets which displayed technically oriented competition. The Commission especially examined whether the R&D activities were pooled in highly concentrated markets. If the parties were competitors or potential competitors, the R&D venture would almost automatically be deemed to violate paragraph 1. However, the main focus appears to have been on the ancillary restraints rather than on the research as such. In fact the Commission never declined an application for exemption under paragraph 3 regarding an R&D venture.[395] Accordingly, it would only refuse an exemption, if the R&D agreement stipulated territorial exclusivity for the distribution of the researched product that would correspond to a violation of the block exemption for vertical agreements (that is, violate the aim of the common or internal market).[396] The Commission never prevented the combination or merger of R&D departments.[397] The general acceptance of R&D agreements was based on a general belief of their contributing effects to technical and economic progress and the aim of creating the internal market.[398]

---

[393]   The Commission's decision was therefore criticised, see Valentine Korah, *R&D and the EEC Competition Rules Regulation 418/85* (ESC Publishing Limited 1986), 13 et seq.

[394]   See, e.g., Commission decision Rank/Sopelem, OJ 1975 L 29/20; Commission decision Vacuum Interrupters Ltd, OJ 1977 L 48/32; Commission decision GEC-Weir Sodium Circulators, OJ 1977 L 327/26; Commission decision Rockwell/Iveco, OJ 1978 L 224/19. Cf. Hanns Ullrich, 'Competitor Cooperation and the Evolution of Competition Law: Issues for Research in a Perspective of Globalisation', in Joseph Drexl (ed.), *The Future of Transnational Antitrust From Comparative to Common Competition Law* (2003), 188 et seq.

[395]   Hanns Ullrich, 'Competitor Cooperation and the Evolution of Competition Law: Issues for Research in a Perspective of Globalisation', in Joseph Drexl (ed.), *The Future of Transnational Antitrust From Comparative to Common Competition Law* (2003), 191 et seq. with references. Correspondingly, the US antitrust enforcement agencies have never opposed a pure joint R&D venture. See discussion *supra* section 3.2.3(iii).

[396]   Ibid.

[397]   Ibid.

[398]   Ibid.

For example in the *Rank/Sopelem* case,[399] where the parties held an aggregated market share of 20 per cent of the common market for television and camera lenses, the parties agreed jointly to conduct research, development and jointly to manufacture the end result (lenses, and so on). They also geographically divided up the world market through a network of exclusive distribution rights.[400] They furthermore agreed to specialise in certain aspects of the research and the production and, thus, to purchase the outsourced R&D service from each other.

The Commission exempted the collective effort after having judged it anticompetitive and in violation of the first paragraph. It found that specialisation agreed upon in *Rank/Sopelem* was in itself anticompetitive, since it eliminated a developer of the outsourced service. Before entering the agreement, the parties were, if not actual, at least potential competitors in these segments of the value chain.[401] Thus, the parties were not

---

[399] See Commission decision Rank/Sopelem, OJ 1975 L 29/20.

[400] Some of these early individual exemption cases also encompassed joint commercialisation. E.g., in the *De Laval-Stork* case, the Commission stated that in particular cases joint marketing is justified. Close technical cooperation with the purchaser was necessary in order for the market to be researched, orders obtained, and purchasers' requirements to be satisfied and for understanding the needs in relation to production and research. All had to be conducted with the same team of technicians that also provide the after-sales service which was of special importance in this industry. See Commission decision De Laval-Stork, OJ 1977 L 215/11.

[401] Interestingly, there seem not to have been any barriers for conducting individual research based on patents held by either party. Several commentators believed that the Commission was too hasty to find the two parties potential competitors. They foremost criticised the *ex post* viewpoint. For example, in the *Vacuum Interrupters* case, Commission decision Vacuum Interrupters Ltd, OJ 1977 L 48/32, the Commission stipulated that even though neither party manufactured vacuum interrupters, their experience in the field of heavy electrical equipment might well have led them to extend the range of products to also include vacuum interrupters. Thus, at least, in the medium term they could conduct business separately. See Commission, Report on Competition Policy 1976, 39 et seq. See also for similar case the *KEWA* case where Bayer, Hoechst, Gelsenberg and Nukem were, according to the Commission, able separately to perform the business that the joint venture was supposed to perform (see Commission decision KEWA, OJ 1976 L 51/16). Some commentators believe that this is a too wide definition, cf., e.g., Frank Fine, 'EEC Anti-Trust Aspects of Production Joint Ventures', (1992) 13 *European Competition Law Review* 206; Tao Xiong & James Kirkbride, 'Controlling Research and Development Co-operation through EC Competition Controls: Some Concerns', (1998) 19 *Comp. Law.*, 296, 300.

competitors when entering the agreement, but their independent development could potentially have led them to become direct competitors. They
were potential competitors, or at least potential unilateral entrants of the
relevant market. In other words, by eliminating the workforce and
thereby the required knowledge needed in order to perform the service
outsourced to each other, the agreement eliminated the potential competitive pressure the parties imposed on each other.[402]

The Commission exempted the *Rank/Sopelem* joint effort under the
then applicable Article 85(3) because the specialisation helped the parties
to acquire economies of scale and scope in R&D.[403] It allowed such
ancillary restraints that it found indispensable for the attainment of the
main purpose of the agreement. This implied that the geographic
exclusivity scheme with absolute sales prohibition had to be modified in
order to allow for either party to make passive sales in the territories
designated to the other party. The absolute protection of national market
was eliminated. However, reimbursement for any costs due to the free
after-sales service provided by the importing party was exempted.
Moreover, in the event the agreement was terminated, the clauses
restricting the freedom of the parties to administer their industrial
property rights, to do research with third parties, and to use trademarks
and company names acquired before the cooperation, had to be either
deleted or limited for the agreement to be exempted under paragraph 3.
The Commission also held that the restriction that both parties had to
approve third party licensing would eliminate access to the result and the
parties deleted the provision.[404]

As the *Rank/Sopelem* case indicates, the Commission generally built its
decisions during this period on the fact that it often found the parties to
be potential competitors. The importance of finding them at least
potential competitors is derived from the standpoint of the Commission
that non-competing parties could enter an R&D agreement without
violating Article 85 EC Treaty (now 101 TFEU).[405] The mere creations of

---

[402] The exclusive distribution rights were also declared incompatible with
Article 85(1) (now 101(1)), see Commission decision Rank/Sopelem, OJ 1975 L
29/20.

[403] Ibid.

[404] Nevertheless, the findings of their research should remain confidential.
See Commission decision Rank/Sopelem, OJ 1975 L 29/20.

[405] See, e.g., the 1968 notice concerning agreements, decisions and concerted
practice in the field of cooperation between enterprises, OJ C 75/3 27.7.1968, 3,
see also Commission, Report on Competition Policy 1971, 46.

a joint venture between actual or potential competitors impaired competition irrespective of restrictive covenants to that effect. The fact that the joint effort was not a distinct incorporated company, but created solely on contracts, did not alter the Commission's standpoint.[406]

The broad definition was also derived from logic of a wide notion of potential competition displayed in the US *Penn-Olin* case.[407] According to the Commission there was an inherent anticompetitive effect within the notion of joint ventures when the parents were potential entrants to the market where the joint R&D would supposedly be active.[408] If they were at least potential competitors or entrants, the joint effort would deter both of them from entering the field of the joint R&D, regardless of restriction in the agreements of that effect. Restrictive clauses to that effect were unnecessary, since the firms would, according to the prevailing logic, not 'cannibalise' their own joint research by initiating unilateral efforts.[409] Thus, non-compete covenants were anticompetitive, but not necessary in order to create a similar anticompetitive effect.

---

[406] The mere setting up of a joint venture can be regarded as anticompetitive, even without any restrictions to that effect and without the parents being actual or potential competitors. See Commission decision GEC-Weir Sodium Circulators, OJ 1977 L 327/26, where the Commission states that 'within the field of the joint venture and in related fields [such] parties are likely to coordinate their conduct and be influenced in what would otherwise have been their independent decisions and activities.' The Commission accordingly found the companies to be potential competitors. However, the Commission was open to stretching the notion further, outside the realm of the definition of competitors. With such a definition, all joint ventures would be anticompetitive and in need of an exemption. Such a conclusion would suffice, considering the fact that the parties would independently conduct some kind of research which would not be performed because of the combined effort. However, these efforts may be totally disconnected from each other and not be in competition and the joint venture would still be considered anticompetitive.

[407] *United States v. Penn-Olin Chemical Co.*, 378 U.S. 158, 172 et seq., (1964).

[408] See Valentine Korah, *R&D and the EEC Competition Rules Regulation 418/85* (ESC Publishing Limited 1986), 5. See the US Supreme Court *Penn-Olin* ruling. See *United States v. Penn-Olin Chemical Co.*, 378 U.S. 158, 172–176, (1964).

[409] This line of reasoning is according to some commentators based on the US Supreme Court *Penn-Olin* ruling. See *United States v. Penn-Olin Chemical Co.* 378 U.S. 158, 172–176, (1964). The logic can be thus taken a step further. The theory stipulates that if the parents are potential entrants to the new market, and if one parent would enter, and the other parent is likely to at least stay on as a potential entrant, i.e., the joint effort eliminates a potential competitor. See

However, in the cases that expressed the, for contemporary antitrust scholars somewhat odd, 'potential competition theory', the Commission also found independent covenants to be anticompetitive. For example, exclusivity clauses were not allowed, in either R&D agreements or in licensing agreements with others. They were, according to the Commission, considered to foreclose the parties from third parties and third parties from the result of the R&D. Also, exclusivity purchasing requirements between the joint venture and the parents, or vice versa, were regarded as limiting competition.[410] Thus, despite the broad definition of potential competitors, the question whether the Commission would have found a joint R&D in breach of Article 85 without finding individual covenants in the agreements anticompetitive is not clear.

Indeed, the Commission never found the main purpose of any scrutinised R&D effort to be in breach of Article 85 (now Article 101 TFEU); only 'ancillary' covenants were found anticompetitive enough to establish that the collaboration as a whole was in breach of Article 85(1). However, the Commission's wide definition of what constitutes a competitor affected the test and the notion of what was an anticompetitive covenant. Since the definition of competitors was wider than it is today, clauses that today would be regarded as ancillary restraints or benign, since the parents are not competitors, were viewed as restrictions between competitors during the 1970–80s and, hence, anticompetitive and in need of an exemption under the third paragraph.[411]

Furthermore, scholars during this period were undecided on the issue. Some commentators believed that EU competition law should not only protect competition when parties enter an agreement, but also during the agreement and after the collaboration ends. Thus, if the parties became competitors during the process of the R&D collaboration because of spillover of knowledge between the firms, the independent status of the firms as competitors would have to be protected *ex post*, when the R&D venture had ended. Firms should always be able to utilise the knowledge

---

also Valentine Korah, *R&D and the EEC Competition Rules Regulation 418/85* (ESC Publishing Limited 1986), 5.

[410]   See, e.g., Commission decision KEWA, OJ 1976 L 51/16 (non-compete covenant); Commission decision Rank/Sopelem, OJ 1975 L 29/20; Commission decision Vacuum Interrupters Ltd, OJ 1977 L 48/32; Commission decision GEC-Weir Sodium Circulators, OJ 1977 L 327/26; Commission decision Rockwell/Iveco, OJ 1978 L 224/19; and Commission decision Olivetti/Cannon, OJ 1988 L 52/51 (exclusive purchasing requirement).

[411]   See Horizontal Guidelines, para 56, indicating that the issue of potential competition has to be assessed on a realistic basis.

gain during the R&D venture after the collaboration. Others purported that the competitive relationship between the parties when entering the agreement was the only interesting subject of analysis, and that their gained knowledge under the collaboration should not be taken into consideration.[412]

Irrespective of the issue of the definition of competitor, commentators also pinpointed other factors for establishing whether an agreement was anticompetitive or not. Foreclosure of essential technology for third parties, which in the end leads to fewer choices for consumers, was also considered anticompetitive. Interestingly, during the 1970s the notion, possibly derived from the 1968 notice, that even a joint R&D between non-competitors could be anticompetitive if a third party was negatively affected by the collaboration, was implemented.

Finally, the objective of the creation of the common market was a guiding principle when scrutinising R&D ventures. If the R&D venture foreclosed national markets, it would presumably have been considered anticompetitive. However, if the joint venture was a collaboration between firms that originated from different member states, such a collaboration could be exempted as furthering the creation of the common market, even though objectively anticompetitive.[413]

(iii) The first group exemption
In the Report on Competition Policy of 1983, the Commission took the first steps to limit the notion of what constitutes a competitor.[414] The Commission focused on what constitutes a potential competitor.[415] It

---

[412] Today the *ex ante* viewpoint has been implemented more widely, see, e.g., Horizontal Guidelines, 56, which clearly stipulate that parties cannot be defined as potential competitors merely because the cooperation enables them to carry out the R&D activity. However, it should be stated that EC competition law even protects competition when the parties are not considered competitors. See, e.g., Valentine Korah, *R&D and the EEC Competition Rules Regulation 418/85* (ESC Publishing Limited 1986), 7 et seq.; Alexis Jacquemin & Bernard Spinoit, 'Economic and Legal Aspects of Cooperative Research: A European View', in Barry E. Hawk (ed.), *Antitrust and Trade Policy in the U.S. and the EC 1985* (Bender, Fordham Corporate Law Institute, 1986), 478 et seq.

[413] See the *Nungesser* case, Case 258/78, *L.C. Nungesser KG and Kurt Eisele v. Commission*, [1982] ECR, 2015.

[414] Commission, Report on Competition Policy 1983, 50 et seq.

[415] Ibid. See also the Commission Notice concerning the assessment of the cooperative joint ventures pursuant to Article 85 of the EEC Treaty OJ C 43, 16.02.1993, 2. These principles appear to have been inspired by the US notion of

stated that it wanted to make its assessment of what constituted a potential competitor in the most realistic way possible. For input joint ventures, which included joint R&D efforts, the relevant questions, according to the Commission, were whether (i) the involved investment expenditure substantially exceeded the financing capacity of each partner; (ii) each partner independently enjoyed the necessary technical know-how and source of supply of input products. If the answer was no to either question, the parties should not be regarded as potential competitors.

For production joint ventures and sales joint ventures, the issues were somewhat different: were the partners familiar with the process technology? Were any of the partners not engaged in production? Was the demand large enough to make it feasible for each of the partners to manufacture the product independently? Did both partners have access to the necessary distribution channels? The issue amounted to the evaluation of risk. Can each partner bear the technical and financial risk of conducting research, developing, producing and marketing the end product on its own? If not, the parties were not potential competitors.

The first block exemption in 1984, concerning R&D, mirrored the statements made by the Commission in the 1983 Report.[416] However, the block exemption was also influenced by other considerations:[417] firstly, the initiation and the development of an EU R&D promotion effort under

---

potential competition. See *United States v. Penn-Olin Chemical Co.*, 378 U.S. 158, 169 (1964).

[416]   For discussion regarding the first group exemption see, e.g., generally Manfred Caspari, 'Joint Ventures – The Intersection of Antitrust and Industrial Policy in the EEC', in Barry E. Hawk (ed.), *Antitrust and Trade Policy in the United States and the European Community, 1985* (Bender, Fordham Corporate Law Institute, 1986); Alexis Jacquemin & Bernard Spinoit, 'Economic and Legal Aspects of Cooperative Research: A European View', in Barry E. Hawk (ed.), *Antitrust and Trade Policy in the U.S. and the EC 1985* (Bender, Fordham Corporate Law Institute, 1986); Jürgen Lindemann, 'A Practical Critique of The EEC Joint Research Rules and Proposed Joint Venture Guidelines', in Barry Hawk (ed.), *United States and Common Market Antitrust Policies* (Fordham Corporate Law Institute, 1986); Angus Maciver, 'EEC Competition Policy in High Technology Industries', in Barry E. Hawk (ed.), *Antitrust and Trade Policy in the U.S. and the EC 1985* (Bender, Fordham Corporate Law Institute, 1986); James Venit, 'The Research and Development Block Exemption Regulation', (1985) 10 *European Law Review*, 151; Eric White, 'Research and Development Joint Ventures under EEC Competition Law', (1985) 16 *IIC*, 663.

[417]   The 1984 block exemption, 5 et seq.

the Community research programmes;[418] secondly, the international debate about competitiveness;[419] and, thirdly, the general workload of the Commission.

The Commission needed to take the new R&D funding programme into consideration when drafting the first group exemption. In contrast to funding schemes under US antitrust law, European joint R&D ventures that receive EU funding can be found anticompetitive under Article 101 TFEU.[420] In comparison, under the US state action exemption, firms receiving aid under public funding schemes would, under certain circumstances, be exempted under the Sherman Act.[421]

The international debate regarding competitiveness raged mostly in the US and resulted in the enactment of the NCRA in 1984. The act stipulated an exemption and safe harbour for R&D collaborations between firms. The first EU R&D group exemption was inspired by the NCRA. However, it was construed differently.

Finally, the Commission had a great backlog of agreements, which had been notified but not yet scrutinised under the individual exemption procedure. By making the block exemption retroactively applicable, the Commission was able to reduce the number of agreements to be analysed.[422]

---

[418] See, e.g., the seventh Cordis Framework programme for R&D, http:// cordis.europa.eu/en/home.html. Last visited 2009-04-01. See also for state aid, The Commission, 'Community Framework for State Aid for Research and Development and Innovation' OJ C 323 of 30.12.2006, 1.

[419] Hanns Ullrich, 'Competitor Cooperation and the Evolution of Competition Law: Issues for Research in a Perspective of Globalisation', in Joseph Drexl (ed.), *The Future of Transnational Antitrust From Comparative to Common Competition Law* (2003), 193 et seq. Regarding the international debate on competitiveness, see Sylvia Ostry & Richard Nelson, *Techno-Nationalism and Techno-Globalism Conflict and Cooperation* (The Brookings Institute 1995), 62 et seq.

[420] Cf. Hanns Ullrich, 'Competitor Cooperation and the Evolution of Competition Law: Issues for Research in a Perspective of Globalisation', in Joseph Drexl (ed.), *The Future of Transnational Antitrust From Comparative to Common Competition Law* (2003), 193 et seq. See also Case 164/98 *DIR International Film Srl et al v. Commission* [2000] ECR I-447, para 29.

[421] Cf. Lawrence Sullivan & Warren Grimes, *The Law of Antitrust: An Integrated Handbook* (Thomson/West 2006), 798 et seq.

[422] At the same time, the Commission also introduced a block exemption for licensing agreements. See, Commission, Report on Competition Policy 1984, 42. It should be acknowledged that some firms possibly stopped sending agreements to the Commission because of the extended time period which they had to endure before getting them exempted. Jürgen Lindemann, 'A Practical Critique of The

The first group exemption cleared joint R&D and joint exploitation of the R&D result.[423] Indeed, cooperation could revolve around R&D, and exploitation of the result through licensing of intellectual property rights and joint manufacturing. Joint sales (that is, distribution) of the innovated products were not included in the group exemption. The parties had to sell the end products independently.[424]

The group exemption actually focused on and gave incentive for specialisation in parts of the joint R&D. The parties could decide unilaterally to research parts of the contemplated result and then later combine the individual findings. Thus, the block exemption regarded specialisation under joint R&D as anticompetitive yet available for exemption.

In comparison with the 1968 notice, the block exemption made clear in the recitals that pure R&D collaboration can – in certain circumstances – fall within the then Article 85(1) EC Treaty where such parties agree not to carry out other R&D in the same field or other fields. Thus, pure R&D collaborations were with the introduction of the 1984 block exemption not considered *per se* legal anymore.

The first block exemption also stipulated a quite far-reaching requirement: the parties needed to stipulate the object of the research. This requirement has, for some reason, been scrapped in the contemporary block exemption. Interestingly, not requiring the parties to state the object of the research limits the possibility for any agency or private plaintiff to determine whether the agreement is, in fact, anticompetitive. By not having to state what the research concerns, the possibility of determining

---

EEC Joint Research Rules and Proposed Joint Venture Guidelines', in Barry Hawk (ed.), *United States and Common Market Antitrust Policies* (Fordham Corporate Law Institute, 1986), 132 et seq.

[423]   See Article 2(e) and (f) of the 1984 block exemption. See also Valentine Korah, *R&D and the EEC Competition Rules Regulation 418/85* (ESC Publishing Limited 1986), 19 et seq. Hanns Ullrich, 'Competitor Cooperation and the Evolution of Competition Law: Issues for Research in a Perspective of Globalisation', in Joseph Drexl (ed.), *The Future of Transnational Antitrust From Comparative to Common Competition Law* (2003), 193. It should be noted that under the notion of permitted exploitation, the parties can license any intellectual property right evolved under the cooperation.

[424]   In this case two firms wanted jointly to produce a product, without prior joint R&D, and the block exemption for specialisation should be utilised. See the 1984 block exemption, 1 et seq. However, if they jointly exploited the results of prior joint R&D between themselves, the old R&D block exemption should have been utilised. See also Commission, Report on Competition Policy 1971, 38 et seq.

whether the parties are competitors in relation to the contemplated R&D is minimised. Moreover, eliminating the requirement of stating the purpose of collaboration eliminates the possibility of analysing whether the objective and breadth of the research would correspond to a standardisation agreement, or a patent pool agreement.

The first block exemption stipulated the restrictive exempted ancillary clauses (the 'grey' list),[425] the ancillary, non-restrictive clauses (the 'white' list)[426] and the hard-core, 'black' clauses.[427] The white list encompassed the clauses which the parties could incorporate in an R&D agreement without running the risk of violating the prohibition in Article 101 TFEU. The black list, on the contrary, contained the clauses which would automatically render the agreement anticompetitive. The grey list, finally, contained the covenants that the firms can use when their collaboration was encompassed by block exemption.

If the specific agreement stipulated covenants that restricted competition and were not anticipated in Articles 4, 5 or 6, the opposition procedure could be implemented.[428] According to the opposition procedure the parties could ask the Commission for an individual exemption of the concerned clauses. If the Commission did not oppose the clauses within six months of the notification, the agreement was automatically exempted.

Furthermore, there was a time limit for the exemption of five years, starting from when the result was jointly introduced into the market.[429] The exemption could, however, be extended if, after these five years, the combined market share of the parties did not exceed 20 per cent. If the parties to the block exemption were competitors in the market for the product, which could be replaced by the result of the R&D, the block exemption was not applicable if their combined market share was to exceed 20 per cent at the time of entering the agreement.[430]

The rule that the immunity elapsed after five years, should the parties hold a combined market share of 20 per cent, implies that the Commission held a so-called *ex post* viewpoint. It took into consideration that the

---

[425]   Article 4 of the 1984 block exemption.
[426]   Article 5 of the 1984 block exemption.
[427]   Article 6 of the 1984 block exemption.
[428]   Article 7 of the 1984 block exemption.
[429]   Article 3 of the 1984 block exemption.
[430]   However, the block exemption was still applicable for five years after entering the agreement, if the parties increased their combined market share above 20 per cent after concluding the agreement. See Article 3 of the 1984 block exemption.

knowledge exchanged and developed during the joint arrangement would ultimately create two competitors out of two non-competitors. Hence, parties that were non-competitors when entering the agreement were, according to the underlying logic of the block exemption, competitors after the five years had passed and therefore the block exemption expired.

In draft versions of the first block exemption regulation, the criterion for creating a market power ceiling originally amounted to no more than one of the three leading firms being allowed to be part of an R&D agreement.[431] However, the Commission found that such a rule was difficult to construe and apply. Instead, the 20 per cent ceiling was enacted. The Commission was also of the opinion that the individual exemption under the third paragraph could be, in individual cases, granted, if the ceiling was breached.[432] Even though the new regulation was enacted, the 1968 notice was left intact. This indicated that pure joint R&D ventures that, according to recital 2 of the block exemption, did not restrict individual R&D fell outside Article 85(1).[433]

In the contemporary R&D block exemption the ceiling and the time limit have been extended. Nonetheless, what is most striking when comparing the old regime under the 1984 block exemption with the new system is the straightforward approach of the old regime. The Director-General for Competition at the time, Manfred Caspari, discussed the steps in the then-applicable R&D block exemption. He stated that the point of departure should be to establish whether the parties are competitors or potential competitors.[434] Such analyses should be done realistically and by making use of the criteria set forth in the Commission Competition Report of 1983. Thus, a crucial issue was whether – taking into account all relevant economic circumstances – the partners could

---

[431]   If the joint effort also includes joint production, the participants could not have a combined turnover exceeding 5,000 million ECU, see Commission, Report on Competition Policy 1983, 44.

[432]   Valentine Korah, *R&D and the EEC Competition Rules Regulation 418/85* (ESC Publishing Limited 1986), 31.

[433]   Commission, Report on Competition Policy 1984, 38.

[434]   However, first establish whether the then Article 85(1) is applicable in light of the Commission Notice on agreements of minor importance which do not appreciably restrict competition. Cf. Manfred Caspari, 'Joint Ventures – The Intersection of Antitrust and Industrial Policy in the EEC', in Barry E. Hawk (ed.), *Antitrust and Trade Policy in the United States and the European Community, 1985* (Bender, Fordham Corporate Law Institute, 1986), 461 et seq.

reasonably be expected to enter the market for the joint venture individu-ally. Would the R&D venture operate actually or potentially in a market where the parents are active or could have entered independently? Thus, even though the joint venture would conduct research with the aim of a product market neither parent was active in, the JV could still be considered an R&D collaboration between competitors if both parents were potential entrants to this product market. In such a case, the horizontal collaboration would run the risk of the Commission consider-ing it as limiting competition. Such a situation would thus inherently be anticompetitive under the first paragraph, at least if the Commission also would have found some restrictive ancillary restraints. If this was not the case, the joint venture would not, by its mere incorporation, restrict competition.

Caspari continued and addressed the issue of joint efforts that operate in an upstream or downstream market (vertically) from its parents. The competition between the parents could then, according to Caspari, be restricted depending on the importance of the upstream (R&D) input for the downstream products. Moreover, third parties could be foreclosed from markets. The anticompetitive or the foreclosing effects could depend on stipulations of exclusivity between the joint effort and the parents.

In these cases there were, according to the Commission, both an inherent anticompetitive effect of the joint effort and a possible anti-competitive effect originating from the restrictions stipulated in the agreement. The inherent risk would increase, depending on the economic importance of the joint R&D effort for the downstream parents. Was the joint effort so important that their cost structures or products became same or similar? In the mind of the representatives of the Commission, the anticompetitive effects of the restraints were mostly to be connected to the stipulation of exclusivity.

According to Caspari, the number of market participants, and the economic strength of the parties, needed to be established within the above analysis of the barriers to entry.[435]

If the joint effort fell within Article 85(1) EC Treaty, applicable at the time, the next step, according to Caspari, was to see whether it was covered by a block exemption. If that was not the case, an independent application of Article 85(3) would follow. Caspari stated that before applying the third paragraph in the individual case, the Commission had to satisfy itself that there is still effective competition present on the

---

[435]   Ibid.

relevant market with the joint venture. In addition, the Commission would make a reasonable economic assessment of whether the restrictions were indispensable with regard to subject matter, geographic extent or duration for the formation and viability of the joint venture.[436]

In the contemporary jurisprudence, firstly, the definition of competitors is restricted. Secondly, there is a large 'grey' area in between the harbour of the R&D block exemption and where Article 101(1) TFEU actually is applicable. In this 'grey' area, a plaintiff needs to show that the collaboration has market power before Article 101(1) is applicable.[437] This can be complicated. The old system, in comparison, was clearer: the first paragraph was quite easily breached when the plaintiff could show that the parties were competitors or potential competitors to each other or to the joint venture or if the market position of third parties was affected by the collaboration. Thereafter, the defendant had to rebut the *prima facie* presumption by showing, for example, that it had no market power, the parties were not competitors or that the collaboration created efficiencies. However, clarity had a price. At least theoretically, joint R&D which was efficient, or enhanced innovation rate or even enhanced rivalry, could be caught by Article 85 if the defendant was not able to convince the court that the requirements in the third paragraph were fulfilled. Thus, the old system, at least potentially, could have had a dampening effect on potential beneficial joint R&D ventures.

3.3.3   Case Law Development

(i)   Definition of competitor
The development of EU competition law which would eventually lead to a narrower application of Article 101(1) started with criticism of the notion of 'competitor' in joint venture cases. Shortly after the inauguration of the first R&D block exemption, specific criticisms were raised. The Commission applied too wide a definition of 'competitor'. The exemption was not wide enough.

One of the first decisions to be criticised, the so-called *BP/Kellogg* case, involved BP International Inc (BP) and the firm MW Kellogg Co.

---

[436]   Ibid.
[437]   Horizontal Guidelines paras 39 et seq. The definition is tangent to the definition of dominance in the 82 Guidelines paras 11 et seq.

(Kellogg).[438] BP had discovered – through individual research – a new way to produce ammonia. Before commercialisation, it needed a processing plant to be designed and built, and since BP lacked experience in building such a facility it approached Kellogg. Kellogg was to design, build and develop the production technique and manage the processing plant. The Commission was notified of the joint production agreement. The Commission found the parties were neither competitors nor potential competitors. Nonetheless, the agreement did not benefit from the group exemption for R&D, since it contained restrictions of exploitation of products and processes that were not *jointly* researched and developed. The agreement stated that BP should not make the catalyst production method available to firms other than Kellogg. Since BP had unilaterally discovered the catalyst method for producing ammonia independently of Kellogg, the restriction of only making the method available to Kellogg violated the group exemption.[439]

The Commission granted an individual exemption under Article 85(3), finding the agreement anticompetitive but eligible for an exemption. According to the Commission, the exclusivity restraint was necessary and reasonable because of the substantial resources both parties needed to invest in the project.

Valentine Korah expressed some concerns regarding the fact that the Commission exempted the agreement instead of finding it a non-infringement of Article 85(1).[440] Referring to the *Remia and Nutricia* case[441] and the *Pronuptia* case,[442] she pointed to the fact that the Court of Justice of the European Communities (CJEU) had implemented the

---

[438] See Commission decision BP/Kellogg, OJ 1985 L 369/6. The *BP/Kellogg* case was the second case the Commission decided under the newly initiated block exemption. See the Commission, Report on Competition Policy, 1985, 77 et seq.

[439] From the Commission, Report on Competition Policy 1985 it seems that there were also restrictions regarding other innovations developed before the initiation of the joint effort, see 39 and 78.

[440] Valentine Korah, 'Critical Comments on the Commission's Recent Decisions exempting Joint Ventures to Exploit Research that Needs Further Development', (1987) 12 *European Law Review*, 18.

[441] Case 42/84, *Remia BV and NV Verenigde Bedrijven Nutricia v. Commission* [1985] ECR 2545.

[442] Case 161/84, *Pronuplia de Paris GmbH v. Pronuptia de Paris Irmgard Scliillgalis* [1986] ECR 353.

ancillary doctrine and that restraints that are indispensable for a pro-competitive agreement were not to be caught by the first paragraph.[443] Accordingly, this was important because if the Commission had found that no violation had been committed, the parties would not have needed to seek an individual exemption and, hence, not been obliged to wait for an answer before initiating the joint effort. This would have saved both cost and time for all parties involved, according to Korah.[444]

(a) Optical Fibres[445]   *Optical Fibres* concerned Corning Ltd, a US firm which invented and developed optical fibres in the 1970s for transferring data and other broadband communication.[446] It was a major invention and breakthrough for communication. Corning held several patents on the technology but there were also competitors and other competing technologies, such as the 'incumbent technology' consisting of copper threads. In fact the incumbent technology of copper threads did have a remarkable comeback when that technology also developed

---

[443]   Both the European and the US ancillary restraint doctrine are applicable also when the main purpose of the agreement is not anticompetitive, see Bellamy & Child, *European Community Law of Competition* (Oxford University Press 2008), 569 et seq. and Lawrence Sullivan & Warren Grimes, *The Law of Antitrust: An Integrated Handbook* (Thomson/West 2006), 702 et seq.

[444]   The Commission probably did not find the restraint ancillary since the non-competition or exclusivity clause restricted not only the parties involved but also foreclosed third party access to BP's new innovation. See Commission, Report on Competition Policy 1994, 106. Today such a clause would probably be regarded as neither restricting the parties nor foreclosing any third parties. The contemplated plant would create more output which would decrease prices. In other words, it would be viewed as ancillary to a benign or pro-competitive joint effort. Third parties, on the other hand, need to come up with competing technologies. The issue today would have been whether, under the ancillary restraints doctrine, Kellogg would have entered into the agreement without the exclusivity clause or perhaps objectively whether any firm in Kellogg's position would have entered into such an agreement without the exclusivity covenant. If not, the exclusivity clause would have been accepted under the ancillary restraints doctrine.

[445]   For a further discussion see Björn Lundqvist, *Standardization under EU Competition Rules and US Antitrust Laws – The Rise and the Limits of Self-Regulation* (Edward Elgar, 2014), 214 et seq. See also Marcus Glader, *Innovation Markets and Competition Analysis* (Cheltenham, Edward Elgar, 2006), 214 et seq.

[446]   See Commission decision Optical Fibres, OJ 1986 L 236/30.

through innovations.[447] Corning had entered into several joint development agreements including either licensing agreements or joint venture
agreements or both with the major cable manufacturers and telecom firms
in the largest EU member states (incumbent former national monopolies).
Subsequently Corning exclusively licensed the optical fibre technology
under its patents in respective member states to the respective joint
venture or in some cases directly to the major national cable manufacturer.[448] The Commission stated that at the time of signing these
agreements the parties were neither competitors nor potential competitors
in the optical fibres technology (market) because of the patents held by
Corning. The major cable manufacture and telecommunication firms and
Corning were not competitors since Corning had invented and fenced off
the optical fibre technology with patents. No one could utilise the
technology without infringing the patents; hence, there were no competitors to Corning.[449]

Given that the parents of the joint ventures were not competitors, the
Commission was mostly concerned about the competition between the
different joint ventures set up in each member state. The joint venture
agreements did not stipulate any restrictions regarding selling into each
other's territories. However, the licensing agreements stipulated restrictions based on the national intellectual property rights limiting parallel
trade. It is moreover alluded to in the decision that Corning as a major
shareholder of the joint ventures could limit each venture's output in
order to limit cross-border sales within the EU, thus preventing the joint
ventures in the different member states from entering each other's
territories and competing.[450]

The Commission granted the Corning system of joint ventures and
licensing agreements an exemption under paragraph 3 only after the
parties minimised some of the restrictive restraints of the agreements.
Corning was given lesser managerial power, and the exclusive territorial
restrictions were dismantled.[451]

---

[447]   For the interesting story about how that innovation became a standard, see
Brian DeLacey et al., 'Strategic Behavior in Standard-Setting Organizations', in
Harvard University Working Paper (SSRN, 2006).
[448]   Ibid.
[449]   Björn Lundqvist, *Standardization under EU Competition Rules and US
Antitrust Laws – The Rise and the Limits of Self-Regulation* (Edward Elgar,
2014), 214 et seq.
[450]   Ibid.
[451]   See Commission decision Optical Fibres, OJ 1986 L 236/30.

Valentine Korah also discussed the *Optical Fibres* case.[452] Korah, together with other commentators, was critical of the fact that the Commission continued to take an *ex post* view of the commercial relationships between the parties.[453] As with the *BP/Kellogg* case, these commentators believe that if the parties are neither competitors nor potential competitors when entering the agreement, they will (or should) not have been deemed to infringe Article 85(1) and thus the exclusive territorial restrictions were only necessary (ancillary) restrictions in an otherwise pro-competitive and pro-innovative joint venture set-up.[454]

From Korah's viewpoint, the Commission should not take into consideration several matters in these circumstances: firstly, it should be ignored that during the period of the joint effort they will acquire status as competitors since relevant know-how will flow between the firms, so that when the agreements eventually terminate they would be full-fledged competitors. For example, non-competitors should be able to enter R&D agreements stipulating market division so that each party would serve only one part of the common market both during the collaboration and after the agreement had elapsed because of a division of the intellectual property right derived from the R&D collaboration. In the event an *ex ante* approach was adopted, primarily absolute territorial restrictions would be transferred from being anticompetitive to being benign and, hence, the policy goal of a common market would be severely limited. Secondly, the fact that the agreement could contain clauses that fore-closed third parties, perhaps to an extent that competition was restricted

---

[452]   Valentine Korah, 'Critical Comments on the Commission's Recent Decisions exempting Joint Ventures to Exploit Research that Needs Further Development', (1987) 12 *European Law Review*, 18, 19 et seq.

[453]   Tao Xiong & James Kirkbride, 'Controlling Research and Development Co-operation through EC Competition Controls: Some Concerns', (1998) 19 *Comp. Law*, 296, 300. See also *Mitchell Cotts/Solfiltra* case, see Commission decision Mitchell Cotts/Solfiltra, OJ 1987 L 41/31 paras 19 et seq. Two similar cases of non-competitor status not concerning joint R&D ventures are the *Eirpagem* case, see Commission decision Eirpagem, OJ 1991 L 306/22, and the *Cekacan* case, see Commission decision Cekacan, OJ 1991 L 299/64.

[454]   Valentine Korah was, and rightfully so, also critical of the amount of time the parties had to wait before the Commission handed down a decision. In *Optical Fibres*, it took the Commission four years from when the first joint venture agreement was notified before a decision was rendered. See Commission decision Optical Fibres, OJ 1986 L 236/30; and Valentine Korah, 'Critical Comments on the Commission's Recent Decisions exempting Joint Ventures to Exploit Research that Needs Further Development', (1987) 12 *European Law Review*, 18, 37 et seq.

even in comparison with a hypothetical situation of no agreement, should not be taken into consideration.[455] For example, explicit or implicit restrictions in an R&D agreement, from an *ex ante* viewpoint, not to enter into R&D collaborations with third parties, should be benign.

(ii) Innovative competition

The *Optical Fibres* case is interesting for several reasons. The case concerned a firm that systematically entered into R&D agreements with, arguably, the most potent potential competitors in the EU. This enabled it to control the evolution of the innovation and keeping the new products within the desired field of technology.[456] Thus, in many ways Corning Ltd., by entering these joint R&D agreements, contractually established the *de facto* standard for the broadband technology. The broadband service became – rightly or wrongly – connected to the optical fibre technology.[457]

Korah did not directly discuss innovation competition or the grant-back clauses but was especially concerned with the limitation on Corning's ability to utilise its intellectual property rights. According to her the limitation set by the Commission on the possibility of Corning stipulating exclusive national licensing agreement with each joint venture would in the end diminish the incentive to invent.[458]

In the *Optical Fibres* case, the Commission eventually approved of Corning's network of inter-related joint ventures all featuring, on the one hand, Corning, the major producer and patent holder of optical fibres, and, on the other, large cable manufacturers in each large member state of the EU.[459] Independently, all the joint ventures were legitimate, since, according to the Commission, the partners in each of the joint ventures

---

[455] See Commission, Report on Competition Policy 1992, 172. For critique of the *ex ante/ex post* viewpoint, cf. Steven Anderman & John Kallaugher, *Technology Transfer and the New EU Competition Rules* (Oxford University Press 2006), 105 et seq.

[456] See Commission decision Optical Fibres, OJ 1986 L 236/30.

[457] Björn Lundqvist, *Standardization under EU Competition Rules and US Antitrust Laws – The Rise and the Limits of Self-Regulation* (Edward Elgar, 2014), 214 et seq.

[458] Valentine Korah, 'Critical Comments on the Commission's Recent Decisions exempting Joint Ventures to Exploit Research that Needs Further Development', (1987) 12 *European Law Review*, 18, 19 et seq.

[459] Compagnie Générale d'Electricité (CGE) in France, Industrie Pirelli S.p.A in Italy, Siemens AG in Germany and N.V. Philips Gloeilampenfabrieken in the Netherlands and in Belgium. See Commission decision Optical Fibres, OJ 1986 L 236/30.

were neither competitors nor potential competitors.[460] However, the Commission still found that the network of joint ventures was anti-competitive since competition between the joint ventures was limited.[461] Given the exclusive licensing agreements, both active and passive sales were prevented. The optical fibres market was, according to the Commission, highly oligopolistic in that it had high entry barriers consisting of patent rights and also the ultimate purchasers of cables were often national authorities favouring local suppliers.[462]

The mere existence of the joint ventures made other cable manufacturers aware of the fact that all large cable manufacturers in Europe had selected to use optical fibres as the technology for the future. Hence, should the manufacturer also choose optical fibres, the manufacturer would likely not choose the wrong technology for the new service market rapidly developing under the notion of 'broadband'.[463]

The ventures were collaboration in the established technology rather than research ventures. They were to develop the cabling technology necessary for cable optical fibres in the respective member states. Corning withheld the possibility of developing the optical fibre technology from the joint ventures. It was only the cable technology that was to be developed.[464]

Irrespective of captioning them R&D agreements or something else, the overall picture underscores that the agreements with each national incumbent were *de facto* agreements to the fact that the European-wide technical standard should be optical fibres for the broadband service or for fast telecommunication in general.[465] Indeed, the system was a standardisation agreement connected with vertical licensing agreements and R&D joint ventures for follow-on R&D.

The research joint ventures into optical fibres technology were effectively prevented by the fact that each joint venture had to grant back to Corning on a non-exclusive basis any improvements, developments, inventions, changes and innovations, to ensure a uniform technology development. Thus, all parties (especially the cable manufacturers),

---

[460]   See Commission decision Optical Fibres, OJ 1986 L 236/30.
[461]   Ibid.
[462]   Björn Lundqvist, *Standardization under EU Competition Rules and US Antitrust Laws – The Rise and the Limits of Self-Regulation* (Edward Elgar, 2014), 214 et seq.
[463]   Ibid.
[464]   Ibid.
[465]   Ibid.

knowing that any improvements would be distributed through the network to all joint ventures, lacked an incentive to do any research regarding optical fibres. The result of this system is that any innovation of the optical fibres technology developed by a party to the joint ventures would wind up through Corning with both its competitors or potential competitors and any potential customer of the improvement.[466] Furthermore, Corning had the right to select a technical manager in each joint venture. The system – being almost all-industry inclusive – logically would eliminate competition for the development of better fibres or cables within the EU.[467]

As stated above, the Commission approved of the system after Corning's influence on the joint ventures was decreased. The joint ventures were allowed to sell all over the Community and managerial influence was limited. The Commission also noted that because of the joint ventures the technology as such was quickly dissolved through the Community. The joint ventures were also limited in time. The grant-back clause was, however, approved, which indicates that the Commission prioritised competition between the joint ventures on the basis of price, instead of safeguarding the possibility of each joint venture developing the product further and, thus, letting innovative competition govern the relationships between the joint ventures.[468]

The Commission's decision in this case should not be regarded as intervening in the 'special subject matter' of national intellectual property

---

[466]   In the case that the proprietor of a patent controls a whole technology, grant-back clauses can be pro-competitive since, firstly, the licensor implicitly accepts that the licensee conducts research within the area of the patent claims. This may otherwise be an infringement under some jurisdictions. Secondly, if a follow-on innovation is perceived, the licensor (proprietor) will not object to the licensee licensing the possibly blocked patent. This line of reasoning makes sense when there are potential customers for the follow-on innovation. However, it seems that in the *Optical Fibres* case possibly all follow-on innovation will be distributed through Corning to all possible customers, without the possibility of the inventing licensee gaining any supra-competitive profit. See Commission decision Optical Fibres, OJ 1986 L 236/30. For a more economic discussion see Susanne Scotchmer, *Innovation and Incentives* (The MIT Press 2004), 137 et seq.

[467]   Björn Lundqvist, *Standardization under EU Competition Rules and US Antitrust Laws – The Rise and the Limits of Self-Regulation* (Edward Elgar, 2014), 214 et seq.

[468]   See Commission decision Optical Fibres, OJ 1986 L 236/30, paras 50 and 57 et seq. It must be stated that these kinds of grant-back clauses are normal in today's patent pool licensing agreements.

rights.[469] The Commission deals with the system as a whole. It limited Corning's managerial influence in the R&D joint ventures. The Commission also tried, with limited effect, to limit the ability of the parties to make the market transparent. It furthermore discussed the grant-back clauses. These limitations do not in hindsight invade on the intellectual property rights of Corning.

An interpretation that would acknowledge these restrictions as limiting Corning's intellectual property rights encourages a very broad scope for intellectual property rights under competition law. It would encourage an interpretation of a wide 'subject matter' doctrine under EU competition law which would exempt almost any action or covenant based on intellectual property rights. Thus, actions which would not reflect the rights, or the parts making up an intellectual property right, under national intellectual property rights would be included under the doctrine.

Actually, the Corning case could be regarded as a failure to protect competition in innovation and competition as a whole in the fibre cable or broadband market. The industry-wide system of joint ventures with grant-back clauses locked in all major potential competitors and purchasers of competing technologies. Neither the cable manufacturers nor any other parties would be able to enter the optical fibres technology with their own innovations. The system created a *de facto* standard under an IP arrangement which belonged to only one firm.[470]

The Commission tried to create price competition between the different joint ventures in Europe. The goal was that each joint venture using the Corning fibre technology should compete in the development of cables. As I have discussed elsewhere, that would probably not happen. Corning was not only a stakeholder in each joint venture, but it also extracted royalties from each joint venture based on the licensing agreements. It would be natural for Corning to set these royalty rates at a level where supra-competitive profits were extracted from the joint ventures. This would, of course, influence the price of the cables and the possibility of the different joint ventures actually competing with price. From this perspective, the decision of the Commission is confusing. The only difference the infusion of competition between the joint ventures created by the Commission would result in was that Corning was forced to stipulate an EU-wide royalty rate rather than being able to fix

---

[469]   Valentine Korah, *Intellectual Property Rights and the EC Competition Rules* (Hart Publishing, 2006), 6 et seq.

[470]   Björn Lundqvist, *Standardization under EU Competition Rules and US Antitrust Laws – The Rise and the Limits of Self-Regulation* (Edward Elgar, 2014), 214 et seq.

supra-competitive royalty rates for each member state. However, given that Corning would still be able to stipulate both a fixed and a running royalty rate in each licensing agreement, the practical difference must be minimal.[471]

(iii) Market power

The *Optical Fibres* case above indicates that the Commission was prepared to accept joint ventures between firms holding substantial market power. Even though the block exemption was updated with the information that the exemption may be withdrawn in these cases (cf. recital 18 R&D block exemption), the Commission would not likely interfere when firms have in fact decided on a technology standard. Likewise, the cases reviewed above indicate that the Commission some-times allowed market power to be built up.[472] There are other cases where it is evident that the market power threshold in the old block exemption did not prevent the agreement in question from not enjoying the exemption stipulated in Article 85(3) [now 101(3)].[473]

A case that further illustrates this is the *KSB/Goulds/Lowara* case regarding an R&D venture with four participants, among them the world's leading and the world's number three pump producing firms. The venture aimed at researching and developing a new sort of water pump.[474] The joint venture was set up in 1985 and the Commission had to scrutinise the agreement in the light of the first block exemption. The most discussed issue in this case was whether the participants could be considered competitors. In fact, the Commission found them to be potential competitors, with a rather broad interpretation of the doctrine of 'potential competitor'.[475] Only one firm had the technical know-how to develop the technology, while the Commission purported that the other participants did have the financial resources to purchase and develop similar capacity. The participants were thereby at least potential competi-tors according to the Commission. And by developing this component

---

[471] Ibid.

[472] See *supra* under section 3.3.2(vi).

[473] Björn Lundqvist, *Standardization under EU Competition Rules and US Antitrust Laws – The Rise and the Limits of Self-Regulation* (Edward Elgar, 2014), 214 et seq.

[474] Commission decision KSB/Goulds/Lowara/ITT, OJ 1991 L 19/25.

[475] For critique see Luis Silva Morais, *Joint Venture and EU Competition Law* (Hart Publishing, 2013), 330 et seq.

jointly rather than individually, they had been involved in a restriction of their freedom of action.[476]

Moreover, it was estimated that the contemplated pump could only be economically successfully produced with an annual production of at least 200,000 pumps. This is why one of the participants was given the task of producing the pumps for the rest of the participants under the joint R&D agreement. The research was divided up between the parties, and the intellectual property derived from the research would belong to the participant that did the research in question. Each participant was granted a royalty-free licence to any intellectual property right derived under the joint effort. In comparison, the agreement stipulated harsh obligations of confidentiality and none of the members were allowed to license the technology to outside parties during the term of the agreement and for a period of five years thereafter.

Competing pump manufacturers expressed concerns to the Commission about the proposed cooperation and especially the stipulation that one firm was to produce the pumps for all participants in the joint venture. If successful, this would create not only more efficient pumps, but also such economies of scale (efficient production) that the competing manufacturers outside the venture would not be able to respond. They would get excluded from the relevant market. This could eventually eliminate any sort of competition, since the competitors would not be able to set up equivalent R&D and manufacturing cooperation. There were simply too few of them to reach a production capacity of 200,000 pumps. Furthermore, the competitors would be prevented from producing similar pumps because of the intellectual property rights held by the participants of the joint venture, and the obligation in the agreement not to license third parties.[477]

The Commission found the agreement anticompetitive under Article 101(1) since the parties were competitors and it restricted their freedom of action. In addition, third parties were potentially foreclosed from the relevant market to be. The Commission issued an exemption under Article 101(3) for a period of five years. The first block exemption was not applicable since the ventures held a combined market share (substantially) above the stipulated thresholds. The Commission was, in the end, not concerned with what the outside pump manufacturers stated as an anticompetitive effect of the cooperation. Instead, the Commission was of

---

[476]   Ibid., 331.
[477]   Ibid., para 13.

the opinion that the cooperation created efficiencies.[478] It allowed the parties to downsize manufacturing capacity and to buy it from the selected producer inside the R&D collaboration. It is clear that the Commission did not conduct a correct and realistic evaluation of whether the parties were potential competitors.[479] However, from the facts given in the opinion, it might be argued that competition in innovation between the parties in the venture and parties outside the venture was limited by the joint effort.[480] There was an element of foreclosure.

The Commission does not reach the ultimate conclusion, that the selected few pump manufacturers in the joint ventures were developing a new form of technology, possibly even a new standard, which could exclude the competitors or firms not inside the collaboration. It seems that the complaining competitors saw this and the adjoining agreement of joint production as in fact a proprietary standard being developed.

Another interesting case regarding the interaction between R&D agreements, standard and the later exploitation by means of a market dominant standard and IP arrangement is the *Continental/Michelin* case.[481] The notified R&D (mainly later stage development) effort aimed at creating tyres which could be used even after they had been damaged and normally would be considered 'flat'. Michelin was the second largest producer of tyres in the world at this time and Continental the fourth largest. Their combined world market share was estimated at 22 per cent, of which they held a 46 per cent share in the EU. The parties would give up their individual research effort in selected areas of the technology for a combined but divided effort to exchange information regarding the mounting systems, architecture and geometry for the new tyres. Each party would hold the intellectual property rights that reflected its innovations, but a common entity was to be set up for granting a worldwide, non-exclusive licence under the technology for anyone interested. The parties would also provide mutual assistance in actions against patent infringements, with the common entity paying for the expenses

---

[478] In a different case, the 'lock-in effects' of the planned technology were considered to be anticompetitive features, see Commission decision BBC Brown Boveri, OJ 1988 L 301/68, para 19.

[479] Ibid., 331 et seq.

[480] Interestingly, there are similar cases concerning pump manufacturers in the US, see *supra* under section 3.2.4.

[481] Commission decision Continental/Michelin, OJ 1988 L 305/33. This case is also discussed in Björn Lundqvist, *Standardization under EU Competition Rules and US Antitrust Laws – The Rise and the Limits of Self-Regulation* (Edward Elgar, 2014), 220.

incurred.[482] Goodyear and Firestone submitted comments stating a concern that the new technology standard would not be made available to them, or would be made available to them in a belated fashion, and that this would seriously affect their ability to compete.[483]

The Commission found that the parties would objectively be able to develop the technology independently, that is, they were competitors. Both were in a very late stage of developing the technology. Elimination of this possibility by the agreement and the prohibition of independently granting licences for the technology rendered the cooperation anti-competitive in the light of Article 101(1) according to the Commission. Nonetheless, the research cooperation was exempted under Article 101(3) for a period of ten years following the first introduction of the new tyre. The joint entity for the exploitation of the intellectual property rights was, however, exempted for 20 years from the time when the 'contracted products' were supposed to be distributed. Thus, the Commission viewed the technology standard agreement with the connected IP arrangement with much more lenient eyes than it viewed the actual research cooperation.[484] The creation of an IP arrangement or a patent pool under a perhaps world-winning standard was supported even though it would most likely extract supra-competitive profit. Under the pool the parties would be able to set royalty rates at a level which could imply not only a cartel price for the technology but also collusion regarding the price of the tyres. From the decision, it may also be concluded that the patents in the IP arrangement vehicle would actually be competing. Or, at least, the Commission failed to address that issue.[485]

(iv) Amendments to the block exemption
The 1984 block exemption can be viewed as a reflection of a more restrictive EU competition law approach to R&D agreements, more restrictive than the approach under previous jurisprudence reflected in the 1968 notice. Indeed, it stipulated that even pure R&D ventures can be anticompetitive. It was structured in the same manner as the other block exemptions with one white list of excused covenants and a rather

---

[482]   Ibid.

[483]   Ibid., under section G. See also Björn Lundqvist, *Standardization under EU Competition Rules and US Antitrust Laws – The Rise and the Limits of Self-Regulation* (Edward Elgar, 2014), 220.

[484]   Ibid., paras 34 et seq.

[485]   Björn Lundqvist, *Standardization under EU Competition Rules and US Antitrust Laws – The Rise and the Limits of Self-Regulation* (Edward Elgar, 2014), 221.

complicated system to exempt other covenants. It did not allow for joint sale schemes. This made the block exemption quite rigid and the room for innovative contract drafting was limited. However, the era of a more restrictive application would soon end. The critique rose against the EU Commission regarding the aforementioned cases and these cases in themselves would soon have an effect on the EU Commission.

The Commission would publish a notice and decide on another group of cases before the block exemption was changed. In 1993, an amendment to the block exemption discarded the ban on joint sales and distribution.[486] The participants of R&D agreements were allowed jointly to distribute the innovated product as long as the parties did not hold a combined market share of more than 10 per cent in the product market. By adding an exemption for joint distribution, the block exemption for cooperative joint ventures also became a plausible alternative to full-functioning joint ventures judged under the merger regulation (Merger Regulation 134/2004).[487] This was one of the purposes of enacting the amendment.[488] Interestingly, after the enactment of the first merger regulation in 1989–90, firms artificially tried to get their joint R&D

---

[486]   See [1993] OJ C43 16.2.1993, 2 et seq. or [1993] 4 CMLR 163.

[487]   See Commission, Report on Competition Policy 1992, 171 et seq. Cf. Hanns Ullrich, 'Competitor Cooperation and the Evolution of Competition Law: Issues for Research in a Perspective of Globalisation', in Joseph Drexl (ed.), *The Future of Transnational Antitrust From Comparative to Common Competition Law* (2003), 196. Concentrative joint ventures are those joint ventures which were scrutinised under the Council Regulation (EC) No 139/2004 of 20 January 2004 on the control of concentrations between undertakings, OJ L 24, 29.01.2004, p. 1 et seq. (Hereinafter the Merger Regulation 134/2004.)

[488]   Thus, the Commission did not seem to have accepted Jorde and Teece's concept of non-linear innovation creation. In the *De Laval-Stork* case the Commission stated that in particular cases joint marketing is justified since close technical cooperation with the purchasers is necessary in order for the market to be researched, orders obtained, the purchasers' requirements and needs in relationship to production and research satisfied. All this must be done through and with the same team of technicians that not only invented the product, but thereafter provided the after-sales service which was of special importance in this industry. See Commission decision De Laval-Stork, OJ 1977 L 215/11. For Jorde and Teece's concept of innovation creation see, e.g., Thomas Jorde & David Teece, 'Rule of Reason Analysis of Horizontal Arrangements: Agreements Designed to Advance Innovation and Commercialize Technology', (1993) Winter *Antitrust Law Journal*, 579.

ventures to be judged according to that regulation.[489] The Article 85 EC Treaty (now 101 TFEU) therefore became the second-best alternative for the parties determining whether a joint R&D project was anticompetitive, or not. It only became available if the joint effort did not meet the definition of concentrative joint venture in the merger regulation.[490] After 1998 the definition would be based solely on the issue of joint control and full functionality of the joint venture.[491]

The amendment to the group exemption in 1993 was an endeavour to create a level playing field between collaborative joint efforts and concentrative joint ventures, so that firms would not prefer concentrative joint ventures. The aim was to promote short-term collaboration, with the benefit for the collaborators that the joint effort under the R&D block exemption did not need to be notified.[492]

---

[489]   Council Regulation (EEC) No 4064/89 of 21 December 1989 on the control of concentrations between undertakings, OJ L395 30.12.1989 (hereinafter the old merger regulation).

[490]   In 1998, the old merger regulation was amended in order to define concentrative joint ventures solely on the basis of whether they are full-functioning or not. See Council Regulation 1310/97 amending Regulation 4046/89, OJ L 180 9.7.1997, 1. Before the amendment, the old merger regulation excluded all joint ventures which had the object or effect of coordinating independent undertakings.

[491]   Ibid.

[492]   Even today, the organisation of a joint effort can be more easily accepted under Merger Regulation 134/2004 than under Article 101. The substantive test is different and the test under Article 101 is stricter in at least two aspects: (i) Article 101(3)(b) provides no exemption if it gives the parties even a possibility to eliminate competition. The Merger Regulation 134/2004, on the other hand, takes a broader view, focusing on the creation of a dominant position (even though the new test, implemented in 2004, is similar to the test under Article 101); (ii) the incorporation of a 'pure' efficiency defence under the Merger Regulation 134/2004, which does not exist under Article 101. Furthermore, the system under the Merger Regulation 134/2004 gives more legal security for the parties involved. However, according to Article 2(4), a joint venture, which has as its object or effect the coordination of the competitive behaviour of undertakings that remain independent, shall be appraised in accordance with the criteria of Article 101(1) and (3) of the EC Treaty (now Article 101(1) and (3) TFEU).

The amendment to the R&D block exemption was also accompanied by changes in the other block exemptions and with the publication of a new notice.[493]

In addition to these two major changes, the Commission initiated a new accelerated procedure for assessing cooperative joint ventures.[494]

(v) The 1993 notice

In addition to the changes made to the block exemption, the Commission wanted to clarify what restraints could be used in R&D agreements and also which R&D agreement would escape Article 85(1) (now 101(1)) altogether, that is, be *per se* legal.

The preamble of the 1985 block exemption stated – in comparison with the 1968 notice – that pure R&D collaborations can be anti-competitive if they restrict the possibility of the parties engaging in same or similar research, independently or together with third parties. The Notice concerning the assessment of cooperative joint ventures pursuant to Article 85 from 1993 (hereinafter the 1993 notice) altered this notion.[495] The 1993 notice stipulated that, in principle, non-competitors' engagement in *inter alia* joint R&D does not fall within Article 85(1). Thus, if the statement in the 1993 notice concerns pure R&D ventures between non-competitors, it should be regarded as a limitation of the

---

[493] Press release, IP/92/1111, 23/12/1992 stating: 'This involves broadening the Group Exemptions on specialisation (No. 417/85), on research and development (No. 418/85), on patent licensing (No. 2349/84), and on know-how licensing (No. 556/89). The Regulations on specialisation and on R&D have been amended to cover also those cooperations which extend beyond the manufacturing stage by including arrangements on joint sales of the contract products. Both "partial function" and "full-function" JVs may therefore enjoy automatic exemption. Production JVs are exempted up to an aggregate market share of 20%. For fully-fledged JVs, which usually pose a greater risk for competition because they stretch to the distribution stage, the maximum market share has been fixed at 10%.' See also [1993] 4 CMLR 163. It thereby made the earlier notice from 1968 obsolete, see OJ C 75/3, 29.7.1968; corrigendum in OJ C 84 28.8.1968, 14. See [1993] OJ C43 16.2.1993, 2 et seq.
[494] Ibid. See also the Commission, Report on Competition Policy 1993, 130 et seq.
[495] See Notice concerning the assessment of cooperative joint ventures pursuant to Article 85 [1993] OJ C43 16.2.1993, 2 et seq.

statement in the block exemption preamble.[496] The 1993 notice specifically stated that this was also the case when the joint R&D has the further
task of granting licences to third parties.[497]

On the whole, the 1993 notice took a positive viewpoint of R&D
collaborations. It stated three situations where competition can be
restricted: (i) when the parties are competitors or potential competitors;
(ii) when the joint venture will foreclose third parties; and (iii) if the joint
venture is part of a network of joint ventures that together can restrict
competition (this last point refers to the Commission's bad experience
with the *Corning* case). Further, the 1993 notice stated three situations
that would normally fall outside Article 101(1): (i) joint ventures created
by firms within the same group; (ii) joint ventures that fall under the
Commission Notice on agreements of minor importance which do not
appreciably restrict competition under Article 81(1) of the Treaty establishing the European Community (hereinafter the *De Minimis* Notice)
threshold;[498] and (iii) joint ventures which do not affect competition
within the meaning of the 1968 notice. Thus, the 1968 notice was granted
a remarkable comeback at the expense of the 1985 block exemption.

The 1993 notice envisioned a two-step analysis. Firstly, the question
was whether the first paragraph was triggered at all in light of the guiding
principles in the 1993 notice. Secondly, if the first paragraph was
triggered, the question would be whether competition was appreciably

---

[496]   The statement in the 1993 notice was subjected to the reservation that
there should remain room for a number of R&D centres in the respective area of
the joint venture. Today the issue whether the parties were competitors or not
appears rather irrelevant. See Commission Notice concerning the assessment of
the cooperative joint ventures pursuant to Article 85 of the EEC Treaty, OJ C 43,
16.02.1993, 2 et seq., para 33. In the Commission, Report on Competition Policy
1994, the Commission stated that under the exemption paragraph (then Article
85(3)), the indispensable requirement implied that there remained effective
competition even though the parties cooperated. Thus, the Commission stated
that it cannot rely exclusively on the internal competition between the parties for
the maintenance of effective competition under Article 85(3). Consequently, an
all-inclusive joint venture would not be granted exemption under Article 85(3)
under any circumstances. See Commission, Report on Competition Policy 1994,
105 et seq.
[497]   Commission Notice concerning the assessment of the cooperative joint
ventures pursuant to Article 85 of the EEC Treaty, OJ C 43, 16.02.1993, 2 et seq.
para 59.
[498]   The current De Minimis Notice: Commission Notice on agreements of
minor importance which do not appreciably restrict competition under Article
101(1) of the Treaty establishing the European Union, OJ C291, 30.08.2014, 1 et
seq.

affected: hence, what market power did the parties have and what restraints were stipulated in the agreement?

The examples of ancillary restraints in the 1993 notice were limited, but can be regarded as including the 'regular restraints', which are now seen in many R&D joint venture agreements. For example, the Commission stated that territorial restrictions limiting the parents had only once been regarded as ancillary and the parties should be cautious when utilising such a covenant.[499]

(vi) The turning point

Already the year after the introduction of the 1993 amendment, the Commission exempted a number of cooperative joint ventures, some where the parents held considerable market share on the relevant market.[500] These decisions were the second group of joint venture cases and the outcome may be viewed as a reply to the general criticism that had been raised at this time not only to the block exemption for R&D, but that all block exemptions were not permissive enough. The block exemptions were regarded as 'straitjackets' for European business. An agreement needed to be individually exempted under Article 101(3) or under opposition procedure if it contained other forms of covenants than those explicitly exempted in the 'white lists'. Since the EU Commission was under-staffed, receiving an individual exemption or an approval under the opposition procedure took a substantial period of time.[501] These delays limited European business in international competition according to the critique.

---

[499] Commission Notice concerning the assessment of the cooperative joint ventures pursuant to Article 85 of the EEC Treaty, OJ C 43, 16.02.1993, 2 et seq., 71 et seq. Making reference to among other cases, the *Mitchell Cotts/ Solfiltra* case, see Commission decision Mitchell Cotts/Solfiltra, OJ 1987 L 41/31.

[500] See the Commission, Report on Competition Policy 1993, 130 et seq. and the Commission, Report on Competition Policy 1994, 105 et seq. An example of the exempted cases was the 1993 Philips-Thomson-Sagem joint venture into development, design and manufacture of matrix liquid crystal displays (LCD). The exemption was granted, by the Commission, in light of Japanese competition. Apart from the *Pasteur Mérieux-Merck* joint venture into development and sales (the manufacturing was performed by respective parent), all other cases in 1994 essentially involved joint R&D, with joint production but separate distribution of the final product, see *Philips/Osram*, *Asahi/St Gobain* and *Fujitsu/AMD*. *Exxon/Shell* concerned final product joint venture. See the Commission, Report on Competition Policy 1994, 105.

[501] Commission, Report on Competition Policy 1992, 171 et seq.

The Commission therefore wanted to show that it considered certain joint ventures favourably when they did not fulfil the condition set out in the block exemption regulations and ventures involving competitors active on oligopolistic markets.

Apart from *Pasteur Mérieux-Merck*,[502] which was a joint venture for joint development and sales (production remained with the parents), all other cases at this point essentially involved R&D and/or production joint ventures but maintained a separate distribution of the final product by the parents (non-full-function joint ventures). In three cases (*Philips/Osram*, *Asahi/St Gobain* and *Fujitsu/AMD*) the joint R&D concerned parts and input to a product mainly sold to the parents for incorporation in a final product, which was produced and sold separately by the parents. Two cases concerned final product joint ventures:

(a) Exxon/Shell   The Exxon/Shell joint venture concerned the development and production of the final product LLDPE (linear low-density polyethylene) which the parent firms would sell independently. The venture combined the fourth and the fifth largest producers in the world and the production joint venture would create the second largest production capacity in Europe. The market for the final product was characterised by an oligopolistic structure with a considerable degree of price transparency and stability of market share and production capacity.

The Commission concluded that the venture had the possibility to suppress competition because the parties were competitors and both were independently able to construct a production facility for the production of the LLDPE. They would also stay in the same product market but independently produce the slightly less developed chemical compound. The parties would, according to the Commission, be able to restrict competition in the following respects: (i) the parents would be obliged to coordinate their investment plans and renounce the possibility of enlarging their polyethylene business by individual action (hence, no overbidding of production capacity);[503] (ii) the parents would inevitably be able to coordinate their production within the joint venture (allocation or collusion in production output); (iii) joint production with separate distribution but without further processing would invite coordination, in particular in relation to price on the end product (spillover effects); and

---

[502]   Commission decision Pasteur Mérieux-Merck, OJ 1994 L 309/1.

[503]   For an economic analysis providing that a joint effort creates the ability to eliminate so-called overbidding and that their feature should be regarded as anticompetitive, see John T. Scott, 'Diversification versus Cooperation in R&D Investment', (1988) 9 *Managerial Decision Economics*, 173, 180 et seq.

(iv) the high joint investment, the joint production and the flow of information between the parties might affect long-term decisions in the polyethylene industry as a whole.[504]

In light of the above, the Commission did not focus on particular provisions in the joint venture agreement but rather made an overall analysis of the inherent effects of such a joint venture.

Instead it focused on the threats to independent decision-making subject to reciprocal influences resulting from the envisioned structure. Interestingly, the Commission found that the joint venture potentially restricted not only output and price in the current market (see (ii) and (iii) above), but also future investment in further output (i) and, perhaps, without explicitly mentioning the concept, future research, development and innovation (iv). These last two points ((i) and (iv)) are inherently anticompetitive features of joint research and production, while the first two concern collusion in the present market. The Commission did not use the words 'innovation' or 'research', which on the whole gives the impression it was more interested in protecting efficiencies, that is, low prices and high output, than innovation, but it is one of few decisions where the Commission acknowledged that restricting innovation may be anticompetitive.

The venture was exempted under Article 85(3) for a period of ten years for several reasons: the plant was the first plant of its kind in Europe, in adding output and capacity on the market, the combined market share of the parties would only slightly exceed 20 per cent; the remaining competitors were able to uphold the competition; and, after some changes in the joint venture agreement, each parent could independently order increases in production.[505]

---

[504]   Commission, Report on Competition Policy 1994, 107. See also Commission decision Exxon/Shell, OJ 1994 L 144/20.

[505]   As a background to this case it should also be mentioned that the low-density polyethylene market and the adjoining market for polypropylene had been plagued with overcapacity since the late 1970s. In 1977, the patents for these products had expired and several firms entered the markets. The Commission published two decisions, *PVC I* and *PVC II*, in 1988 regarding the polypropylene market. Both indicated the existence of price and output cartels. See Commission decision PVC I, OJ 1989 L 74/1 and Commission decision Bayer BP Petroleum, OJ 1988 L 150/35. However, these decisions were appealed. The Court of First Instance did not alter the final conclusion of the existence of anticompetitive agreements. The Commission also rendered a decision for the low-density polyethylene market indicating the existence of a similar collusion; however, that decision was annulled by the Court of First Instance on procedural grounds and then abandoned by the Commission. Both

(b) Pasteur Mérieux-Merck[506]   In Pasteur Mérieux-Merck two leading suppliers of human vaccines with very high market shares in a number of relevant product markets created a joint venture in which they brought together their total European vaccine business relating to existing vaccines and future vaccines. The joint venture would thus develop new vaccines based on previous knowledge and new research performed by the parents. It would exclusively sell these existing and future vaccines in Europe.[507]

The market was highly concentrated, with three world suppliers: Pasteur Mérieux, Merck and Smith Klein Beecham (SKB). The market had high entry barriers: costly and high-risk R&D; production subject to patents, proprietary know-how and national regulatory licences. Cross-licensing between the major suppliers and different distribution methods in various member states added to the difficulties to overcome before entering the market. The Commission concluded that the parties were actual or at least potential competitors for a number of existing and future vaccines. The transfer of their businesses including production, patents and research to a combined entity would eliminate competition (rivalry) between the parents. Furthermore, competition in relation to third parties would be eliminated. The agreement limited the possibility for the parents of licensing third parties under the patent transferred to the joint venture. Third parties were therefore effectively foreclosed from the downstream markets, given the strong position the parents had in the technology market, that is, the IP market.

Interestingly, the Commission also stated that competitors were restricted by the joint venture since their ability to form cooperative arrangements would diminish when two major competitors were no longer eligible for collaboration. Moreover, some ancillary agreements regarding the distribution in France and Germany were considered anticompetitive since they restricted both intra-brand and inter-brand competition. They not only restricted each licensee or distributor in each

---

Shell and Exxon were involved in these decisions (however Exxon to a lesser degree). See Bellamy & Child, *European Community Law of Competition* (Oxford University Press, 2008), 122, 339. It should be noted that in the current edition of Bellamy & Child, these cases are not discussed in such detail as in the preceding, 5th edition, see Bellamy & Child, *European Community Law of Competition* (Sweet & Maxwell, 2001), 206 et seq. with references.

[506]   Commission decision Pasteur Mérieux-Merck, OJ 1994 L 309/1.

[507]   See Commission, Report on Competition Policy 1994, 108 et seq. See also the Commission decision Pasteur Mérieux-Merck, OJ 1994 L 309/1.

member state not to compete with each other, but also foreclosed products and licenses in light of the strong market position of the parent firms.

The joint venture was only exempted after extensive rewriting of the agreements. The parties agreed to open up for competition from the distributors and licensees in Germany and France, that is, making these firms potential competitors. In light of those changes all four conditions in Article 85(3) were fulfilled. R&D competition did not seem to matter and was not taken into consideration. Indeed, there was no indication of protecting poles of research in the *Pasteur Mérieux-Merck* case, for example. The result of that decision was that the Commission accepted the fact that there would only be two research poles in the world *ex post* the implementation of the joint venture agreement and did not accept that the joint venture, nor the parents, was obliged to license third parties.[508]

In the other high-profile joint venture cases from this era (*Philips/ Osram*,[509] *Asahi/St Gobain*[510] and *Fujitsu/AMD*[511]), the Commission followed the same general outline as displayed in the *Exxon/Shell* and the *Pasteur Mérieux-Merck* cases. Even though it concluded that competition was restricted, all the ventures were ultimately exempted under paragraph 3. One major reason why these joint ventures were exempted was that they related to the development and production of new products. The Commission generally favours such ventures because they create new competition and additional output in the market.[512] However, it should be noted that products, produced by the scrutinised joint ventures, did not create new product markets, rather more competition within established product markets where the parents were already active. In some of these cases, the parties held a market share above 50 per cent (cf. *Philips/ Osram* and *Asahi/St Gobain*).

Nonetheless, according to the Commission, it examined both the direct elimination of competition, which resulted from the pooling of development and/or production, and the risk of spillover effects on the separate sales activities performed by the parent firms.

In the cases involving joint input ventures, the spillover effects on the final product market depended, according to the Commission, principally

---

[508] This case has sometimes been referred to as showing that the *Magill* and *IMS Health* line of case law regarding accessing patents under competition law is not applicable when dealing with the pharma sector or pharma patents.

[509] Commission decision Philips/Osram, OJ 1994 L 378/37.

[510] Commission decision Asahi/Saint-Gobain, OJ 1994 L 354/87.

[511] Commission decision Fujitsu AMD Semiconductors, OJ 1994 L 341/66.

[512] Commission, Report on Competition Policy 1994, 110.

on two factors: (i) the importance of the jointly produced input in cost of the final product (ratio common cost/total final cost) and (ii) the market position of the parents. The higher the ratio, that is, the more similar cost structures the buying parents have, the higher the likelihood of coordination of price in the downstream market (spillover effects).

For example, in *Philips/Osram* these effects were considered minimal, since the joint-produced input amounted to only 2–3 per cent of the total cost of the final product.[513] Philips and Osram had to agree to join their development and production of lead glass to a Philips facility in Belgium. The facility would supply 80 per cent of the parent firms' lead glass requirements and any spare capacity would be sold on the open market. The Commission considered the different criteria for exemption under Article 101(3): improving the distribution of production measures allowing the firms to eliminate costs, for example, Osram's obsolete plant, was taken into consideration.

In these decisions, the requirement of a consumer benefit under the third paragraph implied that the consumers would benefit from reduced prices in the future. Interestingly, in the *Philips/Osram* case, the Commission acknowledged – as a consumer benefit – that the quality of the environment would improve because of the new plant. It is not certain that such non-price- or non-output-related effects, which do not benefit consumers but society as a whole, would be taken into consideration today. Indeed, the Commission appears today to view Article 101(3) more as an efficiency exemption rather than as an industry policy exemption.[514] However, bearing in mind that the input produced by the *Philips/Osram* joint venture accorded for only 2–3 per cent of the cost of producing lamps, the benefit for consumers derived from cost efficiencies in this area must be very minimal. Thus, it is likely that the Commission needed to come up with some other justifications apart from potential price reduction. Nonetheless, it must be noticed that this is one of the few cases where the Commission did take other policy goals into consideration apart from pure economically related objectives under Article 101(3).

---

[513]   To this number should, however, be added several other joint ventures that increased the common costs to 8–10 per cent of the final product. See Commission decision Philips/Osram, OJ 1994 L 378/37.

[514]   See generally Communication from the Commission – Notice – Guidelines on the Application of Article 81(3) of the Treaty Official Journal C 101, 27.04.2004, 97-118 (hereinafter 81(3) Guidelines).

Finally, the Commission generally implied that the 'no elimination of competition' requirement is fulfilled as long as there is some other source of supply.

(c) Asahi/St Gobain[515]   The Asahi/St Gobain[516] venture revolved around a joint R&D venture between at that time the two largest producers of automobile glass in the world. When applying for exemption under the then prevailing individual exemption procedure, they stated: 'Any development of a new technology at first requires the selection of a specific R&D track, depending on the existing level of knowledge as well as an assessment of the probability of success of the various lines which are theoretically possible.' The parties therefore agreed on a joint R&D track in the agreement. However, essentially both parties continued to work separately and unilaterally in R&D but they agreed on the framework of a programme defining annual goals for their independent R&D. This allowed each partner to be kept informed of any development made by the other, and permitted joint decisions in relation to the investment in R&D. The parties would also license the technology under the joint venture to each other and third parties when the objective of the agreement was reached and the technology was finally developed. The joint venture would act as a 'medium' through which the selected technology would be licensed.

The parties in all honesty described that they wanted to decide in what direction the technology development in the market should develop and therefore needed to combine forces. Asahi and St Gobain would through the technology secure not only their own existence in the market by the cooperation but also be able to control their competitors' existence and possibly extract licensing fees from them as well by securing the intellectual property rights to the technology. It is difficult to see why they would fail in their pursuit since they were the two leading firms in the market, and, presumably, had strong influence of what should become the technology standard on the market, irrespective of such standard being selected under an SDO's semi-government procedure or *de facto*.

The Asahi/St Gobain joint venture was, according to the Commission, not a final product joint venture. It focused on the pre-final product development. The indispensability requirement in paragraph 3 has often caused problems for parties wanting to limit each other beyond what

---

[515]   Also discussed in Björn Lundqvist, *Standardization under EU Competition Rules and US Antitrust Laws – The Rise and the Limits of Self-Regulation* (Edward Elgar, 2014), 221 et seq.

[516]   Commission decision Asahi/Saint-Gobain, OJ 1994 L 354/87.

might be considered indispensable for the joint venture. The Commission also limited the Asahi/St Gobain joint venture into automotive safety glass to ten years instead of the proposed 30 years. The Commission concluded that bearing in mind the parties' combined market share of more than 50 per cent, the 30-year time period was not indispensable to create the innovation.[517]

As stated above, the Commission granted exemptions in these cases to show that, because of overall economic advantages, it was prepared favourably to consider certain joint ventures even though they involved competitors with market shares exceeding the thresholds laid down in these regulations and did not fulfil the conditions set out in the block exemptions.[518] The economic advantages, efficiencies, referred to by the Commission were all based on the notion of perfect competition or classical price theory, that is, they accomplished cost savings.[519]

(d) Ancillary restraints   The Commission identified a number of ancillary restraints in the context of joint ventures. According to the Commission, ancillary restraints are restrictions imposed only on the parties or the venture, that is, not directly on third parties, which are objectively necessary for the successful function of the joint venture. Thus, they are by their very nature inherent in the operation concerned (for example, non-compete obligation of the parents towards their joint venture). With

---

[517]   The issue of whether the joint R&D was indispensable might be raised since the parties seemed able to conduct the joint R&D independently. Viewed from this perspective, the case clearly indicates how far the Commission was prepared to go to accept joint R&D. See Björn Lundqvist, *Standardization under EU Competition Rules and US Antitrust Laws – The Rise and the Limits of Self-Regulation* (Edward Elgar, 2014), 221 et seq.

[518]   Commission, Report on Competition Policy 1994, 105 et seq. However, it must be stated that the Commission had previously granted exemptions to joint ventures which created combinations with high market shares, see the case ten years previously, Commission decision Bayer/Gist-Brocades, OJ 1976 L 30/13, which bears many similar facts to the *Pasteur Mérieux-Merck* case (among others the market shares), see Commission decision Pasteur Mérieux-Merck, OJ 1994 L 309/1.

[519]   Björn Lundqvist, *Standardization under EU Competition Rules and US Antitrust Laws – The Rise and the Limits of Self-Regulation* (Edward Elgar, 2014), 221 et seq.

regard to joint ventures, ancillary restraints are allowed for the whole duration of the venture, even though they normally were restricted in time.[520]

The benign ancillary restraints identified in the cases referred to above were, *inter alia*: (i) non-compete obligation between the parents and the joint venture during at least the start-up period of the joint venture;[521] (ii) exclusive purchase or sales obligations, with sometimes minimum purchase requirements, at least at the beginning of a joint effort, *vis-à-vis* parents and joint venture (not including exclusive distribution rights for the parents if this would imply territorial limitations);[522] (iii) most favoured nation obligations[523] imposed on the joint effort for the benefit of the parents (also preferential treatment of the parents for supplies in the case of shortage of capacity);[524] (iv) exclusive licensing from the parents to the joint venture with territorial and technical limitations (with

---

[520]   Ibid. This approach had its origin in the *Mitchell Cotts/Solfiltra* case, see Commission decision Mitchell Cotts/Solfiltra, OJ 1987 L 41/31 and the *Elopack/Metal Box* case, Commission decision EloPack, OJ 1990 L 209/15. See also the Commission, Report on Competition Policy 1993, 173; Bellamy & Child, *European Community Law of Competition* (Oxford University Press, 2008), 569 et seq. In regard to other areas such as merger and licensing, the concept of ancillary restraints was well known. See also early case law regarding restraints which were not in breach of Article 101(1). For example the *Nagoya* case where a non-challenge clause was not regarded as infringing Article 101(1), whereas a 'grant-back' clause stipulating the exclusive assignment of any improvement patents was, see Commission, Report on Competition Policy 1972, 53, and Commission, Report on Competition Policy 1980, 88 et seq. See also report from a conference on ancillary restraints in regards to patent licensing agreements held by the Commission in 1974, see Commission, Report on Competition Policy 1974, 20 et seq.

[521]   Commission Notice concerning the assessment of the cooperative joint ventures pursuant to Article 85 of the EEC Treaty, OJ C 43 16.02.1993, 2 et seq., 71 et seq. According to Bellamy a non-compete restriction may today endure the lifetime of the JV and also for parents during a period of at least two years after they transfer the holdings in the JV to a purchaser. Bellamy & Child, *European Community Law of Competition* (Oxford University Press, 2008), 572, with references.

[522]   See, e.g., Commission decision Philips/Osram, OJ 1994 L 378/37.

[523]   Generally also called an 'English clause'.

[524]   Commission decision International Private Satellite Partners, OJ 1994 L354/75 and Commission decision Konsortium ECR 900, OJ 1990 L 228/31. Such a clause seems to encourage collusion, making it odd that it can be regarded as an ancillary restraint. For criticism of these clauses see Commission, Report on Competition Policy 1975, 55.

some exceptions);[525] (v) at least non-exclusive grant-back clauses;[526] (vi) confidential agreements; (vii) not to grant sub-licences; and (viii) post-termination restrictions on the use of technology either by the joint venture or by the parents, for example, prohibitions for assigning the ownership of jointly developed intellectual property rights without the permission of the other party.[527] Interestingly, these restraints resemble the clauses in the 'white list' still at this time included in Article 4 of the R&D block exemption regulation. Thus, accepting them in these cases as ancillary to benign joint ventures was an indirect acceptance of Article 101(1) having been limited in ambit, and the block exemption did not need to be visited before declaring the joint venture benign from an anticompetitive perspective. Here Article 101(1) TFEU and the stipulation of 'anticompetitive effect' for perhaps the first time gets an independent meaning that the plaintiff needs to show. Indeed, it is also now, for the first time, that block exemptions will not be the centre of gravity in EU competition law and slowly become *de minimis* safe harbours rather than indicating the border between benign competition and anticompetitive conduct.

(vii) Conclusion

It is evident that several of the agreements scrutinised by the Commission under the now scrapped individual exemption procedures were captioned R&D agreements and revolved less around creating an innovation or technical solution and more around establishing a standard or a pool for the promotion of the technology, innovation or product in question.[528] Thus, the cooperation consisted of two stages, namely (i) a joint R&D and standards-setting stage and (ii) a joint industrial exploitation of the

---

[525] Commission Notice on restrictions directly related and necessary to concentrations OJ C 56 05.03.2005, 24 et seq., para 42; Commission Notice concerning the assessment of the cooperative joint ventures pursuant to Article 85 of the EEC Treaty, OJ C 43, 16.02.1993, 2 et seq., para 73; Commission decision EloPack, OJ 1990 L 209/15; and Commission decision Asahi/Saint-Gobain, OJ 1994 L 354/87. See comments in Bellamy & Child, *European Community Law of Competition* (Oxford University Press, 2008), 573.

[526] See *inter alia* the *Mitchell Cotts/Solfiltra* case, see Commission decision Mitchell Cotts/Solfiltra, OJ 1987 L 41/31, and Commission, Report on Competition Policy 1986, 78 et seq.

[527] Commission decision EloPack, OJ 1990 L 209/15.

[528] See, e.g., Commission decision Asahi/Saint-Gobain, OJ 1994 L 354/87; and Commission decision Open Group, OJ 1987 L 35/36. See also Björn Lundqvist, *Standardization under EU Competition Rules and US Antitrust Laws – The Rise and the Limits of Self-Regulation* (Edward Elgar, 2014).

results of the joint venture through a pool, where the necessary intellectual property rights are placed for the (sub-) licensing to anyone interested. It is also clear that the R&D block exemption was used in standards-setting activities.[529]

It should moreover be acknowledged that even though this area of competition law went through significant changes towards a more economic approach, and the Commission was indicating that it had a new, more lenient attitude, the Commission also before 1993 was inclined to grant exemptions even for all-industry inclusive R&D ventures. It is therefore questionable whether fewer situations in the end were caught and prohibited by Article 101 TFEU even after 1993–95. Even before 'the turning point', the Commission was not enforcing a stringent policy. The more economic approach in this area implied that there was a restructuring of the method for applying Article 101 rather than an implementation of a more lenient approach or a dismantling of the protection. However, that is not to say that the changes indicated a start to a shift towards a new effect-based approach. The more effect-based Chicago school-oriented approach actually began with these changes in 1993.[530]

There is a body of case law under EU competition law regarding R&D collaborations derived primarily from the decisions made by the Commission under the now scrapped individual exemption procedure under Article 101(3). The US case law in the area of R&D collaboration is minimal and the cases stem from the business review letter procedure. In comparison, the procedure has existed for a long time under the Federal Antitrust jurisprudence. However, since the business review letters are opinions given over hypothetical conduct rather than actual situations, they lack specification and a level of detail often needed in creating precedents. In comparison, the procedure under EU competition law was much more thorough for obtaining the opinion of the Commission in reference to different competition law issues. The individual exemption

---

[529]   The general rules stipulated for standard-setting activities under the Horizontal Guidelines were and are not reflecting reality: '[a]s a general rule there should be a clear distinction between the setting of a standard and, where necessary, the related R&D, and the commercial exploitation of that standard. Agreements on standards should cover no more than what is necessary to ensure their aims, whether this is technical compatibility or a certain level of quality.' See Horizontal Guidelines para 173.

[530]   Björn Lundqvist, *Standardization under EU Competition Rules and US Antitrust Laws – The Rise and the Limits of Self-Regulation* (Edward Elgar, 2014).

procedures created a great body of sometimes very specific and detailed case law. Fortunately for European business, but unfortunately for the development of EU antitrust jurisprudence, this exemption procedure has been scrapped and in addition the block exemptions and the guidelines have become more lenient. Antitrust jurists may have different opinions whether the new system reflects a better competition law. However, everyone must agree that one of the results of the above changes is that there are fewer cases than before. The Commission does not render any decisions and there are fewer cases decided by the courts. Actually, as far as the author knows, there are no, or very few, cases concerning R&D ventures decided after the enactment of the R&D block exemption in 2000.[531] Without a great body of case law, there is no possibility of deriving precedents or rules based on real situations.[532] Possibly the last joint R&D case analysed under the exemption procedure was the *General Electric/Pratt & Witney*[533] joint R&D regarding the joint development of a large airplane engine. The Commission considered that, while it was economically more efficient for the parties to develop the new engine in cooperation, it would have been technically and economically feasible for both parties to develop the new engine independently. The parties were thus potential competitors for the new engine in what would be a tight oligopoly containing, at most, three manufacturers (Rolls-Royce being the independent third producer of similar engines). The creation and functioning of the joint venture appreciably restricted competition for the new engine, according to the Commission, since it reduced the choice of suppliers from three potential suppliers (GEAE, P & W and Rolls-Royce) to two (the joint venture and Rolls-Royce). Nonetheless, the Commission exempted the joint R&D under the third paragraph, finding the joint venture indispensable.

As stated at the beginning of this section, EU competition law became more lenient around 1994 when the Commission approved *inter alia* the

---

[531] See the *Microsoft/Time Warner/ContentGuard* JV case that the parties notified under the EU Merger regulation. The Commission could not establish a change of control so the case was not tried under the Merger Regulation. Nonetheless, the Commission was critical to the collaboration. Discussed *infra*. See http://europa.eu/rapid/press-release_IP-05-295_en.htm. Accessed 24 April 2014.

[532] Instead, the guidelines and block exemptions today often derive their rules from economic theory. Cases have diminished as an important source of competition law.

[533] Commission decision General Electric/Pratt & Witney, OJ 2000 L 58/16.

Asahi/St Gobain and the *Pasteur Mérieux-Merck* joint venture cases.[534] Before these cases, joint R&D, even all-industry inclusive, had been exempted but the business idea of controlling the relevant market by steering innovation under jointly created intellectual property rights and agreement on technology had not been declared benign from a competition law standpoint. These cases were the start of a more forgiving attitude consisting mainly of four changes or developments which are reflected and have been enhanced in the contemporary block exemption and guidelines: (i) a limitation of the notion of 'competitor' to reflect a more realistic market-oriented analysis and thus the ambit of the first paragraph of Article 101 TFEU; (ii) implementing a higher market share threshold for when Article 101(1) TFEU becomes available even though the collaborators are competitors; (iii) the extension of the R&D block exemption in reference to the maximum market share ceiling the collaborators could jointly hold, the time period they could collaborate and the activities that could be conducted (that is, not only joint R&D but production and sales were included in the block exemption); and (iv) the reintroduction and extension of *per se* legal collaborations.[535] It should be noted that these changes in time took place in close symmetry to when changes were made to the US NCRPA.[536]

3.3.4   The System under the Modern Block Exemptions

(i)   R&D block exemptions
On 29 November 2000, the first block exemption for the application of Article 101(3) to R&D agreements was introduced after the introduction of the so-called more economic approach.[537] This block exemption was just one in a series of new block exemptions published from 1999 until 2004, when the Commission implemented a new, more lenient approach towards collaborations between competitors. The 2000 block exemption

---

[534]   See discussion *supra* under section 3.3.2(vi).

[535]   *Per se* legal collaborations were first specified in a 1968 notice and the addition of a third *per se* legal collaboration: when the agreement does not affect 'the relevant parameters of competition'. See Horizontal Guidelines para 24. It should be acknowledged that what (under (i) above) constitutes a competitor and what constitutes *per se* legal collaborations (see (iii) above) interact and overlap. See discussion *infra* under section 3.3.3(iii).

[536]   See discussion *infra* section 3.4.

[537]   Commission regulation No 2659/2000 29 November 2000 on the application of Article 81(3) of the Treaty to categories of research and development agreements OJ L 304, 05.12.2000, 7 et seq. (defined earlier as the 2000 R&D block exemption).

expired in 2010 and was replaced by the current R&D block exemption published on 14 December 2010.[538]

These block exemptions all implemented a market share ceiling for when they are not applicable. The 'white' and the 'grey' lists which were standard paragraphs in the previous block exemptions had been deleted. The opposition procedure and individual exemption procedures not only within the block exemptions but also generally under Article 101(3) had been scrapped. The Commission implemented a parallel substantive and procedural revolution abdicating exclusive power to national courts and competition authorities primarily under Regulation 1/2003. One of the powers abdicated was the exclusive right of granting individual exemptions under Article 101(3) TFEU. National courts were thereby enabled to excuse defendants under the third paragraph.[539]

These legal innovations entailed that the block exemptions in one way lost in importance but also, in another, gained in importance. They do not constitute the demarcation line between prohibited and non-prohibited agreements anymore. The block exemptions have instead become safe harbours, secure places where the parties can rest assured that they do not violate Article 101 TFEU or equivalent rules in the member states. However, falling outside the scope of the block exemptions does not – to an even lesser degree than before – imply violation of Article 101 TFEU. To establish a violation, other requirements also need to be fulfilled. Instead, the Commission's Guidelines have become the important tool for establishing the demarcation line between prohibition and legality. Indeed, the Guidelines have taken over the role of the block exemptions, to distinguish between legal and illegal. The block exemptions have under the new regime acquired the role the *De Minimis* Notice had under the old regime, that is, a low threshold for where the Article 101 TFEU will never in practice be available.[540]

---

[538]   Commission regulation No 1217/2010 14 December 2010 on the application of Article 101(3) of the Treaty on the Functioning of the European Union to certain categories of research and development agreements OJ L 335, 18.12.2010, 36 et seq. (defined earlier as the R&D block exemption).

[539]   This had in practice been possible also before Regulation 1/2003. In Case 47/76 *De Norre v. Brouwerij Concordia* [1997] ECR 65, 89, the Commission argued that national courts were entitled to dismiss objection of nullity under Article 85(2) if it was clear that the anticompetitive agreement fulfilled the requisites in Article 85(3).

[540]   Of course, the *De Minimis* Notice is still available. If the parties have a joint market share of less than 10 per cent or the parties are not competitors at all, the agreement is permissible even if the conditions in the R&D block exemption are not met. However, the black list in the R&D block exemption is

The elimination of the grey and white lists implies a lot more than what might appear at first glance. By eliminating these paragraphs and the opposition procedure, the focus of the whole analysis under Article 101(1) TFEU has shifted 180 degrees. Previously, the structure of, for example, the R&D block exemption was derived from a formalistic point of departure that all R&D agreements which fulfilled the definition in the block exemption were potentially anticompetitive, however, exempted if containing only 'white or grey' clauses. Only the grey or white-listed clauses were actually exempted and if the parties invented new clauses, not to be found in Articles 4–6 of the old block exemption they had to be individually exempted. They were, in accordance with the underlying logic, potentially anticompetitive.

The block exemptions published after the introduction of the more economic approach, by eliminating both the white and grey lists and the opposition procedure, do in fact shift this formalistic foundation. Now the presumption is that all R&D agreements, including joint production and sales, even though including restrictive clauses, are pro-competitive if they do not include the so-called 'black clauses' stipulated in the block exemption. For example, field of use restrictions even between competitors are today presumably pro-competitive according to the R&D block exemption since they are not encompassed by the black list.[541]

Indeed, generally speaking, R&D joint ventures between competitors under EU competition law are considered pro-competitive. The notion that competition is inherently restricted when the parents are competitors or potential entrants to the field dedicated to the joint R&D has been scrapped. The issue whether the parents are competitors or potential competitors has lost importance. This is in stark contrast to the 'old' system, where such harsh words were exchanged in the legal doctrine to establish a correct definition of 'competitor'.[542]

The issue of whether an agreement is pro-competitive, benign or anticompetitive shall be judged under Article 101(1) TFEU, and the main purpose of the agreement shall be scrutinised under paragraph 1 together with the issue of whether a restraint makes a pro-competitive or benign agreement anticompetitive. At least some of the clauses in the former

---

still applicable; Commission Staff Working Document, Guidance on restrictions of competition 'by object' for the purpose of defining which agreements may benefit from the *De Minimis* Notice of 25 June 2014, SWD(2014) 198 final. See Dolmans discussing this point. Maurits Dolmans, 'Standards For Standards', (2002) 26 *Fordham International Law Journal*, 163, 172.

[541] Not included in the black list in Article 5 of the R&D block exemption.

[542] See the 1984 block exemption, 5 et seq.

grey list have been moved from Article 101(3) to Article 101(1). They shall be scrutinised under the EU version of the ancillary restraints doctrine. However, any weighing of pro-competitive versus anti-competitive effects shall be done under Article 101(3).[543] Put differently, if the clause is too restrictive under an Article 101(1) analysis, the efficiencies correlated to the restriction shall be judged against the anticompetitive effects created by the same restrictions under Article 101(3).

What was most striking in the old regime of protecting competition within the field of R&D collaborations was the simplicity of the system. Compared with the system of finding anticompetitive conduct today, the old system was a legal system for establishing anticompetitive conduct, while today the system is more complex.

As mentioned above, then Director-General for Competition Manfred Caspari, in 1985, discussed the steps in the old R&D block exemption stating that the point of departure should be establishing whether the parties are competitors or potential competitors.[544] Thus, the crucial issue was whether the partners could reasonably be expected to enter the market for the joint venture individually. Generally, if that was the case, and the collaboration was not only a pure R&D collaboration but also included joint production and/or sales, the joint effort fell within then Article 85(1) EC Treaty in the old system, the next step was to see whether it was covered by a block exemption. If that was not the case the application of Article 85(3) followed. The Commission would check whether the restrictions imposed on the partners would not exceed the bounds of what on a reasonable economic assessment is indispensable for the formation and viability of the joint venture in subject matter, geographical extent or duration.

Today the method for applying Article 101 is different. The first question after defining the agreement as an R&D collaboration is no longer whether the parties entering the agreement are competitors or not. On the contrary, R&D collaborations between competitors are considered pro-competitive. Instead, initially the agreement should be scrutinised for

---

[543] For example Case T-112/99 *M6 v. Commission* [2001] ECR II-2459, paras 72 et seq.; Case T-65/98 *Van den Bergh Foods v. Commission* [2003] ECR II-4653, para 106; and Case 328/03 *O2 (Germany) v. Commission* [2006] ECR II-1231, paras 66 et seq., 71 et seq., and 116.

[544] Cf. Manfred Caspari, 'Joint Ventures – The Intersection of Antitrust and Industrial Policy in the EEC', in Barry E. Hawk (ed.), *Antitrust and Trade Policy in the United States and the European Community, 1985* (Bender, Fordham Corporate Law Institute, 1986), 461 et seq.

objective hard-core clauses. If no hard-core clauses are present, it is quite clear the agreement will most likely fall outside Article 101(1) according to the rules in the Guidelines or be saved by a safe harbour, if it is not shown that it is very likely that the collaboration would cause anti-competitive harms that would not have existed without it. Does the agreement restrict innovative competition between the parties, does it foreclose third parties to technology (the result), enable the agreement parties to coordinate their behaviour on existing markets (spillover effects) and are there any potential restrictive effects in these regards? Under the few circumstances an agreement would not be saved by having recourse to the Guidelines or the block exemption, thus, an effect analysis under Article 101(3) should be performed. For failing such analysis, the parties need to have market power, be competitors and the collaboration must concern development or later stage application of a technology to a product, that is, research close to the end product. Acknowledging that this description is unclear, a schematic application of Article 101 TFEU to R&D agreements could look like that illustrated in Figure 3.1.

The scheme in Figure 3.1 shows one prominent trend, which perhaps mirrors a broader development under EU competition law. It is getting very complicated; the outcome is based on prediction of the future development of the market rather than objective rules or effects or facts. When eliminating the notion that when two competitors conduct joint R&D Article 101(1) is inherently restricted unless the *De Minimis* Notice was applicable, the application of Article 101 TFEU becomes difficult. What should trigger a more intense scrutiny of the agreement in question?

The reality that no pure R&D collaboration had been declared in violation of Article 101 even before the enactment of the more lenient treatment should be kept in mind.

Below, the application of Article 101 TFEU to R&D collaborations is described and discussed in accordance with the scheme above.

(ii) Objectively restrictive
The first step should be to establish the relevant market(s). At least one market needs to be defined so as to control whether the *De Minimis* Notice is applicable or not.[545] However, *per se* illegal – and to some extent *per se* legal – agreements can be identified without establishing a relevant market. Therefore, agreements could be scrutinised for objective restrictive clauses before the relevant market is established (see Box A in

---

[545]   Commission Notice, O.J. C 291/1 (2014).

Market share above *de minimis* threshold, that is, appreciable effects to competition 5–15%

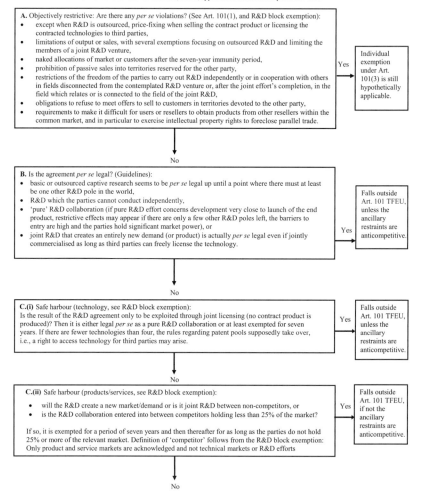

A. Objectively restrictive: Are there any *per se* violations? (See Art. 101(1), and R&D block exemption):
- except when R&D is outsourced, price-fixing when selling the contract product or licensing the contracted technologies to third parties,
- limitations of output or sales, with several exemptions focusing on outsourced R&D and limiting the members of a joint R&D venture,
- naked allocations of market or customers after the seven-year immunity period,
- prohibition of passive sales into territories reserved for the other party,
- restrictions of the freedom of the parties to carry out R&D independently or in cooperation with others in fields disconnected from the contemplated R&D venture or, after the joint effort's completion, in the field which relates or is connected to the field of the joint R&D,
- obligations to refuse to meet offers to sell to customers in territories devoted to the other party, or
- requirements to make it difficult for users or resellers to obtain products from other resellers within the common market, and in particular to exercise intellectual property rights to foreclose parallel trade.

Yes → Individual exemption under Art. 101(3) is still hypothetically applicable.

No

B. Is the agreement *per se* legal? (Guidelines):
- basic or outsourced captive research seems to be *per se* legal up until a point where there must at least be one other R&D pole in the world,
- R&D which the parties cannot conduct independently,
- 'pure' R&D collaboration (if pure R&D effort concerns development very close to launch of the end product, restrictive effects may appear if there are only a few other R&D poles left, the barriers to entry are high and the parties hold significant market power), or
- joint R&D that creates an entirely new demand (or product) is actually *per se* legal even if jointly commercialised as long as third parties can freely license the technology.

Yes → Falls outside Art. 101 TFEU, unless the ancillary restraints are anticompetitive.

No

C.(i) Safe harbour (technology, see R&D block exemption):
Is the result of the R&D agreement only to be exploited through joint licensing (no contract product is produced)? Then it is either legal *per se* as a pure R&D collaboration or at least exempted for seven years. If there are fewer technologies than four, the rules regarding patent pools supposedly take over, i.e., a right to access technology for third parties may arise.

Yes → Falls outside Art. 101 TFEU, unless the ancillary restraints are anticompetitive.

No

C.(ii) Safe harbour (products/services, see R&D block exemption):
- will the R&D create a new market/demand or is it joint R&D between non-competitors, or
- is the R&D collaboration entered into between competitors holding less than 25% of the market?

If so, it is exempted for a period of seven years and then thereafter for as long as the parties do not hold 25% or more of the relevant market. Definition of 'competitor' follows from the R&D block exemption: Only product and service markets are acknowledged and not technical markets or R&D efforts

Yes → Falls outside Art. 101 TFEU, if not the ancillary restraints are anticompetitive.

No

If the R&D collaboration fits neither box above, the effects of the agreement need to be analysed in a joint legal and economic analysis:

D. Overarching Question: Does the agreement cause anticompetitive harms that would not have existed without it? Hence, does the agreement restrict innovation or competition between the parties, foreclose third parties to technology (result), enable the agreement of the parties to coordinate their behaviour on existing markets (spillover effects) or will any network effects between different joint ventures arise?

and

Are there any realistic potential restrictive effects in these regards?

E. (i) R&D efforts:

- R&D collaboration *significantly* reduces competition, e.g. a merger between two of only four poles of research, or will there only be very few innovation efforts left outside the collaboration?
- Does the R&D venture decline new entrants even though in a clear monopoly position and this prevents the emergence of a new product (possibly under the IMS Health Art. 102 TFEU doctrine)?

E.(ii) Spillover effects on other markets:

Do the parties hold *significant* market power in existing markets, i.e. product, service or technology (less than dominance, approx. 40%)? If so:

- will output, price or royalties be affected by the collaboration?
- will commonality of costs greatly affect the price?
- will output, price or royalties be affected by the collaboration?
- will the choice of products or technologies decline because of the joint R&D?

No Market Power, No BER   No   Yes, Market Power. *Prima facie* case established
Presumption of anticompetitive violation
Effect analysis under Art. 101(3).

F. (i) The main purpose of the agreement is not anticompetitive. The ancillary restraints doctrine needs to be analysed before the agreement may be declared falling outside Art. 101(1): are the restraints objectively necessary to implement the agreement? All these clauses are probably benign in the new regime with the black clauses limit:

- prohibition for research in the same or similar fields as the joint effort;
- exclusive purchasing, manufacturing, producing, selling obligations between the parents and the joint venture;
- except for the black-listed situations, field of use restrictions; and
- grant-back obligations (obligations for either party to transfer new innovations or improvements to the other) for related inventions or obligations to communicate experiences gained from commercialisation.

Yes, *Prima facie* case
Presumption of anti-competitive violation
Anti-competitive effects

F. (ii) The main purpose of the agreement is anticompetitive. Individual exemption under Art. 101(3) TFEU must be sought:

(i)   improve the production or distribution,
(ii)   fair share to the consumers,
(iii) indispensable, and
(iv)   no elimination of competition.

Possibly, under Art. 101(3) the 'ancillary' restraints should be weighed. Thus, not only the restraints connected to an anticompetitive R&D venture, but also those ancillary restraints connected to a benign R&D venture but which are not objectively necessary and need individual exemption under Art. 101(3).

Figure 3.1   The system under the new block exemption

Figure 3.1). Hard-core agreements will be regarded as anticompetitive, for example, price-fixing, output restrictions and naked allocation of markets or customers. In addition, the hard-core (black) clauses or agreements listed in the current R&D block exemption must be added.[546] Indeed, those clauses with the object of, for example, restricting the freedom of the participants to carry out R&D independently or in cooperation with others in fields disconnected from the relevant field of research or prohibiting the challenging of the validity of intellectual property rights derived from the finished research cooperation, are objectively anticompetitive also for parties that can take advantage of the *De Minimis* Notice.[547] These black clauses are actually rather far reaching. Indeed, the stipulation that restricting the freedom of the parties to carry out R&D in the field of the contemplated R&D venture, after the completion of the joint effort, should be a black clause is actually surprising. It is clearly more intrusive compared with the ancillary restraints doctrine under the merger regulation that stipulates that when purchasing, for example, an R&D-only firm, the purchaser may restrict the former owner from conducting competing activity (including R&D) with the firm for a period of two to three years.[548] Or, for that matter, in employment relationships a researcher's employment contract may include a non-compete clause or confidential obligation that might limit the employee from taking up employment with competing firms for a

---

[546] Article 5 R&D block exemption. See 81(3) Guidelines, paras 23 and 24, stating that non-exhaustive guidance on what constitutes restriction by object may be blacklisted and hard-core agreements or restrictions; Case C-226/11 *Expedia* [2012] ECR 795. See also Case 5/69, *Völk v. Vervaecke* [1969] ECR 295, para 7.

[547] This could be interpreted the other way around, i.e., if the parties do not reach 5 or 15 per cent market share, depending on the competitive relationship, or where there is no relevant market, then the black clauses in the block exemption should not be applicable. However, under such an interpretation several R&D joint ventures would fall under the *De Minimis* Notice given the fact that R&D ventures often may aim at creating a new product or demand and, hence, the market share of the parties would be non-existent. The R&D block exemption also addresses the issue of R&D joint ventures aiming to create a new market. The black list in the R&D block exemption should thus also be applicable to agreements falling under the *De Minimis* Notice; Commission Staff Working Document, Guidance on restrictions to competition 'by object' for the purpose of defining which agreements may benefit from the *De Minimis* Notice of 25 June 2014, SWD(2014) 198 final. *Contra* Maurits Dolmans, 'Standards For Standards', (2002) 26 *Fordham International Law Journal*, 163, 172.

[548] Commission Notice on restrictions directly related and necessary to concentrations, OJ C 56, 05/03/2005, p. 24 et seq., paras 18 et seq.

period of time (normally less than two years, and as long as the employee receives remuneration). In fact, the R&D block exemption in this regard clearly protects R&D-intensive firms' *ex post* ability to compete with the firms that have given them the assignment to conduct research.

Perhaps to the black list should be added restrictions stating that only one of the parties of the joint R&D may utilise the result after completion of the joint R&D process for further research. If the parties would like to make use of the block exemption, only when one of the parties is a research facility may it be restricted on how to use the result.[549] Nonetheless, perhaps such a restriction may be exempted under the third paragraph.

To the list of hard-core restrictions should also be added agreements with the object of restricting innovation as such. It is interesting to note that the guidelines do not clearly stipulate that an agreement where two or more parties agree not to perform research, or to delay research, or for that matter shelve innovations, is anticompetitive by object.[550] The 'laundry list' in Article 101 states that limiting and controlling technical development implies that naked restriction of R&D should be considered objectively anticompetitive. The black clause in the R&D block exemption stipulating that the parties to a joint R&D venture may not be restricted in conducting research independently or jointly with others outside the scope of their joint efforts would imply that a clear-cut agreement between two parties restricting innovation would be considered anticompetitive by object. The plaintiff should in these situations not be obliged to establish market power, nor anticompetitive effect, before Article 101 TFEU should be applicable.[551] It would be beneficial to have a statement clarifying that naked restrictions of innovation are objective restrictions of competition. However, the guidelines are silent in this regard.

---

[549] R&D block exemption Article 3(2). The *GlaxoSmithKline* case perhaps adds a new dimension to these objectively restrictive clauses. At least it gives an added dimension to the hard-core clauses which protected so-called parallel trade. Case T-168/01 *GlaxoSmithKline v. Commission* [2006] ECR II-2969, paras 121 et seq.

[550] In comparison, under US law such an agreement would be *per se* unlawful, see Phillip Areeda & Herbert Hovenkamp, *Antitrust Law – An Analysis of Antitrust Principles and Their Application* (Aspen Publishers 2005), 113 § 2115b2. *U.S. v. Automobile Manufacturers Association, Inc*, 307 F. Supp. 617, 13 Fed.R.Serv.2d 731, 1970 Trade Cases P73, 070.

[551] C-67/13 P *Cartes Bancaires*, not yet published and Opinion by AG Wahl in the same case.

The 81(3) Guidelines state that 'restrictive by object' does not imply that the agreement needs to include a naked restriction of competition.[552] The nature of the agreement, the aim of the parties and the context of the situation need to be analysed. It should moreover be stressed that the list of anticompetitive behaviour stated in the Guidelines and block exemption is not exhaustive. There might be other objectively anticompetitive agreements not yet discovered.

It is apparent that the Commission in the 81(3) Guidelines promotes a model for defining anticompetitive conduct derived from the *Maschinen-bau Ulm* case[553] rather than from the *Consten and Grundig* case.[554] By stating that even though a clause restricts rivalry the Court should still analyse the nature of the agreement and the context of where it should be applied before rendering it objectively anticompetitive, the Commission supports, not a strict *per se* rule as envisioned in the *Grundig* case, but more of a truncate rule of reason when establishing whether a clause or an agreement is objectively anticompetitive.[555]

(iii) *Per se* lawful conduct

When the agreement is checked for hard-core clauses, the third step is to analyse whether the agreement may be considered *per se* lawful (see Box B in Figure 3.1). The Commission has taken a broad initiative and the Guidelines on the application of Article 101 of the TFEU to horizontal cooperation agreements (hereinafter Horizontal Guidelines) state that some agreements are *possibly* lawful, that is, not falling within the ambit of Article 101(1),[556] even though foreclosing third parties, namely: (i) cooperation between non-competitors; (ii) cooperation between competing companies that cannot independently carry out the project or activity covered by the cooperation; and (iii) cooperation concerning an activity which does not influence the 'relevant parameters' of competition.[557]

---

[552]   81(3) Guidelines para 22 (now 101(3) TFEU).

[553]   See generally Case 56/65 *Société Technique Minière v. Maschinenbau Ulm* [1966] ECR 235.

[554]   See generally Case 56 & 58/64 *Consten and Grundig v. Commission* [1966] ECR 299.

[555]   81(3) Guidelines paras 24 and 31.

[556]   The 2001 Horizontal Guidelines, para 24. See also Horizontal Guidelines, paras 129 et seq.

[557]   See also Björn Lundqvist, *Standardization under EU Competition Rules and US Antitrust Laws – The Rise and the Limits of Self-Regulation* (Edward Elgar, 2014), 197.

These broad statements cannot be considered indicating safe harbours or clear-cut exemptions from EU competition law, but rather general guidance when the collaboration may fall outside the first paragraph. The Commission has also specified in more detail when certain agreements might be regarded as *per se* legal. For example, the above points (i) and (ii) must be rewritten to: if the parties cannot independently carry out the contemplated research, the parties should not be viewed as competitors, and, hence, the agreement does not restrict competition if the collaboration does not foreclose third party access to markets.[558] Firstly, it must be acknowledged that this statement limits the general statement that all cooperation between non-competitors is *per se* legal.[559] Secondly, the declaration by the Commission clarifies statements (i) and (ii) above, indicating that a cooperation between undertakings that cannot independently carry out a project is in fact collaboration between non-competitors. Nonetheless, the statement is based on a somewhat odd definition of competitor which does not correspond to the definition of competing undertaken in the block exemption. Even though the parties cannot independently carry out the research, the parties perhaps independently still contemplate performing research on a product which may replace the competing products currently distributed by the parties. This would make them competitors according to the R&D block exemption, but not trigger Article 101(1) according to the Horizontal Guidelines. The Guidelines must be interpreted as also requiring that the parties create a new market with the contemplated result, which they could not reach independently.

This discrepancy could perhaps also hint that the Commission has taken an *ex ante* viewpoint of who may be competitors in the Guidelines, while still retaining an *ex post* viewpoint in the block exemption.[560]

The standpoint in the Horizontal Guidelines can also only be justified by disregarding the fact that the parties would have performed some kind of research independent of the contemplated joint research. For example, if BMW and Daimler were not able – because of the existing patent situation – independently to create a hybrid engine, should they actually be considered non-competitors for the creation of hybrid cars? They still produce cars, and what if they independently had created something else, for example, lower consumption diesel engines; would that not have created competition? According to the Horizontal Guidelines, BMW and Daimler would possibly be non-competitors in reference to such an R&D

---

[558] Horizontal Guidelines, para 130. See also Luis Silva Morais, *Joint Venture and EU Competition Law* (Hart Publishing 2013), 258 et seq.
[559] Horizontal Guidelines, paras 129 et seq. See also para 147.
[560] However, see Horizontal Guidelines, paras 145–146.

venture. Historically, at least under the guidance paper under US antitrust law, such hypothetical research, in this example into diesel engines, was taken into consideration when establishing whether an agreement was anticompetitive or not. However, if the wording of the Horizontal Guidelines is followed, that is not to be the case anymore. The parties need only to analyse whether their patents block each other.

Furthermore, when a firm outsources previously captive R&D to specialised companies, research institutes or academic bodies, which are not actively exploiting the results, such agreements shall not be regarded as encompassed by Article 101(1) and thus are *per se* legal.[561] It is somewhat difficult to reconcile this statement with what the Horizontal Guidelines generally reflect regarding competition for innovation. It is even harder to reconcile with Article 3(2) the second sentence of the current R&D block exemption, which states that these specialised research institutes may be deprived of access to the result of the joint research for further exploitation.[562] Why is such a clarification in Article 3(2) of the block exemption under 101(3) needed if the entire agreement does not fall under Article 101(1) according to the Horizontal Guidelines? How much needs to be outsourced for the agreement to fall outside 101(1)? Conversely, paragraph 132 of the Guidelines stipulates that so-called pure R&D agreements are not, normally, captured by Article 101(1), but in such case why is there an exemption in Article 3(3) of the R&D block exemption specifically addressing these 'pure' R&D agreements? It should be noted that there might be a difference between basic and 'pure' R&D. A pure R&D agreement can still concern applied research, close to the end product, while basic research is science. Nonetheless, the Horizontal Guidelines and the R&D block exemption are not correlating in some instances and that creates confusion.[563]

---

[561]   Horizontal Guidelines, para 131.

[562]   It should be noted that several researchers asked to delete this limitation for R&D-only firms, when the block exemption was up for revision in 2010. See Joseph Drexl, et al., 'Comments of the Max Planck Institute for IP, Competition and Tax Law on the Draft Commission Block Exemption Regulation on R&D Agreements and the Draft Guidelines on Horizontal Cooperation Agreements' (2010) *Max Planck Institute for IP, Competition & Tax Law Research Paper No. 10-12*.

[563]   Ibid. With this as a starting point, the joint R&D venture needs to be scrutinised to see whether it concerns a slight improvement of the existing products or aims at significantly changing or even developing a new product or technology. If the contemplated product or technology is considerably different from the products marketed by the parties, the emerging new product or technology is not likely to belong to the same relevant market. Correspondingly,

Possibly, the Commission actually has taken a step too far in paragraph 132 and also in preamble 6 of the R&D block exemption; pure R&D collaborations can restrict competition and should not be considered *per se* legal.[564]

Considering that the research institution often becomes foreclosed to third parties after entering an R&D outsourcing agreement, *de lege ferenda*, these situations should be handled with more care and precision.[565] Anecdotal evidence indicates that smaller innovative firms may have been foreclosed by larger firms under R&D agreements in the pharmaceutical sector.[566] Furthermore, it seems that in public–private partnerships between universities (or thereto connected firms) and private undertakings regarding joint R&D collaborations, the agreements often stipulate restrictions for the university also not to conduct competing research after the conclusion of the collaboration. These firms are often research-driven without the possibility of developing drugs. The larger firms often trade their development, testing and distribution skills with the venture. R&D agreements in the pharmaceutical sector have included stipulation that the compound or substance may only (exclusively) be jointly developed under the agreement.[567] Such a covenant gives the larger firms veto power regarding developing the substance or compound. Possibly, the larger firms have other incentives than to develop the substance. Perhaps such development cannibalises on already marketed drugs and the vertically integrated firm decides to delay the development

---

the parties will not be considered competitors. The Guidelines do not stipulate what method should be used for identifying the contemplated market for the new product, but a similar test to the hypothetical SSNIP test may be used. Even if it is established that the contemplated products do not belong in the same market as the current products, the market for existing products may nonetheless be important if the pooling of research efforts may coordinate the parties' behaviour in any way. It may also be a good starting point to identify potential competitors for the contemplated research result.

[564] See Luis Silva Morais, *Joint Venture and EU Competition Law* (Hart Publishing 2013), 252. See also Horizontal Guidelines, para 138.

[565] Horizontal Guidelines, paras 50 et seq. It has been shown that specific research institutions do prefer exclusive licensing arrangements so as to be able to extract supra-competitive profits. Cf. Susanne Scotchmer, *Innovation and Incentives* (The MIT Press 2004), 236 et seq.

[566] Cf. Saami Zain, 'Suppression of Innovation or Collaborative Efficiencies?: An Antitrust Analysis of a Research & Development Collaboration That Led to the Shelving of a Promising Drug', (2006) 5 *J. Marshall Rev. Intell. Prop. L*, 347, 350 et seq., and Davis Hamilton, 'Silent Treatment: How Genetech, Novartis Stifled a Promising Drug', (2005) *Wall. St. J.*, A1.

[567] Ibid.

of the new drug. Under EU competition law, a covenant of exclusive joint development and exploitation would either fall outside Article 101(1) or be captured by the block exemption. Moreover, jointly outsourced R&D by two or more vertically integrated firms to an R&D-specific firm is encompassed in the R&D block exemption.

Interestingly, these specialised research firms are less protected under EU competition law than other firms. Given the clear standpoint by the Commission and generally by European politicians that firms focusing on research and intellectual property creation might increase in number and importance in the future, they should also be encompassed by and protected under EU competition law so they are able to grow also vertically.

Finally, R&D cooperation regarding only basic research does not infringe Article 101(1).[568] Only if the parties retain or acquire substantial market power, such agreements may be considered anticompetitive in the light of Article 101(1).[569] According to the Commission, 'substantial market power' is less than dominance, but probably falling just short of dominance. EU competition law is getting very close (and in some cases beyond) actually requiring market dominance before Article 101 prevents the conduct.[570] Actually, the definition of market power in the Horizontal Guidelines[571] is tangent to the definition of dominance in the 82 Guidelines.[572]

Nonetheless, from a restrictive reading of the guidelines, a summary of the activities which do not fall within Article 101(1) is: (i) except where the parties hold market power in the existing markets, R&D cooperation regarding basic research; (ii) joint research which the parties cannot independently carry out; (iii) captive R&D outsourced to specialised companies, research institutes or academic bodies that are not actively exploiting the results; and (iv) pure R&D collaborations.

---

[568]   Horizontal Guidelines, paras 129 et seq.
[569]   See note 1 of the Horizontal Guidelines, and note 17 of the 2001 Horizontal Guidelines.
[570]   Taking into consideration Article 102 and the fourth condition in Article 101(3) 'no elimination of competition', it might be regarded as difficult to reconcile this narrow interpretation of Article 101(1). It should be noted that in example 2 (para 76) of the Horizontal Guidelines, the parties retain a market share of 75 per cent and the Commission concludes that it will not restrict competition.
[571]   Horizontal Guidelines, paras 39 et seq.
[572]   82 Guidelines paras 11 et seq.

(iv)   The current block exemption

(a)   Introduction   If the agreement is not *per se* illegal or *per se* lawful according to the Guidelines and black list (Boxes A and B in Figure 3.1), the safe harbours or exempted agreements as stipulated in the block exemption may be applicable (see Boxes C(i) and C(ii) in Figure 3.1).

On 14 December 2010, the block exemption for the application of Article 101(3) to R&D agreements was introduced.[573] It reaffirmed the amendment made in 1993 so as to create a fully fledged exemption for firms entering agreements to cooperate in the whole process from research for acquiring new knowledge to the distribution of the end products. Indeed, the parties agree not only to conduct research but also to manufacture and distribute the products under the R&D block exemption.

The Commission also made the exemption more permissive based on its findings in cases decided in 1994.[574] From the outset the new R&D block exemption follows the old block exemption stipulating a time period for when small or midsize firms may exclusively collaborate: Article 2 stipulates the exemption based on Article 101(3), R&D agreements shall not be encompassed by the scope of Article 101(1) as long as the cooperation fulfils the requirements stipulated in the block exemption. Article 1 defines some important notions. Article 3 stipulates the requirement for the exemption. Article 4 states the limitations for the exemption in time and market share. Article 5 stipulates the black list and Article 6 stipulates a list of grey clauses. Article 7 gives the Commission the right to withdraw the exemption in individual cases. Below, these Articles will be discussed in light of the above scheme and in comparison with the 1985 and 2000 R&D block exemptions.

(b)   Definitions   The Commission has in the current block exemption defined R&D agreement in much more detail compared with the 2000 block exemption and also reveals that outsourced or paid-for R&D is included under the block exemption.

The definition of R&D is *inter alia* wide. However, it is less wide than the definition under the 2000 block exemption. It included everything from initial brainstorming to the application for patents. If two large

---

[573]   Commission regulation No 1217/2010 14 December 2010 on the application of Article 101(3) of the Treaty on the Functioning of the European Union to certain categories of research and development agreements OJ L 335, 18.12.2010, 36 et seq. (defined earlier as the R&D block exemption).

[574]   See *supra* under section 3.3.3(vi).

firms, which have some overlapping businesses, would like their researchers to sit down and only brainstorm, based on their know-how, about the future development of the relevant technology or industry, that could have possibly been considered an R&D collaboration under the 2000 block exemption. Now the collaboration needs to be established in an agreement with a concrete aim of developing a commercial and patentable result to benefit from the R&D block exemption.[575]

The notion that joint R&D may imply not only that the research is jointly performed, but also that it may be allocated between the parties, is still intact. Joint research thus by way of specialisation is divided into research, development, production and distribution. In other words, the entering of an R&D agreement may not only oblige the parties to restructure their individual R&D units but, to some extent, also their manufacturing facilities and distribution networks. As long as the collaboration starts out as joint R&D, the R&D block exemption should be applicable. Indeed, a joint R&D agreement does not imply that the parties actually meet to do research. They may share the work. Moreover, several firms may jointly outsource the R&D to a third party. Although it is difficult to see how cross-fertilising of ideas, which is a goal of the block exemption, can materialise in these circumstances, such division of labour enables the parties to become more efficient. They may downsize their own organisations in the areas which have been outsourced to other member(s) of the venture.[576]

A difference compared with the old Regulation 418/85 and the 2000 R&D block exemption is that competing undertakings are defined in more detail in the current R&D block exemption: 'actual competitor' is

---

[575] See, e.g., Article 3(4) R&D block exemption.

[576] Possibly the same effects could come about by using the block exemption for specialisation agreements, see recital 7 Commission regulation No 1218/2010 14 December 2010 on the application of Article 101(3) of the Treaty on the Functioning of the European Union to categories of specialisation agreements OJ L 335, 18.12.2010, p. 43 et seq. See also recital 9 of the Commission regulation No 2658/2000 29 November 2000 on the application of Article 81(3) of the Treaty to categories of specialisation agreements OJ L 304, 05.12.2000, p. 3 et seq. See also Commission decision Bayer BP Petroleum, OJ 1988 L 150/35, where Bayer and BP Chemicals through their R&D agreement effectively made them into non-competitors. They became suppliers for each other within the field of R&D. In the earlier case Commission decision Rank/Sopelem, OJ 1975 L 29/20, the Commission regarded, as an anticompetitive factor, the fact that the R&D agreement introduced specialisation whereby each party to the agreement allows the other to take over R&D work or manufacturing of certain categories of products, which eliminated that party as a developer of those products.

defined as an undertaking active on either the same product or technology market as the result of the R&D will inhabit. 'Potential competitor' means an undertaking that, in the absence of the R&D agreement, would, on realistic grounds and not just as a mere theoretical possibility, in case of a small but permanent increase in relative prices be likely to undertake, within not more than *three* years, the necessary additional investments or other necessary switching costs to supply a product, technology or process capable of being improved, substituted or replaced by the contract product or contract technology on the relevant geographic market.[577]

With this definition the Commission has taken a stand on several issues. Firstly, even though extending the notion of potential entrant from two to three years, the Commission's definition does not encompass the full notion of innovation effort. Even though a decrease in spending on R&D may create a greater difference between price and cost and thus opportunity cost for switching from one product to another, the definition is not focused on innovation efforts.[578] In other words, the rule could hit both ways: (i) the period of three years is to short, not encompassing potential competitors if the Commission would have used the innovation market concept (if such a market concept would work in reality), or (ii) it is too long, actually not fitting very dynamic markets where the rate of innovation is a lot faster than three years and three years would actually encompass too many firms.[579]

---

[577] See Article 1 R&D block exemption. See also Horizontal Guidelines, para 10, fn. 3. In the 2000 R&D block exemption competing undertaking was defined as 'competing undertaking means an undertaking that is supplying a product capable of being improved or replaced by the contracted products (an actual competitor) or an undertaking that would, on realistic grounds, undertake the necessary additional investments or other necessary switching costs so that it could supply such a product in response to a small and permanent increase in relative prices (a potential competitor)'. See also Björn Lundqvist, *Standardization under EU Competition Rules and US Antitrust Laws – The Rise and the Limits of Self-Regulation* (Edward Elgar, 2014).

[578] Regarding the definition of innovation markets, see *supra* and cf. Richard Gilbert & Steven Sunshine, 'Incorporating Dynamic Efficiency Concerns in Merger Analysis: the use of Innovation Markets', (1995) 63 *Antitrust Law Journal*, 569.

[579] This last concern was raised by the scholars at the Max Planck Institute in reference to the draft R&D block exemption. See Joseph Drexl, et al., Comments of the Max Planck Institute for IP, Competition and Tax Law on the Draft Commission Block Exemption Regulation on R&D Agreements and the Draft

Secondly, previously the definition of competing undertakings applied only to goods and service markets and not to technology markets.[580] Indeed, if two firms competed by licensing similar technology but did not sell any competing goods or provided any competing services, they were not to be regarded as competitors according to the 2000 R&D block exemption. The inclusion of technology marks a major improvement in the new block exemption compared with the old block exemption. As a matter of fact, the definition of competing undertaking under the current block exemption is wide, wider than in the Technology Transfer Block Exemption Regulation (TTBER), and also includes potential entrants that would realistically conduct relevant R&D within a period of three years should there be a small but permanent increase in price.[581]

Thirdly, the block exemption might still be interpreted that if the parties contemplate such a ground-breaking invention that a new demand is created, they shall not be regarded as competitors even though they already compete on a product market.[582] A similar exemption exists in the technology transfer block exemption.[583] However, the question is whether this is logical. Parties taking advantage of this exemption are actually claiming that they want to achieve a joint monopoly on a new market. Should such behaviour be promoted? If both competitors have similar aims for a new product or market, should they not compete to attain this goal? Only in rare circumstances where the parties block each other with intellectual property rights so that they cannot compete would such an exemption actually create a new demand. It is also difficult, which the Horizontal Guidelines acknowledge, to draw the line between ground-breaking innovations and innovations that 'only' substitute or replace the current product. The Commission and the Courts

---

Guidelines on Horizontal Cooperation Agreements (2010) *Max Planck Institute for IP, Competition & Tax Law Research Paper No. 10-12*, para 24.

[580]   See R&D block exemption, Article 2 para 5 for definition of 'product'.

[581]   One to three years was the median estimate by industry respondents surveyed about the time required for imitators to duplicate a major patented new process or product and to have a significant impact on the market, see IP 2 Report, fn. 1.

[582]   See Horizontal Guidelines, para 138. Compare Article 1 with Article 4 R&D block exemption. Also Luis Silva Morais has observed this, see Luis Silva Morais, *Joint Venture and EU Competition Law* (Hart Publishing 2013), 266.

[583]   See new TTBER Article 1(n) *e contrario*, i.e., Commission regulation No 316/2014 of 21 March 2014 on the application of Article 101(3) of the Treaty on the Functioning of the European Union to categories of technology transfer agreements.

struggled for example in the *AstraZeneca* case whether the old histamine receptor antagonist (H2 blocker) was a competing drug to AstraZeneca's Losec. AstraZeneca argued that the product's mode of action should be determinative to establish relevant market, while the Commission regarded that therapeutic indication should be the deciding factor when establishing the relevant market. It seems that the Commission in the current block exemption and Guidelines has (again) increased the definition of competitor and possibly the new product really needs to be ground-breaking to be regarded as establishing the parties as non-competitors.

Nonetheless, under US law and more so under EU competition law, there is an acceptance that firms which have achieved a position of monopoly or dominance shall be able to enjoy that position.[584] However, that does not correspond to an exemption, that is, that competition law should stand back in the collective attempt to attain such a position. On the contrary, that is when competition law should apply.

(c) What to research The parties are treated more leniently according to the block exemption if they are not considered competitors. Then it does not matter whether one of the participants has more than 25 per cent market share in the relevant market.[585] Parties are moreover, as discussed above, not considered competitors if they perform joint research they are not able to do on their own.[586] For that reason there exists perhaps an incentive to claim broad and far-reaching aims for the research so as to be able to maintain that the parties are not competitors.

Article 3 states the condition for the exemption. It corresponds in some ways to Article 2 of the 1984 block exemption, albeit with some major differences. The limits to the exemption stated in Article 3 of the block exemption allow, compared with its predecessor, open-ended joint R&D. The research does not need to be qualified within the framework of a programme defining the objectives of the work and the field in which it is to be carried out.

Therefore, in principle, the joint R&D could go on indefinitely as long as there is constant development of new products. Thus, the immunity period is, with some exceptions, seven years for each developed product

---

[584] However, see the rather unnoticed change in Article 7 of Regulation 1/2003.

[585] R&D block exemption Article 4.

[586] See TT Guidelines, para 4, and Horizontal Guidelines, para 130.

or technology, but that does not mean the R&D cooperation has to be confined to seven years. As long as the research develops into new products the parties are, according to the block exemption, free to cooperate beyond the seven years stipulated in the block exemption.[587] In comparison, the US Guidelines stipulate that joint efforts which last beyond ten years should be scrutinised under the Merger Guidelines. Since the question of whether to analyse joint efforts under Merger Regulation 134/2004 or not revolves around the question of 'full functionality', no such definite timeframe can be set up.

Taking the above into consideration, parties holding strong market shares on a product market could join with the objective of creating a new technology under a technology standardisation agreement in the pre-standardisation phase. They would then not be considered competitors under the R&D block exemption since the technology would create a new demand. After the technology is developed the standardisation agreement is entered into, but the parties can continue to collaborate to create SEPs until the end of the seven years.

Interestingly, this might also cause foreclosure effects. It is quite clear that standardisation agreements and patent pools can foreclose competing technologies. It is evident in the area of R&D collaboration that a wide aim for the new technology is allowed. However, if the R&D collaboration is successful the wide definition might be transferred into a technology standard or patent pool definition. These wide definitions might then foreclose new innovators from gaining access to markets.

Another difference between the current block exemption and the 1985 block exemption is the question regarding the parties' access to the results of the R&D, and to prior technology invented by one party to the agreement. It should be noted that the new block exemption compared with the former clarifies in Article 3(3) that if the R&D agreement only provides for joint pure R&D, each party shall independently have the right to exploit the result and any pre-existing *know-how* necessary for the purpose of such exploitation. Thus, *e contrario*, neither party has the right to use any pre-existing rights, for example, background patents to which the other party is the proprietor, when exploiting the result

---

[587]   Confusingly, Article 4(1) of the R&D block exemption states that the exclusivity period is seven years from the time the contracted product or technology is first put on the market. However, if the research continues with the aim of creating another product, the parties seem to be free to continue cooperating. Unfortunately, there is no definition of new product.

independently after the exemption has expired.[588] The party holding background intellectual property rights can thereby foreclose its research colleague making use of the result commercially after the venture. Indeed, even if the proprietor did not disclose the patent before entering the joint research, the other party may be prevented from utilising the result of the joint research.[589] In the draft R&D block exemption the Commission suggested that the parties must agree that prior to starting the research and development all the parties will disclose all their existing and pending intellectual property rights in as far as they are relevant for the exploitation of the results by the other parties.[590] Unfortunately, this requirement was dropped in the final R&D block exemption. The R&D block exemption thereby exempts to some degree patent ambushing or patent hold-up in R&D collaborations. A patentee might lure firms into investing into joint R&D so as to create a technology standard and when such firms have made their investments it reveals the hidden background patent and this behaviour is exempted under the R&D block exemption. Generally, R&D collaborations where the parties want to create a pool of patents but do not want to give access to parties should be exempted under the R&D block exemption.

Interestingly, Article 3(2) is silent regarding pre-existing rights or know-how. It only states that all the parties must have access to the results for the purposes of further research and exploitation. However, such a right may already, to some extent, exist under the research exemption in national patent laws. Or, how do we interpret access? Does this imply access to background IP, that is, technology existing before the joint research and perhaps held by only one party? Or, could it imply even more? The meaning of access for these purposes is not clarified. It is clear, however, that access to the results for the purpose of further research in a connected field may be restricted during the R&D phase.[591] It is equally clear that access to the results for the purpose of exploitation may also be denied for as long as the block exemption applies, provided

---

[588] Compare with the old exemption, which indicated that any pre-existing technical knowledge should be free for the parties to exploit. See Article 2(c), 1985 block exemption.

[589] Perhaps, an analogy with the exemptions stated in national patent laws (e.g., prior user right) may be used by the party foreclosed so as to enable it to access the market.

[590] Draft R&D block exemption, http://ec.europa.eu/competition/consultations/2010_horizontals/draft_rd_ber_en.pdf, accessed 18 March 2011.

[591] Article 5(a) R&D block exemption.

that at least one of the parties is exploiting the result.[592] Access to the result may also be restricted to certain customers and territories for a period of seven years, or as discussed above, and, if the research is continuous, even longer.[593] Finally, however, the possible restriction when the parties were not competitors at the time of entering the R&D agreement, that access to the results for purposes of exploitation may be restricted to one or more technical fields of application has actually been excluded in the new block exemption.[594]

Article 3(4) stipulates the requirement that the joint R&D has to create intellectual property rights or at least licensable know-how; otherwise the group exemption will not be applicable if the parties want to jointly exploit the result. The result must also be of decisive value for the manufacture of the contracted product or the application of the contracted process. The clause prevents the application of the block exemption to sham R&D.

To summarise, the new R&D block exemption generally has a wide definition of R&D and, in comparison, a narrow definition of competitor.[595] The result is nonetheless that firms that in the public opinion would be considered competitors can collaborate about conduct that generally would not be considered R&D. R&D-only firms are also deprived of adequate protection under EU competition law from the competitive threat made up of vertically integrated firms with broad background patents.

(d) The ceiling Compared with the 1984 block exemption, the exemption has been expanded; see Article 4 of the R&D block exemption. The ceiling is now set at 25 per cent market share for joint research, development and joint distribution, compared with 20 per cent for research and development and 10 per cent for joint distribution in the 1984 exemption. The number of years the parties may jointly exploit the invented product has also been extended to seven years, compared with five years in the 1985 block exemption.

It should, however, be noted that the current R&D block exemption compared with the 2000 block exemption is more rigid when establishing how long an R&D collaboration under the exemption might last. Under

---

[592]   Article 5(b) R&D block exemption.
[593]   Article 5(d)(e) (f)(g) R&D block exemption.
[594]   Compare Articles 3(3) in the current and 2000 R&D block exemptions.
[595]   Even though the definition of R&D is less wide in the current block exemption compared with the 2000 block exemption, and likewise the definition of competitor is broader in the current than in the 2000 block exemption.

the 2000 block exemption exploitation in this regard was only initiated when the contract *product* starts being distributed. Thus, if the parties choose only to exploit by the means of licensing the intellectual property invented under the joint effort, a literal interpretation of the 2000 block exemption revealed that the exemption would have continued to be in effect beyond seven years and actually until the parties selected not to cooperate anymore.[596] This was further supported by point 3 in Article 4 of the 2000 block exemption, which stated that the exemption shall apply as long as the combined market share of the participating undertakings does not exceed 25 per cent of the relevant market for the contract products. Thus, if the participating undertakings exploit the technology only through licensing they will never reach and exceed 25 per cent market share for the contract product. With the introduction of the contract technology in the current R&D block exemption, this loophole in the block exemption has been eliminated, so that the seven-year grace period will start from when either product or technology was marketed.

This means that the block exemption could in theory be applicable for the entire duration of the R&D and for seven years after first joint exploitation by means of a patent pool. Some support may be found in the Horizontal Guidelines that this is a correct interpretation. For example, the Commission accepts that joint licensing can be part of an R&D collaboration which would fall outside Article 101(1) altogether.[597] Indeed, the Horizontal Guidelines state that joint licensing of the result of joint R&D is encompassed by the safe harbour even beyond the seven years' immunity in the block exemption and even if the parents would sell 'contracting products', as long as they are open to license third parties.[598] This statement makes the block exemption somewhat superfluous. It is actually a step beyond the block exemption.

In fact, several of the most successful and best known patent pools (MPEG-LA) and the DVD pools originate entirely or in part from joint R&D effort.[599]

Although the TTBER and hence Article 101 TFEU would be applicable for the licensing agreements from the R&D venture to third parties, the interaction between the R&D block exemption and the TTBER is not altogether clear. The TTBER stipulates two different market share

---

[596]   See Article 4 of the R&D block exemption.
[597]   See Horizontal Guidelines, paras 130 and 134.
[598]   See Horizontal Guidelines, para 138.
[599]   For a further discussion see Björn Lundqvist, *Standardization under EU Competition Rules and US Antitrust Laws – The Rise and the Limits of Self-Regulation* (Edward Elgar, 2014).

ceilings depending on whether it is a vertical or horizontal licensing agreement, 20 and 30 per cent, respectively.

Is a licensing agreement from an R&D pool to a licensee a vertical or horizontal agreement? The vertical rules would apply for a third party licensee, but, for the former members of the joint R&D, is their access to the result of the joint R&D regulated by the R&D block exemption or the TTBER (and in that case the rules for horizontal or vertical licensing agreements)?

As discussed above, all parties of the joint R&D should have access to the result according to the R&D block exemption.[600] Since the R&D block exemption stipulates few hard-core restraints in this regard, this access can, however, be limited, perhaps even more limited under the R&D block exemption than if the TTBER would be applicable. Nonetheless, the TTBER should, *perhaps*, be used also in a relationship between an R&D pool and the former R&D participant, at least when the R&D has ended and the centre of gravity of the collaboration has moved from research to exploitation.[601] *De lege lata*, their access to the result, now encompassed in the licensing vehicle, should also be regulated by the rules of horizontal licensing under the TTBER and, if the TTBER is not applicable, the patent pool rules in the TT Guidelines.[602]

Interestingly, the R&D block exemption may in certain cases be applicable also between the original R&D producers setting up 'R&D pools' and third parties. Often pool licensing agreements stipulate far-reaching grant-back clauses, or as a matter of fact cross-licensing obligations for future innovations and patents. Given the broad definition of joint R&D, it would not be difficult to stipulate that licensees should not only grant access to future patents but are also obliged to conduct research or to develop the technology further. Would that meet the threshold in the R&D block exemption? Would these licensing agreements be joint R&D agreements? In comparison with the 2000 block exemption, the Commission has actually created a stand-alone centre of

---

[600]   See discussion *supra* section 3.3.4(iii)(c).

[601]   Not certain, perhaps the R&D block exemption will continue to be applicable. Horizontal Guidelines, paras 13 et seq. See also the new TT Guidelines (Guidelines on the application of Article 101 of the Treaty on the Functioning of the European Union to technology transfer agreements, 2014/C 89/03), paras 69 et seq. stipulating that if the R&D block exemption is applicable, the TTBER will not be.

[602]   Hanns Ullrich, 'Patent Pools – Policy and Problems', in Joseph Drexl (ed.), *Research Handbook on Intellectual Property and Competition Law* (Cheltenham: Edward Elgar, 2008), 143 et seq.

gravity test in the R&D block exemption.[603] The licensing to or from the R&D venture may not constitute the primary objective of the collaboration. It seems close to the conduct of old test, that is, weighing what is the main purpose of the agreement (centre of gravity), technology transfer or R&D in these cases.[604] Presumably, if the R&D pool is set up very early in the lifecycle of the technology, the R&D pool consisting of the background patents could actually be an R&D pool where licensees actually conduct follow-on R&D rather than produce or use the technology licensed. For example, the Corning model, where Corning held background IP rights to the optical fibres technology and entered into follow-on R&D ventures with cable manufacturers, could fall under the R&D block exemption altogether, that is, both the licensing agreements and the R&D agreements.

(e) Conclusion It is clear that few R&D agreements need to fall outside the R&D block exemption. The market share ceiling is not decisive. Even though the current block exemption is a vast improvement and includes joint licensing, and thereby reflects the Commission's ambition to regulate the growing business of R&D-only firms, it is clear that this was done rather mechanically and without analysing whether the licensing of technology actually correlates one-to-one to the sale of products. The difference between a technology and a product might be substantial, especially considering the foreclosure effects. A technology may very well correspond to a standardised technology, that is, a technology that in fact potentially forecloses several product markets.

Thus, the width of the collaborations to benefit from the seven-year immunity could be very different and perhaps the R&D block exemption could have been more flexible in this regard and possibly have different periods of immunity depending on the width of research and, perhaps, market power ambitions of the collaborators. It could be a difference in period of immunity between ventures inventing a single product and when two or more R&D ventures innovate, for example, the new broad telecommunication technology, while this would correlate to a number of different product markets. As I understand the current policy, if the agreement does not contain a black-listed clause, the only agreements which in fact are not covered by the block exemption are, firstly, R&D collaborations, entered into by competitors holding a combined market share of more than 25 per cent, with the aim of slightly improving the

---

[603] R&D block exemption Article 2(2).
[604] See Horizontal Guidelines, para 13.

parents' existing products. Secondly, joint efforts where the seven-year immunity has elapsed and the parties decide to continue the joint effort even though holding a combined market share of 25 per cent or more of the relevant product market. These two situations can be added to the selective situations where an effect-based analysis needs to be conducted. Thus, if the agreement does not contain any black clauses, a 25 per cent market share in the relevant market in these two situations is needed for Article 101 to become applicable in the field of joint R&D.

(v) Effect analysis

Agreements which fall outside the block exemption or are not *per se* illegal or legal, that is, do not fit into Boxes A–C in Figure 3.1, may be declared anticompetitive. However, to be anticompetitive, it must have an effect on competition regarding price, output, innovation or the variety or quality of goods and services (see Boxes E(i) and E(ii) in Figure 3.1). The prevailing overarching question to be analysed is, then, according to the Commission, whether the agreement restricts competition that would have existed or potentially existed without it. One needs to look at the counterfactual situation.

If the R&D agreement would fall outside the R&D block exemption, the first step in the effect analysis under Article 101(1) is (again) to establish and identify the relevant market (see Box D in Figure 3.1).[605]

(vi) What are the relevant market(s) and do we have innovation markets in the EU?

Even though few R&D collaborations ever reach this point of the competition law analysis, the relevant market should be identified on a broader basis than under the R&D block exemption. The definition of competitor was narrower in the 2000 R&D block exemption than outside the block exemption. Within the block exemption the parties did not need to take into consideration the technology market or competition in

---

[605] If an agreement is restrictive by object, the relevant market still needs to be established. There is case law indicating that the relevant market should be established also in these cases, see Case 5/69 *Völk v. Vervaecke* [1969] ECR 295. Nonetheless, the black list in the R&D block exemption should be regarded as such restrictive clauses that a relevant market does not need to be established. However, all this might change because of the *GlaxoSmithKline* case, implying that restrictive effects need to be established also for clauses previously considered objectively anticompetitive. See Case T-168/01 *GlaxoSmithKline v. Commission* [2006] ECR II-2969, paras 121 et seq. See, however, on the contrary, Case C-67/13P *Cartes Bancaires,* not yet published, paras 80 et seq.

innovation when establishing whether they are competitors or not. This was because of the fact that the block exemption defined 'competing undertakings' by referring to whether the contemplated innovation would have replaced products already marketed by the parties to the joint effort. This, of course, limited the notion of competing undertaking in the block exemption but did not influence the notion of competitor outside the block exemption, that is, when the scope of Article 101 TFEU is determined.[606] This has, however, changed in the current block exemption so the relevant market will now be similar inside and outside the block exemption.

To establish the relevant market in reference to R&D agreements, it is necessary to analyse three different segments of the collaboration: the first two being the existing markets, for example, the product market and the technology market, and, thirdly, the competition in innovation or R&D effort.[607]

Defining either the product market or the technology market follows the same principle. Start with the product(s) or technology(ies) currently marketed by the parties and try to identify those products or technologies which customers would switch to in response to a small but significant non-transitory increase in relative price (SSNIP).[608] The market share can then be calculated by dividing the total sum of the firm's sale of the product or the total licensing fees by the total turnover of the market concerned. If the participants are active in the same market, they are normally considered competitors. Interestingly, the new R&D block exemption has defined and also prolonged the notion of potential competitor to a firm which is able to, within a period of three years, enter the relevant market, that is, make the necessary investments, if there is a small but permanent increase in price.[609] This is to encompass some of the innovation markets.

The Horizontal Guidelines state that R&D cooperation may not – or not only – affect competition in existing markets but competition in innovation. Thus, in the cases referred to above where the research efforts

---

[606] See definition of competitor in 2000 Horizontal Guidelines, para 9 with many references.

[607] Horizontal Guidelines, paras 112 et seq. However, possibly this has been done to establish whether the *De Minimis* Notice is applicable or not, and to have a market definition to resort to when the anticompetitive effects of the agreement shall be analysed.

[608] See generally Commission Notice on the definition of the relevant market for the purposes of Community competition law, OJ C372, 9.12.1997, 5 et seq.

[609] R&D block exemption para 1; Horizontal Guidelines, para 10, fn. 3.

aim at developing significant new products or will create a completely new demand, the competition in innovation is not sufficiently assessed under the notion of actual or potential competition on existing markets. According to the Commission, two scenarios can be distinguished: the first scenario is where the R&D is closely linked to a product market. These settings are present in, for example, the pharmaceutical industry, which is structured in such a way that it is possible to detect early on R&D poles, that is, efforts aiming for a certain identifiable result. In these cases it is possible to define rivalry based on different poles aiming for the same demand.[610] The Horizontal Guidelines stipulate:

> Competing R&D poles are R&D efforts directed towards a certain new product or technology, and the substitutes for that R&D, that is to say, R&D aimed at developing substitutable products or technology for those developed by the co-operation and having similar timing. In this case, it can be analysed whether after the agreement there will be a sufficient number of remaining R&D poles. The starting point of the analysis is the R&D of the parties. Then credible competing R&D poles have to be identified. In order to assess the credibility of competing poles, the following aspects have to be taken into account: the nature, scope and size of any other R&D efforts, their access to financial and human resources, know-how/patents, or other specialised assets as well as their timing and their capability to exploit possible results. An R&D pole is not a credible competitor if it cannot be regarded as a close substitute for the parties' R&D effort from the viewpoint of, for instance, access to resources or timing.[611]

R&D efforts in the pharmaceutical sector fit this definition well since the requirement of clinical trials in the pharmaceutical sector prevents the parties from hiding R&D joint ventures. Thus, the Commission can identify overlaps in R&D pipelines in the industry already at the clinical trial phase within the R&D project.

In the second scenario, where the innovation effort of a joint collaboration is not structured clearly enough to identify poles or competitors, the Commission states it will not, barring exceptional circumstances, try to assess the impact of a given effort, but will limit itself to the existing product or technology markets.[612]

One difference between EU competition law and US antitrust law in this regard is, thus, that the notion of the innovation market is still applicable (in theory) in the US. In practice, the innovation market was a

---

[610]   Horizontal Guidelines, para 120.
[611]   Ibid.
[612]   Horizontal Guidelines, para 122.

concept which was difficult to apply. It became evident that the concept of market, be it an innovation, technology or a product/service market, must be based on the notion of some sort of arm's length sales from sellers to purchasers, otherwise the concept of market becomes shallow.[613] As shown above it seems that also the FTC in merger cases started out ambitiously, but has utilised the innovation market concept first more as a test for identifying future product markets, and then with the *Genzyme* case actually limited the concept by indicating that no anticompetitive effect may be shown. It seems to be in very few cases where the US antitrust agencies or the courts use the innovation market concept or underlying idea, at least in reference to R&D agreements/joint ventures. Nonetheless, the EU, as shown above, has rarely accepted the notion of innovation markets.[614] The EU Commission rather uses the innovation competition concept exclusively for the pharmaceutical market, and then only to identify the future goods market, similar to what the FTC and the Justice Department *de facto* did in the end under the notion of the innovation market. The FTC and Justice Department's broad analysis of the innovation market under the merger regime and the Licensing Guidelines (and even more so dictated under the NCRPA) were in fact quite quickly scaled down to a more narrow analysis of the R&D in reference to a clearly defined future market. Nonetheless, there were cases were the US antitrust agencies did prohibit mergers because of the use of the innovation market, mergers that were cleared in the EU.[615]

Also, by stating in the block exemption that if the research development cooperation aims at creating a completely new demand the agreement is exempted irrespective of market share for a period of (at least) seven years indicates a disinterest in innovation markets.[616] The EU competition law therefore disregards the possibility of the joint research

---

[613] Performing an activity which is not directly offered on a market is not to be regarded as an economic activity and the competition rules are hence not applicable, see Case 155/4 *SELEX v. Commission* [2006] ECR II-4797, paras 59 et seq. Appeal rejected, see Case C-113/07 P *SELEX v. Commission* [2009] ECR I-2207. For a comparable US application, cf. Robert Hoerner, 'Innovation Markets: New Wine in Old Bottles?', (1995–1996) 64 *Antitrust Law Journal*, 49, 53 et seq.

[614] One example outside pharma is when the Commission analysed the 6DVD pool. See Commission, Report on Competition Policy 2000, 147 et seq. and Commission, Report on Competition Policy 2002, 194 et seq. See also evidence that the 6DVD patent pool was notified to the EC Commission, OJ C 242 27.08.1999, 5 et seq.

[615] See discussion *supra* section 3.2.3.

[616] See R&D block exemption para 4.

being anticompetitive on an innovation market while still acknowledging that cooperation between firms in research may cause competitive problems.

By not accepting the innovation market, the Commission exempts all kinds of anticompetitive behaviour precisely in those markets where competition in innovation is highest and where patent proliferation is most acute.[617] Thus, the Commission has created a safe harbour. The need of conducting an analysis of the innovation market has, however, been lessened by the fact that the R&D block exemption acknowledges technology markets and potential competitors. As a matter of fact the width of the 'safe harbour' is lessened by the prolongation of the period of time, three years, for which a potential competitor may enter the relevant market.

Perhaps the notion of standards should be taken into consideration. Apart from research poles in the pharmaceutical sector, joint R&D under successful standards should be easily detected and identifiable. If the parties to a joint R&D already hold standard essential patents, they may be considered not only dominant on the relevant technical market but also in innovations because of the interlink between standards and technology market and competition in innovation.

When the relevant market or markets have been identified, the issue will be whether the joint R&D restricts competition in any material way. Does the R&D collaboration foreclose competition which might have existed *ex ante* the collaboration?

(vii)   Restrictive by effect

The main anticompetitive harms arising from R&D joint venture are limiting innovation, foreclose technology or markets for third parties, or enable firms to coordinate their behaviour (spillover effects) on existing product markets.[618]

However, the question is what anticompetitive effect for these harms needs to be established? When is it likely that anticompetitive harm and effect will materialise?

---

[617]   John Barton, 'Antitrust Treatment of Oligopolies with Mutual Blocking Patent Portfolios', (2002) 69 *Antitrust Law Journal*, 851, 874 et seq. Barton discusses the US approach and that the research poles approach worked well for analysing pharmaceutical companies in the 1990s, but not for contemporary 'high-tech' markets.

[618]   Luis Silva Morais, *Joint Venture and EU Competition Law* (Hart Publishing 2013), 254 et seq.

The new regime implies that parties must have some form of market power before Article 101 TFEU is triggered. The *De Minimis* Notice from 2014 states that the Commission will not initiate actions due to agreements entered into between competitors which have a combined market share of below 10 per cent or due to an agreement entered into by non-competitors which each hold a market share below 15 per cent on the relevant market.[619] The need to establish market power is further emphasised in the 81(3) Guidelines, which indirectly state that a 25 per cent combined market share, which makes the block exemption non-applicable, does not imply that the market power needed for establishing a breach of Article 101(1) is reached.[620]

Interestingly, the new Horizontal Guidelines compared with the old guidelines do not elaborate on the notion of 'significant market power', especially not in connection with R&D collaborations.[621] Significant market power was a notion used in the old Horizontal Guidelines, which was supposed to be less than dominance according to the same guidelines, but not far from it.[622] Thus, probably the parties need to reach 35–40 per cent market share on the relevant markets, be it technology or product market, before the first paragraph could have been utilised under the old Horizontal Guidelines.[623] Now it perhaps has been lowered somewhat.

However, establishing some kind of market power is still needed for establishing a breach of Article 101(1) under the effect doctrine. The Horizontal Guidelines stipulate that a market share of more than 25 per cent does not necessarily give rise to restrictive effects on competition. This would imply that the parties need 25 per cent or more market presence to trigger Article 101(1).[624] In one of the examples given (example 5) in the Horizontal Guidelines, the combined market shares of the firms involved was 35 per cent in the EU and 45 per cent worldwide; still, the Commission does not state that the combination would cause

---

[619] *De Minimis* Notice, para 8.

[620] 81(3) Guidelines, paras 23 et seq.

[621] See the new Horizontal Guidelines, paras 44, 134 et seq. compared with the old Horizontal Guidelines, e.g. paras 24, 28, 61 and 66. But see new Horizontal Guidelines, para 130, fn. 1.

[622] Old Horizontal Guidelines, fn. 17.

[623] See Morais, who believes that a threshold of 40 per cent for any form of joint venture to trigger Article 101(1) is too high. Luis Silva Morais, *Joint Venture and EU Competition Law* (Hart Publishing 2013), 281.

[624] Morais purports that the threshold should be 25 per cent. Luis Silva Morais, *Joint Venture and EU Competition Law* (Hart Publishing 2013), 287.

anticompetitive effects under Article 101(1), only: 'to the extent that the joint venture has restrictive effects on competition within the meaning of Article 101(1), it is likely that it would fulfil the criteria of Article 101(3).'[625]

According to the old Horizontal Guidelines, R&D agreements were anticompetitive if they restricted innovation, foreclosed technology or markets for third parties, or enabled firms to coordinate their behaviour (spillover effects) on product markets. However, with the exception of when there are only two or three R&D poles left in the relevant field of research, to trigger Article 101(1) by restricting innovation, more constraint is needed than the natural restriction of two or more parties (poles) entering a collaboration agreement.[626] The fact that all cooperation limits competition between the partners because neither is capable of securing a technology advantage over the other, and thereby improving its position in the market, was thus, normally, not enough, except when very few poles are left.[627]

Surprisingly, here the new Horizontal Guidelines actually seem to have tightened the analysis and reflect a view that R&D collaborations should benefit from a heightened antitrust scrutiny since the anticompetitive effect of the fact that the two competitors collaborate is enough to at least potentially trigger Article 101(1).[628]

Nonetheless, the *ex ante/ex post* debate which started in the 1980s concerning whether the definition of competitor was too wide was dismantled or became somewhat obsolete, not by limiting the definition of competitor but by the fact that the Commission does not (on good grounds) mind collaboration between competitors anymore, as long as there is no creation of market power – at least not until the relevant market is foreclosed for third parties, which may be much later than at the 25 per cent market share stipulated as the ceiling in the R&D block exemption.

The anticompetitive effect displayed in some older cases, that is, the removal of the parties as potential research partners for others, is now again sufficiently anticompetitive to be in violation of Article 101(1)

---

[625] Horizontal Guidelines, para 149 et seq.

[626] See old Horizontal Guidelines, para 19.

[627] This has thus been regarded as anticompetitive, see Commission, Report on Competition Policy 1978, 78; however, not anymore, see Horizontal Guidelines, para 19.

[628] Horizontal Guidelines, para 27.

TFEU.[629] However, only if the collaboration affects competition in the market to such an extent that negative effects, such as output limitation, can be expected do they become anticompetitive.[630] Indeed, the Guidelines indicate that both market power and likely negative effects should be present before paragraph 1 would be breached.[631]

It seems that the new Horizontal Guidelines compared with the previous guidelines are less restrictive when Article 101(1) can become applicable under the effect doctrine. Nonetheless, perhaps, if we look at Article 101 in its entirety (including 101(3)), we probably demand for establishing an infringement both market power and negative effects under Article 101 on a similar level as for establishing dominance and abuse under Article 102 TFEU. The power to act independently of market forces is inherent in establishing dominance under Article 102, but now also under Article 101 TFEU. Thus, by demanding that it is established that competition has been or will be restricted under Article 101 TFEU also when taking efficiencies of the collaboration into consideration, in the area of R&D collaboration, it implies a showing of collective dominance and abuse. Thus, possibly the Commission or the plaintiff still needs to establish realistic *prima facie* cases that innovation will be restricted, of foreclosure of technology or markets for third parties, or firms are likely to coordinate their behaviour (spillover effects) on existing product markets. For such a *prima facie* case the plaintiff

---

[629] See, e.g., Commission decision Rank/Sopelem, OJ 1975 L 29/20, para 4. Actually the issue can be divided into two groups: (i) the removal of potential research partners; and (ii) that the joint R&D venture thus could force other competitors to seek alliances, once confronted with the market power created by the joint research venture. Perhaps the second argument would still have prevailed with the Commission under the old Horizontal Guidelines, since it implies that the anticompetitive effects of the agreement actually extend beyond the parties involved. However, since neither (i) nor (ii) can be measured from an efficiency standpoint, these anticompetitive features of a joint venture probably fall outside Article 101(1) even though the partners hold market power. Some more recent cases reveal that such an argument presented by competitors of the research participants was not accepted by the Commission, see the *Michelin/Continental* case, Commission decision Continental/Michelin, OJ 1988 L 305/33.

[630] Thus, even though an agreement only affects the two partners because neither is capable of securing a technology advantage over the other and thereby improving its position on the market, it can be anticompetitive if they possess market power, see Horizontal Guidelines, para 19.

[631] Horizontal Guidelines, paras 133 et seq.

probably still needs to show a market share for the joint venture of at least 35–40 per cent (perhaps more) under Article 101(1).[632]

On the 'innovation market', when the R&D collaboration does not generate any market shares yet, anticompetitive effects under EU competition law must be judged in light of whether we can identify R&D poles or centres. One example in the Horizontal Guidelines hints at the fact that the EU Commission would allow combination of poles to the extent that there exists at least two other R&D poles *ex post* the JV, that is, apart from the scrutinised merged pole.[633] However, combining the last two existing poles of research would be regarded as elimination of competition under Article 101(3) and thus such a joint effort would not be exempted under Article 101(3).[634] From this it must be derived that according to the Commission a joint R&D venture may, under certain circumstances, be exempted as long as there is another independent effort striving for the same or similar goal.[635] This should perhaps be compared with the Guidelines for technology transfer, which state a safe harbour for parties to licensing agreements beyond the ambit of the TTBER in the event that there are four substitutable technologies in addition to the technology controlled by the parties to the relevant agreement.[636] However, it seems that when judging R&D collaboration and competition in innovation, the effect doctrine under Article 101(1) must be judged together with Article101(3) before rendering a conclusive answer. It is difficult to judge these under 101(1) without taking into consideration the contemplated research.

(viii) Ancillary restraints

As stated above, even if the collaboration – after being analysed step-by-step, box-by-box, according to the scheme in Figure 3.1 – is

---

[632]   Luis Silva Morais, *Joint Venture and EU Competition Law* (Hart Publishing 2013), 254 et seq.

[633]   See Horizontal Guidelines, para 147, example 2 stating that a market share of 75 per cent in the existing product market would not alter the conclusion that the joint research is benign.

[634]   Horizontal Guidelines, para 144. The comparable US rule is that at least three research poles must exist before Section 1 of the Sherman Act is applicable, see *supra* 3.2.3(vii).

[635]   Interestingly, formally the parties could still claim that their research will create a new market and they should, hence, be exempted under the R&D group exemption. Indeed, even before Article 101 can be utilised, the R&D block exemption must in these cases be withdrawn; otherwise it would exempt the effort for at least seven years. See Horizontal Guidelines, para 126.

[636]   TT Guidelines, 25 et seq., para 131.

considered not restrictive of competition either by object or by having the anticompetitive effect of parties holding market power, while still falling outside the block exemption, the ancillary restraints still need to be analysed to see whether they are proportionate to the main purpose of the agreement (see Box F(i) in Figure 3.1). Are the restraints objectively necessary for implementing the collaboration? In other words, without them would implementing the transaction be difficult or impossible?

When comparing the 81(3) Guidelines and the Commission statement in 1993 when the concept of ancillary restraints was newly introduced under EU competition law, the requirements for what constitutes an ancillary restraint have lessened. The requirement of objectively necessary has been made more permissive and ancillary terms in the agreement can also restrict third parties, whereas in 1993 they could only restrain the parties directly involved.[637] By enlarging the number of legitimate ancillary restraints, the area of applying Article 101(1) is minimised. Some restraints, which before caused the whole purpose of the agreement to be considered anticompetitive by object, are now considered ancillary.[638] Thus, are the restraints objectively necessary for implementing the collaboration? In other words, without them would implementing the transaction be difficult or impossible?

(ix) The application of Article 101(3)
The question is then when to apply Article 101(3) independently (see Box F(ii) in Figure 3.1).[639] A plaintiff following the guidelines has to a great extent already visited steps in application of Article 101(3) under the effect analysis in Article 101(1). The Commission has to some extent abandoned the third paragraph for an effect analysis under the first paragraph. The general Court has, however, not abandoned the third paragraph.[640] Any efficiency claimed by the parties should be judged under Article 101(3) TFEU.

Apart from claims of efficiency, that is, cost savings, the parties should not be considered competitors if they, respectively, do not have the

---

[637] See 81(3) Guidelines paras 28 et seq., and Commission, Report on Competition Policy, 1993, 106.

[638] Ibid.

[639] For a good analysis of Article 101(3), see generally Brenda Sufrin, 'The Evolution of Article 81(3) of the EC Treaty', (2006) 51 *Antitrust Bulletin*, 915.

[640] For example Case T-112/99 *M6 v. Commission* [2001] ECR II-2459, paras 72 et seq. Case T-65/98 *Van den Bergh Foods v. Commission* [2003] ECR II-4653, para 106; and Case 328/03 *O2 (Germany) v. Commission* [2006] ECR II-1231, paras 66 et seq., 71 et seq., and 116.

economic possibility of performing the contemplated research. The Court has stated that a deliberation concerning pro-competitive and anti-competitive features of the agreement, including the question of whether each party, independently, profitably could perform the research in question, should be made under Article 101(3), instead of Article 101(1).[641] Nonetheless, there should be some possibilities of arguing that R&D projects, which are so ambitious that it is evident that the parties would not independently have the economic resources to perform them, will not be captured by Article 101(1) at all.[642]

The division between what to analyse under Article 101(1), that is, whether it is legally and technically impossible to perform the research unilaterally, compared with the economic weighting in Article 101(3), is not easy to grasp since all legal and technical problems ultimately boil down to a question of cost. Thus, the analysis in Article 101(1) must to some extent be economic rather than legal.[643] The Court and the Commission would have been better off stating that for the agreement to fall outside Article 101(1) TFEU, a totally new market needs to be established as a consequence of the agreement or the clause.

The case law decided around 1993–94 may shed some light on the question when recourse may be had to the third paragraph.[644] The Asahi/St Gobain venture, for example, revolved around a joint R&D venture between, at that time, the two largest producers of automobile glass in the world. The parties described that they, through the R&D, wanted to control and direct where the technical development in the market should evolve. Indeed, they wanted to control the technology market by making their jointly developed technology the technology standard. Asahi and St Gobain would thereby secure not only their own existence in the market by the cooperation; they would also be able to control their competitors' existence and possibly extract licensing fees from them as well by securing the intellectual property rights to the *de facto* standard for the market. As stated above, it is difficult to see why

---

[641]   Ibid.

[642]   Commission decision EloPack, OJ 1990 L 209/15, support this view.

[643]   81(3) Guidelines para 30, see also Case T-112/99 *Metropole Television (M6) et al. v. Commission* [2001] ECR II 2001, 2459 paras 76 et seq. See also COMP/29.373 Commission decision Visa International, OJ 2002 L 318/17, 27.

[644]   See discussion *supra* section 3.3.2(vi). Commission decision Fujitsu AMD Semiconductors, OJ 1994 L 341/66; Commission decision Asahi/Saint-Gobain, OJ 1994 L 354/87; Commission decision Philips/Osram, OJ 1994 L 378/37 and also the Commission decision Pasteur Mérieux-Merck, OJ 1994 L 309/1. See also Commission, Report on Competition Policy 1994, 108 et seq.

they would fail in their pursuit since they were the two leading firms in the market.[645]

The Commission granted exemption in this case to show that, because of overall economic advantages, it was prepared to consider certain joint ventures favourably even though they did not fulfil the conditions set out in the block exemptions and even if they involved competitors with market shares exceeding the thresholds laid down in these regulations.[646] The economic advantages referred to by the Commission were all based on the notion of perfect competition or classical price theory, that is, they accomplished cost savings, because of the joint research. However, can Article 101(3) actually be used with the argument that the parties aim at monopolising the technology market as long as costs are saved? This line of reasoning would take Article 101(3) very far from rivalry and turn it into an efficiency defence that trumps R&D rivalry. Indeed, it also circumvents the indispensable requirement in the third paragraph.

The interesting conclusion when scrutinising the cases discussed above is that several of the high-profile R&D cases (for example *Asahi/St Gobain*,[647] *KSB/Goulds/Lowara* and *Continental/Michelin*[648]), where the Commission allowed for collaboration between firms holding both much market power on 'old' markets and also being two of few research poles in the relevant industries, was that they aimed to create new technology standards, that is, new basic technologies for future markets. Perhaps it is this aim which actually allows for the collaborations to be accepted. While combining R&D poles for the development of follow-on innovation, even though the parties do not hold any market power on that market, may cause the Commission to scrutinise the collaboration more closely, R&D collaborations by consortia consisting of the system leaders of the industry to create new technical global standards are accepted, even though they aim to substitute the current technology.

---

[645]   Björn Lundqvist, *Standardization under EU Competition Rules and US Antitrust Laws – The Rise and the Limits of Self-Regulation* (Edward Elgar, 2014).

[646]   Commission, Report on Competition Policy 1994, 105 et seq. However, it must be stated that the Commission had previously granted exemptions to joint ventures which created combinations with high market shares, see the Commission decision Bayer/Gist-Brocades, OJ 1976 L 30/13, which bears many resembling facts to the *Pasteur Mérieux-Merck* case (among others the market shares). See Commission decision Pasteur Mérieux-Merck, OJ 1994 L 309/1.

[647]   Commission decision Asahi/Saint-Gobain, OJ 1994 L 354/87.

[648]   Commission decision Continental/Michelin, OJ 1988 L 305/33.

Notwithstanding that this conclusion is somewhat dysfunctional, possibly we must allow for all-industry joint ventures when establishing the technical infrastructure and interoperability standards for the new economy. Since the new economy is plagued by network and tipping effects, an R&D consortium is a less anticompetitive solution than the development of *de facto* standards which may be in the hands of a monopolist.

(x) Summary

Figure 3.1 shows the steps needed to establish a violation of Article 101(1) TFEU in the field of R&D collaboration. Moreover, conduct which today is regarded as falling outside Article 101(1), that is, *per se* legal, should be taken into consideration in order to stake out the area of antitrust scrutiny. The primary situations where the block exemption exempts any form of anticompetitive conduct are: collaboration between competitors or non-competitors, irrespective of market share, for the attainment of a new product, creating an entirely new demand, for the period of seven years after the contracted product was first put on the market, or longer if the combined market share does not exceed 25 per cent; collaboration between competitors holding a combined market share of less than 25 per cent for the period of seven years after the contracted product was first put on the market, or longer if the combined market share does not exceed 25 per cent; collaboration between non-competitors for a period of seven years after the contracted product was first put on the market, or longer if the combined market share does not exceed 25 per cent; and, more controversially, if the parties decide to exploit the result on the technology market only, the block exemption exempts the entire collaboration including the joint licensing for the duration of the collaboration.

3.3.5   Is There a Right to Access Joint R&D Ventures under Article 101 TFEU?

The case law from the European courts could be interpreted that Article 101 also includes the right to access collaborative joint ventures under the TFEU.[649] In several decisions regarding joint ventures the Commission required the parties to open up the ventures for third parties.[650] One

---

[649]   See, e.g., Joint Cases T-374-388/94 *European Night Service v. Commission* [1988] ECR II-3141, para 209. See also Case T 504/93 *Tiercé Ladbroke AS v. Commission* [1997] ECR II-923, paras 11 et seq.

[650]   See, e.g., Commission decision Telecom Development, OJ 1999 L 218/24, paras 28 and 41.

observation is, however, the total lack of any discussion in the Guidelines or block exemption that third parties should be granted access to joint research ventures. In comparison, both the TT Guidelines, when analysing patent pools, and the Horizontal Guidelines, in respect to standardisation agreements, state that there certainly is a point where the main concern is not to prevent the building-up of market power but to ensure access to the dominant standard or patent pool for competitors.[651] Similarly, recent decisions by the Commission in reference to Motorola and Samsung, respectively, clearly stipulate a right to access standard essential patents (SEPs) under industrial standards.[652] The Commission even purports that these cases draw up a 'safe harbour' for accessing SEPs. Thus, when a technology standard or a pool has become *de facto* essential, the task for competition law is no longer to prevent it from being dominant but to prevent abuse and actually to facilitate access for competitors to the intellectual property rights. If competition by substitute cannot be upheld due to market failure, competition by imitation must be granted under competition law. This enables the competitors to get access to, at least, the product market and possibly also the technology market, governed by the standard or the pool.[653]

Thus, the Commission does not acknowledge foreclosure problems at the level of contemplating innovations. Indeed, competitors can only access the result of joint R&D under EU competition law.

By only partially accepting the notion of innovation markets, the EU Commission may *de facto* allow firms not only jointly to dominate the innovation markets but also totally to monopolise them.[654] For example,

---

[651] The Horizontal Guidelines, paras 257 et seq., and TT Guidelines, para 226. Regarding the interaction between Articles 101 and 102 it may, e.g., be easier to prove concerted practices under the *Dyestuff* case, see Case 48-69 *Imperial Chemical Industries v. Commission* [1972] ECR 619, paras 8 et seq., than collective dominance under the *Airtours* case, see case 342/99, *Airtours v. Commission* [2002] ECR II-02585.

[652] See press releases regarding Samsung and Motorola from 29 April 2014: http://europa.eu/rapid/press-release_IP-14-489_en.htm and http://europa.eu/rapid/press-release_IP-14-490_en.htm. Accessed 7 May 2014.

[653] See T-504/93 *Tiercé Ladbroke v. Commission* [1997] ECR II 923 § 131; T-374/94 *European Night Service et al v. Commission* [1998] ECR II-3141, para 209.

[654] Correspondingly, the US approach not to oblige a party to create competition in its own technology might prevent a third party from getting access at least to one firm's research effort, see *supra*. However, when discussing collaborative joint efforts there should be, theoretically, some right to access

if a joint R&D effort (consortia) in the pre-standardisation phase brings together parties with significant resources to perform repeated research so as to create dominant technologies to create a whole new demand, there is limited possibility of accessing such a venture for a smaller competitor under EU competition law.[655] They will only be able to access the result. In academia there seems to be a line of discussion that there must be a possibility to access joint R&D ventures. Both Morais in 2013 and Gutterman in 1997 seem to imply that access to joint R&D ventures in exceptional cases must be granted by the courts, based on the essential facility doctrine.[656]

Probably a court would not agree and perhaps only in exceptional cases open up a joint R&D venture for non-wanted entrants. For example, the test stipulated in *IMS Health* for accessing intellectual property rights could become applicable through analogy under Article 101 TFEU for accessing R&D collaborations, but it seems unlikely.[657] Moreover, perhaps, the new cases regarding accessing SEPs may also by analogy be applicable to certain consortia in the pre-standardisation phase, but this also seems somewhat unlikely.

---

based on the notion of innovation markets and the antitrust violation group boycott, for discussion see *supra*.

[655]   Baumol technology consortia are thus legally benign under EU competition law. Cf. William Baumol, *The Free-Market Innovation Machine* (Princeton University Press 2002), 73 et seq. See discussion *infra* under section 4.

[656]   Luis Silva Morais, *Joint Venture and EU Competition Law* (Hart Publishing 2013), 257. Alan S. Gutterman, *Innovation and Competition Policy – A Comparative Study of the Regulation of Patent Licensing and Collaborative Research & Development in the United States and the European Community* (London & Boston, Kluwer Law International, 1997), 339 et seq.

[657]   Case T-418/01 *IMS Health Inc & Co v. NDC Health GmbH & Co* [2001] ECR II-3193. See also the interesting German case Federal Supreme Court (Bundesgerichtshof) July 13, 2004 – Case No. KZR 40/02 ('Tight-Head Drum' (Standard-Spundfass) where a patentee who set up a standard together with three other firms was obliged to license a foreign entrant an essential patent under the standard. For comments, cf. Matthias Leistner, 'Federal Supreme Court (Bundesgerichthof)', (2005) 6 IIC, 741). Such a right could be based on the reasoning of the *IMS Health* case, see Case T-418/01 *IMS Health Inc & Co v. NDC Health GmbH & Co* [2001] ECR II-3193. See also Commission decision Konsortium ECR 900, OJ 1990 L 228/31.

3.3.6 Standardisation Agreements[658]

(i) Introduction

Where participation in the standard-setting procedure is unrestricted and the process for adopting the standard in question is transparent, standardisation agreements which contain no obligation to comply with the standard and provide access to the standard on fair, reasonable and non-discriminatory terms will normally not restrict competition within the meaning of Article 101(1).[659] This safe harbour was introduced in 2010 with the new Horizontal Guidelines.[660] The Horizontal Guidelines stress that high market share held by the parties in the markets affected by the standard will not necessarily be a concern for the competition law analysis of a standardisation agreement.[661] Thus, the agreement establishing the standard is legitimate even though entered into by parties which jointly or separately hold a dominant position on the product market as long as the standard is free for other (competitors) to adopt and influence.

The *De Minimis* Notice can be utilised so that joint standard-setting activities escape Article 101(1) TFEU. The *De Minimis* Notice may become more often available in reference to standard-setting activities rather than in other activities given that standard-setting activities often aim at developing rules for new products and markets,[662] markets where no one yet holds market power. As with joint R&D efforts, standard-setting activities enjoy an indirect exemption under EU competition law as innovation markets are only to a limited extent acknowledged. The market share ceiling in the *De Minimis* Notice is thus only interesting in reference to the technology and products market(s) defined or created by the standardisation agreement.

Neither the R&D nor the other block exemptions are directly concerned with standard-setting activities in the way that the NCRPA is after the latest amendment. Nonetheless, SSOs have made use of the broad

---

[658] For a further discussion see Björn Lundqvist, *Standardization under EU Competition Rules and US Antitrust Laws – The Rise and the Limits of Self-Regulation* (Edward Elgar, 2014).

[659] Horizontal Guidelines, para 280.

[660] Also the EU Commission states that this is a safe harbour, see Commission Press Release, 'Competition: the Commission adopts revised competition rules on horizontal co-operation agreements', IP 10/1702.

[661] Horizontal Guidelines, para 296.

[662] Maurits Dolmans, 'Standards for Standards', (2002) 26 *Fordham International Law Journal*, 163, 172.

definition of research under the R&D block exemption also for pre-standardisation activities, including standard-setting activities.[663] Moreover, the Commission has addressed standard-setting activities in some individual decisions.[664]

If an agreement falls within Article 101(1), it may benefit from the application of Article 101(3) TFEU.[665] There is no block exemption for standard-setting activities under EU competition law.[666] However, can the R&D block exemption become available for standard-setters? The definition of R&D under the R&D block exemption is, as discussed above, wide.[667] The issue has not been firmly decided by any European court, but it is clear that in practice many standard-setting efforts are joint standard-setting and R&D efforts, and that standard-setting activities are encompassed by the definition of R&D in the R&D block exemption.[668]

Small groups of firms may prepare standards *en petit comite inter alia* in a consortium by entering into joint R&D agreements in the pre-standardisation phase, so as to present a joint solution for adaptation of a standard.[669] The R&D block exemption may very well be applicable if the collaboration meets the conditions stipulated therein.[670] This could,

---

[663]   Ibid.

[664]   See discussion *infra* section 3.3.3(v).

[665]   For example, generally Commission decision Open Group, OJ 1987 L 35/36.

[666]   Under the enabling Regulation Council Regulation (EEC) No 2821/71 of 20 December 1971 on the application of Article 85(3) of the Treaty to certain categories of agreements, decisions and concerted practices, OJ L 285 29.12.1971, p. 46. Vol II, App C.2, Article 1(l)(a), the Commission has the power to grant block exemptions to agreements which have as their object 'the application of standards or type', but that power has not been exercised in a broader sense.

[667]   However, not as wide as the definition of research in the previous block exemption. The old R&D block exemption Article 2(4) stated 'research and development means the acquisition of know-how relating to products or processes and the carrying out of theoretical analysis, systematic study or experimentation, including experimental production, technical testing of products or processes, the establishment of the necessary facilities and the obtaining of intellectual property rights for the results.'

[668]   Cf. Maurits Dolmans, 'Standards for Standards', (2002) 26 *Fordham International Law Journal*, 163, 166, 172.

[669]   Maurits Dolmans, 'Standards for Standards', (2002) 26 *Fordham International Law Journal*, 163, 172.

[670]   The *De Minimis* Notice should presumably apply. The interaction between the *De Minimis* Notice and the R&D block exemption is not clear, given the fact that the R&D block exemption specifically addresses the issue of R&D

for example, enable the parties to explicitly agree not to admit outsiders. Also, outside the R&D block exemption, standard-setting activities may be exempted under Article 101(3) TFEU even though, for example, being limited to a few firms if that can be motivated by competitive reasons.[671]

As long as the standard-setting organisations follow these basic rules regarding transparency and accountability, the result is safe within the harbour. This seems to be, apart from the safe harbour for patent pools, one of the first exemptions under mainstream competition law for a vehicle that in all honesty may have all the features that a price cartel normally has, solely based on procedure rules.

(ii) What might be anticompetitive?

Standard-setting activities might be violations of EU competition law. Article 101(1) TFEU might, in theory, be triggered because of a number of reasons: (i) open access to the standardisation process is restricted or limited; (ii) 'over-standardisation', that is, the breadth and depth of the technology standard excludes new and competing technologies;[672] (iii) 'under-standardisation', that is, the technology is still regulated under the standard, however the breadth or depth of the standard is too narrow, granting exclusive field of use to certain intellectual property holders; (iv) even collusion in choice of technology, that is, the technology selected under a technology standard, is neither the best nor the technology which should have been selected through a free innovation and competition process conducted through customer selection not influenced by the standardisation agreement; (v) the result of the standardisation process is not open to every firm; and (vi) spillover effects, information exchange between competitors, commercial collusion, collective boycotts and market allocation under the supervision of an SSO.[673]

---

agreements between non-competitors. The black list contained in the R&D block exemption should be applicable also for agreement which could fall under the *De Minimis* Notice. See discussion *supra* under section 3.3.3(ii).

[671] See, e.g., Commission decision Open Group, OJ 1987 L 35/36, where the Commission agreed to a limitation on the number of participants in a joint R&D and standard-setting joint venture.

[672] Cf. Dolmans regarding standardisation depth, i.e., what freedom is left for firms to develop future improvements under a technology standard. Maurits Dolmans, 'Standards for Standards', (2002) 26 *Fordham International Law Journal*, 163, 172 et seq.

[673] For a similar but different list, cf. the headings of Maurits Dolmans, 'Standards for Standards', (2002) 26 *Fordham International Law Journal*, 163.

These six anticompetitive features essentially boil down to two concerns: exclusion of competitors and the restriction of the innovation process by the selection of a low-key technology.[674]

In addition, vertical concerns regarding standardisation agreements may emerge: hold-up and patent ambush problems. Correspondingly, reactions to these problems might create horizontal problems: IP policies of dominant SSOs can reduce incentive to innovate by firms focusing on R&D and compulsory licensing covenants can be imposed on members of SSOs, that is, innovators might be exposed to buyer cartels and monopsony power.

The Commission has seldom found standardisation agreements anticompetitive. An agreement on standards must, however, according to the Commission, not reduce product diversity. Licensees should be able to develop products outside the technology standardised under the agreement. For instance, Sony and Philips entered into a patent pool/cross-licensing agreement with other VCR producers on the uniform application of technical standards for the VCR system which the Commission found anticompetitive.[675] Under the agreement the parties were not allowed to implement and develop other systems or to develop the Philips system without the consent of the other parties. The Commission refused an exemption on the ground that implementation of the agreement would lead to exclusion of other, perhaps better, systems.[676] In other words, the parties must be free to develop the technology.[677]

---

[674]   They are the same essential concerns the antitrust authorities should be worried about when analysing the horizontal part of technology pools. See discussion *supra* section 3.2.2(iv) and *infra* section 3.4.

[675]   The Philips and Sony VCR cross-licensing agreement, which was found to have negative effects upon competition within the European Community since the system foreclosed perhaps better systems, was not granted exemption under the third paragraph. Commission decision Videocassette recorders, OJ 1977 L 47/42. The US FTC also did an early analysis of the Philips and Sony licensing agreements for CDs in the 1980s, see Carl Shapiro, 'Navigating the Patent Thicket: Cross Licenses, Patent Pools and Standard Setting', in Adam Jaffe, et al. (eds), *Innovation Policy and the Economy* (2001), 20.

[676]   For comment on the *Videocassette* case, see Maurits Dolmans, 'Restriction on Innovation: An EU Antitrust Approach', (1997–1998) 66 *Antitrust Law Journal*, 455, 480 et seq.

[677]   Grant-back clauses might lessen the incentive to innovate, see discussion *infra* under section 3.3.

(iii) What the Commission fails to address and what it disregards

The old Horizontal Guidelines stipulated several 'regulatory goals' for the antitrust treatment of standard-setting activities: (i) standardisation agreements must not reduce product diversity any more than is reasonably necessary to achieve the legitimate objective of the standards;[678] (ii) standardisation agreements may be caught by Article 101(1) insofar as they grant the parties joint control over production and/or innovation, thereby restricting their ability to compete on product characteristics, while affecting third parties like suppliers or purchasers of the standardised products;[679] (iii) standards should be set in a transparent manner, be non-discriminatory and, ideally, technologically neutral. Finally, (iv), according to the old Horizontal Guidelines, as a general rule, there should be a clear distinction between the setting of a standard and, where necessary, the related R&D, and the commercial exploitation of that standard. Agreements on standards should cover no more than what is necessary to ensure their aims, whether this is technical compatibility or a certain quality.[680]

It should be emphasised that these provisions were regulatory goals rather than rules and it is therefore difficult to extract anything material from these goals and for that matter attribute them any weight. Nonetheless, compared with the current Horizontal Guidelines, none of these goals are present and instead the safe harbour stipulates the rules for winding up outside Article 101(1) altogether.

The Commission should instead acknowledge that standardisation inherently reduces technological variety and stifles dynamic competition but should still benefit from being exempted under Article 101(3).[681]

Consumers may be deprived of a particular product, attribute or quality that they want. Depending on the breadth or depth of a standard, competition is also narrowed down to imitation and copying rather than creating new and improved technology and products.[682] Competition is narrowed down to price and image, while competition as an innovation and discovery process is restricted. R&D competition will be restricted. Furthermore, price competition may also be restricted. Firstly, if the technology is over-standardised, the reduction in product diversity will create cost commonalities and facilitate at least parallel pricing on

---

[678]   The old Horizontal Guidelines, para 167.
[679]   Ibid., para 166.
[680]   Ibid., para 173.
[681]   Cf. Maurits Dolmans, 'Standards for Standards', (2002) 26 *Fordham International Law Journal*, 163, 174 et seq.
[682]   Ibid.

product markets, irrespective of whether price-fixing or maintenance clauses are utilised. Secondly, in the technology markets IP arrangements (and patent pools) where substitute patents are involved are exempted royalty cartels.

It is clear that a selection of a technology under a standard often concerns negotiations between technology holders rather than a selection of the most advanced or best technology.[683] This implies that the firms with the most intellectual property rights, the largest market share and the most resources to spare for lobbying often might have the greatest influence on an SSO.

Provocatively, the Commission has addressed problems such as patent ambush and hold-up which generally appear only when the general rule has not been adhered to and a smaller technology-only firm manages to insert a patent as essential under a relevant technology. Of course, this is important; there are important cases of patent ambush and hold-up as well as cases where monopsony power by the SSO has resulted in the application of technologies of lesser quality than actually present and available for the SSO.[684] However, the Commission does not address the larger picture to an adequate extent from a competition law perspective.

---

[683]   Cf. Maurits Dolmans, 'Standards for Standards', (2002) 26 *Fordham International Law Journal*, 163, 178 et seq.; Douglas Melamed, 'Patents and Standard: The Unimportance of Being Essential', (2006), 12 et seq. [the document is on file with the author]; and Rudi Bekkers, 'Patent Drag and Stacking IPR fees – Are the IPR policies of standard bodies failing or should we better address excessive technology inclusion?', (2007) *Position Paper for High level Workshop on standardization, IP Licensing and Antitrust* [the document is on file with the author].

[684]   See the ETSI DVSI case reported by Dolmans, see Maurits Dolmans, 'Standards for Standards', (2002) 26 *Fordham International Law Journal*, 163, 176 et seq. A more current concern regarding standard-setting activities is the implication of the possibility of *ex ante* licensing negotiations before a technology standard is set. It has even been suggested that technology standards should be auctioned out. See Daniel Swanson & William Baumol, 'Reasonable and Nondiscriminatory (RAND) Royalties, Standards Selection, and Control of Market Power', (2005) 73 *Antitrust Law Journal*, 1, 15 et seq. Under US antitrust law, the NCRPA clearly encompasses not only IP negotiations before a standard is agreed upon but also IP arrangements and agreements. The US Justice Department has not yet taken a clear stand regarding IP arrangements but clearly stated under the two SDO business review letters in 2006 and 2007 that patentees may publicly state on what terms essential patents will be made available if their patents would be selected. Business review letters from Thomas O. Barnett to Robert Skitol and Michael A. Lindsay, regarding the VITA and EEEI standards, respectively, dated October 30 and April 30, 2007. The letters address the issue

Notwithstanding the above, of course, Article 101(3) may often be applicable for parties to standard-setting agreements. Efficiency benefits may very well triumph over the anticompetitive effects. However, that would motivate a block exemption in this regard and not merely a chapter in the Horizontal Guidelines. The establishment of a standard may only happen when it is indispensable.

Lastly, there is a clear connection between market integration and European-wide standard-setting. Private or semi-private organisations such as the ETSI regulate trade on the internal market in a way that makes not only the EU competition law rules potentially applicable, but also the free trade and free movement rules could be infringed. Interestingly, the right to free movement and to access markets is a horizontal right under the TFEU, that is, horizontal in the sense that these rules also govern the conduct of private individuals and firms *vis-à-vis* each other.[685] This would imply that also privately drafted, industry-wide standards must be possible to scrutinise under, for example, the free goods provisions. Clearly, private organisations may also be scrutinised under the, for example, free movement of goods, services or the right of free establishment even though lacking any official connection to a member state or not being able to produce official public rules.[686] This is possibly a way to address standardisation agreements under the TFEU apart from the competition rules.

(iv) Conclusion

In several aspects, the standard-setting industry is dominant in those industries where the patent system has failed in the sense that there are too many patents on too narrow a technology. These industries face a mosaic of patents and the SSO can from the mosaic create a new technology reflecting a demand and, thus, create a new market, product or demand.

To allow full and workable competition between technologies in the standardisation process, and to ensure that the benefits of standardisation

---

of negotiations of the term of licensing under a conceived industrial standard. For the letters, see http://www.usdoj.gov/atr/public/busreview/letters.htm, last visited 2009-04-04.

[685] See generally Case C 415/93 *Union royal belge des societes de football association ASBL et al v. Jean-Marc Bosman* [1995] ECR I-4921, where private regulations of UEFA and FIFA were scrutinised under the rules of free movement.

[686] See, e.g., the Case C 415/93 *Union royal belge des societes de football association ASBL et al v. Jean-Marc Bosman* [1995] ECR I-4921, para 83.

are maximised so that they outweigh the inherent restrictions on innovation, the selection process should be based on objective, relevant, qualitative and verifiable criteria. The technology selected needs to represent a technological leap, that is, create a new market, demand or product, or create such efficiencies that a standard is indispensable. Equal treatment regardless of origin of the technology needs to be ensured and selection of the technology needs to be done in a fair, open and verifiable manner and by objective personnel. The standard selected needs to be drafted so that it is neither too broad nor deep, nor too narrow. Of course, this could be too much for a competition authority to handle. Indeed, IP offices should be assigned to scrutinise standardisation agreements. The criteria are very similar to what is required for a patent and, hence, possibly patent offices should be selected to scrutinise SSOs and standardisation agreements whether the standard selected is both the most adequate for the demand and reflects a slim tradable property/technology.

In light of the above, standardisation agreements and SSOs should be addressed from different viewpoints. Not only competition law is triggered, but also the EU free movement regulations and national intellectual property laws should be scrutinised given the goal of creating and maintaining an internal market. To protect competition in the standard-setting process, the Commission needs to take the broadest viewpoint possible.

3.3.7   Concluding Remarks and the Very Latest Development

The intensity of the scrutiny under EU competition law of R&D collaborations has come in waves over the years. Initially, under the 1968 notice, pure R&D collaborations and similar arrangements were not the focus of the EC Commission and were disregarded. R&D collaborations solely between non-competitors or arrangements between competitors that neither limited the parties' competitive behaviour nor affected the market position of third parties were deemed not to fall under the first paragraph, that is, they were *per se* legal. In practice, the 1968 notice was shortly after its inauguration limited to small and medium-sized firms, even though on the face of it, it applied to firms of all sizes.[687]

The threshold for what would be considered anticompetitive under the first paragraph was lowered with the 1985 block exemption, which stipulated that pure R&D collaborations were also anticompetitive if the

---

[687]   See *supra* under section 3.3.4(i).

firms were prevented from conducting unilateral research regarding the same subject matter as contemplated to be conducted under the joint R&D.[688]

Both under the 1968 notice and the 1985 block exemption, the first paragraph of the collusion prohibition (cf. Article 85(1), later changed to Article 101(1) TFEU) was interpreted as having a wide application. This generous interpretation was derived from a wide notion of competitor, and, more importantly, from the notion that restrictive covenants limit competition when they are enforceable beyond a shorter period of time, limiting freedom of decision. *Ex post* competition, that is, that the parties when ending the collaboration may, due to the spillover effects (transfer of knowledge between each other), be competitors even though when entering the contract they were not, was also protected. Thus, not only *ex ante* competition, that is, that two competitors should not be allowed to collude, was prohibited, but EU competition law also tried to facilitate competition when a collaboration ended.

The point when EU competition law in this area became more lenient was around 1993, with some joint venture cases where the parties held substantial market power.[689] These cases were the starting point of three developments: (i) a limitation of the notion of competitor and introducing different definitions of competitor in the block exemption and outside the block exemption; (ii) implementing a high market share threshold for when Article 101(1) TFEU becomes available, and the increase of the market share ceiling and the time period for when the block exemption is available; and (iii) the reintroduction of the *per se* legal collaborations from the 1968 notice and adding a third *per se* legal collaboration: when the agreement does not affect 'the relevant parameters of competition'. The reintroduction of the notion that pure R&D agreements are *per se* legal implied that EU competition law repudiated the notion of innovation market. Thus, as a fourth point for limiting the ambit of EU competition law and the definition of competitor, it should be noted that the notion of innovation market was not implemented under EU competition law. Ultimately, with the introduction of the 2000 block exemption and later the current block exemption, the discussion regarding the definition of competitor became obsolete. Collaborations between competitors are no longer considered infringing the first paragraph *per se*. Instead, collaborations between competitors are *per se* legal unless

---

[688] See *supra* under section 3.3.4(ii).
[689] See *supra* under sections 3.3.4(iv) and 3.3.4(v).

proven to decrease the prevailing notion of competition. Thus, there must be an antitrust harm and likely effect connected to that harm.

With the introduction of the 2000 block exemption, the era of a less burdensome application of the Article 101 TFEU to joint venture was at its peak. Consequently, few cases have emerged and private plaintiffs are even less prevalent than before.

In addition, joint licensing of the result was accepted together with global private standardisation agreements. This became a plausible business model for small groups of firms.[690] It became possible to initiate joint R&D under the block exemption with the aim of creating a technology which would monopolise the market as a standard. This enables the participants to create collaborations that would be exempted from competition law scrutiny entirely.[691]

Nonetheless, the very latest development shows that the Commission possibly have a nascent interest in R&D collaborations. The current block exemption is in some ways more stringent than the 2000 block exemption and also the Commission has actually initiated investigations into development agreements.

In October 2014, the Commission sent a Statement of Objection to Honeywell and DuPont and stated it had concerns that a series of agreements concluded between Honeywell and DuPont in 2010 may have hindered competition on the market for new refrigerant for air-conditioning systems in cars, R-1234yf.[692] The selection of 1234yf as the standard was the result of a process conducted under the auspices of the Society of Automotive Engineers, which represents the interests of all groups involved in the automotive sector.[693] Honeywell's and DuPont's agreements relate notably to both the development and production arrangements of the R-1234yf.[694]

---

[690] The Commission accepts that joint licensing can be part of a pure R&D collaboration which could fall outside Article 101(1) altogether, see Horizontal Guidelines paras 130, 134.

[691] Actually, the Horizontal Guidelines encompass joint licensing of the result of joint R&D in the safe harbour (of the Horizontal Guidelines) even beyond the seven-year immunity in the block exemption and even if the parents would sell contracting products, as long as they are open to license third parties, see Horizontal Guidelines, para 138.

[692] See EU Commission press release: http://europa.eu/rapid/press-release_IP-14-1186_en.htm. Accessed 27 January 2015.

[693] Ibid.

[694] See EU Commission press release: http://europa.eu/rapid/press-release_IP-11-1560_en.htm?locale=en. Accessed 1 May 2013.

According to the Commission, Honeywell and DuPont are the only two suppliers of R-1234yf to carmakers. The Commission's provisional finding is that the cooperation between Honeywell and DuPont on production of R-1234yf has reduced their decision-making independence and resulted in restrictive effects on competition. These effects include a limitation of the available quantities of the new refrigerant that would have otherwise been brought to the market, as well as a limitation of related technical development.

Indeed, the Commission seems to address R&D collaborations and the interface R&D collaborations, standardisation and production, and conclude that the parties agreed to restrict development.

3.4 A COMPARATIVE STUDY: IS THERE A PRACTICAL DIFFERENCE IN THE TREATMENT OF RESEARCH AND DEVELOPMENT AGREEMENTS BETWEEN THE TWO JURISDICTIONS?

3.4.1 Introduction

It is clear that in the field of R&D competition policy, the United States, with the introduction of the NCRA in 1984, took command of what should be regarded as benign collusion in the area of R&D collaborations. The US initiative was triggered by the competitive fear of the perceived collaborative Japanese industry. When analysing the different bills regarding an exemption from antitrust law that were in circulation during this period on Capitol Hill, it is obvious that for several senators, and the Reagan administration, the aim was not only to create an exemption for joint intellectual property creation, that is, research, but also for collective exploitation of intellectual property rights. Thus, the liberation from the *per se* threat for collaborations as such was an objective irrespective of whether they originated from joint R&D or not. During the legislative process in 1983 and 1984 the NCRPA was, however, limited to joint R&D (and the joint licensing of the R&D result).[695]

The EU quickly followed suit with the first R&D block exemption in 1984. Ironically, the 1984 block exemption, by following the then standard structure of EU block exemptions, actually imposed a more

---

[695] See discussion *supra* under section 3.2.

stringent analysis of R&D collaborations than was previously the case under the 1968 notice. The scrutiny was tightened also since pure R&D collaborations needed to adhere to the block exemption to be exempted in some cases.[696]

On a general level, the approach taken by the EU in the area of antitrust scrutiny of R&D collaborations has been, and still is, to place the level of benign collusion as close to the US application of antitrust law to joint R&D efforts as possible, but still be a bit more lenient. Under the old regime, this policy was foremost implemented on a case-by-case level under the exemption procedure under paragraph 3 of the Article 85 EC Treaty (now Article 101 TFEU). Unfortunately, the internal disagreements within the EU antitrust community on the general system of the application of Article 101 TFEU, which emerged after 1985 especially concerning the breadth of 85(1), interrupted this strategy and a new form for the implementation of EU antitrust policy towards, for example, R&D collaborations needed to be invented.[697]

The 1993 amendment to the NCR(P)A to also include joint production was *inter alia* inspired by the fact that the EU block exemption included joint production from the beginning of 1985.[698] Interestingly, in the same year, 1993, the EU R&D block exemption was amended to also include

---

[696]   See discussion *supra* under section 3.3.

[697]   The combination of the block exemptions and the exemption procedure under the first paragraph were in 1985 considered a straitjacket. For example, only R&D agreements including white-listed covenants were *per se* legal under the R&D block exemption. If the parties wanted to have other covenants not listed in the white list in the R&D block exemption, they had to make use of the individual exemption procedure. However, to obtain an individual exemption could take some time. The long period firms had to wait to obtain an exemption under the third paragraph was therefore a problem. The block exemption procedure, on the whole, was perhaps too legalistic and rigid. It created straitjackets in certain areas. However, it would still take some time before the general system of the block exemptions, and thus the broad application of the first paragraph, was overhauled and changed. See *supra* under sections 3.3.2(iii) and 3.3.2(v).

[698]   Jorde and Teece argued to this effect, cf., e.g., Thomas Jorde & David Teece, 'Innovation, Cooperation and Antitrust', (1989) 4 *High Tech Law Journal*, 1; Thomas Jorde & David Teece, 'Acceptable Cooperation among Competitors in the Face of Growing International Competition', (1989) *Antitrust Law Journal*, 529; Thomas Jorde & David Teece, 'Innovation and Cooperation: Implications for Competition and Antitrust', (1990) 4 *Journal of Economic Perspectives*, 75; and Thomas Jorde & David Teece, 'Innovation, Cooperation, and Antitrust', in Thomas Jorde & David Teece (eds), *Antitrust, Innovation, and Competitiveness* (Oxford University Press, 1992), 47 et seq.

joint distribution or joint sales up to a combined market share of 10 per cent. Correspondingly, the EU Commission still wanted the R&D block exemption to be slightly more lenient than its US equivalent, the NCRPA.[699] However, joint distribution may 'slip' under the NCRPA.[700]

The intertwined development of the US and EU R&D antitrust policy after 1993 has continued both under the NCRPA and the R&D block exemption. The US Licensing Guidelines re-adopted the safe harbour or safe zone of the four technologies threshold in 1995 and the general safe harbour of 20 per cent market share.[701] This was followed by the four technology threshold in the EU TT Guidelines published in 2000. That same year the R&D block exemption was introduced.[702] In the new block exemption the Commission increased the ceiling of the safe harbour from 20 per cent for joint R&D and 10 per cent for joint distribution to 25 per cent market share on the relevant product market. Moreover, it implemented the paradigm shift that joint R&D should be presumed pro-competitive rather than presumed anticompetitive. In 2000 the US Justice Department and the FTC in the Collaboration Guidelines increased the safe zone for R&D collaborations by decreasing the remaining free technologies needed on an innovation market to three technologies instead of four.[703]

In 1995 the innovation market concept was (re-)introduced by the IP Guidelines and the efforts by Gilbert and Sunshine. Several cases followed where the innovation market was used foremost by the FTC in mergers in the pharmaceutical sector. The wide innovation market as envisioned in the legal history of the NCRPA was not in practice utilised. Neither was the test drawn up by Gilbert and Sunshine.[704] Instead, in the 10–15 cases where it was used during the 1990s, the FTC and the Justice

---

[699]   John T. Scott purports that joint ventures under the NCRPA can conduct joint sales, see John Scott, 'The National Cooperative Research and Production Act', in ABA (ed.), *Issues in Competition Law and Policy* (ABA Section of Antitrust Law 2008), 1316.

[700]   Ibid.

[701]   See *supra* section 3.2.3(vii).

[702]   See *supra* section 3.3.3.

[703]   See *supra* section 3.2.3(vii).

[704]   Two Deputy Assistant Attorneys initiated the discussion in an article, outlining the innovation market concept, see Richard Gilbert & Steven Sunshine, 'Incorporating Dynamic Efficiency Concerns in Merger Analysis: the Use of Innovation Markets', (1995) 63 *Antitrust Law Journal*, 569, 574 et seq. Several commentators have commented and criticised their views. See, e.g., Robert Hoerner, 'Innovation Markets: New Wine in Old Bottles?', (1995–1996) 64 *Antitrust Law Journal*, 49; George Hay, 'Innovations in Antitrust Enforcement',

Department focused on rather clear cases of correlation between identified future markets and innovations that would potentially or likely lead to dominance or monopoly position on these markets. There were exemptions to this rule, but mostly the antitrust agencies focused on the merger where it seemed that rivalry would be exchanged for monopoly position, and where there would only be one or few innovation efforts pursued. As discussed above, the FTC and Justice Department during this period were more ambitious than the Commission and several cases which were prohibited by the FTC were cleared by the Commission. The effort to make use of the innovation market concept, at least by the FTC and the Justice Department, seems to have died down with the 2003 FTC case.

In 2004, the US enacted the Standards Development Organization Advancement Act, which gave SDOs access to the NCRPA. The implications of the latest amendment are difficult to establish without case law. 'Standard-setting activities' include a great variety of conduct disconnected from R&D. A special reference is made to intellectual property rights. SDOs' handling of intellectual property rights is semi-immune under the Act. Does that imply that setting up *ex post* a patent pool under a technology standard may be included under the NCRPA? Or, at least, that a horizontal agreement, negotiations or public declarations regarding the terms on which access to essential patents should be granted *ex ante* the decision of the SDO is included as standard-setting activities?

Standard-setting activities in the pre-standardisation phase under SSOs were already included under both the NCRPA and the R&D block exemption.[705] Indeed, firms joining up in consortia to conduct or outsource R&D so as to match a contemplated standard were encompassed by the NCRPA and the R&D block exemption, respectively.[706]

(1995–1996) 64 *Antitrust Law Journal*, 7; and Richard Rapp, 'The Misapplication of Innovation Market Approach to Merger Analysis', (1995–1996) 64 *Antitrust Law Journal*, 19. See also Gilbert and Sunshine's reply: Richard Gilbert & Steven Sunshine, 'The Use of Innovation Markets: A Reply to Hay, Rapp, and Hoerner', (1995–1996) 64 *Antitrust Law Journal*.

[705]   See discussion *supra* under sections 3.2.4 and 3.3.5, respectively.

[706]   Cf. Carl Cargill, 'Intellectual Property Rights and Standard Setting Organizations: An Overview of Failed Evolution', (2002) 27 March *FTC/DOJ Hearings on Competition and Intellectual Property Law and Policy in the Knowledge-Based Economy*, 1 regarding the NCRPA; and Maurits Dolmans, 'Standards for Standards', (2002) 26 *Fordham International Law Journal*, 163, 166 et seq. and 172, regarding the R&D block exemption.

Given this practice, the issue is what value the latest amendment added. The 2004 amendment was enacted to include SDOs under the NCRPA and to circumvent the three technology safe harbours in the Collaboration Guidelines. An additional reason was to include 'standard-setting activities' under the NCRPA, activities that are not connected to or derived from joint R&D whatsoever. The SDOs are semi-immune under the NCRPA for such activities, while the members are not. However, presumably the members of the SDO are also immune if they are joint R&D ventures.[707] At least granting of licences, under the notion of joint venture in the NCRPA, could include agreement, negotiations and public declarations of terms of licensing.[708] That would imply that not only the SDOs and the joint ventures are immune from antitrust suits but also the interaction between joint R&D and SDOs. Whether Congress actually took notice of the fact that the members of an SDO could be the already semi-exempted joint venture is not clear. This is also a point where the legislators and the antitrust agencies have failed to address the whole picture of the model of innovation business, even though actually inserting all conduct under an act.

In the end, depending on the interpretation of the interface between joint R&D and standard-setting activities, the latest amendment to the NCRPA can take away decades of case law where the Supreme Court has declared that patent pools including competing patents are *per se* illegal. Competing patents can, presumably, be licensed jointly under a joint R&D venture and the joint venture should still be judged under the NCRPA irrespective of whether the parties to a joint R&D have agreed on a technology or not under an SDO.

The latest changes to the US antitrust policy possibly influenced the newly introduced R&D block exemption and Horizontal Guidelines. The EU Commission acknowledged that the result of joint R&D is not only intellectual property rights but also technology standards. Thus, stand-alone technology standardisation agreements without connection to joint R&D have been exempted under the Horizontal Guidelines.[709]

---

[707] Even if horizontal agreement between joint R&D ventures on the terms for licensing are not exempted under the NCRPA, the joint ventures might set up a patent pool in accordance with the rules from the patent pool business review letters from the end of the 1990s and then also be (*per se*) legal. See RFID business review letter from Thomas O. Barnett to William F. Dolan and Geoffrey Oliver dated October 21, 2008, 8.

[708] See discussion *supra* section 3.2.3(xii).

[709] Horizontal Guidelines, paras 280 et seq. See discussion *supra*.

The above is a short and general historical exposé of the intertwined development of R&D competition law on both sides of the Atlantic. There certainly are differences between the US and the EU application of competition law to R&D collaborations, of which the recognition of the innovation market under US law is the most prominent. Nonetheless, the general notion that these collaborations are promoted under US and EU law rather than restricted is obvious. However, in more detail, if the two policies are juxtaposed, what is similar and what is different?

3.4.2   What is Anticompetitive?

The US Collaboration Guidelines stipulate:[710]

> An exercise of market power may injure consumers by reducing innovation below the level that otherwise would prevail, leading to fewer or no products for consumers to choose from, lower quality products, or products that reach consumers more slowly than they otherwise would. An exercise of market power also may injure consumers by reducing the number of independent competitors in the market for the goods, services, or production processes derived from the R&D collaboration, leading to higher prices or reduced output, quality, or service. A central question is whether the agreement increases the ability or incentive to reduce R&D efforts pursued independently or through the collaboration, for example, by slowing the pace at which R&D efforts are pursued. Other considerations being equal, R&D agreements are more likely to raise competitive concerns when the collaboration or its participants already possess a secure source of market power over an existing product and the new R&D efforts might cannibalize their supra-competitive earnings. In addition, anticompetitive harm generally is more likely when R&D competition is confined to firms with specialized characteristics or assets, such as intellectual property, or when a regulatory approval process limits the ability of late-comers to catch up with competitors already engaged in the R&D.

In general, an EU competition lawyer would agree to this definition of what anticompetitive harm may arise out of joint R&D collaborations. One difference would be that by not accepting an innovation market to the extent that the US antitrust agencies did, an agreement or joint conduct to decrease R&D efforts or R&D investments without any consequences for either a technology or product market can theoretically not be anticompetitive conduct under EU competition law, even though the innovation market would become monopolised. However, the question is whether this could ever happen in practice. Perhaps the rule could,

---

[710]   Collaboration Guidelines, 15.

under EU competition law, be that an intentional reduction of intellectual property rights production, that is, output reduction on a relevant technology market, would be anticompetitive. For such competition harm, EU competition law would not need to use innovation markets. In addition, it should be noted that Article 101 TFEU directly stipulates that limiting or controlling technical development is a violation of Article 101(1) TFEU.[711] Thus, an agreement where the parties agree not to undertake R&D should therefore be objectively anticompetitive. With this in mind, US and EU antitrust law create a similar outcome in practice.[712]

Moreover, the difference in scope for unlicensed experimental use defence between the US and Europe, discussed at the beginning of the book, may influence when identifying 'competitors' and harm to competitors. When comparing the European statutory exemption in UPCA with the case-law-based experimental use defence in *Madey* and *Bolar*, it is obvious that the EU exemption is wider. Does that imply that on US innovation markets, firms in the US are less likely to be considered competitors since patents are, in theory, also blocking experimental use? Since patents are blocking, should firms that are possibly competitors in relevant product markets be allowed to collaborate on the relevant innovation market since they hold blocking patents (one-way or cross-blocking patents) to the specific aim of their research? While in the EU, the wider experimental use exception together with the fact that innovation markets are not recognised imply that firms, pre-competition, when conducting R&D, either are or are not competitors. A dogmatic view on the effect of a patent to the definition of competitor may have this effect in the US and EU. The *Summit* and *VISX* patent pool cases[713] are a good example of where the FTC, initially, was able to show that the alleged patent pool concerning eye surgery technology was in fact a collusion agreement, while it was later proven that the patents held by the parties were blocking. When discovering that the parties did hold blocking

---

[711] However, trade between member states has to be affected for Article 101(1) TFEU to be violated. That might be difficult in reference to an innovation market which is perhaps more theoretical than a real relevant market.

[712] In addition to the above R&D-oriented anticompetitive conduct, anticompetitive spillover effects on technology and product markets and foreclosure of third parties to the result of the joint effort are considered anticompetitive conduct. See *supra* section 2.1. Finally, the enactment of the Standards Development Organization Advancement Act in 2004 also enlarges the number of anticompetitive conducts which might fall, and thus are exempted, under the NCRPA compared with the R&D block exemption.

[713] *In re* Summit Tech. Inc., 127 F.T.C. 208 (1998). *In re* VIXS Inc., 127 F.T.C. 136 (1999).

patents, the FTC re-opened the case and dismissed it, hence, the collaboration went from being a cartel to a legitimate patent pool.[714]

The limited experimental use defence under US intellectual property law thereby creates a defence under US antitrust law. Firms may claim that they hold either cross-blocking patents or one of them holds a single blocking patent and collaborative R&D should be allowed since the parties are not competitors on the innovation market.

An argument for not utilising the concept of innovation market is that it is conceptually wrong, since there is no real 'market'.[715] A second argument for not using the concept of 'innovation market' is what is discussed above, which is that it lends its support to the idea of limiting the unlicensed experimental defence to non-business or only ideal research.

3.4.3   Definition of Joint R&D, Joint Production and Sales

With reference to Box 3.1a, there is a clear difference in scope. The NCRPA includes not only joint R&D but also joint production of results originating from joint R&D. Also, joint production ventures are encompassed by the Act. In comparison, the R&D block exemption is more focused on joint R&D and the exploitation of the result of such collaborations. Joint production not originating from a joint R&D effort is instead, under the EU competition law system, included in the block exemption for specialisation. The NCRPA, therefore, encompassed not only the R&D block exemption but also, from an EU perspective, parts of the specialisation block exemption. Moreover, it should be noted that the limitation to actual damages also applies to joint production of products, processes and services if such joint production takes place within the US and the venture and the parties controlling the venture are either US persons or foreign persons from a country that treats US persons no less favourably than domestic persons under its antitrust laws.[716] Furthermore, again the Standards Development Organization Advancement Act needs

---

[714]   Ibid.

[715]   Josef Drexl, 'Anti-competitive Stumbling Stones on the Way to a Cleaner World: Protecting Competition in Innovation without a Market', (2012) 8 *Journal of Competition Law & Economics*, 507.

[716]   See 15 U.S.C.A § 4306. Interestingly, the requirement that the place of production should be in the US would probably disqualify the US from treating foreign firms no less favourably under its antitrust laws.

to be taken into consideration. It enlarges the NCRPA to also include standard-setting activities and – according to my interpretation – patent pool activities, without these activities originating from a joint R&D effort. The definition of standard-setting activities under the NCRPA is shown in Box 3.1b.

BOX 3.1A   JOINT VENTURE

US – joint venture is:

(i) theoretical analysis, experimentation or systematic study of phenomena or observable facts;

(ii) the development or testing of basic engineering techniques;

(iii) the extension of investigative findings or theory of a scientific or technical nature into practical application for experimental and demonstration purposes, including the experimental production and testing of models, prototypes, equipment, materials and processes;

(iv) the production of a product, process or service;

(v) the testing in connection with the production of a product, process or services by such venture;

(vi) the collection, exchange and analysis of research or production information; or

(vii) any combination of the purposes specified in the paragraphs above, and may include the establishment and operation of facilities for the conducting of such a venture, the conducting of such a venture on a protected and proprietary basis, and the prosecution of applications for patents and the granting of licences for the results of such ventures.

EU – research and development agreement means:

(i) joint research and development of contract products or contract technologies and joint exploitation of the results of that research and development;

(ii) joint exploitation of the results of research and development of contract products or contract technologies jointly carried out pursuant to a prior agreement between the same parties;

(iii) joint research and development of contract products or contract technologies excluding joint exploitation of the results;

(iv) paid-for research and development of contract products or contract technologies and joint exploitation of the results of that research and development;

(v) joint exploitation of the results of paid-for research and development of contract products or contract technologies pursuant to a prior agreement between the same parties; or

(vi) paid-for research and development of contract products or contract technologies.

BOX 3.1B   STANDARD-SETTING ACTIVITIES – US

A Standard Setting Activity means any action taken by a standards development organization for the purpose of developing, promulgating, revising, amending, reissuing, interpreting, or otherwise maintaining a voluntary consensus standard, or using such standard in conformity assessment activities, including actions relating to the intellectual property policies of the standards development organization.

Under EU competition law, both the Horizontal and the TT Guidelines need to be visited to find how these collaborations are perceived.

BOX 3.1C   STANDARD-SETTING ACTIVITIES – EU

Where participation in standard-setting is **unrestricted** and the procedure for adopting the standard in question is **transparent**, standardisation agreements which contain **no obligation to comply** with the standard and provide **access to the standard on fair, reasonable and non-discriminatory terms** will normally not restrict competition within the meaning of Article 101(1).

The US Justice Department has not stated whether IP arrangements under standards should be judged as patent pools or whether it approves of *ex ante* IP negotiations in the pre-standardisation phase. In comparison, the EU Commission states that *ex ante* unilateral disclosure of most restrictive licensing terms will not in principle violate Article 101(1).[717] However, the EU Commission in the ETSI IP Policy stated that *ex ante* negotiations and agreements should be judged according to the TT Guidelines.[718] Accordingly, the EU Commission must have meant the patent pool rules in the TT Guidelines, which would imply that even *ex ante* negotiations would be benign.[719]

---

[717]   Horizontal Guidelines, para 299.
[718]   See the EC Commission acclamation of the ETSI IP policy indicating that *ex ante* licensing negotiations or agreement under an SSO can have pro-competitive benefits, see Press Release IP/05/1565, 12 December 2005.
[719]   More specifically TT Guidelines, para 225.

3.4.4 The General Exempted Area

The NCRPA is both an exemption and a safe harbour. It is an exemption in the sense that private parties are entirely discouraged from launching any suits against conducts encompassed by the Act. Collaborators become immune from private litigation because of the mix of the rule of reason, the innovation market concept, no treble damages and the possibility of having to pay the winning party's litigation costs. The incentives for challenging anti-competitive conduct are eliminated. Interestingly, that mix exists as a general rule under EU competition law. There is no treble damages rule under EU competition law and normally in civil law countries the losing party has to pay the litigation costs of the winning party. The counterweight in such systems is that public bodies, such as the EU Commission, should be able to protect competition on the behalf of the citizens.

The innovation market concept – as originally envisioned by the legislator of the NCRPA or by Gilbert and Sunshine – does not exist under EU competition law. Disregarding the concept of the innovation market could be interpreted as exempting anticompetitive conduct on such markets. The innovation market concept is, however, somewhat of a double-edged sword. It increases the likelihood of two firms being 'competitors' since innovation markets are often larger than technology or product markets.[720] But at the same time, an innovation market, by being connected to several product and technology markets, diminishes market power of single firms that might be dominant on a connected product market. Two firms jointly dominating a product market may be able to conduct joint R&D if their combined market power on the innovation market is low and the barriers to enter the product market are low. However, as seen in the development of the innovation market concept in the US, the concept narrowed and was used mostly in the pharmaceutical sector to identify either innovation conducted on product markets or future goods markets. This implied that only one goods market was connected to the identified innovation market, making the investors of the R&D for that goods market likely to be dominant on the innovation market.

In conclusion, it must therefore be clear that today neither jurisdiction invites private antitrust suits in the area of R&D collaborations and the later exploitation of the R&D result. In reference to the public antitrust suits initiated in the US by either the federal government, consisting of either the Justice Department and the FTC, or a state attorney general, or in the EU by either the Commission or a national competition authority, the initial question is when the safe harbour or block exemption, respectively, is situated.

---

[720] See for example the GE/ZF case discussed *supra*, where the parties had few overlaps on any product market in the US, while still found to be close competitors on the innovation market.

BOX 3.2   US AND EU SAFE HARBOURS

US

EU

Innovation market: three research efforts.

Technology market: 20 per cent market share, or if market share figures are not available, four technologies on either the technology or the innovation market or in combination.

Product/service markets: 20 per cent market share.
Joint R&D ventures that last more than ten years should be analysed under the merger rules.

Generally, non-competitors conducting research, which includes R&D ventures with an aim that neither firm could manage on their own, are *per se* legal. Thus, the parties are neither competitors nor potential competitors, and the collaboration should not violate the Sherman Act or equivalent. However, the notion of innovation market does increase the relevant 'market' for finding competitors. If the firms are competitors on the innovation market, the three technology safe harbours stipulated in the Collaboration Guidelines become available.

Innovation markets are generally exempted from antitrust scrutiny.

Technology markets: under the R&D block exemption, research into new technology is generally exempted from antitrust scrutiny during seven years and thereafter until the parties reach a market share of 25 per cent on the relevant product market. Licensing agreements from the joint R&D to third parties should be judged under the TTBER, i.e., 30 per cent in vertical relationships and 20 per cent in horizontal.

Product/service markets: after seven years the block exemption stipulates a market share ceiling of 25 per cent.

Special not *per se* legal rules, but where it may be unlikely that Article 101 will be considered infringed:
(i)   basic research,
(ii) captive research outsourced,
(iii) R&D which the parties cannot conduct independently,
(iv) 'pure' R&D collaboration, or
(v)   joint R&D that creates an entirely new demand (product)?
In addition there are three general rules of limitation: (i) collaboration between non-competitors, (ii) joint conduct which the parties cannot conduct independently, (iii) conduct which does not affect the relevant parameters to competition.

Outsourcing basic and captive research seems to be *per se* legal up until a point where there must be at least one other R&D pole in the world. If the pure R&D effort concerns development very close to launch of the end product, restrictive effects may appear if there are only a few other R&D poles left, the barriers to entry are high and the parties hold significant market power. New demand R&D seems to be *per se* legal even if jointly commercialised as long as third parties freely can license the technology.

Initially, it should be noted that it is difficult to compare exemptions. Nonetheless, in reference to Box 3.2, the exempted area and the safe harbours are wider under EU competition law than under US antitrust law. The close to *per se* legal rules stipulated in Box 3.2 are mainly derived from the 2000 Horizontal Guidelines, and interestingly these *per se* legal rules are not so clearly indicated in the 2010 Horizontal Guidelines. On the contrary, the Commission states that pure R&D collaborations may also be considered anticompetitive. EU competition law still stipulates that the block exemption expires after the collaboration has continued for seven years and the parties have reached a combined market share on the product market of 25 per cent. This indicates that there still is some notion of protecting *ex post* competition under EU competition law.[721] Thus, EU competition law allows that the parties during the lifespan of the joint venture to acquire a position of competitors by stipulating that they, after the joint venture has terminated, should be allowed to use the result of the joint R&D (and background know-how) in competition with each other. In comparison, the NCRPA does not stipulate an end to when it is not applicable anymore. Instead, the Collaboration Guidelines state that a joint venture lasting more than ten years should be regarded as a merger. Given that the NCRPA has a higher judicial order than the Guidelines, the question is to what extent the ten-year rule applies for R&D ventures that fulfil the definition stipulated in the NCRPA.

The next question would be whether US antitrust law in practice would strike down conduct which is considered *per se* legal under EU antitrust law. When utilising the notion of innovation market and by acknowledging that basic research and applied research should be judged similarly, the US approach in practice would not consider the conduct deemed *per se* legal under EC antitrust law as violating section 1 of the Sherman Act.

Thus, the EU *per se* legal rules are corresponding to the innovation market concept in correlation to the notion that basic and applied research should be judged similarly under US antitrust law. For example, outsourced R&D would not concentrate the innovation market and would be legal under the innovation market similar to the EU *per se* legal rule.[722]

---

[721] However, the seven-year rule can be circumvented, see *supra* section 3.3.3.

[722] However, when two or more firms outsource R&D to one special R&D vehicle, this would concentrate the market and here is perhaps a difference between US and EU antitrust law, where EU antitrust law is more lenient given its *per se* legal rules. The EU competition law non-recognition of innovation

3.4.5   Black Lists

Judging from the black lists (Box 3.3a), the EU Commission is somewhat more interested in *ex post* competition (for example non-access to the R&D result clauses are black-listed[723]) and protection of the internal market. Indeed, as I have discussed elsewhere, small intensive R&D-only firms should also have access to the result of the joint or

---

markets is understandable, from one perspective, since they are theoretical. For critique of the notion of innovation markets, see William Tom & Joshua Newberg, 'Antitrust and Intellectual Property: From Separate Spheres to Unified Field', (1997) *Antitrust Law Journal*, 167, 222 et seq., see fn. 271 for references. However, EU competition law also limits the potential competitor doctrine and generally the notion that competitors under EU competition law holding blocking patents are non-competitors. However, that can create awkward results: in the practical world of uncertainty, the breadth of patents is not necessarily certain, given the progress of the technology and the likelihood of invalid patents or claims under patents. Such realities are normal and part of firms' competitive analysis and strategies. For example, suppose that prior to a joint R&D agreement, both the technology patented by A and the technology patented by B are required to produce a commercial product. But each set of patents is also associated with a certain risk that either the other patent owner or a third party licensee may invent around the patents, or have necessary claims declared invalid. The two parties may be potential competitors on the technology market or real competitors on the innovation market, and there is some probability that a third party licensee may license from one and try to invent around or invalidate the patents from the other – in a sense, a market displaying normal dynamic competition based on the logic enshrined in the patent laws of the world. The price of the licences from the two firms would reflect these risks and potential. However, after the two firms pool their intellectual property rights under a joint R&D agreement, the probability of competition is greatly reduced. Both the licensors have implicitly agreed on a technology path, especially if the agreement even stipulates joint future R&D obligations. A potential entrant will have to invent around or declare invalid a much greater array of patents, irrespective of the stipulation of the pool licence agreement. It seems clearly benign under EU competition law for the two firms to enter an R&D agreement in the above scenario given that EU competition law does not recognise innovation markets or the notion that patents can be circumvented. In contrast, under US antitrust law, the above could trigger Sherman Act section 1 without the safe harbours being applicable. Thus, non-recognition of an innovation market creates *per se* legal conduct under EU competition law which actually might be anticompetitive under US antitrust law. For a similar example, cf. William Tom & Joshua Newberg, 'Antitrust and Intellectual Property: From Separate Spheres to Unified Field', (1997) *Antitrust Law Journal*, 167, 218 et seq.

[723]   However, in comparison with the 2000 R&D block exemption, non-challenge clauses are not black-listed but grey-listed.

BOX 3.3A BLACK LISTS

Covenants making the NCRPA non-applicable:

(i) the obligation to exchange commercial information, e.g. costs, and prices, of any product sold by the parties if not reasonably necessary to conduct the research;

(ii) restrictions regarding the marketing or distribution of products, other than distribution of goods from the venture to the parents or the commercialisation of intellectual property;

(iii) restrictions limiting the output of other products, services or innovation not produced by the venture and also requiring the sale, licensing or sharing of other innovations not encompassed by the venture (restricting grant-backs);

(iv) restricting the parties from doing research if not appropriate to restrict the use of proprietary information contributed by one party to the venture, or to require that party to do certain research;

(v) agreement on allocation of markets with a competitor;

(vi) the obligation to exchange information regarding the production of products or services other than that produced by the venture;

(vii) requirements to use existing facilities to produce the product, service or process in question unless it involves the production of a new product or technology; and

(viii) apart from (ii), (iii) and (vii), restricting or requiring participation of a participant in the joint effort of unilateral or joint activity, if not reasonably required.

Objective restrictions under EU antitrust law:

- except when R&D is outsourced, price-fixing when selling the contract product or licensing the contracted technologies to third parties;
- limitations of output or sales, with several exemptions focusing on outsourced R&D and limiting the members of a joint R&D venture;
- naked allocations of market or customers after the seven-year immunity period;
- prohibition of passive sales into territories reserved for the other party;
- restrictions of the freedom of the parties to carry out R&D independently or in cooperation with others in fields disconnected from the contemplated R&D venture or, after the joint effort's completion, in the field which relates or is connected to the field of the joint R&D;
- obligations to refuse to meet offers to sell to customers in territories devoted to the other party;
- non-access to the result for participants in joint R&D or prohibition to exploit, except in some exceptional cases, creates non-application of exemption (grey);
- requirements to make it difficult for users or resellers to obtain products from other resellers within the common market, and in particular to exercise intellectual property rights to foreclose parallel trade.

outsourced R&D *ex post* the joint venture collaboration has ended. This is actually the most pro-rivalry stipulation of the whole R&D block exemption, and should be extended. If an R&D-intensive firm enters into a joint exclusive development agreement with a firm focused on, for example, the clinical testing for getting a drug approved by national or regional drug authorities, or on standard-setting activities in SDOs, it should be protected from this firm 'shelving' or stalling the development of the innovation. If an innovation is shelved or it is clear that one party to an exclusive development agreement is stalling the process for a period of, for example, three years, the block exemption should not be available anymore.

Any comparable rules protecting R&D-intensive firms are missing from the NCRPA. The US Congress was more concerned with the fact that a joint R&D venture can be used as a vehicle for cartels (cf. the restriction on covenants for transferring information under the joint R&D venture), even though also stating that participants must be free to conduct research unilaterally and in combination with other firms. Competitors are also prevented from dividing the market between them. Nonetheless, the parties under the NCRPA can restrict the use of the result to only one party.[724]

In general, the black lists are short given that the NCRPA and to a lesser degree the R&D block exemption include many different types of conduct: from the creation of an idea until the exploitation of intellectual property rights under patent pools and thereto connected agreements on joint royalty fees, technology and access for third parties. The black lists have also gained in importance. Joint R&D is now considered pro-competitive both under US and EU antitrust laws. In other words, the definitions of joint venture, research or joint R&D are not conclusively determining what collaborations are encompassed by the more lenient approach under either the NCRPA or the R&D block exemption. Instead, the black lists should be read *e contrario*. Only then can the collaborations encompassed by the Acts be determined. For example, see Box 3.3b.

---

[724] Björn Lundqvist, *Standardization under EU Competition Rules and US Antitrust Laws – The Rise and the Limits of Self-Regulation* (Edward Elgar, 2014), 365 et seq.

BOX 3.3B   BLACK LIST STANDARD-SETTING ACTIVITIES

The black list for standard-setting activities under the NCRPA states:

(i)   exchanging information among competitors relating to cost, sales, profitability, prices, marketing, or distribution of any product, process, or service that is not reasonably required for the purpose of developing or promulgating a voluntary consensus standard, or using such standard in conformity assessment activities;

(ii)   entering into any agreement or engaging in any other conduct that would allocate a market with a competitor;

(iii)   entering into any agreement or conspiracy that would set or restrain prices of any good or service.

Number (iii) in Box 3.3b gives away the fact that Congress actually wanted to include technology pool activities under the NCRPA. Read *e contrario* Congress includes the negotiation and agreement on royalty rates under the notion of standard-setting activities. This is an accurate interpretation given that handling of intellectual property rights is included as a standard-setting activity.

Congress wanted to prevent and hinder so-called 'patent ambush' and patent hold-ups with the 2004 amendment; however, exempting patentees that agree on royalty rates under a technology standard is a great step towards dismantling protection under US antitrust law. There is no prohibition under the NCRPA for patentees who are not competitors or hold competing patents to agree on royalty rates.[725] Actually, the interface between the NCRPA and the patent pool case law and guidance given in the business review letters from the end of the 1990s is not clear.[726] Is it only patentees of essential patents in relation to a technology standard that may negotiate under the NCRPA, or should all patentees claiming to have a patent covered by the standard be allowed to negotiate?

In comparison, the new EU Horizontal Guidelines do not really stipulate any clear black list. Agreements that use a standard as part of a broader restrictive agreement aimed at excluding actual or potential competitors restrict competition by object. Likewise, any agreements to reduce competition by using the disclosure of most restrictive licensing terms prior to the adoption of a standard as a cover to jointly fix prices either of downstream products or of substitute IPR or technology will

---

[725]   See discussion *infra* section 3.4.2.

[726]   Ibid.

constitute restrictions of competition by object. Furthermore, the standard development organisation is obliged to have an IPR policy to take advantage of the safe harbour, but the requirement is not really a black clause.

As will be discussed in detail in the next chapter, IP arrangements and technology pools are not purportedly dealt with under any block exemption under EU competition law. Instead, technology pools and standard-setting activities are dealt with in the TT Guidelines and the Horizontal Guidelines. Patentees holding competing patents are generally not allowed to enter into a patent pool agreement.

Given the increase in importance of technology markets and the increase of patent pools and the licensing business as a whole, the black lists in both the NCRPA and in the R&D block exemption should, *de lege ferenda*, be amended by the black lists normally connected to intellectual property licensing, technology transfer and patent pools.

3.4.6   Outside the Safe Zones

It is clear that falling outside the safe harbours stipulated in the NCRPA or the R&D block exemption does not automatically cause the collaboration to be anticompetitive.[727] On the contrary, the US rule of reason or the EU effect doctrine requires that the parties have enough market power so that anticompetitive conduct actually has the potential of being successfully implemented. This would generally require at least 40 per cent market share in a technology or product market. Thus, the general thresholds from the merger regulation or dominance/monopolisation could be used by analogy.[728] Furthermore, for example, the Horizontal Guidelines stipulate what constitutes antitrust harm and how to address these cases:

> 120. In the first scenario, which is, for instance, present in the pharmaceutical industry, the process of innovation is structured in such a way that it is possible at an early stage to identify competing R&D poles. Competing R&D poles are R&D efforts directed towards a certain new product or technology, and the substitutes for that R&D, that is to say, R&D aimed at developing substitutable products or technology for those developed by the co-operation and having similar timing. In this case, it can be analysed whether after the agreement there will be a sufficient number of remaining R&D poles. The

---

[727]   For a different view see fn. 37 in the IP Guidelines.

[728]   Compare for example the definition of market power in the Horizontal Guidelines, paras 39 et seq., with the definition of dominance in the 82 Guidelines, paras 11 et seq.

starting point of the analysis is the R&D of the parties. Then credible competing R&D poles have to be identified. In order to assess the credibility of competing poles, the following aspects have to be taken into account: the nature, scope and size of any other R&D efforts, their access to financial and human resources, know-how/patents, or other specialised assets as well as their timing and their capability to exploit possible results. An R&D pole is not a credible competitor if it cannot be regarded as a close substitute for the parties' R&D effort from the viewpoint of, for instance, access to resources or timing.

121. Besides the direct effect on the innovation itself, the co-operation may also affect a new product market. It will often be difficult to analyse the effects on such a market directly as by its very nature it does not yet exist. The analysis of such markets will therefore often be implicitly incorporated in the analysis of competition in innovation. However, it may be necessary to consider directly the effects on such a market of aspects of the agreement that go beyond the R&D stage. An R&D agreement that includes joint production and commercialisation on the new product market may, for instance, be assessed differently than a pure R&D agreement.

This rule above, which many US antitrust lawyers probably think could or should also be the rule in the US, makes it possible to define anticompetitive conduct in the innovation race. However, given the lenient approach towards R&D collaborations in the case law, does it really matter what the Horizontal Guidelines stipulate?

The *Asahi/St Gobain* case,[729] the joint R&D venture between, at that time, the two largest producers of automobile glass in the world, states quite clearly what joint R&D in many cases, in all essence, consists of: two leading firms in a market deciding on a technology for the future. In the pre-standardisation phase, they conduct either separate research or jointly outsource the R&D, under a joint R&D agreement stipulating the definition of the technology and where the development is heading. The technical avenue selected is bordered in with intellectual property rights so that the market is shielded from outsiders. Thereafter the parties cross-license each other, or at least agree on the non-assertion of patent rights, they produce products under the technology and the technology is also licensed to third parties. By carefully drafted licensing agreements, perfect price discrimination may be achieved.[730] By selecting both fixed and running royalty rates together with field of use and market allocation restrictions, discriminating supra-competitive profit can be extracted from

---

[729] Commission decision Asahi/Saint-Gobain, OJ 1994 L 354/87.

[730] For definition of perfect price discrimination and the possibility of implementation, cf. Susanne Scotchmer, *Innovation and Incentives* (The MIT Press 2004), 37 et seq. and 162 et seq.

not only the technology market but also the product market. Thus, the licensors keep for themselves some segment of the product market, while they give access to other segments through licences. The royalty rates are set at a level where the licensees only get a small return based on invested capital. The rest of the profit from the product market is transferred to the patentees. The patentees create a *de facto* standard and implicitly agree not to develop it further.

In the *Asahi/St Gobain* case, the parties stated their objective for the joint R&D was to create a standard and a pool. The Commission accepted it.[731] In other words, it is quite obvious that collusion under the shield of an R&D pool is accepted today. Agreement on price of the product or territorial exclusivity is not allowed. However, when both the innovation and technology markets are monopolised, no such agreement is necessary.[732] The royalty rates may be set so as to extract discriminating monopolistic profits also from different geographic product markets.

In the US, an example is the case from 2004, *Genzyme/Novazyme*,[733] where the FTC analysed innovation competition in reference to two firms being the only source of research for a treatment for the rare Pompe disease. While, as I discussed above, both firms were in pre-clinical testing for a drug/treatment against Pompe disease, the FTC Commissioners were not in agreement and the FTC decision to close the case without remedies was heavily criticised by the dissenting commissioner and abstinent commissioner. The majority pointed to the fact that the FTC could not decline a merger simply based on the number of independent R&D programmes: '[t]he Commission has been cautious in using innovation market analysis,' Chairman Muris stated, because 'economic theory and empirical investigations have not established a general

---

[731] Commission decision Asahi/Saint-Gobain, OJ 1994 L 354/87.

[732] An agreement on what price licensees should market goods for is perhaps not infringing US antitrust law. See *U.S. v. General Electric Company et al.*, 272 U.S. 476, 477 (1927). It is questionable whether this precedent still reflects the applicable law, see Lawrence Sullivan & Warren Grimes, *The Law of Antitrust: An Integrated Handbook* (Thomson/West 2006), 910 et seq. However, by overruling *Dr. Miles* in the newly decided *Leegin Creative Leather Products, Inc. v. PSKS, Inc et al.*, 127 S. Ct. 2705, U.S., 2007, perhaps the *General Electric* case from 1927 should be viewed with new eyes.

[733] See press release 13 January 2004, FTC Closes its Investigation of Genzyme Corporation's 2001 Acquisition of Novazyme Pharmaceuticals, Inc., http://www.ftc.gov/news-events/press-releases/2004/01/ftc-closes-its-investigation-genzyme-corporations-2001, last visited 12 January 2013. See also In the Matter of Genzyme Corp. Docket c 4126 File no 0410083 (2005).

causal relationship between innovation and competition.' Rather, a 'careful, intense factual investigation is necessary' to 'distinguish between pro-competitive and anticompetitive combinations of innovation efforts.' Furthermore, there were substantial efficiencies to be gained by the merger. Perhaps, the FTC did something similar as to what now is stipulated in the Horizontal Guidelines, while the majority also found great efficiencies in this specific merger.

Interestingly, under these cases, the firms can combine market power to an extent beyond the scope of what would be allowed under the merger regulations.

If the parties are unsure whether the collaboration would be anti-competitive or not, they may file for a business review letter with the Justice Department under US antitrust law and a comfort letter under the implemented equivalent comfort letter with the EU Commission under EC competition law. In light of the case law derived from business review letters and the decisions under the scrapped individual exemption procedure under EC competition law, it is likely that a joint R&D effort might be given the green light. Few, if any, R&D collaborations have been prohibited on either side of the Atlantic. Indeed, they are instead promoted.

3.4.7 Standard-setting Consortia[734]

As I have discussed in the book regarding standard-setting, firms perhaps do not conduct unilateral R&D and then present and discuss their findings in the technical committees of the SDOs. Instead, as is clear from the cases presented above, they often conduct joint R&D under a consortia-driven standard-setting model. It seems clear that the standard-setting consortia model may also imply jointly developing the technology to be implemented.[735] Thus, it is difficult to defend collaboration in standard-setting and patent-pooling because rivalry exists at the R&D stage. Pre-competition rivalry implies that there is some kind of race in which entrepreneurial skills are matched against each other, but is that really true? In light of the above, it is possibly not. Moreover, in this book several examples of standards and pharma innovations that were

---

[734] For a further discussion see Björn Lundqvist, *Standardization under EU Competition Rules and US Antitrust Laws – The Rise and the Limits of Self-Regulation* (Edward Elgar, 2014).

[735] See Steven Anderman & Hedvig Schmidt, *EU Competition Law and Intellectual Property Rights – Regulation of Innovation* (Oxford University Press 2011), 293 et seq.

created by joint R&D collaborations/mergers have been given. Actually, one could argue that the consortia model of standard-setting includes joint R&D as well.

Baron and Pohlmann's recent in-depth research seems to support this conclusion. It shows that firms with substitutable R&D programmes or patent portfolios are more likely to be members of the same pre-standardisation consortium.[736] In fact, Baron and Pohlmann's research, based on a database including all ICT standards issued between 1992 and 2009, shows that consortia have been formed for all standards with an unusually high number of patent holders.[737] Baron and Pohlman also warn that if the major economic function of consortia is to reduce technological rivalry, competition authorities should monitor SDO cooperation with standards consortia carefully.[738]

Thus, the question is whether there actually is competition *for* a standard, or whether we have standards that are a collaborative effort from innovation to patent pool.

The interesting conclusion when scrutinising the cases discussed above, for example *Asahi/St Gobain*,[739] *KSB/Goulds/Lowara, Continental/Michelin*[740] and *Genzyme/Novazyme*,[741] was that they aimed to create new technology standards, that is, new basic technologies for future markets, or a new drug without any competing substances available on the market. As stated above, in *Asahi/St Gobain*, the parties even state this aim. The Commission or the FTC in these cases either found that the joint venture/mergers would create substantial efficiencies, or, what is more likely, embraced a Schumpeterian belief that competition does not favour innovation – that innovation as a process is not driven or connected to the existence of competitive pressure.

---

[736]   Justus Baron and Tim Pohlmann, 'Who Cooperates in Standard Consortia – Rivals or Complementors' (2013) 9 *Journal of Competition Law & Economics*, 905, 921, 928.

[737]   Justus Baron and Tim Pohlmann, 'Who Cooperates in Standard Consortia – Rivals or Complementors' (2013) 9 *Journal of Competition Law & Economics*, 905, 912, 921 et seq., 928.

[738]   Ibid., 928.

[739]   Commission decision Asahi/Saint-Gobain, OJ 1994 L 354/87.

[740]   Commission decision Continental/Michelin, OJ 1988 L 305/33.

[741]   See press release 13 January 2004, FTC Closes its Investigation of Genzyme Corporation's 2001 Acquisition of Novazyme Pharmaceuticals, Inc., http://www.ftc.gov/news-events/press-releases/2004/01/ftc-closes-its-investigation-genzyme-corporations-2001, last visited 12 January 2013. See also In the Matter of Genzyme Corp. Docket c 4126 File no 0410083 (2005).

It is clear that competition law has a problem with the conduct that takes place before and during the standard-setting procedure. There is no real relevant market. An innovation 'market' is theoretically wrong, while still at least useful as a concept. Several commentators argue that agreement on a research path or on technology may be exclusionary and/or collusive conduct, although the problem is that there is no market yet to show actual market effect.[742] Then it becomes too speculative to be taken into consideration. If the notion of an innovation market is not accepted, there are no relevant markets to establish anti-competitive effects.

Establishing an interoperability standard is furthermore clearly not a rigorous, scientific process driven by identifying the 'best' technology in a particular field.[743] Technology is selected to become a standard through a collaborative process. Based on prior R&D and former standards, the selection of a new standard may involve evaluation of, or selection and even compromise among, competing technical approaches.[744] While we may analyse, with the help of engineers, whether intellectual properties reflect substitute technologies,[745] it is very difficult to establish what constitutes the best technology and what might not be competition on the merits, especially when it comes to interoperability standards for the new economy. We just do not know what should be considered pro-competitive or anticompetitive.

Notwithstanding the above, we should still not lose sight of the 'but for' case. For product standards specifically, a situation without a standard would imply competition between technologies. Even with reference to interoperability standards, the 'but for' reality is competition between technologies. Perhaps it is not the competition we want because one firm will probably gain monopoly power due to network effects, but it will, at least, be in competition and rivalry with other firms. Furthermore, maybe these monopolies in the new economy will not last because new innovations will soon follow.[746] It seems that we sometimes are too afraid to allow the market to find this solution (if it is available).

---

[742] See Jonathan J. Rubin, 'Patents, Antitrust, and Rivalry in Standard-Setting', (2007) 38 *Rutgers Law Journal*, 509, 520.

[743] Ibid.

[744] Ibid.

[745] Identifying substitute technologies may be very difficult, which the analysis of the several pools has shown.

[746] See generally, Carl Shapiro and Hal R. Varian, *Information Rules* (Harvard Business School Press, 1999), 173 et seq.

Joint research and development under US and EU law

However, to state that standard-setting would not take place in a 'market' seems to disregard the fact that standard-setting is often the alternative to competition for consumers in a market based on price, quality and design.

If the latest empirical research by Baron and Pohlmann is correct,[747] it seems to imply that pre-standardisation consortia, where competing firms engage in joint R&D, with the intent to be able to conclude majority voting blocks when the standard is decided in the more official SDOs, is common. As I have stated elsewhere, could it then not be a misuse of the standard-setting procedure if *de facto* the procedure in the SDO is irrelevant or a sham, while the larger IP holders already have decided on what technology to select in the pre-standardisation phase in a closed and confidential R&D consortium? At least we could agree that it could be a misuse of the standard-setting procedure, while there is still the issue to resolve whether this behaviour effectively excludes competing or rival technologies. Indeed, the issue is still whether the market can sustain several standards or technologies (effectively excluding several inter-operability standards) and that the decision on a product standard *de facto* excludes a competitor or potential competitor by excluding a competing or substitute standard or technology from the market. Thus, the plaintiff needs to show at least potentially anti-competitive effect, while the members of the consortia may refute any allegation by providing support for the idea that the collaboration created efficiencies. Of course, consortia increase efficiency in R&D and also eliminate duplicate or wasteful R&D.[748]

In a similar vein, could one argue that joint R&D ventures for the establishment of a standard should be regarded as a joint monopoly or collective dominance if the parties to the joint R&D actually hold majority power in the relevant technical committee in the relevant SDO where the future standard will be adopted, if this is possible to identify? Or, the parties to a joint R&D that aims to replace a standard, or come up with a substitute standard, should be regarded as dominant if they own or hold the majority of SEPs to the standard to be replaced? In fact, the new definition of competitors in the current R&D block exemption –

---

[747]   Justus Baron and Tim Pohlmann, 'Who Cooperates in Standard Consortia – Rivals or Complementors' (2013) 9 *Journal of Competition Law & Economics*, 905, 907, 928.

[748]   Björn Lundqvist, *Standardization under EU Competition Rules and US Antitrust Laws – The Rise and the Limits of Self-Regulation* (Edward Elgar, 2014).

stipulating a broad definition that also includes market power in the current product market to be replaced by the joint R&D result and the extended definition of a three-year period for potential competitors – implies that dominance may be identified in these cases. If the consortia members are active on the market where their joint R&D will create a standard, they may be competitors according to the R&D block exemption. Furthermore, the *Motorola* and *Samsung* cases recently decided by the Commission also imply that competition law in reference to standard-essential conduct perhaps is more easily triggered.[749] In the Samsung and Motorola cases, the Commission draws up a 'safe harbour' for when firms may access SEPs without the holder of the SEP denying access. As long as the infringer/potential licensee is a 'willing licensee' access must be granted and the patentee may not utilize the procedural tool of injunction. 'Willing licensee' implies according to the Commission that the infringer would like to enter a license agreement on fair, reasonable and non-discriminatory (FRAND) terms, while still may disagree on the level of the royalty or for that matter whether the SEP is essential or valid. Those issues can still be left for the court to decide as long as the infringer commits to abide to the result of the court proceeding.[750] The *Samsung* and *Motorola* cases seem to imply that accessing SEPs should be granted based on the *ipso facto* establishment that the patent is standard-essential. Thus, it seems that the Commission bases its decision on a rather legal analysis of dominant position, based on the technical essentiality of the patents, in light of the fact that interoperability standards, for example the 3G UMTS standard, inherently imply that standard-essential patents must be accessed to be able to access the connected product markets. The question is if this line of reasoning may also apply to those pre-standardisation consortia that seem to proliferate. Then depending if the standard to be developed is an infrastructure, interoperability or product standard, the antitrust reaction could be that access to certain R&D ventures could be granted.

As stated above, if the parties to the joint R&D actually hold majority power in the relevant technical committee in the relevant SDO where the future standard will be adopted, and the R&D aims to replace a standard, or come up with a substitute standard, should they be regarded as dominant? Or, if they own or hold the majority of SEPs to the standard to

---

[749] See press releases regarding Samsung and Motorola from 29 April 2014. http://europa.eu/rapid/press-release_IP-14-489_en.htm and http://europa.eu/rapid/press-release_IP-14-490_en.htm. Accessed 7 May 2014.
[750] Ibid.

be replaced, and presumably in the standard to be, are they dominant under the Commission's *Motorola* and *Samsung* decisions? Hence, should access to the potential joint R&D be granted, if the aim is infrastructure or an interoperability standard? Or, should such joint R&D to establish SEPs potentially be in violation of Article 101(1) TFEU to the extent that it cannot be considered 'competition on the merits' or because such joint R&D is likely to create a dominant position? Article 101(3) TFEU will still be available.

3.5 CONCLUSION

Superficially there are differences between the EU and the US jurisdictions in the application of competition law to R&D collaborations. For example, under EU law the joint research may also include joint sales for a period of seven years after the sale of the first contemplated products, while there is no such corresponding exemption under US law. There is no market ceiling for when the NCRPA should not be applicable, whereas there is a 25 per cent cap on the EU block exemption.

However, the question is whether this is actually a true indication of different attitudes towards R&D collaborations. Firstly, joint sales may be 'exempted' under the US business review letter procedure or even without having recourse to that scheme. Secondly, from a close reading of the block exemption, it is evident that the market share threshold does not reflect the true upper limit after which Article 101(3) is not applicable.

Possibly, there is a difference in approach concerning whether the research is of basic or applied type. The EU approach still is based on the notion that research develops in a linear fashion, starting with basic research. Cooperation in basic research would then be less suspicious than joint applied research. In the US, after the implementation of a more complex innovation model, this is not true anymore. Whether this difference actually makes a distinction is unclear. Both EU and US jurisdictions take such a lenient approach to joint research that the difference can be neglected.

Moreover, the now more academic difference between the innovation market of the US and the innovation competition of the EU could imply a difference if the US antitrust agencies had embraced the large innovation market as they were stated in, for example, the License Guidelines, and even more so in the NCRPA. However, that has not happened, and after the 1990s the concept of, at least, the 'large' innovation market has vanished.

Presumably, the remaining differences are negligible. The preferred result in both jurisdictions is to increase the amount of research carried out, as well as to increase the number of jointly owned intellectual property rights. Both jurisdictions therefore have a lenient attitude, or even an encouraging attitude towards R&D collaborations. It is also evident that the level of protection of competition is decreasing on both sides of the Atlantic. Joint efforts that before were considered anti-competitive are today declared benign or even pro-competitive. On the whole, market power is tolerated, or, perhaps, even encouraged.

The most striking difference before 14 December 2010 between the US and EU approaches was the latest enactment to the NCRPA.[751] Standard-setting activities, encompassing agreements on royalty rates by competitors, are encompassed by the Act. However, with the introduction of the safe harbour in the Horizontal Guidelines, this difference has also been eliminated – with one twist. The NCRPA is only applicable to the SDO, not its members, while this restriction does not apply to the EU safe harbour.

The conclusion is thus rather depressing and the question would then be: can this be changed? What should a policy for innovation, and the protection of innovation and the innovation process under antitrust law that does not rely on neoliberal *laissez faire* be?

---

[751] Some differences remain: the US cases concerning research efforts including all US-based firms in one industry do not have their equivalent under EC case law. The lack of pan-European industry-wide collaborations is not the result of them not being allowed to collaborate in such a fashion under Article 101(3); rather, it is very seldom that all firms in Europe in one industry join together. One exemption would be the 3G platforms, see discussion *infra* under section 3.5.5. The integration of the common or internal market has not yet reached the point where all firms in one industry join together.

4. Innovation policy to be implemented

The object of this book is thus to dissect the antitrust treatment in the US and under EU law of joint research and development (joint R&D) with thereto connected agreements for the implementation of the result of such R&D collaboration. Special focus has been on the new economy, mainly the network industries and the pharma and biotech industries.

An initial proposal would be that the US and Europe, not having a unified experimental use exemption, need to align (harmonise) their experimental use defences under intellectual property law. Under competition law, the consequence of different experimental use defences, between the EU and the US, is difficult to establish. As discussed above, in theory, it creates unexpected effects. Firms are forced to collaborate since the experiment use exemption never or seldom applies.

Moreover, it is clear, from the above, and also from Peritz's research, that a limited or very restricted unlicensed experimental use defence increases transaction costs.[752] Firms must at least enter into licence negotiations and agreements, which, if the transaction cost increases, will imply that scarce resources are not allocated in the most efficient way.[753]

One of the ideas or theses of the book is to propose a way to identify dominance or market power for the participants of an R&D collaboration in the innovation segment without the establishment of an innovation 'market'. As several scholars have pointed out, for example Josef Drexl, there are no innovation markets.[754] This is correct.

Nonetheless, the reason for this quest is that in the network as well as pharmaceutical industries there seems to be a clear need for a test to establish dominance in reference to the development and selection of

---

[752]   Rudolph J.R. Peritz, 'Freedom to Experiment: Towards a Concept of Inventor Welfare', (2008) 90 *Journal of the Patent and Trademark Office Society*, 245, 250 et seq.

[753]   Ibid.

[754]   Josef Drexl, 'Anti-competitive Stumbling Stones on the Way to a Cleaner World: Protecting Competition in Innovation without a Market', (2012) 8 *Journal of Competition Law & Economics*, 507.

future successful innovations, while anticompetitive exclusionary conduct may very well materialise in the innovation process. Indeed, there is a 'boom' of contracts entered into in the pharma and biotech sectors by firms often of different size and market power. In fact, it seems clear that much exclusionary anticompetitive conduct may take place before any markets have materialised. Great rivalry 'for market' may imply extensive fair or unfair exclusionary conduct.

Several scholars[755] have divided the pharmaceutical cases and other innovation market cases into two groups: (i) whether the agency took innovation into consideration when analysing the product market and product market competition, or (ii) whether the agency defined a future goods market or second-generation product market, or even took into consideration R&D or innovation as such, that is, competition in far-reaching (basic) R&D.

Under economic theory and empirical research there seem to be two main groups of innovations. The first group includes incremental innovations (research), where the firm diligently develops the next model or generation of products.[756] Large firms often conduct these innovations on oligopoly markets. These firms can be highly specialised or have R&D groups that are highly specialised. These groups can also be structurally outside the firms, while assignments are outsourced to them. The research conducted may be expensive, while the success rate may also be – if not high – predictable, since the research aims to protect, hold and possibly gain in market share in already established markets or in the next generation of such markets.

The other group of innovations are the radical innovations that create new markets and destroy old markets. These innovations create new demand and demand creativity, ingenuity and other talents to be created. Here economic research tells us that small pioneering firms are often active and most successful: they can harbour the entrepreneurs, the generalists and the rebels.

The innovation process presumably needs to be protected differently for these two groups. Innovation for both groups is important. For incremental innovation to flourish, and for large firms to be able to price above marginal cost in mature markets, competition must prevail. And while this is perhaps most probably done by upholding competition on

---

[755] See discussion in section 3.2.2 *supra.*
[756] See discussion in Chapter 2 *supra.*

product markets, the antitrust agencies also need to analyse the innovation race to the market. Will the joint R&D venture (or merger) eliminate R&D tracks, where these tracks in this setting were likely to lead to marketed products? Nonetheless, patent law and copyright law could be of importance in upholding competition by supplement and by diversity. Patent rights force firms to innovate and innovate around, while competition law should still prevent mergers and joint ventures that concentrate on the innovation process. That would be the formula for creating innovation while upholding the goals of competition.

Radical innovations need to be protected by competition law. Entrepreneurs for the creation of new demand need access to the markets and supply – access that competition law should uphold. Also, these are the R&D-intensive firms that need to be developing at a distance from larger firms while still making use of the large firms' infrastructure and investments. For example, R&D-intensive firms should be able to exit long-term agreements with large firms when it is obvious that the large firms try to buy out or prevent radical innovation to destroy their markets by 'shelving' their drugs or conduct similar actions. Large technical or pharmaceutical companies may try to foreclose small firms from accessing customers or developing innovations. Therefore, joint R&D ventures or mergers need to be scrutinised so that the concentration is not likely to decrease or lessen research tracks in order that anticompetitive effects will materialise – while of course taking the smaller firms' need of investment and efficiency into consideration.

Carrier's suggestion of creating a new innovation 'market' test while acknowledging that it is not a market in a general sense is commendable and necessary. If biotech or pharmaceutical firms have developed substances and are clinically testing them, the antitrust agencies should make a thorough analysis of whether a merger or an R&D collaboration will decrease the innovation rate or the incentive to innovate, or create a joint production and product and, hence, align prices. Using the different phases of clinical testing under the FDA procedure is an elegant way of circumventing the uncertainty inherent when measuring innovation and concentration. Mergers or joint R&D ventures between firms with drugs in Phase III testing should be the concern, even though possible mergers or collaborations regarding compounds not yet in the late clinical testing phases may also in certain circumstances be scrutinised more carefully. It all depends on the likelihood of the firms actually agreeing on pursuing only one drug when both drugs actually could have been marketed. In fact, these cases are somewhat similar to the pay-for-delay cases, where we are dealing with firms conducting R&D (and not generic producers) and the transfer of money happens before eminent entry on the product market.[757] Large firms pay small innovative firms to exit future goods markets. Of course, a prohibition may be available only if the antitrust agencies can prove that it was likely that there would have been two drugs or substances on the market. Any such findings may be rebutted, as Carrier proposes, through showing efficiencies and Schumpeter defences.

Joint R&D ventures should be judged in a similar fashion as mergers if they create lasting structural effects by eliminating innovation avenues or tracks. Several of the joint R&D ventures discussed in this book lasted for many years or for entire product cycles. Joint R&D ventures (for example a joint exclusive development agreement) in, for example, the pharmaceutical sector may also *de facto* have the same effect as a merger between two firms pursuing rival R&D tracks. It implies that the firms will pursue only one track. Joint R&D ventures are not as far reaching as mergers in reference to the structure of the firms, while the structural effects on innovation may be similar since they often include an agreement not to conduct separate research. Moreover, the efficiencies gained by a joint R&D venture are probably less than what parties gain in a merger. Similarly, as I have purported here and discussed elsewhere, the procedure for obtaining technical standards and the work in the relevant technical committees may indicate early in the process what research pole and avenue will be successful. These very different procedures may have similar effects to the FDA procedures for pharmaceuticals. This creates transparent R&D to competitors. Thus, in the interface between standard-setting and joint R&D, the antitrust agencies may also very well map out what joint R&D effort would indicate dominance. In fact, under the pre-standard process in the consortia, the firms themselves agree on the success of innovations and thereby concentrations in the R&D segment can be foreseen, measured and prevented. Large firms that in fact represent voting power or majorities in the technical committees of

---

[757] Interestingly, in the EU Commission investigation of the conduct of Servier, the Commission stated that it had objections to specific sets of practices by Servier, which appears to be dominant in the market for Perindopril. The first practice being that Servier purportedly acquired scarce competing technologies to produce Perindopril, rendering generic market entry more difficult or delayed. This behaviour (and the purported settlement agreements with other generic manufacturers), if established, infringes EU antitrust rules that prohibit restrictive business practices and the abuse of a dominant market position (respectively Articles 101 and 102 of the Treaty on the functioning of the European Union – TFEU). What Servier purportedly conducted is a combination of reducing R&D efforts by competitors and the pay-for-delay abuse. See press release from June 2014: http://europa.eu/rapid/press-release_IP-14-799_en.htm, accessed 27 January 2015.

established SDOs may inhibit the innovation process, especially by preventing radical innovations from being adopted by markets. They may agree on one avenue of innovation and deliberately forgo other forms of innovation track. A similar test to that of Carrier could also be implemented for these forms of collaborations. Do the parties to the joint R&D venture represent the voting majority in the technical committee of the relevant SDO? In some SDOs, large firms have up to 50 votes each in the technical committees, while smaller firms may have a lot less. Is it likely that they would have developed two or several competing technologies while competing instead of collaborating that would have been able to sustain competition on the market? If the answer is yes, the R&D collaboration should perhaps be considered as having anticompetitive effects. Such an R&D venture could cause competitors to stop conducting competing R&D. Or, are we dealing with a network market, where only one standard or technology may prevail, and thus efficiencies of having one technology outweigh the benefits of having competing technologies? In that case, even joint R&D ventures and mergers between firms with combined public power (voting majority) in the technical committee should be allowed to concentrate.

I also propose that the block exemption for R&D agreements or the IP Guidelines in the US are amended so that a small R&D-intensive firm may not enter into a joint exclusive development agreement for a period longer than two or three years without the large pharmaceutical firm (the other party to the agreement) being obliged to *de facto* develop the drug or substance that the agreement concerns. No shelving of drugs or other technology innovations should be allowed. And should an R&D-intensive firm enter such an agreement and its partner does not develop the drug, it should be possible to exit the joint exclusive development agreement. The large firms may in these situations of course purchase the smaller firm to circumvent this black clause, but then the merger regulation may become applicable or the innovators may exit the small R&D firm with a substantial remuneration and start again.

Bibliography

1. REGULATIONS, GUIDELINES AND NOTICES

A. EU Regulations, Guidelines, Notices, Reports and Press Releases

(i) Regulations, guidelines, notices and reports

Council Regulation (EEC) No 2821/71 of 20 December 1971 on the application of Article 81(3) of the Treaty to certain categories of agreements, decisions and concerted practices, OJ L 285, 29.12.1971, 46.

Council Regulation (EEC) No 4064/89 of 21 December 1989 on the control of concentrations between undertakings, OJ L 395, 30.12.1989, 1.

Council Regulation (EC) No 1310/97 amending Regulation 4046/89, OJ L 180, 09.07.1997, 1.

Council Regulation (EC) No 1/2003 of 16 December 2002 on the implementation of the rules on competition laid down in Articles 81 and 82 of the Treaty, OJ L 1, 04.01.2003, 1.

Council Regulation (EC) No 139/2004 of 20 January 2004 on the control of concentrations between undertakings (the EC Merger Regulation), OJ L 24, 29.01.2004, 1.

Commission Regulation (EEC) No 418/85 of 19 December 1984 on the application of Article 85(3) of the Treaty to categories of research and development agreements, OJ L 53, 22.02.1985, 5.

Commission Regulation (EC) No 2658/2000 of 29 November 2000 on the application of Article 81(3) of the Treaty to categories of specialisation agreements, OJ L 304, 05.12.2000, 3.

Commission Regulation (EU) No 1218/2010 of 14 December 2010 on the application of Article 101(3) of the Treaty on the Functioning of the European Union to categories of specialisation agreements, OJ L 335, 18.12.2010, 43.

Commission Regulation (EU) No 1217/2010 of 14 December 2010 on the application of Article 101(3) of the Treaty on the Functioning of the European Union to categories of research and development agreements, OJ L 335, 18.12.2010, 36.

Commission Regulation (EC) No 2659/2000 of 29 November 2000 on the application of Article 81(3) of the Treaty to categories of research and development agreements, OJ L 304, 05.12.2000, 7.

Commission Regulation (EU) No 316/2014 of 21 March 2014 on the application of Article 101(3) of the Treaty on the Functioning of the European Union to categories of technology transfer agreements, OJ L 93, 28.3.2014, 17.

Commission Notice concerning agreements, decisions and concerted practises in the field of cooperation between enterprises, OJ C 75, 27.07.1968, 3.

Commission Notice – Guidelines on the application of Article 81 of the EC Treaty to horizontal cooperation agreements, OJ C 3, 06.01.2001, 2.

Commission Notice – Guidelines on the application of Article 81 of the EC Treaty to technology transfer agreements, OJ C 101, 27.04.2004, 2.

Commission Notice on agreements of minor importance which do not appreciably restrict competition under Article 101(1), OJ C 291, 30.08.2014, 1.

Commission, Report on Competition Policy 1971.
Commission, Report on Competition Policy 1972.
Commission, Report on Competition Policy 1974.
Commission, Report on Competition Policy 1975.
Commission, Report on Competition Policy 1978.
Commission, Report on Competition Policy 1976.
Commission, Report on Competition Policy 1980.
Commission, Report on Competition Policy 1981.
Commission, Report on Competition Policy 1983.
Commission, Report on Competition Policy 1984.
Commission, Report on Competition Policy 1985.
Commission, Report on Competition Policy 1986.
Commission, Report on Competition Policy 1992.
Commission, Report on Competition Policy 1993.
Commission, Report on Competition Policy 1994.
Commission, Report on Competition Policy 1997.
Commission, Report on Competition Policy 2000.
Commission, Report on Competition Policy 2002.

(ii) Press releases

EC Commission press release IP/00/1135; 09.10.2000, The DVD 6C pool.

EC Commission press release IP/03/1152; 07.08.2003, Commission clears Philips/Sony CD Licensing program.

EC Commission press release IP/06/139; 09.02.2006, Commission closes investigation following changes to Philips CD-Recordable Disc Patent Licensing.

EC Commission press release IP/05/1565; 12.12.2005, ETSI IPR rules.

EC Commission's Memo/Press Release, MEMO/07/389; 01.10.2007, Commission initiate formal proceedings against Qualcomm.

B. US Acts, Governmental Guidelines, Business Review Letters and Speeches

(i) US Acts and governmental guidelines

Sherman Act of 1890, 15 U.S.C. § 1–7.

Clayton Antitrust Act of 1914, 15 U.S.C. § 12–27, 29 U.S.C. § 52–53.

Federal Trade Commission Act of 1914, 15 U.S.C §§ 41–58.

The National Cooperative Production Amendments of 1993, Pub. L. No. 103-42, [amended the National Cooperative Research Act of 1984, Pub L. No. 98-462, renamed it the National Cooperative Research and Production Act of 1993. The Standards Development Organization Advancement Act of 2004, Pub. L. No. 108-237, extended the provisions of the NCRPA to standards development organisations.], 15 U.S.C § 4301–4307.

U.S Department of Justice & Federal Trade Commission, 'Antitrust Guide Concerning Research Joint Ventures' (1980).

U.S Department of Justice & Federal Trade Commission, 'Antitrust Guidelines for the Licensing of Intellectual Property' (1995).

U.S Department of Justice & Federal Trade Commission, 'Antitrust Guidelines for Collaborations Among Competitors' (2000).

Federal Trade Commission, 'To Promote Innovation: The Proper Balance of Competition and Patent Law and Policy' (2003).

U.S Department of Justice & Federal Trade Commission, 'Antitrust Enforcement and Intellectual Property Rights: Promoting Innovation and Competition' (2007).

(ii) Department of Justice business review letter procedure

Business Review Letter to Samuel Weisbard, dated Feb. 10, 1975.

Business Review Letter to John Buckley, dated Jan. 17, 1978.

Business Review Letter to John Schafer, dated July 29, 1987.

Business Review Letter from Mark Gidley to Michael I. Miller, dated Sept. 2, 1992.

GPRI Business Review Letter from Joel Klein to Rufus Oliver, dated April 23, 1997.

MPEG-2 Pool Business Review Letter from Joel Klein to Gerrard Beeney, dated June 26, 1997.

3 DVD Pool Business Review Letters from Joel Klein to Gerrard Beeney, dated Dec. 16, 1998.

PRT Business Review Letter from Joel Klein to David William Livingston, dated Mar. 20, 1998.

6 DVD Business Review Letters from Joel Klein to Carey Ramos, dated June 10, 1999.

American Welding Society Business Review Letter from Charles James to Douglas McDonald, dated Oct. 7, 2002.

VITA Business Review Letter from Thomas O. Barnett to Robert A. Skitol, dated Oct. 30, 2006.

IEEE Business Review Letter from Thomas O. Barnett to Michael A. Lindsay, dated April 30, 2007.

AEC Business Review Letter from Thomas O. Barnett to Rufus Oliver dated Aug. 23, 2007.

RFID Business Review Letter from Thomas O. Barnett to William F. Dolan and Geoffrey Oliver dated Oct. 21, 2008.

(iii) Speeches

Masoudi, Gerald, 'Antitrust Enforcement and Standard Setting: the VITA and IEEE Letters and the IP2 Report', before the Spring Meeting of the American Intellectual Property Law Association 2007.

Masoudi, Gerald, 'Efficiency in Analysis of Antitrust, Standard Setting, and Intellectual Property', before High-Level Workshop on Standardization, IP Licensing, and Antitrust 2007, TILEC, University of Tillberg.

Masoudi, Gerald, 'Objective Standards and the Antitrust Analysis of SDO and Patent Pool Conduct', before Annual Comprehensive Conference of Standard Bodies and Patent Pools, 2007.

2. AUTHORS

ABA, *The Federal Antitrust Guidelines For Licensing of Intellectual Property Origins and Applications* (Chicago, American Bar Association, Section of Antitrust Law, 2002).

ABA, *Intellectual Property and Antitrust Handbook* (Chicago, American Bar Association, Section of Antitrust Law, 2007).

Adamsson, Peter, et al., *Lagarna inom Immaterialrätten* (Stockholm, Norstedts Juridik, 2008).

Anderman, Steven, 'Technology Transfer and the IP/Competition Interface', in Ehlermann, Claus-Dieter and Atanasiu, Isabela (eds), *European Competition Law Annual 2005: The Interaction between*

Competition Law and Intellectual Property Law (Oxford, Hart Publishing, 2007), 211.

Anderman, Steven and Kallaugher, John, *Technology Transfer and the New EU Competition Rules* (Oxford, Oxford University Press, 2006).

Andewelt, Roger, 'Analysis of Patent Pools under Antitrust Laws', (1985) 53 *Antitrust Law Journal* 611.

Archibugi, Daniele and Iammarino, Simona, 'The Globalization of Technological Innovation: Definition and Evidence', (2002) 9 *Review of International Political Economy* 98.

Areeda, Phillip and Hovenkamp, Herbert, *Antitrust Law – An Analysis of Antitrust Principles and Their Application*, 2nd ed. Volume XIII (Boston, Aspen Publishers, 2005).

Armentano, Dominick, 'Competition Theory and the Market Economy', in High, Jack and Gable, Wayne (eds), *A Century of The Sherman Act: American Economic Opinion, 1890–1990* (Fairfax, George Mason University Press, 1992), 201.

Arrow, Kenneth, 'Economic Welfare and the Allocation of Resources for Invention', in Groves, Harold (ed.), *The Rate and Direction of Inventive Activity: Economic and Social Factors* (Cambridge, Nat'l Bureau of Econ. Research, 1962), 609.

Bagley, Constance E. and Tvarnø, Christina D., 'Pharmaceutical Public-private Partnership: Moving From Bench To the Bedside' (2014) 14 *Harvard Business Law Review* 373.

Baldwin, William and Scott, John, *Market Structure and Technological Change* (New York, Harwood Academic Publishers, 1987).

Barton, John, 'Patent and Antitrust: A Rethinking in Light of Patent Breadth and Sequential Innovation', (1997) 67 *Antitrust Law Journal* 449.

Barton, John, 'Antitrust Treatment of Oligopolies with Mutual Blocking Patent Portfolios', (2002) 69 *Antitrust Law Journal* 851.

Baumol, William, 'Horizontal Collusion and Innovation', (1992) 102 *The Economic Journal* 129.

Baumol, William, *Entrepreneurship, Management and the Structure of Payoffs* (Cambridge, MIT Press, 1993).

Baumol, William, *The Free-Market Innovation Machine* (Oxford, Princeton University Press, 2002).

Beeney, Garrad, 'Pro-Competitive Effects of Intellectual Property Pools: A Proposal for Safe Harbor Provisions', in, *Patent Pools and Cross-Licensing: When Do They Promote or Harm Competition? Under the Antitrust Enforcement and Intellectual Property Rights: Promoting Innovation and Competition Hearings* (U.S Dep't of Justice & Fed. Trade Comm'n, 2002).

Bekkers, Rudi, 'Patent Drag and Stacking IPR fees – Are the IPR policies of standard bodies failing or should we better address excessive technology inclusion?', (2007) *Position Paper for High Level Workshop on Standardization, IP Licensing and Antitrust*.

Bekkers, Rudi, et al., 'Case studies on the interface between research and standardisation, and case studies on patent pools as a coordination mechanism', in, INTEREST Consortium Priority 8 No. Contract 503 594, EU 6th Specific Targeted Research Project, 2006.

Bekkers, Rudi, et al., 'Patent pools and non assertion agreements: Coordination mechanisms for multi-party IPR holders in standardisation', (2006) *EASST 2006 Conference*.

Bekkers, Rudi and Liotard, Isabella, 'European Standards for Mobile Communication: The Tense Relationship between Standards and Intellectual Property Rights', (1999) 21 *European Intellectual Property Review* 110.

Bellamy and Child, *European Community Law of Competition* (London, Sweet & Maxwell, 2001).

Bellamy and Child, *European Community Law of Competition* (Oxford, Oxford University Press, 2008).

Blair, Roger and Harrison, Jeffrey, *Monopsony Antitrust Law and Economics* (Princeton, Princeton University Press, 1993).

Bowman, Ward, *Patent and Antitrust Law: A Legal and Economic Appraisal* (Chicago, University of Chicago Press, 1973).

Brodley, Joseph, 'Joint Ventures and Antitrust Policy', (1981–1982) 95 *Harvard Law Review* 1521.

Brodley, Joseph, 'Antitrust Law and Innovation Cooperation', (1990) 4 *Journal of Economic Perspectives* 97.

Brown, Jack, 'Technology Joint Ventures to set Standards or Define Interfaces', (1992–1993) 61 *Antitrust Law Journal* 921.

Bulow, Jeremy, 'An Economic Theory of Planned Obsolescence', (1986) 101 *The Quarterly Journal of Economics* 729.

Cargill, Carl, 'Intellectual Property Rights and Standard Setting Organizations: An Overview of Failed Evolution', (2002) *FTC/DOJ Hearings on Competition and Intellectual Property Law and Policy in the Knowledge-Based Economy*.

Carlson, Steven, 'Patent Pools and the Antitrust Dilemma', (1999) 16 *Yale Journal of Regulation* 359.

Carrier, Michael A., *Innovation for the 21st Century: Harnessing the Power of Intellectual Property and Antitrust Law* (Oxford Scholarship Online, May 2009).

Caspari, Manfred, 'Joint Ventures – The Intersection of Antitrust and Industrial Policy in the EEC', in Hawk, Barry E. (ed.), *Antitrust and*

Trade Policy in the United States and the European Community, 1985 (New York, Bender, Fordham Corporate Law Institute, 1986), 449.

Cerny, Philip, 'Gloablisation, and the Changing Logic of Collective Action', (1995) 49 *International Organisation* 595.

Cerny, Philip, 'Globalization, Governance, and Complexity', in Prakash & Hart (eds), *Globalization and Governance* (London, Routledge, 1999).

Choumelova, Dessy, 'Competition law analysis of patent licensing arrangements – the particular case of 3G3P', (2003) 1 *EU Commission, Competition Policy Newsletter* 39.

Chronopoulos, Apostolos, 'Patenting Standards – A Case for US Antitrust Law or a Call for Recognizing Immanent Public Policy Limitations to the Exploitation Conferred by the Patent Act', (2009) 40 *IIC* 782.

Ciborra, Claudio, 'Alliances as Learning Experiments: Cooperation, Competition and Change in Hightech Industries', in Mytelka, Lynn (ed.), *Strategic Partnerships and the World Economy* (London, Pinters Publishers, 1991), 51.

Coller, Gillbert, 'Competing, Complementary and Blocking Patents: Their Role in Determining Antitrust Violations in the Area of Cross-Licensing, Patent Pooling and Package Licensing', (1968) 50 *Pat. Off. Soc'y* 723.

Crane, Daniel M., 'Joint Research and Development Ventures and the Antitrust Laws', (1984) 21 *Harvard Journal of Legislation* 405.

David, Paul, 'Intellectual Property Institutions and the Panda's Thumb: Copyrights and Trade Secrets in Economic Theory and History', in Wallerstein, Mitchel, et al. (eds), *Global Dimensions of Intellectual Property Rights* (Washington D.C., National Academy Press, 1993), 19.

de Jong, Gjalt, et al., 'The Content and Role of Formal Contracts in High-tech Alliances', (2009) 11 *Innovation: Management, Policy & Practice* 44.

DeVellis, James, 'Patenting Industry Standards: Balancing the Rights of Patent Holders with the Need for Industry-Wide Standards', (2003) 31 *AIPLY Quarterly Journal* 301.

Dolmans, Maurits, 'Restriction on Innovation: An EU Antitrust Approach', (1997–1998) 66 *Antitrust Law Journal* 455.

Dolmans, Maurits, 'Standards for Standards', (2002) 26 *Fordham International Law Journal* 163.

Dolmans, Maurits and Piilola, Anu, 'The New Transfer Block Exemption: A Welcome Reform, After All', (2004) 27 *World Competition* 351.

Drexl, Josef, et al., 'Comments of the Max Planck Institute for IP, Competition and Tax Law on the Draft Commission Block Exemption

Regulation on R&D Agreements and the Draft Guidelines on Horizontal Cooperation Agreements', (2010) *Max Planck Institute for IP, Competition & Tax Law Research Paper No. 10-12.*

Drexl, Josef, 'Anti-competitive Stumbling Stones on the Way to a Cleaner World: Protecting Competition in Innovation without a Market', (2012) 8 *Journal of Competition Law & Economics* 507.

Dutfield, Graham and Suthersanen, Uma, 'The Innovation Dilemma: Intellectual Property and the Historical Legacy of Cumulative Creativity', (2004) 8 *Intellectual Property Quarterly* 379.

Farell, Joseph and Merges, Robert, 'Incentives to Challenge and Defend Patents: Why Litigation Won't Reliably Fix Patent Office Errors and Why Administrative Patent Review Might Help', (2004) Summer *Berkeley Technology Law Journal.*

Farrell, Joseph, et al., 'Standard Setting, Patents, and Hold-up', (2007) 74 *Antitrust Law Journal* 603.

Farrell, J., 'Complexity, Diversity, and Antitrust', (2006) *Antitrust Bulletin* 51, 165–173.

Feldman, Gabe, 'The Misuse of the Less Restrictive Alternative Inquiry in Rule of Reason Analysis', (2009) 58 *American University Law Review* 561.

Fine, Frank, 'EEC Anti-Trust Aspects of Production Joint Ventures', (1992) 13 *European Competition Law Review* 206.

Fine, Frank, 'The EU's New Antitrust Rules for Technology Licensing: A Turbulent Harbour for Licensors', (2004) 29 *European Law Review* 766.

Fine, Frank, *The EC Competition Law on Technology Licensing* (London, Sweet & Maxwell Ltd, 2006).

FTC, *To Promote Innovation: The Proper Balance of Competition and Patent Law and Policy* (FTC, 2003).

Fuchs, Andreas, *Kartellrechtliche Grenzen der Forschungskooperation* (Baden-Baden, Nomos Verlaggesellschaft, 1989).

Gandal, Neil, 'Compatibility, Standardization, and Network Effects: Some Policy Implications', (2002) 18 *Oxford Review of Economic Policy* 80.

Geradin, Damien, 'Standardization and Technological Innovation: Some Reflections on Ex-ante Licensing, FRAND, and the Proper Means to Reward Innovators', (2006) 29 *World Competition* 511.

Geradin, Damien et al., *Elves or Trolls? The Role of Non-Practicing Patent Owners in the Innovation Economy* (SSRN, 2008).

Geradin, Damien and Rato, Miguel P., *Can Standard-Setting Lead to Exploitative Abuse? A Dissonant View on Patent Hold-Up, Royalty Stacking and the Meaning of FRAND* (SSRN, 2006).

Gilbert, Richard, 'Antitrust for Patent Pools: A Century of Policy Evolution', (2004) April *Stanford Technology Law Review* 3.

Gilbert, Richard and Newberry, David, 'Preemptive Patenting and the Persistence of Monopoly', (1982) 72 *The American Economic Review* 514.

Gilbert, Richard and Sunshine, Steven, 'Incorporating Dynamic Efficiency Concerns in Merger Analysis: The Use of Innovation Markets', (1995) 63 *Antitrust Law Journal* 569.

Gilbert, Richard and Sunshine, Steven, 'The Use of Innovation Markets: A Reply to Hay, Rapp, and Hoerner', (1995–1996) 64 *Antitrust Law Journal* 75.

Gilbert, Richard and Tom, William, 'Is Innovation King at the Antitrust Agencies? The Intellectual Property Guidelines Five Years Later', (2001) 69 *Antitrust Law Journal* 43.

Ginsburg, Douglas, 'Antitrust, Uncertainty and Technological Innovation', (1979) 24 *Antitrust Bulletin* 635.

Gitter, Donna, 'International Conflict over Patenting Human DNA Sequences in the United States and the European Union: An Argument for Compulsory License a Fair-use Exemption', (2001) 76 *New York University Law Review* 1623.

Gordon, George and Hoerner, Robert, 'Overview and Historical Development of the Misuse Doctrine', in Koback, James (ed.), *Intellectual Property Misuse Licensing and Litigation* (Chicago, ABA Section of Antitrust Law, 2000), 1.

Grossman, Gene and Shapiro, Carl, 'Research Joint Ventures: An Antitrust Analysis', (1986) 2 *Journal of Law, Economics and Organization* 315.

Hamilton, Davis, 'Silent Treatment: How Genetech, Novartis Stifled a Promising Drug', (2005) *Wall Street Journal* A1.

Hansen, Marc and Shah, Omar, 'The New EU Technology Transfer Regime – Out of the Straitjacket into the Safe Harbour?', (2004) 25 *European Competition Law Review* 465.

Hawk, Barry, *United States, Common Market and International Antitrust: A Comparative Guide* (New York, Law & Business Inc., 1985).

Hay, George, 'Innovations in Antitrust Enforcement', (1995–1996) 64 *Antitrust Law Journal* 7.

Hayek, Friedrich A., *New Studies in Philosophy, Politics, Economics, and the History of Ideas* (London, Routledge and K. Paul, 1978).

Heller, Michael and Eisenberg, Rebecca, 'Can Patents Deter Innovation? The Anticommons in Biomedical Research', (1998) 280 *Science* 698.

Heller, Michael, 'The Tragedy of the Anticommons: Property in the Transition from Marx to Markets', (1998) 111 *Harvard Law Review* 621.

Hoerner, Robert, 'Innovation Markets: New Wine in Old Bottles?', (1995–1996) 64 *Antitrust Law Journal* 49.

Hovenkamp, Herbert, 'United States Antitrust Policy in an Age of IP Expansion', in Hawk, Barry E. (ed.), *International Antitrust Law & Policy 2006* (New York, Juris Publ. Fordham Competition Law Institute, 2007), 230.

Hovenkamp, Herbert, 'Signposts of Anticompetitive Exclusion: Restraints on Innovation and Economies of Scale', in Hawk, Barry E. (ed.), *International Antitrust Law & Policy 2006* (New York, Juris Publ., Fordham Competition Law Institute, 2007), 409.

Huaiwen, He, 'A Self-Defeating Framework: How Far Could ITU Policy Go', (2009) 31 *E.I.P.R.* 343.

Iandiorio, Joseph, 'Patent Pools and the Antitrust Laws', (1964) 46 *Journal of the Patent Office Society* 712.

Jacquemin, Alexis and Spinoit, Bernard, 'Economic and Legal Aspects of Cooperative Research: A European View', in Hawk, Barry E. (ed.), *Antitrust and Trade Policy in the U.S. and the EC 1985* (New York, Bender, Fordham Corporate Law Institute, 1986), 487.

Jaffe, Adam, 'The U.S. patent system in transition: policy innovation and the innovation process', (2000) 29 *Elsevier Research Policy* 531.

Jaffe, Adam and Lerner, Josh, *Innovation and its Discontents* (Princeton, Princeton University Press, 2004).

Jorde, Thomas and Teece, David, 'Acceptable Cooperation among Competitors in the Face of Growing International Competition', (1989) 58 *Antitrust Law Journal* 529.

Jorde, Thomas and Teece, David, 'Innovation, Cooperation and Antitrust', (1989) 4 *High Tech Law Journal* 1.

Jorde, Thomas and Teece, David, 'Innovation and Cooperation: Implications for Competition and Antitrust', (1990) 4 *Journal of Economic Perspectives* 75.

Jorde, Thomas and Teece, David, 'Innovation, Cooperation, and Antitrust', in Jorde, Thomas and Teece, David (eds), *Antitrust, Innovation, and Competitiveness* (New York, Oxford University Press, 1992), 47.

Jorde, Thomas and Teece, David, 'Rule of Reason Analysis of Horizontal Arrangements: Agreements Designed to Advance Innovation and Commercialize Technology', (1993) 61 *Antitrust Law Journal* 579.

Katz, Michael, 'An Analysis of Cooperative Research and Development', (1986) 17 *Rand Journal of Economics* 527.

Katz, Michael and Shapiro, Carl, 'Systems Competition and Network Effects', (1994) 8 *Journal of Economic Perspectives* 93.

Kerber, Wolfgang, 'Competition, Innovation and Maintaining Diversity Through Competition Law', in J. Drexl, W. Kerber and R. Podszun (eds) *Economic Approaches to Competition Law: Foundations and Limitations* (Edward Elgar, 2010).

Kirslow, Samuel, *Nations Choose Product Standards and Standards Change Nations* (Pittsburgh, University of Pittsburgh Press, 1997).

Kitch, Edmund W., 'The Nature and Function of the Patent System', (1977) XX *The Journal of Law and Economics* 265.

Kjölbye, Lars and Peeperkorn, Lucas, 'The New Technology Transfer Block Exemption Regulation and Guidelines', in Ehlermann, Claus-Dieter and Atanasiu, Isabela (eds), *European Competition Law Annual 2005: The Interaction between Competition Law and Intellectual Property Law* (Oxford, Hart Publishing, 2007), 161.

Klemperer, Paul, *Auction Theory – A guide to the literature* (SSRN, 1999).

Koelman, Kamiel J., 'An Exceptio Standardis: Do We Need an IP Exemption for Standards', (2006) 7 *International Review of Intellectual Property and Competition Law* 823.

Korah, Valentine, *R&D and the EEC Competition Rules Regulation 418/85* (Oxford, ESC Publishing Limited, 1986).

Korah, Valentine, 'Critical Comments on the Commission's Recent Decisions exempting Joint Ventures to Exploit Research that Needs Further Development', (1987) 12 *European Law Review* 18.

Korah, Valentine, *Intellectual Property Rights and the EC Competition Rules* (Oxford, Hart Publishing, 2006).

Lang, John Temple, 'European Community Antitrust Law: Innovation Markets and High Technology Industries', in Hawk, Berry E. (ed.), *International Antitrust Law & Policy 1995* (London, Sweet & Maxwell, Fordham University School of Law, 1996), 519.

Layne-Farrar, Anne, et al., 'Pricing Patents for Licensing in Standard-Setting Organizations: Making Sense of FRAND Commitments', (2007) 74 *Antitrust Law Journal* 671.

Lee, Nari, 'Patented Standards and the Tragedy of Anti-commons', (2006) *Forthcoming in Teollisoikeudellisia Kirjoituksia*.

Leistner, Matthias, 'Federal Supreme Court (Bundesgerichthof)', (2005) 6 *International Review of Intellectual Property and Competition Law* 741.

Lemley, Mark, 'Antitrust and the Internet Standardization Problem', (1996) 28 *Connecticut Law Review* 1041.

Lemley, Mark, 'Intellectual Property Rights and Standard-Setting Organizations', (2002) 90 *California Law Review* 1889.

Lemley, Mark, 'Ten Things to Do About Patent Holdup of Standards (and One Not to)', (2008) 48 *Boston College Law Review* 149.

Lemley, Mark and McGowan, David, 'Legal Implications of Network Economic Effects', (1998) 86 *California Law Review* 479.

Lemley, Mark and Shapiro, Carl, 'Patent Holdup and Royalty Stacking', (2007) 85 *Texas Law Review* 1991.

Lerner, Josh, 'Patenting in the Shadow of Competitors', (1995) 38 *Journal of Law and Economics* 463.

Lerner, Josh and Merges, Robert, 'The Control of Technology Alliances: An Empirical Analysis of the Biotechnology Industry', (1998) 46 *Journal of Industrial Economics* 125.

Lerner, Josh, et al., 'The Structure and Performance of Patent Pools: Empirical Evidence', in, *NBER* (Harvard University, 2003).

Levang, Bradley, 'Evaluating the Use of Patent Pools for Biotechnology: A Refutation to the USPTO White Paper Concerning Biotechnology Patent Pools', (2002–2003) 19 *Santa Clara Computer & High Tech Law Journal* 229.

Lim, Daryl, 'Misconduct in Standard Setting: The Case for Patent Misuse', (2011) 51 *IDEA: The Journal of Law and Technology* 557.

Lindemann, Jürgen, 'A Practical Critique of The EEC Joint Research Rules and Proposed Joint Venture Guidelines', in Hawk, Barry E. (ed.), *Antitrust and Trade Policy in the U.S. and the EC 1985* (New York, Bender, Fordham Corporate Law Institute, 1986), 343.

Lundin, Pernilla, et al., 'International Collaboration in R&D Structure and Dynamics of Private Sector Actors', in Europe, Gaia Rand (ed.) (Gaia Group Oy, 2004).

Maciver, Angus, 'EEC Competition Policy in High Technology Industries', in Hawk, Barry E. (ed.), *Antitrust and Trade Policy in the U.S. and the EC 1985* (New York, Bender, Fordham Corporate Law Institute, 1986), 701.

Majewski, Suzanne E., *How Do Consortia Organize Collaborative R&D? Evidence from the National Cooperative Research Act* (SSRN, 2004).

Majewski, Suzanne E. and Williamson, Dean V., *Endogenous Spillovers, Strategic Blocking, and the Design of Contracts in Collaborative R&D: Evidence from NCRA filings of R&D Joint Ventures* (SSRN, 2002).

Martin, Stephen, 'The Evaluation of Strategic Research Partnerships', (2003) 15 *Tech. Analysis & Strategic MGMT* 159.

Martin, Stephen and Scott, John T, 'The nature of innovation market failure and the design of public support for private innovation', (1999) 29 *Research Policy* 437.

Maurer, Stephen and Scotchmer, Suzanne, 'Profit Neutrality in Licensing: The Boundary Between Antitrust Law and Patent Law', (2006) 8 *American Law and Economics Review* 476.

Melamed, A. Douglas, 'Identifying Exclusionary Conduct under Section 2: The No Economic Sense Test Symposium – Identifying Exclusionary Conduct under Section 2', (2006) 73 *Antitrust Law Journal* 375.

Melamed, A. Douglas and Lerch, David, 'Uncertain Patents, Antitrust, and Patent Pools', in Ehlermann, Claus-Dieter and Atanasiu, Isabela (eds), *European Competition Law Annual 2005: The Interaction Between Competition Law and Intellectual Property Law* (Oxford, Hart Publishing, 2005), 273.

Melamed, Douglas, 'Patents and Standard: The Unimportance of Being Essential', in, *unpublished work* (2006).

Merges, Robert, 'A Brief Note on Blocking Patents and Reverse Equivalents: Biotechnology as an Example', (1991) 73 *Journal Pat. & Trademark Off. Soc'y* 878.

Merges, Robert, 'Contracting into Liability Rules: Intellectual Property Rights and Collective Rights Organizations', (1996) 84 *California Law Review* 1293.

Merges, Robert, 'Institutions for Intellectual Property Transactions: The Case of Patent Pools', in Dreyfuss, Rochelle, et al. (eds), *Expanding Boundaries of Intellectual Property* (Oxford, Oxford University Press, 2001), 123.

Merges, Robert and Nelson, Richard, 'Market Structure and Technical Advance: The Role of Patent Scope Decision', in Jorde, Thomas and Teece, David (eds), *Antitrust, Innovation and Competitiveness* (New York, Oxford University Press, 1992), 185.

Meyer, Martin, *Academic Entrepreneurs or Entrepreneurial Academics? Research-Based Ventures and Public Support Mechanisms* (SSRN, 2003).

Mireles, Michael, 'An Examination of Patents, Licensing, Research Tools, and the Tragedy of the Anticommons in Biotechnology Innovation', (2004) 38 *University of Michigan Journal of Law Reform* 141.

Monopolkommission, 'Huaptgutachten: Wettbewerbspolitik vor neuen Herausforderungen', (1988/89).

Motta, Massimo, *Competition Policy* (Cambridge, Cambridge University Press, 2004).

Narula, Rajneesh, 'Globalisation and Trends in International R&D Alliances', in, MERIT, Maastricht Economic Research Institute on Innovation and Technology in its series Research Memoranda, Nr 001, 2003.

Narula, Rajneesh, *Globalization and Technology* (Cambridge, Polity Press, 2003.

Narula, Rajneesh and Dunning, James, 'Explaining International R&D Alliances and the Role of Governments', (1998) 7 *International Business Review* 377.

Narula, Rajneesh and Hagedoorn, James, 'Innovating through strategic alliances: moving towards international partnerships and contractual agreements', (1998) 19 *Technovation* 283.

Nelson, Philip, 'Patent Pools: An Economic Assessment of Current Law and Policy', (2007) 38 *Rutgers Law Journal* 539.

Newberg, Joshua, 'Antitrust, Patent Pools, and the Management of Uncertainty', (2000) 3 *Atlantic Law Journal* 1.

OECD, 'OECD Science, Technology and Industry Outlook 2008: Highlights', (2008).

Ogus, Anthony, 'Rethinking Self-Regulation', (1995) 15 *OJLS* 97.

Ohana, Gil, et al., 'Disclosure and Negotiation of Licensing Terms Prior to Adoption of Industry Standards: Preventing another Patent Ambush', (2003) 24 *European Competition Law Review* 644.

Ostry, Sylvia and Nelson, Richard, *Techno-Nationalism and Techno-Globalism Conflict and Cooperation* (Washington D.C., The Brookings Institute, 1995).

Pál, Szilágyi, 'Bidding Markets and Competition Law in the European Union and the United Kingdom Part I', (2008) 29 *European Competition Law Review* 16.

Patterson, Mark, 'The Role of Power in the Rule of Reason', (2000) 68 *Antitrust Law Journal* 429.

Patterson, Mark, 'Inventions, Industry Standards, and Intellectual Property', (2002) 17 *Berkeley Technology Law Journal* 1043.

Peritz, Rudolph J.R., 'Thinking about economic progress: Arrow and Schumpeter in time and space' in Josef Drexl (ed.), *Technologie et Concurrence – Liber Amicorum Hanns Ullrich* (Bruxelles: Larcier Pub., 2009).

Peritz, Rudolph J.R., 'Freedom to Experiment: Towards a concept of Inventor Welfare', (2008) 90 *Journal of the Patent and Trademark Office Society* 245.

Peterson, Scott, 'Consideration of Patents during the Setting of Standards', (2002) *DOJ/FTC Hearings on Competition and Intellectual Property Law and Policy in the Knowledge-Based Economy*.

Peterson, Scott, 'Patent and Standard Setting Process', (2002) *FTC/DOJ Hearings on Competition and Intellectual Property Law and Policy in the Knowledge-Based Economy*.

Petit, Maria Luise and Tolwinski, Boleslaw, 'Technology Sharing Cartels and Industrial Structure', (1996) 15 *International Journal of Industrial Organisation* 77.

Pfeffer and Nowak, 'Patterns of Joint Venture Activity: Implications for Antitrust Policy', (1976) 21 *Antitrust Bulletin* 315.

Pitofsky, Robert, 'Antitrust and Intellectual Property: Unsolved Issues at the Heart of the New Economy', (2001) 16 *Berkeley Technology Law Journal* 535.

Plompen, Peter, 'The New Technology Transfer Guidelines (TTG) as Applied to Patent Pools and Patent Pool Licensing: Some Observations

Regarding the Concept of "Essential Technologies"', in Ehlermann, Claus Dieter and Atanasin, Isabela (eds), *European Competition Law Annual 2005: The Interaction between Competition Law and Intellectual Property Law* (Oxford, Hart Publishing, 2005), 295.

Priest, George, 'Cartels and Patent Licensing Arrangements', (1977) 20 *Journal of Law and Economics* 309.

Queen, Thomas W., 'Recent Development in Federal Antitrust Legislation', (1984–1985) 53 *Antitrust Law Journal* 443.

Rapp, Richard, 'The Misapplication of Innovation Market Approach to Merger Analysis', (1995–1996) 64 *Antitrust Law Journal* 19.

Robinson, D. T. and Stuart E. T., 'Financial Contracting in Biotech Strategic Alliances', (2007) 50 *Journal of Law and Economics* 559.

Ritter, Cyril, 'The New Technology Transfer Block Exemption under EC Competition Law', (2004) 31 *Legal Issues of Economic Integration* 161.

Salop, Steven C., 'Exclusionary Conduct, Effect on Consumers, and the Flawed Profit-Sacrifice Standard', (2006) 73 *Antitrust Law Journal* 311.

Samuelson, Pamela, et al., 'A Manifesto Concerning the Legal Protection of Computer Programs', (1994) 94 *Columbia Law Review* 2308.

Saunders, Kurt M. and Levine, Linda, 'Better, Faster, Cheaper-later: What Happens When Technologies are Suppressed', (2004) 11 *Mich. Telecomm. & Tech. L. Rev* 23.

Schallop, Michael, 'The IPR Paradox: Leveraging Intellectual Property Rights to Encourage Interoperability in the Network Computing Age', (2000) 28 *AIPLY Quarterly Journal* 195.

Schepel, Harm, *The Constitution of Private Governance – Product Standards in the Regulation of Integrating Markets* (Oxford, Hart Publishing, 2005).

Scherer, F.M. and Ross, David, *Industrial Market Structure and Economic Performance* (Boston, Houghton Mifflin Company, 1990).

Scherer, Fredric, *Industrial Market Structure and Economic Performance* (Chicago, Rand McNally, 1980).

Scherer, Fredric, 'The Innovation Lottery.', in Dreyfuss, Rochelle, et al. (eds), *Expanding the Boundaries of Intellectual Property* (Oxford, Oxford University Press, 2000), 3–21.

Schrijver, Steven de and Marquis, Mel, 'Licensing Technology in the EU after the Big Bang: the New Technology Transfer Block Exemption Regulation and Guidelines', (2004) 25 *Business Law Review* 161.

Schumpeter, Joseph, *The Theory of Economic Development* (Cambridge, MA., Harvard Univ. Press, 1934, reprinted 1961).

Schumpeter, Joseph, *Capitalism, Socialism and Democracy* (London, George Allen & Unwin, 1976, first published in 1943).

Scotchmer, Suzanne, 'Standing on the Shoulders of Giants: Cumulative Research and the Patent Law', (1991) 5 *Journal of Economic Perspectives* 29.

Scotchmer, Suzanne, *Innovation and Incentives* (London, The MIT Press, 2004).

Scott, John, 'Diversification versus Cooperation in R&D Investment', (1988) 9 *Managerial Decision Economics* 173.

Scott, John, 'The National Cooperative Research and Production Act', in ABA (ed.), *Issues in Competition Law and Policy* (Chicago, ABA Section of Antitrust Law, 2008), 1297.

Serafino, David, 'Survey of Patent Pools Demonstrates Variety of Purposes and Management Structures', (KEI Research Note 2007:6, 2007).

Shapiro, Carl, 'Navigating the Patent Thicket: Cross Licenses, Patent Pools and Standard Setting', in Jaffe, Adam, et al. (eds), *Innovation Policy and the Economy* (Cambridge Massachusetts, MIT Press, 2001), 119.

Shapiro, Carl, 'Setting Compatibility Standards: Cooperation or Collusion?', in Dreyfuss, Rochelle, et al. (eds), *Expanding the Boundaries of Intellectual Property* (Oxford, Oxford University Press, 2001), 81.

Siegel, Donald, 'Data Requirements for Assessing the Private and Social Returns of Strategic Research Partnerships: Analysis and Recommendations', (2003) 15 *Tech. Analysis & Strategic MGMT* 207.

Skitol, Robert, (2002) *DOJ/FTC Hearings on Competition and Intellectual Property Law and Policy in the Knowledge-Based Economy.*

Skitol, Robert A., 'Buyer Power and Antitrust: Concerted Buying Power: Its Potential For Addressing the Patent Holdup Problem in Standard Setting', (2005) 72 *Antitrust Law Journal* 727.

Smith, Joel, 'EC: Competition – Revised Technology Transfer Block Exemption Rules in Force', (2004) 26 *European Intellectual Property Review* 113.

Sufrin, Brenda, 'The Evolution of Article 81(3) of the EC Treaty', (2006) 51 *Antitrust Bulletin* 915.

Sullivan, Lawrence and Grimes, Warren, *The Law of Antitrust: An Integrated Handbook* (St. Paul, Thomson/West, 2006).

Swanson, Daniel and Baumol, William, 'Reasonable and Nondiscriminatory (RAND) Royalties, Standards Selection, and Control of Market Power', (2005) 73 *Antitrust Law Journal* 1.

Tassey, Gregory, 'Standardization in Technology-Based Markets', (2000) 29 *Res. Pol'y* 587.

Tom, William and Newberg, Joshua, 'Antitrust and Intellectual Property: From Separate Spheres to Unified Field', (1997) 66 *Antitrust Law Journal* 167.

Treacy, Pat and Heide, Thomas, 'The New EC Technology Transfer Block Exemption Regulation', (2004) 26 *European Intellectual Property Review* 414.

Ullrich, Hanns, *Kooperative Forschung and Kartellrecht* (Heidelberg, Verlag Recht und Wirtschaft, 1988).

Ullrich, Hanns, 'Intellectual Property, Access to Information, and Antitrust: Harmony, Disharmony, and International Harmonization', in Dreyfuss, Rochelle, et al. (eds), *Expanding Boundaries of Intellectual Property* (Oxford, Oxford University Press, 2001), 365.

Ullrich, Hanns, 'Competitor Cooperation and the Evolution of Competition Law: Issues for Research in a Perspective of Globalisation', in Drexl, Josef (ed.), *The Future of Transnational Antitrust From Comparative to Common Competition Law* (Berne, Kluwer Law International, 2003), 159.

Ullrich, Hanns, 'IP-antitrust in context: approaches to international rules on restrictive uses of intellectual property rights', (2003) 48 *Antitrust Bulletin* 837.

Ullrich, Hanns, 'Legal Protection of Innovative Technologies: Property or Policy?', in Granstrand, Owe (ed.), *Economics, Law and Intellectual Property* (Dordrecht, Kluwer Academic Publishers, 2003), 439.

Ullrich, Hanns, 'Expansionist Intellectual Property Protection and Reductionist Competition Rules: A TRIPS Perspective', (2004) 7 *Journal of International Economic Law* 401.

Ullrich, Hanns, 'The Interaction between Competition Law and Intellectual Property Law – An Overview', in Ehlermann, Claus-Dieter and Atanasiu, Isabela (eds), *European Competition Law Annual 2005: The Interaction between Competition Law and Intellectual Property Law* (Oxford, Hart Publishing, 2007), xvii.

Ullrich, Hanns, 'Patent Pools: Approaching a Patent Law Problem via Competition Policy', in Ehlermann, Claus-Dieter and Atanasiu, Isabela (eds), *European Competition Law Annual 2005: The Interaction Between Competition Law and Intellectual Property Law* (Oxford, Hart Publishing, 2007), 305.

Ullrich, Hanns, 'Patente, Wettbewerb, und technische Normen: Recht- und ordnungspolitische Fragestellungen', (2007) 10 *Gewerblicher Rechtsschutz und Urheberrecht 2007* 817.

Ullrich, Hanns, 'Patent Pools – Policy and Problems', in Drexl, Josef (ed.), *Research Handbook on Intellectual Property and Competition Law* (Cheltenham, Edward Elgar Publishing Limited, 2008), 139.

Ullrich, Hanns, 'Patents and Standards – a comment on the German Federal Supreme Court decision Orange Book Standard', (2011) 41 *IIC* 337.

Ullrich, Hanns, 'Patente under technische Normen: Konflikt under Komplementarität in patent- und wettbewerbsrechtlicher Sicht', in Leistne Matthias (ed.), *Europäische Perspektiven des Geistigen Eigentum* (2010).

Ullrich, Hanns and Heinemann, Anders, 'Competition Policy and Intellectual Property Rights A Comparative Analysis of the Competition Rules Relating to IPR in the European Union, the USA, Japan and in International Law' (1999).

Waldman, Michael, 'A New Perspective on Planned Obsolescence', (1993) 108 *The Quarterly Journal of Economics* 273.

Wallace, James H., 'Recent Development in Federal Antitrust Legislation', (1983) 52 *Antitrust Law Journal* 479.

Wallace, Joel, 'Rambus v. F.T.C. in the Context of Standard-Setting Organizations, Antitrust, and the Patent Hold-Up Problem', (2009) 24 *Berkley Technology Law Journal*, 661.

Wells, Wyatt, *Antitrust and the Formation of the Postwar World* (New York, Columbia University Press, 2002).

White, Eric, 'Research and Development Joint Ventures under EEC Competition Law', (1985) 16 *International Review of Intellectual Property and Competition Law* 663.

Venit, James, 'The Research and Development Block Exemption Regulation', (1985) 10 *European Law Review* 151.

Vollebregt, Erik, 'The New Technology Transfer Block Exemption: From Straitjacket to Moving Targets', (2004) 10 *Computer and Telecommunications Law Review* 123.

Xiong, Tao and Kirkbride, James, 'Controlling Research and Development Co-operation through EC Competition Controls: Some Concerns', (1998) 19 *Competition Law Journal* 296.

Zain, Saami, 'Suppression of Innovation or Collaborative Efficiencies?: An Antitrust Analysis of a Research & Development Collaboration That Led to the Shelving of a Promising Drug', (2006) 5 *John Marshall Review of Intellectual Property Law* 347.

Zhang, Liguo, 'How IPR Policies of Telecommunication Standard-Setting Organizations can Effectively Address the Patent Ambush', (2010) 41 *IIC* 380.

Index

actual damages 54, 61, 228
agencies, antitrust 54, 58, 74–6, 101, 103, 107, 224–5, 250–1
allocation of markets 92, 118, 120, 176, 213, 235
ancillary restraints 43–5, 49–50, 130, 132, 134, 166–7, 174, 176–8
  benign 167
  EU 204–5
  restrictive 57, 141
  test 50
  United States 91–3
anticompetitive agreements 1, 57, 62, 64, 180
anticompetitive conduct 168, 174, 180, 200, 208, 226, 231, 238–9
  definition 180
anticompetitive effects 68–9, 83–4, 88, 141, 174, 199–200, 202–5, 243–4
anticompetitive features 90, 161, 203, 206, 214
anticompetitive harms 54, 175, 177, 200, 226
  direct 62, 83
anticompetitive R&D ventures 122, 177
anticompetitive risks 76, 89, 95, 119
anticompetitiveness, United States and European Union compared 226–8
antitrust agencies 54, 58, 74–6, 101, 103, 107, 224–5, 250–1
  US 27, 199, 226, 246
applied research 47, 57–8, 70, 72–3, 111, 129, 182, 233
appropriability 7, 9–10, 12, 19, 80, 83, 102
Arrow, Kenneth 6–7, 9, 12–13, 22
Asahi/St Gobain 163, 165–6, 171, 206–7, 239–40, 242
AstraZeneca 189

Automobile Manufacturing Association 56, 96

background patents 86–7, 93, 190, 192, 195
Baron, Justus 16, 242, 244
barriers to entry 18, 43, 45–6, 70, 102, 105, 129, 141
basic research 57–8, 70, 72–4, 110–11, 182, 184, 232–3, 246
Berkey 41–3, 96
biotech industries 1, 14, 18, 25, 248–9
black clauses 139, 173, 178–9, 196, 238, 252
black lists 92, 139, 173, 179, 185, 213, 234–8
blanket licences 39–40
block exemptions 136–42, 154–9, 168–76, 178–86, 188–97, 199–202, 211–13, 217–24
  1993 notice 157–9
  amendments 154–7
  current 138, 171, 171–208, 219–20, 245
  first 127, 135–54, 171, 221
  specialisation 228
  technology transfer *see* TTBER
  turning point 159–68
blocking patents 227–8, 234
BMI 39
Bolar 23–6, 227
business review letters 27, 96, 106–16, 123, 169, 237, 241
buyer cartels 120–1, 214

cable manufacturers 147–8, 150, 195
cannibalising 7, 9–10, 133
Capitalism, Socialism, and Democracy 6